INTASC Standards	Chapters
1. Making Content Meaningful	
a. understands central content concepts	3, 5, 6
b. links curriculum to prior learning	3, 5, 6, 9, 11
c. evaluates and chooses appropriate materials	2, 5, 6, 9
d. engages students in interpreting ideas	3, 4, 5, 6, 7, 8, 9
e. uses interdisciplinary approaches	4, 7, 8, 9, 11
f. uses methods of inquiry central to the discipline	4, 6, 7, 8, 9, 11
2. Child Development and Learning Theory	
a. evaluates student performance to design instruction	6, 7, 8, 11
b. links teaching to students' prior experiences	2, 3, 4, 6, 10
c. provides opportunities for active student engagement	3, 10
d. encourages student reflection	7, 8, 9, 10
e. accesses student thinking in multiple formats	4, 6, 7, 9, 11
3. Learning Styles/Diversity	
a. designs instruction appropriate to student needs	2, 3, 4, 5, 9, 11
b. provides student performance opportunities	3, 4, 5, 6, 9, 11, 12
c. accesses support services when needed	7, 8, 10
d. adjusts instruction to learning differences	3, 4, 5, 9, 10, 12
e. uses and connects cultural factors and instruction	3, 4, 5, 6, 10, 12
f. creates a learning community with respect	2, 10, 11, 12
4. Instructional Strategies/Problem Solving	
a. selects multiple teaching strategies to foster thinking and problem solving	2, 3, 4, 5, 6, 7, 8, 9, 11
b. encourages student use of learning resources	2, 5, 8, 9, 11, 12
c. uses multiple strategies and roles to meet learner needs	2, 3, 4, 5, 6, 7, 9, 10
5. Motivation and Behavior	
a. encourages clear procedures and expectations	1, 2, 5, 6, 9, 10, 11
b. engages students through their interests, choices, and problem solving	1, 5, 6, 8, 9, 10
c. organizes time, space, and activities to support learning	2, 7, 9, 11, 12
d. organizes, prepares students for meaningful group work and full participation	1, 2, 3, 4, 5, 6, 9, 11
e. analyzes and adjusts classroom environment to enhance social relationships, student engagement, and productive work	2, 3, 4, 9

INTASC Standards	Chapters
6. Communication/Knowledge	
a. models effective communication skills	2, 3, 5, 6, 8, 11, 12
b. provides support for learner expression	3, 4, 5, 6, 8, 9, 10, 11
c. demonstrates that communication is sensitive to gender and cultural differences	2, 9, 10, 11
d. uses a variety of media communication tools to enrich learning	3, 9, 10, 11, 12
7. Planning for Instruction	
a. plans lessons and activities to address various learning styles, performance modes, problem solving, and exploration	2, 3, 4, 5, 9, 11
b. develops plans appropriate for curriculum goals, and based on effective instruction	3, 4, 5, 6, 9, 11
c. develops short- and long-range plans	3, 4, 9, 10
8. Assessment	
a. selects, constructs, and uses assessment strategies appropriate to the learning outcomes	3, 4, 6, 9, 11
b. uses a variety of formal and informal assessments	3, 5, 4, 6, 9, 10
c. uses assessment strategies to involve students in self-assessment activities	4, 10, 11
d. evaluates activities, student performance through observation and analysis of student work	4, 5, 6, 10
e. maintains and employs useful records of student work	10, 11
f. involves parents and other professionals in student evaluation	12
9. Professional Growth/Reflection	
a. evaluates and revises teaching practices	3, 4, 5, 9, 10, 12
b. uses professional literature and colleagues, other resources to support self-development	1, 2, 3, 4, 5, 9, 12
c. consults with other professionals as support for self-reflection and problem-solving	1, 2, 3, 4, 6, 11, 12
10. Interpersonal Relationships	
a. participates in activities to support a strong learning environment	1, 2, 3, 4, 5, 9, 10, 11, 12
b. links with other professionals to support student learning and well-being	1, 2, 3, 4, 5, 6, 10, 12
c. seeks to establish cooperative partnerships with parents/guardians to support student learning	2, 10, 11, 12
d. advocates for students	4, 9, 11, 12

TEACHING IN K-12 SCHOOLS

A REFLECTIVE ACTION APPROACH

FIFTH EDITION

Judy W. Eby
Reflective Action Research Center
San Diego, California

Adrienne L. Herrell
Florida State University

Michael Jordan
California State University, Fresno

Allyn & Bacon
Boston   Columbus   Indianapolis   New York   San Francisco   Upper Saddle River
Amsterdam   Cape Town   Dubai   London   Madrid   Milan   Munich   Paris   Montreal   Toronto
Delhi   Mexico City   São Paulo   Sydney   Hong Kong   Seoul   Singapore   Taipei   Tokyo

Acquisitions Editor: Kelly Villella Canton
Editorial Assistant: Annalea Manalili
Vice President, Director of Marketing: Quinn Perkson
Senior Marketing Manager: Darcy Betts Prybella
Production Editor: Gregory Erb
Operations Supervisor: Central Publishing
Project Manager, Central Publishing: Laura Messerly
Senior Art Director: Jayne Conte
Cover Designer: Central Design
Cover Art: Vaciav Volrab/Shutterstock
Full-Service Project Management: Aparna Yellai, GGS Higher Education Resources, A division of
    PreMedia Global Inc.
Composition: GGS Higher Education Resources
Printer/Binder: Edwards Brothers
Cover Printer: Lehigh-Phoenix
Text Font: Janson Text-Roman

For related titles and support materials, visit our online catalog at www.pearsonhighered.com.

Between the time website information is gathered and then published, it is not unusual for some sites to have closed. Also, the transcription of URLs can result in typographical errors. The publisher would appreciate notification where these errors occur so that they may be corrected in subsequent editions.

Library of Congress Cataloging-in-Publication Data
Eby, Judy W.
    Teaching in K-12 schools : a reflective action approach / Judy Eby,
Adrienne Herrell, Michael Jordan.—5th ed.
        p. cm.
    Includes bibliographical references and index.
    ISBN-13: 978-0-13-704705-5
    ISBN-10: 0-13-704705-3
    1. Effective teaching. 2. Thought and thinking. 3. Educational tests
and measurements. 4. Lesson planning. I. Herrell, Adrienne L. II. Jordan,
Michael, 1944- III. Title.
    LB1025.3.E28 2011
    371.102—dc22

                                                    2009050094

Printed in the United States of America
10 9 8 7 6 5 4 3 2 1

Allyn & Bacon
is an imprint of

www.pearsonhighered.com

ISBN-13: 978-0-13-704705-5
ISBN-10:   0-13-704705-3

To our sons, daughters-in-law, and nieces who have chosen this rewarding profession of teaching.

JE, AH, and MJ

BRIEF CONTENTS

CONTENTS

Chapter 5
Assessing and Meeting Students' Diverse Needs   107

Chapter 6
Establishing a Basis for Active, Authentic Learning   129

Chapter 9
Balancing Standards and Creative Activities: The Importance of the Arts   187

Chapter 10
Assessing and Reporting Student Accomplishments   207

PREFACE

Beginning with the first edition of this book, we have aspired to make it much more than an academic textbook. Our goal has always been to inspire and encourage teachers to become as reflective, creative, and independent as possible throughout their teaching careers. We have tried to achieve this goal by searching for the most creative and adventurous teachers and weaving their real-life stories into the text.

At this time, we recognize that creativity and independence do not appear to be as highly valued as being able to follow guidelines and meet standards. We struggled with how to balance the reality of today's rather uniform educational expectations with our message that true satisfaction in teaching comes from being a caring and creative artist in the classroom. At first, the fifth edition of *Teaching in K-12 Schools* seemed like it was going to be difficult to write. But as we began to collect the stories of teachers who are not only coping in a standards-based environment but also excelling at it, we became much more positive. So we are happy to be able to offer this edition with what we believe is a balanced description of the realities of a standards-based curriculum with the truly exhilarating stories of teachers who see these standards not as a goal, but as a baseline.

Our new aspiration is to inspire teachers to view federal, state, and local standards as meaningful and important, but not the end goal of teaching. We provide the stories of real teachers who begin with standards and then exceed them by creating highly original and creative curricula that take into account and meet the diverse needs of their students. The fifth edition provides you with the knowledge base you need to become a highly professional and creative teacher who meets and exceeds standards with confidence.

WHAT'S NEW IN THIS EDITION

To accomplish our new aspiration, we have revised *Teaching in K-12 Schools* to emphasize the following new features:

- A new, updated Reflective Action in Teaching Model is introduced in Chapter 1. This model takes into account the need to plan with standards in mind. Teachers can learn how to become more reflective and proactive in the thousands of decisions they face every day.

- The Continuous Improvement Model (CIM) is explained and referenced throughout this new edition. This model is based on the book closing the Achievement Gap: NO EXCUSES (Davenport and Anderson, 2002.) The infusion of this information provides an introduction to a valuable approach to improving student outcomes being implemented, with great success, throughout the United States.

- Chapter 9, "Balancing Standards and Creative Activities: The Importance of the Arts," is new to the fifth edition. This chapter explores the possibilities of meeting standards while encouraging higher-level problem solving and creativity.

- The fifth edition is updated to align with the revised Bloom's taxonomy (Anderson et al., 2001), which highly supports our assertion that higher-level problem solving and creativity are uniquely intertwined.

- Video Examples demonstrating many of the strategies recommended in this text are included on the brand new General Methods MyEducationLab website, www.MyEducationLab.com. Margin notes throughout the textbook direct the reader to the video at relevant points in the narrative. A table of the video clips related to the content of the text is included in the instructor's manual.

- Because we strongly advocate active involvement throughout this text, we have added a new feature entitled Guided Group Exploration to each chapter. These activities provide hands-on engagement for the teacher candidate reading this text for a course and serve to explore the concepts featured in each chapter. They also give teacher candidates examples of various hands-on activities that they can use with their students in elementary and secondary classrooms.

- New end-of-chapter material now includes a feature called Reflective Action Experiences for Your Portfolio of Professional Practices that provides simulated experiences and essays that invite reflection and focus the teachers on ways that they can meet standards while still providing a rich, meaningful curriculum for their students. These activities serve as the basis for an interview portfolio that teacher candidates may use when they apply for their first teaching positions.

- Two new features, Playing Catch Up and Communicating with Parents, have been included in this edition. Playing Catch Up focuses on strategies for working with students who are not working at grade level. Communicating with Parents offers suggestions for encouraging parents to become members of the learning team.

- Technology applications are marked with a special icon throughout the text to highlight ways that the use of technology can be infused into the curriculum.

- Updated information on two vital classroom management issues, conflict resolution and bullying prevention, is included in the fifth edition.

- Many new Reflective Action Case Studies and classroom vignettes from a variety of grade levels model how teachers create school curricula and programs, select teaching strategies, and plan appropriate assessments for their students that achieve the standards of their school districts. These real-life examples of teachers' reflections can serve as models for beginning teachers to think and act with creativity and originality. They can be found in Chapters 2, 7, 10, and 11.

MYEDUCATIONLAB

The power of classroom practice.

Teacher educators who are developing pedagogies for the analysis of teaching and learning contend that analyzing teaching artifacts has three advantages: It enables new teachers time for reflection while still using the real materials of practice; it provides new teachers with experience thinking about and approaching the complexity of the classroom; and in some cases, it can help new teachers and teacher educators develop a shared understanding and common language about teaching. . . .[1]

As Linda Darling-Hammond and her colleagues point out, grounding teacher education in real classrooms—among real teachers and students and among actual examples of students' and teachers' work—is an important and perhaps even an essential part of training teachers for the complexities of teaching in today's classrooms. For this reason, we have created a valuable, time-saving website—MyEducationLab—that provides you with the context of real classrooms and artifacts that research on teacher education tells us is so important. The authentic in-class video footage, interactive skill-building exercises, and other resources available on MyEducationLab offer you a uniquely valuable teacher education tool.

[1]Darling-Hammond, L., & Bransford, J., Eds. (2005). *Preparing Teachers for a Changing World*. San Francisco: John Wiley & Sons.

MyEducationLab is easy to use and integrate into both your assignments and your courses. Wherever you see the MyEducationLab logo in the margins or elsewhere in the text, follow the simple instructions to access the videos, strategies, cases, and artifacts associated with these assignments, activities, and learning units on MyEducationLab. MyEducationLab is organized topically to enhance the coverage of the core concepts discussed in the chapters of this book. For each topic on the course, you will find most or all of the resources discussed in the sections that follow.

Connection to National Standards

Now it is easier than ever to see how your coursework is connected to national standards. In each topic of MyEducationLab, you will find intended learning outcomes connected to the appropriate national standards for your course. All of the Assignments and Activities and all of the Building Teaching Skills and Dispositions in MyEducationLab are mapped to the appropriate national standards and learning outcomes.

Assignments and Activities

Designed to save instructors preparation time, these assignable exercises show concepts in action (through video, cases, or student and teacher artifacts) and then offer thought-provoking questions that probe your understanding of these concepts or strategies. (Feedback for these assignments is available to the instructor.)

Building Teaching Skills and Dispositions

These learning units help you practice and strengthen skills that are essential to quality teaching. First, you are presented with the core skill or concept, and then you are given an opportunity to practice your understanding of this concept multiple times by watching video footage (or interacting with other media) and then critically analyzing the strategy or skill presented.

General Resources on Your MyEducationLab Course

The Resources section in your MyEducationLab course is designed to help students pass the licensure exam; put together an effective portfolio and lesson plan; prepare for and navigate the first year of their teaching careers; and understand key educational standards, policies, and laws. This section includes the following:

- *Licensure Exams:* Access guidelines for passing the Praxis exam. The Practice Test Exam includes practice questions, case histories, and video case studies.
- *Portfolio Builder and Lesson Plan Builder:* Create, update, and share portfolios and lesson plans.
- *Preparing a Portfolio:* Access guidelines for creating a high-quality teaching portfolio that will allow you to practice effective lesson planning.
- *Licensure and Standards:* Link to state licensure standards and national standards.
- *Beginning Your Career:* Educate yourself by accessing tips, advice, and valuable information on:
  - Résumé writing and interviewing: Expert advice on how to write impressive résumés and prepare for job interviews.
  - Your first year of teaching: Practical tips to set up your classroom, manage student behavior, and organize for instruction and assessment.
  - Law and public policies: Specific directives and requirements you need to understand under the No Child Left Behind Act and the Individuals with Disabilities Education Improvement Act of 2004.

- *Special Education Interactive Timeline:* Build your own detailed timelines based on different facets of the history and evolution of special education.

Visit www.myeducationlab.com for a demonstration of this exciting new online teaching resource.

INSTRUCTOR SUPPLEMENTS

The following ancillary materials have been created for the third edition. These instructor supplements are available for download from the password-protected Instructor Resource Center at www.pearsonhighered.com/irc. Please contact your local Pearson representative if you need assistance.

Instructor Manual/Test Bank

The guide to the textbook developed for instructors provides concrete chapter-by-chapter overviews and notes as well as teaching ideas and assignment suggestions, and test questions.

PowerPoint® Presentation

PowerPoint® slides have been developed for the new edition that may be used "as is" but lend themselves well to customization to meet the instructor's specific needs.

ACKNOWLEDGMENTS

We gratefully acknowledge the contributions made by professors and students who have provided us with meaningful feedback on our previous editions. We also thank the reviewers of the fifth edition: Jim Codling, Mississippi State University; Ethel King-McKenzie, Kennesaw State University; Andrea Malmont, Shippensburg University; Mark Seaman, Stephen F. Austin State University; and Sammie Stephenson, Arkansas Tech University. You are our eyes and ears. With your feedback, we are confident that we can continue to provide a realistic and hopeful view of the teaching profession today.

We would also like to acknowledge our second-generation teachers: our sons, daughters, and nieces in the education profession. You will note their experiences throughout the book. Alex Eby, Judy's son in Montana; Adrienne's sons, Sean Bateman, technology coach at Eden Prairie High School in Minnesota, and Dr. Colin Bateman, chemistry and physics teacher at Astronaut High School in Titusville, Florida; and Adrienne's daughter-in-law, Diana Bateman (wife of son Andy) who is now teaching kindergarten at Imperial Estates Elementary School in Titusville, Florida. Adrienne also has another daughter-in-law, Jennifer (wife of son David), who teaches second grade in Georgia and whose stories will be added in future editions. Daughter-in-law Melanie (wife of son Colin) is currently completing her teaching degree. Michael's niece and two great-nieces are teachers in the Mobile, Alabama, area. We're very proud of our teaching families and sincerely hope that our beliefs and work in the educational field have inspired all of the younger-generation teachers in our families.

ABOUT THE AUTHORS

Judy Eby, Ph.D., began her teaching career at a Head Start program in Coronado, California. She has been a classroom teacher, a gifted program coordinator, a teacher educator (at DePaul University, University of San Diego, and San Diego State University), and a mentor teacher in the Beginning Teacher Support Academy with the San Diego Unified School District. In 1983, she wrote a master's thesis on gifted behavior and published two articles on that subject in *Educational Leadership* in 1983 and 1984. One of those articles caught the attention of Benjamin S. Bloom, who corresponded with Judy and wrote, "I think you are on the right track."

This led to the opportunity to do her Ph.D. at Northwestern University with Professor Bloom as her dissertation chairman and adviser. In 1986, she wrote her dissertation on gifted behavior as a developmental process rather than an innate and unchanging trait. Essentially, she asked the question, "What are the behaviors that people use to originate and create high-quality original products in the talent area of their choice?" The 10 behaviors that she found to be correlated with this type of success are perceptiveness, active interaction with the environment, reflectiveness, persistence, independence, goal orientation, originality, productivity, self-evaluation, and communication of findings. She published the *Gifted Behavior Index* and her first book, *A Thoughtful Overview of Gifted Education,* in 1990.

Turning her attention to teacher education as a professor of education at DePaul University in Chicago, Judy reinterpreted her construct of gifted behavior in terms of teacher education, and called this related construct *reflective action in teaching.* This time she asked the question, "What are the behaviors or actions that teachers use to create high-quality original school curricula and programs to meet the needs of their students?" The answers to this question form the basis of this textbook.

You can learn more about Judy at her website: *www.reflectiveaction.com.* There, you can learn about her new Reflective Action Book Clubs for Teachers that might benefit you and your faculty in your search for ways to improve your teaching effectiveness, especially in terms of becoming more perceptive, reflective, and proactive in meeting the needs of your students. This process doesn't end when you are awarded your first teaching credential—it continues throughout your career.

One of the central concepts of reflective action is to seek feedback from treasured colleagues. Judy has been very fortunate to have the advice and counsel of her coauthors, Adrienne Herrell and Michael Jordan. Her best critic, however, is her son Alex Eby, a teacher in Bozeman, Montana and is now in his first year of teaching. His feedback and encouragement keep Judy both honest and realistic about what it is like to be a beginning teacher in the 21st century.

Adrienne Herrell, Ph.D., has retired from California State University, Fresno (2004), where she was a professor of reading and language arts and taught classes in early literacy, assessment, and strategies for teaching English language learners. *Teaching in K-12 Schools: A Reflective Action Approach* is Adrienne's fourteenth book for Pearson. Her previous books include *Camcorder in the Classroom* with Joel Fowler, and *Fifty Strategies for Teaching English Language Learners* with Michael Jordan. Adrienne taught and directed the ESOL program at Florida State University during 2006–2008 and currently continues to teach part time for FSU. Adrienne's writing and research are built on her experiences teaching in Florida's public schools for 23 years. She and Michael Jordan are currently engaged in research in public schools in California and in Florida, where they now reside.

Michael Jordan, Ed.D., has recently retired as associate professor at California State University, Fresno. He has taught primary grades through high school in Georgia, Alabama, Florida, and California. Michael is also an actor, education director, and is dedicated to providing access to live theatre to children and youth. He and Adrienne incorporate many dramatic reenactment strategies in their joint research, working with vocabulary and comprehension development in children learning English in the public schools of Alaska, California, Florida, Pennsylvania, Ohio, and Oregon. This is Michael's seventh book for Pearson.

CHAPTER

1

Reflective Action in Teaching

■■■■■■■■■■■■■■■■■■■■■■■■■■■■■■■■■

Jane Speidel teaches junior-year courses in English at Astronaut High School in Titusville, Florida. Academically, Jane's students are at a midlevel; many of them have not yet passed the Florida Comprehensive Assessment Test (FCAT), which is required to receive a high school diploma.

One semester, a few years ago, the principal of Jane's school decided to ban parties held to celebrate the end of the school year. Jane and her students responded by doing a research and writing project to provide the principal with justification for such a celebration. Their project had a positive outcome. The principal reinstated the celebrations, and Jane has made this project a tradition in her classes. Each year, her students write persuasive essays that the principal uses to justify end-of-year parties. The process is eagerly anticipated by Jane's students and the administration.

Her students read novels and respond to these literary pieces using a variety of writing forms. They write letters to Mrs. Speidel, responding to specific prompts such as "If you were going to take this author to dinner, where would you take him, and why?" These prompts require the student to research the background of the books they read, thinking about the setting and plot of the story. They also research local restaurants to find a match for the backgrounds and interests of the author and the literature they are reading. In answering the question of why a particular restaurant was chosen, the student must justify the choice with information gained through research, citing the sources of the information.

Her students produce a cookbook each spring centered on a new theme. The students interview local residents, collect recipes, and research the history of their topic and the recipes. In the past few years, they have chosen themes such as the historical recipes of their community, traditional family recipes, and favorite desserts.

The first year of this project, the classes were made up of about 50% African-American students. They decided to research the African-American culture and traditional foods.

Each student found a favorite recipe and researched its origin, preparation, and use. Students also researched traditional celebrations and interesting facts about the African-American culture that related to food. Each page in the cookbook typically displays a recipe and a sidebar with information about the cultural origins, traditional use, and other interesting information related to the recipe. The students make oral presentations to explain their research and demonstrate some of the discoveries they've made. One student demonstrated the games played by slave children as they shucked the corn used in the traditional sweet cornbread served at African-American meals. The culminating activity is a "cookbook reception" where the recipes included in the cookbook are prepared and served: a great occasion attended by parents, students, and school administrators.

In this 3-week project, many of the Sunshine State Standards for 9th- to 12th-grade English/Language Arts are addressed. One reading standard addressed is the writing of a formal report using information gleaned from reading, interviewing, and relating the information to personal experiences. Another reading standard involves selecting and using appropriate research skills and tools according to the type of information being gathered and organized. A great many of the standards are addressed as the students select and use appropriate prewriting strategies, draft and revise their writing, and produce a final document that has been edited for mechanics and is supported by appropriate graphics. The students address the viewing, speaking, and listening standards as they create an oral presentation supported by visuals, and ask and answer questions about their research and the research of their peers. This project encourages students to read widely and respond in written and oral formats; perhaps most important, it provides an authentic reason for celebration that is enthusiastically supported by the school administration.

Like Jane Speidel, you can become a teacher who reflects deeply and decisively on the actions you take in your own classroom. We can help you reach that goal by sharing real-life classroom experiences related by the teachers who lived them. We've chosen stories like Jane's that clearly illustrate the reflective-action process.

Our first chapter describes a method teachers can use to reflect on the many issues that arise in their classrooms each day. We call our concept **reflective action** *in teaching*.

Our *reflective action* model might envision a teacher pondering over the problem of what to do with a class that does not pay attention and does not seem to want to learn the lesson being taught. After considering the problem and talking to colleagues, the teacher determines that the students were not engaged in learning because the original lesson plan did not provide any opportunities for students to be active learners. As the teacher reflects on the failed lesson, an "aha" moment occurs: "They didn't have anything in their hands!" The teacher adjusts her plan so that the students are actively engaged in learning by doing. The teacher has demonstrated both the willingness and the ability to reflect on what can be done to build bridges between what her students know and can do and what they are capable of learning, given appropriate teaching methods.

In a recent study funded by the National Institutes of Health and cited in *USA Today* (3/27/07), researchers found that children have only a 1 in 14 chance of having a rich, supportive elementary school experience. The findings suggest that not enough time is focused on teachers being engaging and supportive. The overwhelming majority of classroom time, based on the observations of this study, is spent in passive, teacher-directed activity. They also noted that classrooms can be dull, bleak places where students don't get much teacher feedback or personal attention. These teachers consistently scored low on measures such as "richness of instructional methods" and "providing evaluative feedback. Studies such as these point out the importance of teachers constantly recognizing the need to evaluate their own teaching, especially as it relates to student needs and interests. The "whole child" is such an important part of our educational pursuits.

This model is a way of clarifying just how teachers think systematically about their practice and learn from their experiences. We wholeheartedly agree that accomplished teachers are inventive in their teaching. They recognize the need to explore new findings and continue learning while incorporating ideas and methods developed by others. It is important for teachers to seek the advice of others and draw on education research and scholarship to improve their practice. We illustrate this concept by showing a teacher investigating new methods that may help students learn better and by discussing the problem with trusted colleagues. Our teacher uses *reflective action* to take new actions that will better fit students' needs. We cannot stress too much the importance of teachers thinking systematically about their practice and learning from experience.

DEFINITIONS OF REFLECTIVE THINKING AND ACTION

In *How We Think: A Restatement of the Relation of Reflective Thinking to the Educative Process*, Dewey (1993) defined reflective thinking as the "active, persistent and careful consideration of any belief or supposed form of knowledge in light of the grounds that support it" (p. 9). An analysis of this carefully worded statement creates a powerful verbal image of the reflective thinker and correlates with the concept presented here of a person consciously choosing to use reflective action in teaching.

The first descriptive adjective, *active*, indicates one who voluntarily and willingly takes responsibility for considering personal actions. Reflective action includes an energetic search for information and solutions to problems that arise in the classroom. In teaching, this involves identifying the strengths and needs of individual students and being responsible for finding teaching approaches that work for a diverse group of students. Dewey's use of the word *persistent* implies a commitment to thinking through difficult issues in depth, continuing to consider matters even though it may be uncomfortable or tiring to do so. Although some teachers may begin to seek knowledge and information, they may be satisfied with easy answers and simple solutions. In contrast, reflective teachers are rarely satisfied with quick answers. Instead, they continually and persistently seek to fine-tune and improve ways to teach students and manage classroom events.

The careful thinker is one who has concern for both self and others. Teachers who use reflective action care deeply about ways to improve their own classroom performance and how to bring the greatest possible benefit to the lives of their students. They believe that teaching is relational—meaning that the quality of interactions in the classroom sets the tone for learning. Using reflective action, such teachers set out to create positive, nurturing classroom environments that promote high self-esteem and concern not only between the teacher and students, but also among students and their peers. Less caring teachers are likely to consider their own needs and feelings to be of greater importance than those of their students. Because they do not reason with care, they may make unreasonable demands on their students or fail to sense and address important student needs. In today's schools, the focus is on meeting standards. One of these standards involves the establishment of an effective learning environment. Teacher caring and reflection are important elements of the leadership that creates a safe and effective learning environment.

Dewey's (1993) phrase "belief or supposed form of knowledge" implies that little is known for sure in the teaching profession. The teacher who uses reflective action recognizes the value of informed practice but maintains a healthy skepticism about various educational procedures and theories. While a less reflective teacher might be persuaded that there is only one right way to teach, the reflective teacher observes that individual students may need different conditions for learning and a variety of incentives in order to be successful. A less reflective teacher might adopt each new educational fad without questioning its value; the reflective teacher greets each of these new ideas with an open but questioning mind, considering whether it is valuable and how it can be adapted to fit the needs of individuals within the class.

The final phrase in Dewey's (1993) definition, "in light of the grounds that support it," directly relates to the reflective thinker's practice of using evidence and criteria in making judgments. While less reflective teachers may jump to quick conclusions based on initial observations or prior cases, the reflective teacher gathers as much information as possible about any given problem, weighs the value of the evidence against suitable criteria, and then draws a tentative conclusion. After a conclusion is made, the less reflective teacher may stick to it rigidly, but the reflective teacher will reconsider his or her judgments when new evidence or information becomes available. The reflective teacher is also willing to adapt teaching strategies when it becomes evident that the students' needs are not being met.

Although persistent and careful thinking is important to the reflective teacher, such thinking does not automatically lead to change and improvement. Dewey (1993) also acknowledged the importance of translating thought into action, and specified that attributes of open-mindedness, responsibility, and wholeheartedness are needed for teachers to translate their thoughts into reflective actions.

Schon (1990) concurs with Dewey's (1993) emphasis on action as an essential aspect of the reflective process. He defines the reflective practitioner as one who engages in "reflection-in-action." This kind of thinking includes observing and critiquing our own actions and then changing our behaviors based on what we see. Reflection-in-action gives rise to an on-the-spot experiment. We define a problem, consider how we have addressed it in the past, and then try out new actions to test our tentative understandings of them. This process helps us determine whether our moves change things for the better. An on-the-spot experiment may work, or it may produce surprises that call for further reflection and experiment.

Schon (1990) also notes that reflectivity in teaching leads to "professional artistry," a special type of competence displayed by some teachers when they find themselves in situations full of surprise, ambiguity, or conflict. Just as physicians respond to each patient's unique array of symptoms by questioning, inventing, testing, and creating a new diagnosis, Schon believes that reflective teachers also respond to the unexpected by asking questions such as, "What are my students experiencing?" "What can I do to improve this situation?" "How does my students' performance relate to the way I am teaching this material?"

Often, during the process of reflection, teachers find that a new, surprising event contradicts something they thought they already "knew." When this happens, reflective individuals are able to cope with paradoxes and dilemmas by reexamining what they already know, by restructuring strategies or reframing the problem. They often invent on-the-spot experiments to put their new understandings to the test or to answer the puzzling questions that have arisen from the event.

Reflective action is made up of many elements and is related to an individual's willingness to be curious and assertive in order to increase self-awareness, self-knowledge, and new understandings of the world in which we live and work. It is not something that occurs easily for most of us, and it takes time to develop. Writing of this idea, Brubacher, Case, and Reagan (1994) cite the children's story *The Velveteen Rabbit* to suggest that becoming a reflective practitioner has much in common with the process of becoming "real." As the Skin Horse explained to the Rabbit, becoming "real" takes time, and it happens after a toy has been loved so much that it loses its hair and becomes shabby. In the same way, becoming a truly reflective teacher involves time, experience, and inevitably a bit of wear around the edges!

REFLECTIVE ACTION BUILDS ON WITHITNESS

This book describes classroom strategies and methods that you can use to become a caring and reflective teacher so that you will *thrive* in the classroom, not just "get by." We believe that two major traits help teachers achieve the kind of caring relationships that encourage students to relate to ideas, to their peers, and to others in their worlds. The first trait is *withitness*, which refers to a combination of caring and perceptiveness that allows teachers to focus on the needs of their students. The second trait, *reflective action*, is rooted in withitness. It is the ability to monitor your own behaviors, feelings, and needs and to learn from your mistakes. One of the most important things you can do to develop both withitness and reflective action is to get to know yourself and understand your own needs and desires for approval and acceptance from your prospective students. We will return to this theme repeatedly because your need to receive respect and affection from your students is something you must come to recognize and deal with effectively before you can care for others.

We will begin by examining the concept of withitness, and then describe reflective action as it relates to withitness.

Withitness

When you go into classrooms and observe teachers at work, you probably are curious to discover the differences between classrooms that are well managed and those that are disorderly and chaotic. Kounin (1977) hypothesized that smoothly functioning classrooms were governed by a clear set of rules and that chaotic classrooms had vague rules and discipline strategies. When he took his video cameras into classrooms, however, he found that his hypothesis was wrong. What he observed was that the most smoothly functioning classrooms were those that were led by a teacher whose management style was characterized by a high degree of alertness and the ability to pay attention to more than one thing at the same time.

Kounin (1977) labeled the teacher characteristic that distinguished good classroom managers from poor ones as *withitness*. Good classroom managers, he observed, knew what was going on in their classrooms at all times. They were aware of who was working and who was not. They were also able to carry out their instruction while at the same time monitoring student behavior. They were willing and able to alter their lessons at the first sign of student restlessness or boredom, even if they were in midsentence. If a minor disruption occurred between students, the teacher perceived it immediately and was likely to walk toward a student, using eye contact that said, "I am watching you. You can't get away with that behavior in here."

Withitness is expressed more through teacher perceptiveness and behavior than through rules or harsh words. Eye contact, facial expressions, proximity, gestures, and actions such as stopping an activity demonstrate teacher withitness to students. These teachers are able to continue teaching a lesson while gesturing to a group or standing next to an overactive student who needs to refocus on the lesson. These are examples of the concept of overlapping, in which the teacher is able to deal both with student behavior and the lesson at the same time.

Kounin (1977) also studied what he called the *ripple effect*, a preventive discipline strategy that he found to be particularly useful in elementary classrooms. Kounin observed a student in his own college class reading a newspaper during the lecture. When Kounin reprimanded the student, he observed that his remarks caused changes in behavior among the other members of the class as well. Side glances to others ceased, whispers stopped, eyes went from windows or the instructor to notebooks on the desk. In subsequent observations in kindergarten classrooms, Kounin found that when teachers spoke firmly but kindly to a student, asking that student to desist from misbehavior, the other students in the class were also likely to desist from that behavior as well. When teachers spoke with roughness, however, the ripple effect was not as strong. Children who witnessed a teacher reprimand another child with anger or punitiveness did not conform more nor misbehave less than those witnessing a teacher desist another without anger or punitiveness.

Herrell and Jordan (2007) added another dimension to withitness, that of cultural sensitivity. They found that a culturally sensitive teacher not only evoked positive responses from students of other cultures but also started a ripple effect of cultural sensitivity among the English-only-speaking students. This cultural sensitivity involved the recognition of word meanings and nuances in the students' first languages and the recognition of special aspects of a second culture, and it expressed general admiration of a student's ability to function in more than one language. Cultural sensitivity will be explored in more depth in a later chapter.

Reflective Action As It Relates to Withitness

We all hear that it is good to be reflective and that teachers who are reflective are likely to grow and mature into excellent teachers. But what does it mean to be reflective and how do you get that way? As educators, we want to create a word picture in our readers' minds that describes positive, caring, reflective teachers in action. We believe that reflectiveness starts with withitness because it is first and foremost a type of perceptiveness. Perceptive, with-it teachers constantly observe conditions and gather information to make good judgments about what is happening in a classroom and what can or should be done to address it. Withitness continually raises the quality and level of reflective thinking because it helps teachers observe more accurately and collect more complete information about classroom conditions. Reflective teachers plan for variations in student response, constantly monitor students' reactions to classroom events, and are ready to respond when students show confusion or boredom. Reflective teachers actively monitor students during group activities and independent seatwork, looking for signs that students need clarification of the task or the teacher's expectations. They also consider the quality of developing student relationships, and not how students interact with ideas, peers, and others in various settings.

Can withitness and reflective action be learned? We believe so. If you are willing to examine the cause-and-effect relationships in your classroom honestly and search for reasons for students' behaviors, then you are likely to develop withitness in the process. If you are willing to ask other adults to observe your interactions with students and give you feedback on how you respond to various situations, then you will be able to make changes and improve the quality of your withitness radar and responses. If you are willing to discuss classroom problems openly and honestly with your students, in a problem-solving manner, then you are likely to learn from them what their signals mean.

For example, Judy once visited a second-grade classroom where a teacher planned the morning activities to go from reading to math to science without a break. By the time the teacher asked the students to put away their math books and take out their science books, the grumbling and murmuring and shuffling feet had grown to intolerable proportions. With no trace of withitness, this teacher's voice went higher and higher as she scolded the children and told them to be quiet and listen, keep their hands and feet still, sit up, and pay attention. This happened over and over until lunchtime. A reflective, caring teacher using withitness as a tool would have perceived that student grumbling signaled a planning problem—one that could be easily solved by allowing the children to move and stretch for a few minutes before starting another lesson.

Principals and supervising teachers often note that withitness and reflective thinking grow with experience. They grow in a symbiotic way. The more withitness teachers develop, the more reflective they are likely to become. Similarly, the more reflective teachers are about how their own needs may conflict with the needs of their students, the more withitness they display. Few first-year teachers exhibit consistent and accurate withitness. It is gradually developed by teachers as they actively reflect on the effects of their actions and decisions on their students' behavior.

For example, a beginning teacher may gradually become aware that her lessons are too long for the students' attention spans. From that time on, she will be sensitive to whether a particular lesson is moving too slowly or lasting too long. On another day, the teacher may notice that whenever a certain student is made to establish eye contact, the student ceases to misbehave; the teacher reflects on this and actively begins to use eye contact as a way to connect not only with this student but also with others. Then, after further observation and discussion with a colleague, the teacher may also become aware that in some cultures children fail to make eye contact with adults as a sign of respect. In response to a serious disruption, the teacher may notice that using a strong, confident voice causes the students to pay attention, whereas using a tentative, meek voice causes their attention to wander. Through reflecting on these experiences, the teacher develops two effective strategies for redirecting student behavior, and begins to learn which is more effective in a given situation. Her active self-reflection is the first step toward developing greater withitness, and her increasing withitness contributes to greater self-reflection.

STANDARDS THAT APPLY TO REFLECTIVE ACTION IN TEACHING

Certain guidelines assist teachers in making good decisions about their curricula and other classroom management issues. Each state has a board of education that publishes a set of standards for teachers to use when planning school programs. A *standard* is a goal or expectation intended to ensure high-quality educational experiences for all students. In the past, school districts made most curriculum decisions independently, but now each state has adopted standards that apply to all schools. It is important for you to become familiar with those published by your state. Content standards describe what the state wants students to learn for each subject in the elementary curriculum: reading and language arts, mathematics, science, history and social science, physical education, and visual and performing arts. These content standards identify or define the curriculum and grade-level goals that you as teacher will be responsible for teaching. It is the standards, not the textbooks, that constitute the curriculum. The textbooks adopted by your state are simply classroom resources you can use to help your students gain the knowledge and skills defined in the content standards.

As a teacher, you will be planning a sequence of lessons designed to help your students learn and grow toward the grade-level expectations defined in each of the content standards. You will be responsible for monitoring their performance and progress throughout the year and must be ready to plan and adapt your lessons to support their achievement of the state standards. State assessments will be used to determine whether students in your school are mastering the content standards.

National Standards

State boards of education also have responsibility for awarding teachers with teaching credentials or licenses. When you complete your teacher education program, you will be awarded a license or credential to teach in your state. However, if you move to another state, you must satisfy the requirements for that state's teaching credential as well. A new, national organization has been formed that awards nationally recognized teaching credentials. The National Board for Professional Teaching Standards (NBPTS) has a mission to advance the quality of teaching and learning by providing rigorous standards for teachers. While state boards of education provide certificates for beginning teachers who demonstrate competence in teaching, the NBPTS provides the voluntary opportunity to experienced teachers to earn an additional certificate that demonstrates their high levels of proficiency in their chosen profession. This organization synthesized the research on teaching excellence and has produced a document describing five core propositions that define standards of excellence that teachers may attain during their careers. The NBPTS seeks to identify and recognize teachers who effectively enhance student learning and demonstrate a high level of knowledge, skills, abilities, and commitment to the teaching profession.

Reflecting on Your Ethics and Principles

Reflective action is a time-consuming practice that requires a willingness to examine why you choose to do something, how you can do something better, and how your actions affect other people. When you engage in reflective thinking about actions you have just taken or are about to take, you may become critical of your own behavior or your motives. Peters (1991) observes that reflective practice involves a personal risk because it requires that practitioners be open to an examination of beliefs, values, and feelings about which there may be a great sensitivity.

When teachers are engaged in reflection about their decisions, actions, and behaviors, they are likely to begin asking themselves questions such as, "Why do I have this rule?" "Why do

I care so much about what happens in my classroom?" "How did I come to believe so strongly about this element of my teaching?"

As teachers ask themselves this type of searching question, they are likely to reexamine their core beliefs and values. For example, if a teacher has grown up and gone to school in a traditional setting where children were "seen but not heard" unless they were responding to a direct question by an adult, then the teacher may expect the same type of behavior from students. But imagine that this teacher observes a classroom where students are allowed to interact, discuss their ideas with other students, and take part in spirited discussions with the teacher. Based on past assumptions, the beginning teacher may feel uncomfortable in a classroom with this noise level and consider the behavior of the students to be rude. This teacher should then ask the following questions: "Why am I uncomfortable with this noise level? Is it because I was never allowed to speak up when I was a child? How did I feel about the rules when I was a child? How do I feel about them now? What are the differences in the way these children are learning and the way I learned? What do I want my future students to learn: how to be quiet and orderly or how to be curious and assertive?"

When you confront confusing and ambiguous questions like these with honesty, your self-reflection can lead to new understandings of how your beliefs influence your present choices and actions. Continued reflective thinking can lead you to begin to clarify your philosophy of life and teaching, your ethical standards and moral code.

Do you think that it is necessary for you as a teacher to know what you stand for, what you believe and value? Is it important that you be able to state clearly the ethical and moral basis for your decisions? Strike (1993) notes two important reasons for teachers to have a well-articulated philosophy of teaching and code of ethics: (1) They work with a particularly vulnerable clientele, and (2) the teaching profession has no clear set of ethical principles or standards. Strike believes that, in the matter of discipline and grading, the most important ethical concepts are honesty, respect for diversity, fairness, and due process. He also believes that teachers must be willing to consider the ethical implications of equity in the way teachers distribute their time and attention to students, and avoid playing favorites. Are these ideas part of your personal code of ethics?

It is likely that you believe your students ought to have the attributes of honesty, respect for diversity, and fairness. If so, it is vital that you demonstrate these behaviors for them because it is well known that teachers are important models of moral and ethical behavior for the students they teach. When you begin teaching, we want you to accept the responsibility for beliefs and ethics. Teachers are important role models for behavior and character. In classrooms that we observe, the teacher's character and moral code set the standards and the tone or climate for the classroom. If the teacher is fair, students are influenced to treat others fairly. If the teacher is impulsive and selfish, students are likely to behave in the same way. When teachers demonstrate a willingness to listen openly and honestly to others' points of view, students begin to respect the opinions of others as well. When teachers are closed and rigid in their approach to teaching and learning, students mold their behavior into a search for right answers and rote learning.

The National Association for the Education of Young Children (NAEYC) recognizes that many daily decisions required of those who work with young children are of a moral and ethical nature. The association has produced a code of ethical conduct that offers guidelines for responsible behavior and sets forth a common basis for resolving the principal ethical dilemmas encountered in early childhood care and education. The following core values of their document offer a basis for ethical and moral decision making:

Appreciating childhood as a unique and valuable stage of the human life cycle

Basing our work with children on knowledge of child development

Appreciating and supporting the close ties between the child and family

Recognizing that children are best understood and supported in the context of family, culture, community, and society

PRAXIS

Knowledge of the code of ethics from professional organizations and in the literature is tested in PRAXIS™ Exam 4a.

Respecting the dignity, worth, and uniqueness of each individual (child, family member, and colleague)

Helping children and adults achieve their full potential in the context of relationships that are based on trust, respect, and positive regard. (NAEYC, 1997)

Noddings (2005) expresses the need for ethical caring in schools because schools are places where human beings learn how to interact. She proposes that caring is the basis of the Golden Rule. Caring as a moral attribute is no doubt high on the list of most aspiring teachers. Many people choose the career of teaching because they care deeply about the needs of children in our society. They are also likely to feel responsible for meeting the needs of their students. Occasionally, you may observe teachers who seem to have lost the ability to care for others because they are overwhelmed with meeting their own needs. They tend to blame others when their students fail to behave or achieve. Reflective, caring teachers, however, willingly accept that it is their responsibility to design a program that allows their students to succeed. They take responsibility for problems that occur during the school day rather than blaming others. They work every day to balance their own needs with the needs of their students. They are committed to growing as professional educators. To achieve these goals, they are willing to learn systematic ways of reflecting on their own practice so that they can enhance their students' likelihood to succeed. Other moral attributes that teachers cite as important in their personal lives and in their work with children are honesty, courage, and friendliness.

A GRAPHIC MODEL OF REFLECTIVE ACTION IN TEACHING

Consider that, as writers, it is our responsibility to connect with you in the same way teachers must connect with their students. We reflect on memories of ourselves as beginning teachers and think about what we wanted to learn and needed to know to be successful. In this fifth edition, we use feedback from readers of previous editions, as well as our own continuing research, to fine-tune the material we want to present.

We know that sometimes students learn better by seeing a picture or a graphic model of a complicated idea. The model of reflective action we present in this edition has changed from earlier editions because we are continually reflecting on how to make it more understandable and usable. Still, we recognize that any model is oversimplified and relies on the readers to fill in details and examples with their own imagination. With feedback from you, we will continue to refine our thinking in future editions. This is exactly how your own teaching can improve over the years if you are willing to seek critical feedback, reflect, and grow as a result of your experiences. In addition, changes in education policies and current research often influence what is expected of teachers. Standards-based teaching requires that you focus on a set of predetermined goals established by your state board of education. This may cause stress for teachers who want to design programs to meet the diverse needs of their students. When all students must meet the same standards, teachers have an enormous task to create lessons that also allow each student to experience success.

Jerome Bruner (1960) described children as active problem solvers who are ready and eager to take on difficult learning tasks in a supportive learning environment. His now classic text *The Process of Education* describes the concept of the spiral curriculum, which "revisits basic ideas repeatedly, building upon them until the student has grasped the full formal apparatus that goes with them" (p. 13).

When you think of your school years, perhaps you recall subjects that were taught year after year, each time reviewing past learning and then revisited with increased complexity. The concept of the spiral curriculum allows teachers to adapt lessons to ensure that all students succeed. Maybe you had a favorite teacher who made a recurring subject such as U.S.

Figure 1.1 Different perspectives create a point of view.

history or geometry come "alive" to you in a way that made you feel stimulated and motivated to learn very difficult material. Perhaps one of the reasons you are reading this book is because your interactions with a caring teacher helped instill in you the desire to awaken a love of learning in others in the same way you were influenced.

You have probably heard the term *the art of teaching*. One aspect of the art of teaching is that each of us enters the teaching profession with a unique set of experiences with people and with institutions. From these individual experiences, each teacher develops a unique perspective, or set of expectations, through which we view the world and from which we determine what we think life in a classroom should be like.

In the field of education, our perspectives or expectations work a little bit like the visual artist's perspective. For example, imagine that three different artists have been asked to paint the same landscape. Figure 1.1 shows the artist on the left painting the scene as she views it. Notice how she has chosen to depict the boat in relation to the sunset and the lake.

In contrast, note how the middle artist's view differs. He focuses on a close-up of the pine tree, with the boat further in the distance. If you compared the two paintings, you might not realize at first that there were pine trees in the original scene. Finally, look at the third artist's canvas. How does her view compare to the first two? There is no lake at all in her painting.

Over time, artists develop particular perspectives that become associated with their style of art. In the same way, your unique teaching and learning perspective will lead you to notice some things and overlook others—during your teacher preparation courses and throughout your teaching career. There is nothing wrong with having a perspective or set of expectations about teaching—in fact, you can't help having one. However, it is important to remember that your personal perspective is not the only view or interpretation of events. As a teacher you need to look at events and planning as if you were using a three-way mirror. In fact, there are at least as many different perspectives for an event as there are participants in it!

The process of planning any type of classroom event is also unique for each teacher. The particular steps you take in planning a lesson or other types of classroom activities will be unique, and they may vary from day to day or lesson to lesson. As a teacher, you will consider some aspects such as the students' prior knowledge, what the standards call for the students to learn, and what your expectations are for the outcome of the lesson. We are proposing a general set of steps or guidelines here that we call a model of *reflective action in teaching*.

Reflective action is a series of steps or processes in which you reflect on what you want to occur in your classroom, then take some type of action. While you are taking the action,

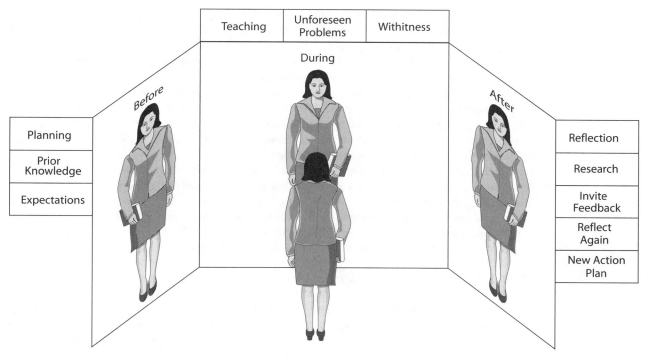

Figure 1.2 Graphic model of reflective action in teaching.

you are also likely to be evaluating how well it is working. That evaluation may cause you to adapt or modify your course of action or plan an entirely new and different action.

Teachers establish learning goals in response to state standards, district requirements, students' needs, availability of resources, time commitments, and personal limits of energy and creativity. The process that teachers use is most likely to be reflective in nature. At the beginning, teachers sketch out in their minds a teaching action in the simplest terms first. For example, a teacher may have a simple vision of teaching a math lesson on fractions, using pizza to motivate the students. The teacher sees students cutting pizzas into halves, quarters, sixths, etc. Upon further reflection, however, the teacher sees the possibility of a huge clean-up to follow, and modifies the plan from cutting pizzas to cutting up cardboard "pizzas." The teacher may even prepare cardboard circles and pass them out to the students. But as the lesson develops, the teacher reflects on how difficult it is for students to cut accurate fractional sections of the cardboard circles. Seeing the ragged "fourths" and "sixths" cut by the students, the teacher re-evaluates the lesson to improve it. Each time the teacher modifies this lesson and plans a new set of actions, more details are added to ensure success. In this way, the reflective actions resemble looking in a three-way mirror in order to see a reflection from multiple perspectives.

In Figure 1.2, we represent the multiple perspectives involved in reflective action. The figure shows some of the many adaptations teachers make, from their first vision of a teaching event to the first attempt to teach the event and then subsequent modifications that are made over time.

In the left-hand mirror, the **Teacher begins to plan** a lesson based on state content standards for the grade level and subject matter and to meet school district requirements and goals. Many teachers form a picture in their heads of what is about to occur. This mental image may even be in the form of a moving picture, with a script that the teacher intends to follow. The teacher expects that, by following the script, the goal for this lesson will be achieved.

Next, the **Teacher considers the students' prior knowledge** and what they need to learn next. Reflective teachers think about the general needs or readiness of their class as a whole, and they also consider the individual needs of students. Some students will need more scaffolding in order to be successful, while others may have already mastered the material and need a more challenging assignment.

During the teaching of the lesson, **Unforeseen problems may occur** and students' responses may not match what was expected. Reflective teachers immediately begin to rethink their lesson plans. This can occur for a number of reasons. Perhaps the students' experiences with school differ greatly from those of the teacher, or perhaps a physical need (e.g., hunger, fatigue) prevents a student from paying full attention to the teacher's input. For any number of reasons, an unforeseen problem or challenge may (and often does!) arise during even the best-prepared lessons.

Non-reflective teachers may try to ignore warning signals and continue to teach their lessons just as planned, without adapting them to fit the needs of their students. When the inevitable confusion and inattention occurs, they tend to focus only on students who fulfill their expectations and try to ignore the students who don't understand or are not paying attention. These teachers lack *withitness*. Sometimes, their lack of withitness can result in such frustration with their careers that they leave teaching forever.

Reflective Teachers Use *Withitness*.   They notice the behavior of all students and respond quickly to unexpected events. Caring, reflective teachers monitor the ever-changing climate of the classroom by paying close attention to students' nonverbal and verbal responses. When events deviate from expectations, a teacher who uses reflective action responds by changing pace in a lesson, moving about the room, and interacting with students in an effort to redirect and refocus attention and learning.

Withitness is a form of *reflection-in-action* (Schon, 1990). This means that the teacher is perceiving cues from students, pondering what they mean, and talking out loud or continuing with a demonstration—all at the same time! This is an amazingly difficult feat to accomplish, and most beginning teachers do not achieve this easily. It takes practice and more practice. It also takes commitment and more commitment to teach and reflect at the same time. You will find that your withitness grows as you become more practiced at looking at events from multiple perspectives.

After the teaching event, the teacher reflects again and tries to understand the reasons that problems may have occurred. This is also known as **reflection-on-action** (Schon, 1990). Reflective teachers do not stop thinking about a problem when the bell rings. They try to understand what happened and why. They want to know how the problem might have been prevented. While non-reflective teachers may blame it all on the students, reflective teachers will not be satisfied with such a hasty conclusion. We cannot emphasize enough the importance of this step. Without reflection-on-practice, there is unlikely to be any growth of withitness. Without reflection, there is little or no opportunity to be creative, identify and solve problems, or devise and take a new approach.

Teacher Invites Feedback.   A teacher's honest self-reflection leads to the next important action step on the reflective-action model, inviting the feedback of respected colleagues or looking for other resources to help explain the unexpected classroom event. A concerned teacher might share a discouraging classroom experience with a colleague, who is likely to have a different perspective to offer.

Teacher Does Proactive Research.   Perhaps the colleague will recommend a book or an article about the subject, or suggest a workshop the teacher could attend. By taking the pro-active step of seeking new information, the reflective teacher grows stronger and more capable with each such learning experience. These teachers are increasing their capacity for planning, teaching, and evaluating interesting learning events, tailored to fit the needs of the students they teach. Rather than simply adopting a colleague's perspective or ideas, the reflective teacher formulates a unique and creative idea of how to re-teach the lesson.

Teacher Creates a New Action Plan.   The next step is to devise a new action plan. The teacher imagines the scene in the classroom again and writes a new script—with greater and more accurate awareness of the students' existing knowledge, skills and interests. There are likely to be additional action steps needed, such as locating appropriate materials and getting them set up in the classroom in time for the next lesson. The entire reflective action process begins again with this newly adapted lesson. Perhaps all will go smoothly, but if a new problem occurs, the reflective teacher uses withitness to perceive the problem and begins the whole reflective action process again.

We hope that you can adapt this reflective action model to situations that arise in your classrooms. We hope that you will recognize the importance of reflecting before, during, and after a lesson is taught. By reflecting before the lesson, you may be able to imagine or picture what is likely to occur. Then you can take preventive action by changing your lesson plan to better fit the needs of your students.

In the midst of the lesson, we hope that you will use your withitness and reflect on the actions you are taking in real time. What is happening? How are the students responding? Who is paying attention and who isn't? Why do some students seem overwhelmed or bored by this lesson? What can I do to improve the learning experience for them right now? These are questions that reflective teachers ask themselves while they are in front of their class.

After the lesson is history, it is time to reflect on what went well and what didn't. Beginning teachers may tend to get discouraged when lessons don't go as planned, but experienced teachers know that unforeseen circumstances are not only possible; they're likely. They reflect on what happened without assigning blame to themselves or to their students. They recognize that by reflecting and adapting this lesson, they are learning from their own experience.

The reflective-action model never really ends. Instead, caring, reflective teachers begin the whole process again: planning, teaching, using withitness, feedback, research, and creativity. We believe that reflective action is an integral part of creativity. In addition, the self-awareness that grows from reflection-on-practice enhances teachers' self-confidence and makes them thrive and grow in their chosen career.

Communicating with Parents

This reflective model extends beyond planning for individual lessons or units of teaching. It also involves considering the multiple perspectives of the broader community responsible for educating our children. Involving parents is a crucial part of this model.

Sharing your philosophy of education with parents is an important aspect of enlisting them as members of the learning team. Use back-to-school night, parent meetings, and parent conferences to help parents understand your beliefs about education and the ways in which they are implemented in your classroom. For example, if you believe that children should develop their intrinsic motivation, and you don't believe in giving rewards and prizes in the classroom, you need to share this with the parents. You need to become familiar with research that supports your beliefs and be prepared to defend them and the related practices. You can then enlist parents in helping to develop the students' intrinsic motivation by using encouraging words or special time to work together on projects as incentives rather than buying them presents or giving them material rewards.

Developing your philosophy of education will be an ongoing project. As you study educational psychology and teaching methods, your ideas and beliefs will change. For this reason, revisiting your ideas and the related philosophy should become part of your reflection on teaching. Every time you observe in a classroom or plan a lesson, you should get into the habit of reflecting on the practices you've seen or planned. In this text, we will include regular activities that will support your reflection and help you develop a clear and concise philosophy of education.

GUIDED GROUP EXPLORATION

After the teaching event, the teacher should reflect again and try to understand the reasons for any problems that might have occurred or ways in which the lesson might be strengthened, then try to understand what happened and why. While non-reflective teachers may blame it all on the students, reflective teachers will not be satisfied with such a hasty conclusion. Without reflection-on-practice, any professional growth is unlikely.

1. Divide the class into groups.
2. Assign one teaching scenario to each group and distribute blank transparencies and non-permanent markers to each group.
3. Place the task directions on the board or overhead:
   a. Read the scenario your group is given (see Figure 1.3).
   b. Discuss what happened and why.
   c. Discuss resources that might be accessed for deciding what action you could take.
   d. Decide on an appropriate action(s).
   e. Write responses (actions) on the transparency provided.
   f. Share your group's suggestions at the overhead.

While teaching a math lesson on multiplication, I realize that several of my students haven't mastered their addition facts. They have to count each item to figure out the arrays that I am using to demonstrate that multiplication is repeated addition. They are not able to complete the repeated additions because their lack of basic skills.

While teaching a social studies lesson about the Civil War, I realize that my students are obviously disinterested: passing notes, having to be redirected to the text, and talking to one another. We are reading a chapter in the social studies book and answering the questions at the end of the chapter.

My second-grade class and I read a descriptive paragraph and discuss the words that make it descriptive. I ask my students to write a paragraph about their favorite place using as many descriptive words as possible. About half of my students seem to have no idea how to begin.

Several of my third-graders have great difficulty reading the third-grade textbooks. I have them placed in books appropriate for their reading instruction, but they can't read the social studies and science textbooks. I'm at a loss as to how to help them.

I have several students in my class who are just learning English. They all speak Spanish at home. I need to do something to help them understand the instruction in my class. What can I do?

I have a child included in my classroom from a learning disabilities resource class. He has great difficulty keeping up with any writing tasks in my class due to his poor fine-motor skills. He tries to keep up, but it takes him twice as long as any of my other students to do any written work.

I have several students who don't seem to be able to pass their spelling tests. They go through the weekly routines: looking up the words in the dictionary, writing sentences using the words, and filling in the blanks in sentences. In spite of all this, they continue to fail their tests each week.

There is a child in my class who is being left out of everything by the others. He is overweight and prefers to read a book on the playground instead of joining in the games. The other students won't pick him for teams anyway. He is becoming increasingly isolated.

Figure 1.3 Teaching scenarios

This activity provides an opportunity to explore a variety of resources available for reflecting on and implementing modifications to instruction.

REFLECTIVE ACTION ACTIVITY FOR YOUR PROFESSIONAL PORTFOLIO

PRAXIS
The use of professional development to support ongoing personal reflection is tested in PRAXIS™ Exam Section 4a.

To help you develop your philosophy of education (a personal statement of your values and beliefs relating to the education of children), it is important for you to explore position statements and codes of ethics adopted by professional organizations in the field. This begins the process of developing and clarifying your personal philosophy of education. Visit the following websites to select statements that reflect your personal beliefs related to teaching at this stage in your professional development. List those statements and paraphrase them in a format that best suits your personal philosophy.

http://www.nea.org/aboutnea/code.html   National Education Association

http://www.naeyc.org/about/position/PSETH05.asp   National Association for the Education of Young Children

References

Brubacher, J., Case, C., & Reagan, T. (1994). *Becoming a reflective educator: How to build a culture of inquiry in the schools*. Thousand Oaks, CA: Corwin Press.

Dewey, J. (1993). *How we think* (rev. ed.). Lexington, MA: D.C. Heath.

Herrell, A., & Jordan, M. (2007) *Fifty strategies for teaching English language learners* (3rd ed.) Upper Saddle River, NJ: Pearson Education.

Kounin, J. (1977). *Discipline and group management in classrooms*. New York: Holt, Rinehart and Winston.

Martin-Kniep, G. (1999). *Capturing the wisdom of practice: Professional portfolios for educators*. Alexandria, VA: Association of Supervision and Curriculum Development.

National Association for the Education of Young Children (NAEYC). www.naeyc.org

National Board for Professional Teaching Standards. (2002/2003a). *Middle childhood/generalist portfolio*. Washington, DC: NCATE Webmaster. Access at www.nbpts.org/candidates/portfolios.cfm

National Board for Professional Teaching Standards. (2002/2003b). *What teachers should know and be able to do*. Washington, DC: NCATE Webmaster. Access at www.nbpts/standards/intro.html

Noddings, N. (2005). *The challenge to care in schools* (2nd ed.). New York: Teachers College Press.

Peters, J. (1991). Strategies for reflective practice. *Professional and Continuing Education, 51*, 83–102.

Schon, D. (1990). *Educating the reflective practitioner*. San Francisco: Jossey-Bass.

Strike, K. (1993). The legal and moral responsibility of teachers. In J. Goodlad, R. Soder, & K. Sirotnik (Eds.), *The moral dimensions of teaching* (pp. 188–223). San Francisco: Jossey-Bass.

PEARSON
myeducationlab
The Power of Classroom Practice

Now go to Topics #16: Professional Responsibilities in the MyEducationLab (www.myeducationlab.com) for your course, where you can:

- Find learning outcomes for these topics along with the national standards that connect to these outcomes.
- Complete Assignments and Activities that can help you more deeply understand the chapter content.
- Apply and practice your understanding of the core teaching skills identified in the chapter with the Building Teaching Skills and Dispositions learning units.

CHAPTER

2

Creating a Safe, Healthy, and Happy Classroom

■ ■

One thing that has not changed, despite rapid growth and dependence on technology, is that we all still need to feel that someone cares for us. Every student who enters a classroom to begin a new year yearns for a teacher who will like her, inspire her to do her very best, listen to her, and respond to her needs and longings. There is no high-tech shortcut for this fundamental truth.

Nel Noddings (2005) recognized that "the desire to be cared for is almost certainly a universal human characteristic. Not everyone wants to be cuddled or fussed over. But everyone wants to be received, to elicit a response that is congruent with an underlying need or desire" (p. 17). Caring is a way of relating to one another's needs and points of view, not a set of specific behaviors.

The best, most creative, caring, and reflective teachers realize that, like parenting, good teaching takes time and understanding. Good teaching resembles good parenting in that both require long periods of time and continuity to develop. Good parents and teachers start by creating an environment that encourages trusting relationships, and they work continually to strengthen that foundation of trust (Noddings, 2005).

Diana Bateman is a third-grade teacher at Lewis Carroll School in Cape Canaveral, Florida. Here is her story of how she and other teachers at her school work together to establish an environment for learning that supports children and helps them to feel that they are all part of the school community.

Our faculty operates as if we are part of the same family of learners. We all want to know how the brain works and how children learn best. We have participated in the same in-service trainings and have selected three philosophical bases for our learning programs and our discipline and classroom management procedures. The three philosophies that we have adopted and adapted are William Glasser's (2001) quality school model, Susan Kavalik's

> **PRAXIS**
> This chapter prepares you to address PRAXIS™ Exam Section 1c: Student Motivation and the Learning Environment.

(1994) integrated thematic instruction (ITI) model, and Jeanne Gibbs's (2001) tribes model. Basically, I manage my classroom by teaching my students how to use the life skills that are the basis of Kavalik's ITI model.

Integrity—Act on what's right

Initiative—Do what needs to be done

Flexibility—Alter plans when necessary

Perseverance—Keep at it

Organization—Plan, arrange, and implement in an orderly way

Sense of humor—Laugh and be playful without harming others

Effort—Do your best

Common sense—Use good judgment

Problem solving—Create solutions to problems that arise

Responsibility—Be accountable for your actions

Patience—Wait calmly

Friendship—Make and keep friends through mutual trust

Curiosity—Show a desire to investigate and find out things

Cooperation—Work together toward common goals

Caring—Feel and show concern for others (Kavalik, 1994, pp. 29–30)

I never assume that my students come to school knowing these life skills. I believe it is my responsibility to teach them each and every skill. I also give them examples of how to use them and plenty of opportunities to apply them.

THE FIRST WEEK OF SCHOOL

For the past 4 years, I taught a third- and fourth-grade combination class. I loved it because, at the beginning of the school year, the fourth-graders already knew what was expected and they could model the life skill behaviors for the third-graders. This year I am teaching a standard third grade, and at the beginning of the year they all seemed very young and immature to me. I introduced the life skills and class procedures and told the students what I expected in terms of behavior, but they didn't all get it the first time they heard it. Every night during that first week of school, I would reflect on the day and try to decide what to do next. I had to decide whether to spend my energy on creating great math and reading lessons or thinking of new ways to help my students understand the importance of our class rules and procedures. I decided that, for the first week, the most important thing for me to do was teach my students how to live and work together as a family and to practice and rehearse our class procedures.

On the first day of school, I form "tribes" (Gibbs, 2001), but I prefer to call them learning clubs. Each learning club consists of four students, two boys who are paired and two girls who are paired. The way I assign pairs of students is to think of one as a rookie and one as a veteran. That was a natural effect of having a third- and fourth-grade combination class, but this year all my students are rookies. I try to pair up a more mature student with one who might be somewhat less mature.

Every morning in my class, after we have completed some basic housekeeping procedures, we come together in a community circle. This is our relationship-building time. The first day of school, I use activities that will help us all get to know one another. I teach the life skill of problem solving right away on the first day of school by calling one learning club to come and sit near me in a circle. Then, when I call the second learning club to come to the circle, I ask the first group to use their problem-solving skills to make room for the second group. As each group of four students comes to the circle, I say, "How can you use problem solving to figure out how to incorporate the new students into the circle?"

Our school administrators use these same processes with the faculty to build a sense of community among the teachers and the rest of the staff. Before a staff meeting, we might do a tribe activity, which is basically a relationship-building activity. This relationship encourages us all to be more reflective about the thousands of decisions we make each day, and we know we can go to our colleagues to discuss problems we are having and get feedback and new ideas.

I have two basic rules that I use for myself in my classroom. I have promised myself that I will never yell at students and I will always speak to them with respect. During the first week of school I tell my students that I respect them too much to yell at them. I feel that the minute I yell, I lose their respect, and respect is what I am trying to earn from the first minute I greet them at the door of my classroom.

To avoid raising my voice, I use other methods to get their attention, such as chimes or hand-clapping signals. I teach my students the expected procedures so that they know exactly what to do. For example, when I clap three times, I teach my students to respond by clapping three times themselves, indicating they have heard me. I then teach them to direct their attention to me, raise their hands up into the air and then, as a group, we lower our hands as if we are pushing the noise down, down, down. At the same time, we all say a long drawn out "whooooooooooosh," which sounds like letting all the air out of a balloon. When the whoosh ends, it is quiet. We use this noise control method school-wide. That is one reason it is so effective. When it is completely quiet, the students know that the next step in our class procedure is for them to be ready to work and to listen attentively.

This strategy comes from Gibbs's (2001) *Tribes*. In the first week of school, I teach the class what attentive listening is and how to do it. I tell them that when they are listening attentively, their eyes need to be on the speaker and their hands have to be still. They learn to nod their head to show that they are listening. I help them to visualize and practice this procedure with the use of a T-chart. On one side of the T-chart I write, "What attentive listening looks like"; on the other side I write, "What does it sound like?" Together we fill in the chart with their ideas, such as "All eyes are on the speaker" or "It sounds like a train stopping at a station."

I have found that by using *consistent* morning procedures, we get the day off to a smooth start. The children have four things to do in the morning:

1. Come in and greet the teacher by giving her a hug, a handshake, or a high five. I stand at the door to greet them. I think that this lets them know that I value them and that I'm glad to see them.
2. Sign up for lunch. From this procedure, I also take the attendance. They learn that when they come in the room, they are expected to put their nametag either in the *lunch* or *no lunch* folder. Two helpers count the number of lunches and take the number to the office.
3. Unpack their belongings and make sure they have a pencil sharpened.
4. Take their seat and do a short learning activity that we call our "morning work." I prepare this morning work ahead of time and have it on their desks when they come in the room. This can be half a piece of paper that reviews a math concept or a grammar skill from the day before.

DIANA'S REFLECTIVE PROCESS

If I didn't have these four procedures and provide them with their morning work, they wouldn't know what to do. They might wander around, make noise, or play. I want them to know that school is a place to learn, and these four procedures make that very clear to everyone in the room. I have the four procedures written on a chart stand near the front door. But this year, with my classroom full of rookies, some children would see the procedures on the chart but not pay attention to them. They didn't seem to understand that it was their responsibility to sign up for lunch. After class, I would reflect on this problem and try to decide how to teach it again more effectively. The next day I pulled the chart stand up and we read the four steps again. I then asked if there was one learning club that was brave enough to use their life skill of courage to model all four steps for the rest of the class. They all wanted to do it. I chose one group and asked the group members to go outside again and come in the door, acting out all the procedures. As they came in, I pointed to procedure one and they greeted me. Then they acted out putting their nametags in the lunch folder, unpacking their belongings, sharpening their pencils, and getting started on their morning work.

If I could tell beginning teachers one important thing, it is that these types of reteaching, practicing, and rehearsing procedures are absolutely necessary. Children need much more modeling and practice than we believe is necessary.

Even when most of the class comes to know and accept the procedures, it is likely that one or two children will need even more reinforcement. For example, this year I had one child who seemed particularly immature and impulsive to me. He needed several rehearsals to learn the morning procedures, and when I asked the children to line up for lunch, he got down on his hands and knees and crawled on the floor. I didn't say anything at the time, but when the other children left the classroom, I tapped on his shoulder and asked him to stay and talk with me. I described his own behavior to him and asked him how he thought his actions affected other children. We looked at the chart to read the class procedure for lining up. It read, "When I call your learning club, push your chairs in and line up at the door."

I asked him if he understood that sentence. He said that he did. I asked him, "Is this something you can do?" and he answered yes. Then I asked him, "Is it something you are willing to do?" When he agreed that he would follow the procedure, I asked him to show me how to line up and walk to the lunchroom.

I believe in these procedures because I think that they free up the class and me to spend our energy on learning. When children know what is expected of them, then they know how to succeed. They feel safer in a classroom where the rules are consistent and well understood by everyone. These procedures take a lot of time at the beginning of the school year, but after that, I believe that I spend less time on discipline the rest of the year. The end result is that we can all focus on learning together as members of a happy, purposeful learning community. I always type these procedures up and have students put them in their notebooks. When we have guest teachers, the students are expected to refer to their procedures. Also, their parents can look at their notebooks and see exactly what my expectations are.

As Diana Bateman demonstrates in her story about setting up her classroom for the first day of school, caring, reflective teachers have an intense commitment to meet the needs of their students.

In this text, we use the term *withitness* to refer to this attitude teachers have that compels them to listen, watch, and learn from their students. In their daily practice, reflective, with-it teachers adjust their expectations, plans, and schedules to attain and keep students interested and motivated to do well in their studies. If a reflective teacher becomes aware of a family circumstance that may prevent a student from paying full attention to school tasks, then the teacher will talk with the student to learn more about the situation and then modify the classroom expectations accordingly.

In this chapter, we will provide descriptions and examples of classroom management strategies and discipline techniques that respect the rights of each individual in the classroom and promote growth of self-esteem and self-responsibility. While there are many discipline methods that seem to work in the sense that they cause students to listen quietly and perform adequately, they are not included here if they rely on bribery, threats, sarcasm, or harsh punishments. We believe that you can establish classroom rules and expectations with your students, respecting their rights as well as your own. We believe that you can create a classroom community where the character of each student is encouraged to grow and expand during the school year. We hope that you want to be the type of teacher that is recalled by students later in life as the one who helped them understand the need for self-responsibility and respect for others. We also hope that you want to establish a classroom environment that is a happy and satisfying place to work and learn.

PRACTICAL CLASSROOM MANAGEMENT STRATEGIES
Connectedness

Joy! Does this word remind you of classroom environments you have participated in as a student or an observer? Glasser has been researching classroom management methods that have this goal since the early 1960s. His original work (1969), *Schools Without Failure*, persuaded teachers to see the necessity for creating a therapeutic environment that would allow all students to succeed. Today, Glasser (2001) continues to create models of school environments that are characterized by joy, cooperation, and a feeling of connectedness.

In classrooms where students and teachers alike appear to be doomed to fail, there is a noticeable lack of teacher reflectiveness. Glasser (2001) observes nonreflective teachers who seem trapped into seven deadly habits: criticizing, blaming, complaining, nagging, threatening, punishing, and rewarding to control the behaviors of their students. The mistaken goal of the teacher who uses these negative habits is to control the behavior of students. Teachers use these habits on students; students respond by using them on teachers, thus creating a dismal, joyless environment that leads to a downward spiral of failure.

Glasser (2001) suggests that we replace these deadly habits with seven connecting habits: caring, listening, supporting, contributing, encouraging, trusting, and befriending. The teacher's goal should be to connect with students rather than attempt to control them.

But teachers may say, "What am I supposed to do when a kid in my class is disruptive and obviously testing my authority?" Glasser (2001) responds, "Students who give you a hard time have already chosen to separate from you. That's why they're disrupting. If you can't connect with them, they'll give you a hard time all year, resisting your direction, which is their way of trying to control you" (p. 25). Such a student may keep disrupting the classroom until you start to threaten and punish. It's like a game of "Gotcha!" When students see that you have lost control, they may surmise that they are now in control. As the situation escalates, the students are very likely blaming the entire situation on the teacher, who has "lost it."

How do you avoid this nightmare? Glasser describes a couple of familiar situations and suggests a way to use connecting behaviors rather than resorting to blaming behaviors. A teacher in a seventh-grade history class notices that a boy starts to hum and keeps humming louder, while watching carefully to see what the teacher will do about it. Other students are also aware of the situation and are watching to see what will happen. This is a situation that demands withitness, followed by an appropriate and constructive response. Glasser suggests that the teacher stop teaching, look at the boy, and say, "Tom, I'm having trouble teaching with what you're doing. I'd like to talk with you for a few minutes." Tell the other students to go back to their work, but do not be concerned if they watch and listen as you talk with Tom because they can learn from this lesson on human interaction.

When you and Tom are sitting eye to eye, begin by saying, "Tom, I'm concerned about you. I don't think you are happy in this classroom. I'd like you to be happier. I think if you were happier, you wouldn't have been humming this morning. What do you think?"

Tom may be surprised and disarmed by this approach. He expects anger, threats, and punishment. His surprise will likely mean that he is paying attention to you, but he may not know how to answer your question. Instead, he may try to ignore or pretend that he does not need you to care about him. He may answer, "I'm okay, don't worry about it." This is a weak effort to suggest that he does not need a connection with you. But he does. All children need to feel connected to the important adults in their lives and, as their teacher, you are one of the most important adults in your students' lives.

Continue to talk quietly with Tom. You might say, "I'm worried about you. If I weren't worried about you, I wouldn't take this time to talk with you about it. You are a smart kid.

PRAXIS
Principles of classroom management are tested in PRAXIS™ Exam Section 1c.

I'd like to help you get some good work done in this class. I think you'd feel a lot better if you did some work that you are proud of."

Tom may respond with something like, "I hate history. It's boring. Who cares about that old stuff anyway?"

To continue your connective interaction, you might respond, "That's a good question. Why should anyone care about history? We can talk about that with the whole class later this morning. But, for now, I need to get back to teaching. I hope that you will get back to your report and finish it in a way that will make you proud of your work. I am not going to try to make you work, but please sit quietly and think about all of this until the period is over."

Tom and the whole class have heard this important exchange. If Tom cooperates at this point, an important compromise has been achieved for all members of the class. If Tom begins to hum again with a defiant look in his eye, it may be necessary to send Tom to the principal's office or another quiet place. You can say quite honestly, "Tom, I can't devote any more time to this problem right now. Go to the principal's office and wait for me there. I will come and talk to you during recess." After Tom leaves, you may want to talk to the class about what just happened. Ask the students to give their opinion of what just happened. Allow them to give suggestions for what you might say to Tom when you meet with him during recess. Explain to your students that you want to create a classroom where everybody can work and where everyone feels connected and supported.

Strategies to Meet Students' Needs

PRAXIS
Knowledge of important theorists is tested in PRAXIS™ Exam Section 1a: Student Development and the Learning Process.

In *Motivation and Personality*, Maslow (1954) first described a hierarchy of human needs. He recognized that people have basic physical and emotional needs that must be satisfied before they can attend to the higher need for achievement and recognition. If the lower needs are not satisfied, an individual is preoccupied by trying to meet them, and other, higher level needs are pushed into the background. This explains why hungry or tired students cannot learn efficiently. All their capacities are focused on satisfying the need for food or sleep. To satisfy the real hunger needs experienced by many students, some schools provide breakfast or snacks so that students can pay attention to school tasks.

What happens when the student has plenty of food and adequate shelter and is well rested? Then "at once other (and higher) needs emerge" (Maslow, 1954, p. 375) and these become dominant. Once basic physiological needs are met, humans need safety and security. Next come the needs for love and belonging. Imagine two classrooms, one led by either an autocratic or a permissive teacher, in which students feel threatened, insecure, and isolated, and the other led by a democratic teacher, in which students feel safe, secure, cared for, and connected with other members of the class community. In the latter setting, students are more likely to have their needs met and therefore be ready and able to achieve greater success in academic work.

Glasser (2001) believes that students need to feel safe, happy, and proud of themselves in a classroom if they are going to become convinced that schoolwork is worth the time and effort. To enlist their support, he recommends that you allow your students to know you as a human being, not just as an authority figure. Isn't it true that the better you know someone and the more you like them, the harder you will work for that person? Glasser asks you to use that same principle when establishing the expectations and procedures for your classroom. He suggests that, during the first few months you are with your students, you look for natural occasions to tell them about the following:

Who you are

What you stand for

What you will ask them to do

What you will not ask them to do

What you will do for them

What you will not do for them

Glasser suggests that you may want to begin the school year in a way that creates a sense of connectedness between you and your students. One way to accomplish this is to involve your students in decisions about how to arrange the desks and tables in order to promote good two-way communication and make the students feel connected to you and to one another.

Organization Strategies

When your students walk into your classroom for the first time, they can sense a particular climate or environment within a few moments. A multitude of sensory images enters their consciousness—sights, sounds, and smells, for the most part. The way the room is arranged, its messiness or neatness, wall decorations, open or shut windows, and the smell of chalk dust or an animal cage all combine to create a unique atmosphere or climate in a classroom.

What do you want your students to see, hear, smell, and feel when they enter your classroom? The appearance of your classroom makes a statement about the extent to which you care for the environment in which you and your students will spend several hours each day. It may be untidy, neat, colorful, drab; filled with objects, plants, animals, and children's art; or left undecorated and unkempt. No two classrooms are alike; each has its unique environment. However, some classrooms (and their occupants) bloom with health, vitality, and strength, whereas others appear sickly, listless, and debilitated.

Reflective teachers may want to come to school several days before their contract calls for them to be there. They can hang posters, decorate bulletin boards, and carefully consider ways to arrange the students' desks, tables, bookcases, and other furniture to fit their curriculum plans and the needs of their students. You know from the many years you have spent in classrooms as students that a bright, colorful, and stimulating classroom leads you to expect that school will be interesting and that the teacher celebrates life and learning. You also know that drab, undecorated spaces lead to expectations of dullness and boredom.

How to arrange the desks is a complex issue. Even though you may decide to involve your students in helping to rearrange the furniture as a way of connecting with them during the first week of class, you must still select an arrangement for the first day of school. Often the room contains many more desks than it was designed to hold comfortably. The number of students in a classroom may vary from 15 to 35, and the precise number of students is not known until the last minute, making preplanning difficult. Generally, though, teachers know approximately how many students they will have in their classrooms, and they set about arranging the desks in a way that uses space economically and strategically. Their plans are governed by an image of themselves and their students in teaching and learning experiences.

While arranging the classroom, reflective teachers envision its activity flow—what it will be like when the classroom is filled with students. This imaging process helps reflective teachers decide how to arrange the furniture in the room. As with other important decisions, each option has both advantages and disadvantages. Desks can be arranged in rows, circles, semicircles, and small groups. Each arrangement influences how students work and how they perceive their environment. Rows of desks provide an advantage in keeping order but leave little space for activities (Figure 2.1). A large circle of desks can be used if the teacher envisions that teaching and learning experiences will take place in the center of the circle, but it will be difficult for all students to see the chalkboard (Figure 2.2).

Arranging desks into small groups results in students' spending more time working together, initiating their own tasks, and working without teacher attention when compared with students in traditional rooms. Teachers who value cooperative group learning experiences over teacher-centered learning experiences often use clusters of four to six desks (Figure 2.3).

Activity and workspaces can be arranged by using bookcases and room dividers or simply by arranging tables and chairs in the corners of the room. Some teachers bring in comfortable furniture and rugs to design a space just for quiet reading. Computer or listening stations must

myeducationlab
The Power of Classroom Practice

For an example of one teacher's approach to arranging furniture and materials, go to the Video Examples section of Topic #3: Classroom Management in the MyEducationLab for your course and view the video entitled Arranging Furniture and Materials.

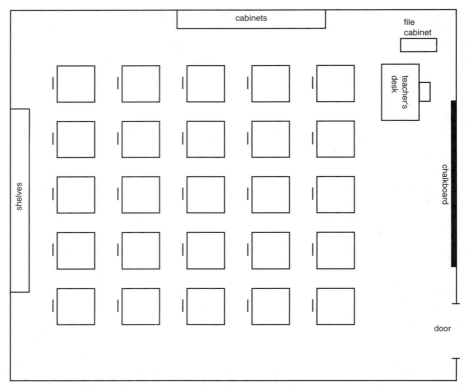

Figure 2.1 Classroom arrangement: rows of desks.

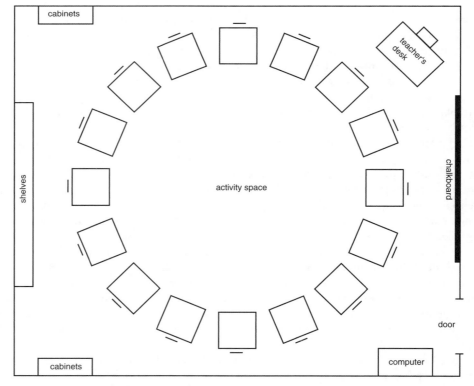

Figure 2.2 Classroom arrangement: circle of desks.

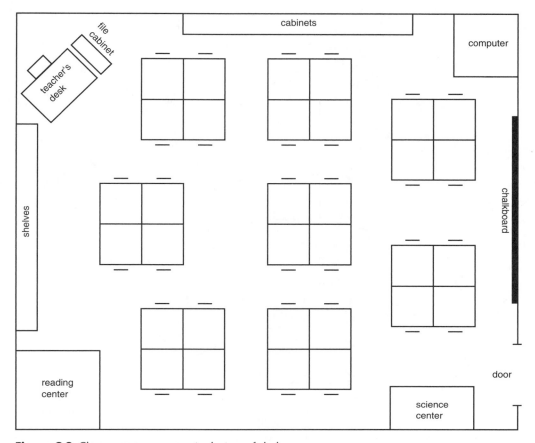

Figure 2.3 Classroom arrangement: clusters of desks.

also be designated. Room arrangement and the use of space are highly individualized decisions. Teachers make these decisions to fit their personal image of what a classroom should be, by considering what they value most highly and how the room arrangement fits their values as well as the curriculum and grade level of the class.

Reflective teachers also consider the effects of the physical arrangement of the room on developing a healthy classroom environment. Rows of desks imply order and efficiency but do little to build a sense of community. Clusters of desks promote cooperation and communication among groups of students. A large circle or concentric arcs arrangement (Figure 2.4) encourages communication and sharing among the entire class. Many reflective teachers change their room arrangements from time to time, depending on the goals of a particular learning experience, and thus create a variety of classroom environments to fit a variety of purposes.

Planning for the First Day of School

The physical environment and schedule of the classroom may lead students to expect certain things about the way teaching and learning will occur during the school year. Thus, as you will recall from your own experiences, students look forward to meeting their new teacher for the first time so that they can discern what life will be like in this classroom. Students create lasting expectations during the first few minutes of the first day of school. For example, consider Figure 2.5, which describes students' experiences on their first day of school in four hypothetical classroom scenarios. You can probably recognize the teachers in these opening-day scenarios and can give them different names and faces from your own experiences in school. You have been exposed to a variety of teaching styles, methods, attitudes, and philosophies as

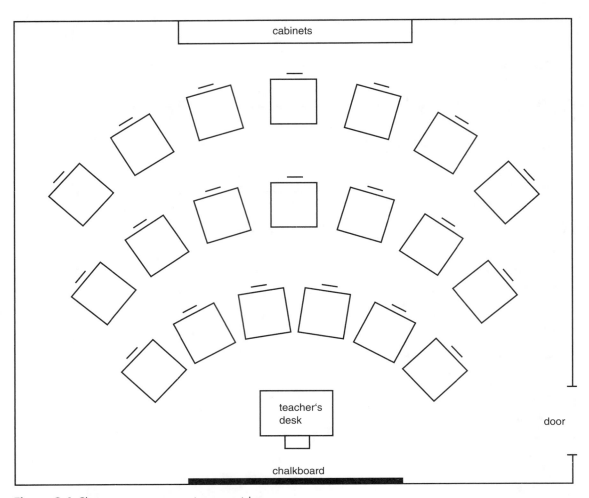

Figure 2.4 Classroom arrangement: concentric arcs.

consumers of education. Now you will soon become a teacher yourself. What style will you have? How will your igstudents perceive you? What values and principles will you model? How will your students feel when they walk into your classroom on the first day of school?

Each scenario depicts a variation of what we call a teaching style. A ***teaching style*** is a highly individualized and complex concept made up of personality, philosophy, values, physical and emotional health, past experiences, and current knowledge about the effects of a teacher's behavior on the classroom environment.

Perhaps you may be considering the important question, "Is it possible to control and decide on my teaching style, or is it simply a function of my personality?" The more information you can gather about how teachers create healthy climates for learning, the more power you have to gain self-understanding and control over this and other important matters pertaining to teaching and learning.

To identify the most effective classroom management strategies, Evertson and Harris (2002) reviewed and evaluated the findings of many major studies on classroom management strategies. They found that, even under the best circumstances, half or less of the school day is used for instruction. They also noted that the more effective classroom managers were able to conserve instruction time and minimize noninstruction time by appropriately sequencing, pacing, monitoring, and providing feedback for student work. The most effective managers were those who had rules and procedures planned for their classes. During the first week of school, the more effective managers spent a major part of the first day and much time during the next 3 weeks helping their students adjust to their classroom expectations and learn to understand the rules and procedures established for the class. Like

Miss Adams and Mr. Catlin from Figure 2.5, the teachers began describing the rules and procedures they had selected as soon as most students had arrived. In some cases, but not always, students were asked to suggest rules for the class. The rules and procedures were explained clearly, with examples and reasons.

More effective managers did not rely simply on a discussion of the rules. They spent a considerable amount of time during the first week of school explaining and reminding students of the rules. One of the most effective ways to communicate your expectations to your class is to lead them through a rehearsal on how to follow the procedures. More effective teachers take time to rehearse procedures, such as how to line up for lunch or what students should take out of their desks for math class. Many teachers teach students to respond to

---

The scene is an elementary school. It is the first day of the new school year. In one corridor, several classroom doors are open. We see and hear four teachers greet the students in their classes.

Room 101

Miss Adams is standing at the doorway. As children walk in, she says, at a calm, even-toned voice, to each of them, "You'll find your name on a desk," as she gestures toward clusters of desks. "Sit in that desk and wait quietly." The children obey and the room is quiet within. When all the children have entered, Miss Adams goes into her classroom and quietly shuts the door behind her. The beginning bell rings at precisely that moment.

Room 102

Mr. Baron is nowhere to be seen. Children enter the classroom looking for him, but when they don't see him, they begin to talk and walk around the room. The desks are arranged haphazardly. Two boys try to sit in the same desk, and a scuffle breaks out. The beginning bell rings. Suddenly Mr. Baron comes running down the hall, enters the room, and yells, "All right, you guys, sit down and be quiet. What do you think this place is? A zoo?"

Room 103

Mr. Catlin is standing at the door wearing a big smile. As each child enters, he gives the child a sticker with his or her name on it. "Put this sticker on a desk that you like and sit at it," he says. The children enter and quickly claim desks, which are arranged in concentric arcs facing the front of the room. They talk with each other in the classroom. When the bell rings, Mr. Catlin enters, leaving the door ajar for latecomers.

Room 104

Mrs. Destry is sitting at her desk when the children enter. Without standing up, she tells the children to line up along the side of the room. They comply. When the bell rings, she tells a student to shut the door. Begins to call the class role, seating the students in alphabetical order. begins to call the class role, seating the students in alphabetical order.

If we were able to enter the classrooms with the students, this is what we might see, hear, and experience.

Room 101

Miss Adams stands in front of the class. She has excellent posture and a level gaze. As she waits quietly for the children to find their seats, she looks each child in the eye. They settle down quickly. When the classroom is perfectly quiet, she begins to talk.

"I see that you have all found your desks. Good. Now we can begin. I like the way you have quieted down. That tells me that you know how to behave in school. Let's review some of the important rules of our classroom."

Pointing to a chart entitled "Class Rules," she reads each aloud and tells the children its significance. "Rule 1: Students will pay attention when the teacher is speaking. This is important because we are here to learn and there can be no learning if you do not hear what the teacher is saying. Rule 2: Students will use quiet voices when talking in the classroom. This rule is important because a quiet, orderly classroom is conducive to learning. Rule 3: No fighting, arguing, or name calling is allowed."

The children listen attentively to all items. They do not ask questions or comment on the rules. After the rules are read, Miss Adams assigns helpers for class jobs. The newly appointed monitors pass out the reading books, and the children begin to read the first story in their books. Miss Adams walks quietly from desk to desk to see that each child is reading.

Figure 2.5 Scenarios of the first day of school.

Room 102

Mr. Baron rushes in and slams some books and papers on the desk. Some of them land on the floor nearby. Stooping to pick them up, he says, "Sit down, sit down or I'll find cages for you instead of desks." The children sit down, but the noise level remains high.

"Enough! Do you want to begin the school year by going to the principal's office? Don't you care about school? Don't you want to learn something?" Gradually, the noise diminishes, but children's voices continue to interrupt from time to time with remarks to their teacher or to fellow classmates.

Mr. Baron calls roll from an attendance book. He does not even look up when a child says "Here" but stares intently at the book. He has several children pass out books at one time, resulting in more confusion about whether each child received all the necessary books. Finally he tells them to begin reading the first story in their reading books. Some do so, others do not. Mr. Baron begins looking through his file cabinet, ignoring the noise.

Room 103

Mr. Catlin walks through the room as he talks to the class. From time to time, he stops near a child and puts his hand on the child's shoulder, especially a child who appears restless or insecure. This action seems to help the child settle down and pay attention.

"Welcome back to school! This year should be a good one for all of us. I've got some great new ideas for our math and social studies programs, and we'll be using paperback novels to supplement our reading series. But first, let's establish the rules for our classroom. Why are we here?"

A student raises her hand. Mr. Catlin reads the name tag sticker on her desk and calls on her by name. "To learn," she says timidly.

"Exactly!" Mr. Catlin agrees. "And, what rules can help us to learn the most we've ever learned in a single year?"

Several children begin to call out responses at the same time.

"Wait a moment, class. Can we learn anything like this?"

A chorus of "No's" is heard.

"Then what rule do we need to solve this problem?"

A child raises his hand, is called on, and says, "We need to raise our hands before we talk."

"What a fine rule," Mr. Catlin says with a broad smile. "How many agree?" The hands of most children go up. Mr. Catlin spots one child whose hand is not raised. He walks over to that child, kneels next to the child's desk and says, "Do you agree that this rule will help you learn this year?" "Yes," says the child and his hand goes up.

After the class has established and agreed on several other class rules, Mr. Catlin talks about the reading program. He offers the children their choice of five paperback novels, distributes them, and tells the children to begin reading. As they read, he circulates around the room, stopping from time to time to ask questions or make comments about the stories to individual children.

Room 104

Mrs. Destry regards the children in their line with an unfriendly gaze. When a child moves or talks, she gives that child a withering stare. From a class list, she begins to read the students' names in alphabetical order, indicating which seat they are to take. The students sit down meekly. No one says a word or makes a sound.

"Now, class, you will find your books in your desks. Take out your reading books and turn to the first page." Going down the rows, each child reads a paragraph aloud while the other children sit silently and listlessly, following along in their books.

Figure 2.5 (Continued)

specific signals, such as a bell or a hand signal to call for attention. Evertson and Harris (2002) observe that the more effective managers begin the school year by clearly establishing themselves as the classroom leaders. They prepare and plan classroom procedures in advance, communicate their expectations clearly, and demonstrate their withitness by signaling their awareness of disruptive student behavior when it occurs. *After the first 3 weeks, teachers who use these methods have few major discipline problems for the rest of the year.*

The reflective teacher, guided by moral principles, also recognizes that it is not simply a matter of establishing leadership that is important; the style of leadership counts as well. Miss Adams and Mr. Catlin quickly established that they were the classroom leaders, but Mr. Catlin's style of leadership best exhibited the underlying moral principles of caring, consideration, and honesty as he interacted with his students. The result is that students in such an environment return the caring, consideration, and honesty to the teacher and exhibit it in their interactions with one another.

In contrast, less effective managers (exemplified by Mr. Baron) did not have well-thought-out classroom procedures. Although teachers like Mr. Baron always have rules, the rules are often vague and the teachers tend to tell the class the rules and procedures quickly without spending time discussing and rehearsing what they really mean. Others, like Mrs. Destry, try to move quickly to academic matters. They seem to expect the students to be able to comprehend and retain the rules from a single, brief statement. They do not teach the class routines and procedures. As a result, they often find themselves wasting many hours of class time during the year as they remind the students again and again how to behave.

The way teachers monitor the behavior of their students is also a critical factor in establishing a clear set of expectations for students. The Evertson and Harris (2002) study disclosed that less effective teacher-managers did not actively monitor students' behavior. Instead, they busied themselves with clerical tasks or worked with a single student on a task while ignoring the rest of the class. The consequence of vague and untaught rules and poor monitoring was that the children were frequently left without enough information or a good enough example to guide their behavior.

From this study, you can conclude that if you expect your students to obey the rules of your classroom, you must give them clear directions, allow them to rehearse the procedures until they get them right, actively monitor your students at work, and show them that you expect them to pay attention to the task and do their work. Remember the sad finding that less than half of the school day is actually used for teaching and learning itself. Resolve to use your time as effectively as possible by using your withitness and other strategies to prevent time from being wasted unnecessarily.

Teacher Body Language

Jones (2000) found that effective classroom management and control of student behavior depends a great deal on the teacher's body language. Strong, effective teachers are able to communicate many important things with eye contact, physical proximity, bodily carriage, gestures, and facial expressions. These teachers do not have to be 6 feet 5 inches tall and weigh 230 pounds. Indeed, it is fascinating to observe teachers who are small in stature manage classrooms with a glance by standing next to a student who is disturbing the classroom.

Consider the eye contact of the teachers in the first-day scenario. Miss Adams had a level gaze and met the students' eyes as she looked at each of them at their first meeting. In a positive and nonthreatening manner, she communicated that she was aware and in control. In contrast, Mrs. Destry gave the students "withering stares" that probably caused them to feel anxious and fearful about the year ahead. Mr. Baron never met the eyes of his students at all, communicating his lack of preparedness and confidence to manage the classroom. Mr. Catlin used physical proximity as well as eye contact to put his students at ease and to communicate that he was in charge.

Jones (2000) recommends the concentric circle desk arrangement that Mr. Catlin used because it causes students to focus their attention on the teacher and enables the teacher to provide help efficiently by moving quickly to the side of any student who is having difficulty. A teacher can help students allay their fears and turn the focus to the classroom activity by moving close to the restless student and placing a hand on the student's shoulder. However, to use physical proximity effectively, the teacher must be able to step quickly to the side of the misbehaving student, as Mr. Catlin did. Thus, room arrangement can help or hinder a teacher's ability to control children's behavior.

A teacher's personal bearing also sends messages to students. The strong, straight posture of Miss Adams reinforced the students' perception that she was an authority worthy of their respect. Good posture and confident bodily carriage convey strong leadership, whereas a drooping posture and lethargic movements convey weakness, resignation, or fearfulness (Jones, 2000).

PRAXIS
This section prepares you for PRAXIS™ Exam Section 3a: Verbal and Nonverbal Communication Techniques.

Gestures are also a form of body language that can communicate positive expectations and prevent problems. Teachers can use gestures to mean "stop," "continue," or "quiet, please" without interrupting their verbal instruction. When used with positive eye contact, physical proximity, bodily carriage, or facial expression, gestures can prevent small disruptions from growing into major behavior problems.

Facial expressions also vary greatly among teachers. They can show enthusiasm, seriousness, enjoyment, and appreciation, all of which encourage good behavior; or they can reveal boredom, annoyance, and resignation, which may tend to encourage misbehavior (Jones, 2000). Facial expressions that display warmth, joy, and a sense of humor are those that students themselves report to be the most meaningful. You may even want to look in the mirror to see how students will see you when you are happy, angry, feeling good about yourself, or upset.

Establishing Rules and Consequences

In a healthy democratic community, the citizens understand and accept the laws that govern their behavior. They also understand and accept that if they break the laws, certain consequences will follow. Healthy democratic classrooms also have laws that govern behavior, although they are usually called rules. In the most smoothly managed classrooms, students also learn to understand and accept the consequences for breaking a rule from the very first day.

In the first-day scenarios, each teacher established rules and consequences for the classroom differently. Miss Adams established a set of rules before school began. She read them to the class and explained why each was important. Neither Mr. Baron nor Mrs. Destry presented a clear set of rules. Their actions indicated that they expected the students to discover the rules of the classroom. These are likely to be quite consistent in Mrs. Destry's classroom, but in the case of Mr. Baron, we suspect that the rules may change from day to day. Mr. Catlin had planned an entire process for establishing rules. His process involved the students in helping to establish the class rules based on shared expectations and consequences.

Two different types of consequences are used to guide or shape student behavior. Natural consequences are those that follow directly from a student's behavior or action. For example, if a student gets so frustrated while working on an assignment that he rips the paper in half, the natural consequence is that the work will have to be redone, from the beginning. If another student wakes up late, the natural consequence is that she misses the bus and has to walk to school, arrives late, and suffers the embarrassment of coming to class tardy. In these cases, there was no adult intervention; the consequence grew directly from the student's behavior.

Logical consequences are those the teacher selects to fit students' actions; they are intended to cause students to change their behavior. For example, a teacher may decide that the logical consequence for not turning in a paper on time is that the student must stay in for recess or come in for a detention after school to finish the paper. When the paper is turned in, the logical consequence is that the student may go out to recess or leave the detention hall.

The difference between a punishment and a consequence is that a consequence is not arbitrary, and it is not dispensed with anger or any other strong emotion. In his book, *What Works in Schools*, Marzano (2003) recommends seven action steps in establishing rules and procedures that will have the effect of managing your classroom with a sense of success for you and a sense of belonging and acceptance for your students:

Action Step 1: Articulate and enforce a set of classroom rules and procedures.

Action Step 2: Use strategies that reinforce appropriate behavior and recognize and provide consequences for inappropriate behavior.

Action Step 3: Institute a schoolwide approach to discipline.

Action Step 4: Develop a balance of dominance and cooperation with students.

Action Step 5: Develop your awareness of the needs of different types of students and learn ways to meet those needs.

Action Step 6: Use withitness to heighten your awareness of the actions of your students in your classes.

Action Step 7: Maintain healthy emotional objectivity with your students. (pp. 95–102)

By establishing a clear set of rules with objective consequences and clearly communicating these rules and their consequences to your students, you can fulfill many of these seven action steps. In many classrooms, teachers write a set of rules on a large piece of poster board that is prominently displayed. Many teachers try to word the rules in positive ways, describing what they expect rather than what they forbid. They write specific consequences for each rule on the same poster for all students to see. For example:

Our class rules	Consequences if you do not follow this rule
We wait in line courteously.	You will go to the end of the line.
We listen to the teacher.	You will lose 5 minutes of free time.
We turn in work on time.	You will do your work at free time.
We work and talk quietly.	You will take a timeout.
We treat others with respect.	You will write a letter of apology.

Using Positive Consequences and Rewards

Many beginning teachers believe that they can reward students with tokens or awards to earn their cooperation and respect. Jones (2000) examined the familiar incentive systems of grades, gold stars, and being dismissed first. He discovered that these systems appear to benefit only the top achievers; they are not genuine incentives for students who cannot realistically meet the established criteria. Jones (2000) also notes that if teachers offer incentives that are not particularly attractive to many students, then the incentives will not positively affect student behavior or achievement. He uses the term *genuine incentives* to distinguish those that students perceive as both valuable and realistic for them to earn from those that students perceive to be of little benefit or impossible to achieve. His system of "responsibility training" focuses on preventing discipline problems by helping students develop self-control and insight into what is meaningful and important in life.

One important way to develop self-responsibility is a form of time-management training that provides genuine incentives for students to waste less time during the day. If they work efficiently and cooperatively, they can earn their own time to do what they want with it. Jones (2000) has observed enough classrooms to conclude that, without genuine incentives to save time, many students will simply fritter it away. They move slowly getting to their seats in the morning. They waste time coming to attention, getting out their materials, or lining up. Jones suggests that teachers think about time in the same way they think about money.

To train children to become more responsible with money, it is essential that they earn some money in the first place. Once they have money of their own, it is the adult's responsibility to help them learn how to manage their money effectively. They have to learn that they cannot use credit or borrow more money. They need to learn that if they want more money, they have to earn it. Responsibility training with time is analogous to learning to manage money. Teachers can establish a classroom system that allows students to earn *preferred activity time (PAT)* to make their own choices. If they fritter away their class work time, then they earn less PAT. If they work effectively and cooperatively during work periods, they become rich (!) in time for their own preferred activities. In this type of system, you can maintain an objective demeanor that is nicely balanced between dominance and cooperation because you are not rewarding or punishing student behavior as much as you are simply keeping an accurate record of the students' decisions and giving them their payoff in time.

If students are to continue to perceive these favored activities as genuine incentives, they must be delivered as promised. Some teachers promise the incentive but run out of time and do not deliver on their promises. Another counterproductive practice is to continually threaten to reduce or eliminate the incentive if students do not cooperate. Still others deliver the reward even when the work is not done acceptably. When this occurs, the students learn that they can have dessert even if they do not eat their dinner—that is, they can get the reward without doing their work. This practice can destroy the balance of trust between student and teacher so that, when the teacher establishes incentives, the students are skeptical that they will be delivered as promised.

When delivered as promised and as earned, genuine incentives can promote increased achievement among individuals and groups and can cause peer pressure to encourage good behavior. Caring, reflective teachers attempt to understand the real needs and desires of their students and to provide incentives that meet these needs.

✳ REFLECTIVE ACTION CASE STUDY ✳

Using active learning to reinforce relevant learning while managing classroom behavior

Dr. Colin Bateman, Honors Chemistry and Physics Teacher, Astronaut High School, Titusville, Florida

Teaching Students to Apply Science Concepts to Everyday Life

I had been assigned an integrated science class for the first time. This class was much larger than my regular honors chemistry and physics classes of 12 to 15 highly motivated students. The idea of maintaining effective lessons with 36 students who had little or no science background was a bit daunting.

Teacher Begins to Plan

I looked over the standards for the course and tried to match the standards with hands-on lessons to help the students become actively involved.

Teacher Considers What Students Already Know

I reviewed the students' records to determine which science courses the students had taken previously, and I found that few of them had taken any science courses in their freshman year. The class was mostly comprised of sophomores but included a few juniors who had failed general science the year before.

I decided I needed to give some type of pretest before each unit to identify what type of background knowledge I would need to explore before launching the unit. I designed the first pretest as a Jeopardy game with individual answer keys to make it less stressful for the students.

Reflective Teacher Uses Withitness and Reflects on the Event

The first class was a disaster. The students knew very few of the answers to the Jeopardy questions and I had to keep redirecting them to their individual answer keys, reminding them that I didn't expect them to know all the answers since we hadn't yet studied the topic (oceanography). I heard a lot of muttering about, "Why do we need to know this stuff anyway?"

Teacher Does Research and Invites Feedback

I decided that I needed to find a way to motivate the students and find a classroom management strategy that would keep them on task. I read up on motivational theory and management strategies for adolescents. As a result, I designed a unit that would demonstrate practical ways that the knowledge could be used in their everyday lives. This wasn't too difficult since the students all live on the Atlantic coast and like to go to the beach and surf. I also noted that an important aspect of motivation is the student's ability to see him- or herself as having the potential to be successful.

Teamwork and the importance of social interaction were stressed in the classroom management strategies I read for adolescents. I decided to have the students work in teams while I provided a structure to keep them on task.

I asked my colleagues on my teaching team to review the plans. They were a bit skeptical about a classroom management technique that involved earning and losing team points over a month in order to earn a team pizza party before the teams were shuffled. They were, however, eager for me to try it and see how it worked. They were also concerned that I would be taking up teaching time keeping track of team points. I explained that I had devised a record-keeping system that would not detract from the lesson. I would provide each group with a set of five clothespins on a cup in the middle of their table. During a lesson, if anyone on the team was off task, I would simply remove a clothespin without comment. If the group got back on track I would replace their lost clothespin. Each group would have a point keeper who would enter the number of clothespins left on their cup at the end of each period.

Teacher Reflects Again, Using Feedback, Research, and Creativity

After the first few days of the unit, I reflected on the way it was working. I found that I had a few students who were not motivated, in spite of the team approach. They were often off task and their teammates were getting frustrated with them. I talked to the class and asked them what should be done about students who were not putting effort into the team assignments. One student suggested that a group be allowed to "vote a member off the island" if they weren't trying. I asked how the excluded team member could complete the assignment without being part of the team. One student said, "If they won't work as a team member, let them be responsible for the assignment on their own." After that discussion, I found that the team pressure seemed to have worked well. If I removed a clothespin all the others at the table would say, "Frank" or "Maggie" under their breath and the offender would quickly get back on track.

Teacher Creates a New Action Plan

I reflected on the plan almost weekly and fine-tuned it. I assigned some students to work by themselves if it became obvious they were hindering the group's progress. I had some individual conferences with students and put two of them on individual contracts. I also planned a culminating activity in which the students presented at least one practical reason for learning the material we had studied. They provided many good examples of the importance of oceanography to their safety, modern medicine, and dietary needs.

Classroom Meetings

One method that democratic teachers often use to build mutual caring, consideration, and honest expression of opinions and perceptions is to hold classroom meetings to discuss problems confronting the class. Some teachers hold regularly scheduled classroom meetings each week; others schedule them only when necessary. When Judy taught fifth grade, she scheduled her meetings just before lunch on Wednesdays so that they were in the middle of the week. She found that one of the most important effects of a classroom meeting is the sense of community created when the students and teacher sit down to solve problems together.

The seating arrangement for a class meeting is a single circle of chairs so that each member of the class can see both the teacher and all other members of the class. The teacher has the responsibility of establishing rules and consequences for the meeting. These usually consist of a rule about one person speaking at a time and accepting the ideas and opinions of others without criticism or laughter. It is important that, as the leader of the meeting, the teacher be nonjudgmental. When expressing anger or other feelings, class members are encouraged to use I-statements.

The meeting may be divided into several parts. For example, the teacher may choose to open with an unfinished statement such as "I sometimes wonder why . . ." or "I am proud of . . ." or "I am concerned about . . . ." Going once around the circle, every member of the class is encouraged to respond to this opening statement, while the teacher encourages communication from every member of the group. While all class members are encouraged to respond, the teacher makes it clear that any individual can simply say, "Pass." Opening the class meeting in this way has the advantage of allowing everyone to speak at least once during the meeting and may bring out important issues that need discussion.

The second part of the meeting can be devoted to students' concerns. The teacher opens this discussion by asking who has a concern. When a problem is expressed, the teacher moderates discussion on that issue alone until it is resolved. Issues are seldom resolved easily in one meeting, but class members can raise a problem, express different ideas and opinions, then offer possible solutions. When a reasonable solution is worked out, the teacher's role is to restate the solution, suggest that the class try it for a time, and discuss how it worked at the next classroom meeting. Other student concerns can then be expressed.

The third part of the class meeting can address the teacher's concerns. The teacher can bring up a problem by expressing personal feelings or stating expectations for future work. Students' responses can be brought out and discussed and solutions proposed. The sense of community that develops from expressing needs and opinions, hearing other perspectives, and solving problems together is translated into all aspects of life in the classroom. When an argument occurs during recess or when students perceive something as unfair, they know they can discuss it openly and freely in a class meeting. When the teacher needs more cooperation or wants higher quality work, this issue can be brought up in a class meeting. Mutual understanding, tolerance for opposing views, and developing a way to resolve conflicts result in a strong sense of ownership and commitment to the academic, social, and emotional goals of the class as a whole.

ISSUES IN CLASSROOM MANAGEMENT

Economic and Social Differences May Cause Varied Expectations of Students

Laughter and fun may seem to be scarce commodities in many school districts today. School violence, bullying, and suicide make the headlines these days, even in elementary schools.

Many people think that inner-city schools serving less affluent students are deadly and sterile, whereas suburban schools serving middle-class students are vital and stimulating. In reality, though, within each school a great variety of classroom environments exists. Talented, caring, and reflective teachers in inner-city schools can and do make learning a joyful experience, and their classrooms shine with goodwill, understanding, wit, and creativity. There are, however, just as many careless, nonreflective teachers in rural areas and in the suburbs as there are in the inner cities. In any environment, such teachers give little thought to their job or to their classrooms, which are filled with anxiety, disorder, anger, and despair.

Unfortunately, great social and economic disparities exist in the world. Children who have not created these differences are their victims. Historically, school has been the great equalizer, the means to rising out of poverty, the chance to make the most of one's potential. Reflective, caring, and creative teachers know they can make a significant difference in students' lives, and they work especially hard at creating a positive, healthy classroom environment to counteract the effects of poverty, discrimination, and neglect.

Whether you teach in a small town, a wealthy suburb, or the inner city, some social issues are universal and seem to be growing at an alarming pace. One of these problems is a trend toward ethical and moral bankruptcy. As national corporations demonstrate, there is a growing sense that winning is everything and that rules are for the other guys. As a classroom teacher, you will have an uphill struggle to convince your students that honesty and integrity matter. You will have to model it for them if you expect them to understand or accept that moral discipline is worth achieving.

Lickona (2004) says that some many schools turn to character education because they are distressed by the decline they see in student respect and responsibility. He has observed student teachers and first-year teachers confront the harsh realities of working with students who bring their anger and resentment to school each day. Character education programs provide activities to support student attitude changes and lead them to want to behave differently and develop respect and empathy for others.

Teachers and administrators often have concerns about the time needed to facilitate character education programs. The good news is that schools and districts that have implemented character education programs have been rewarded with increased academic achievement. To view a comprehensive report on the results in character education, see the Character Education Partnership's website, CEP.org (Likona, 2004, p. 123.)

Lickona believes that the teacher is the central moral authority in the classroom and for many children, the teacher functions as the primary moral "mentor" in their lives. "Exercising authority, however, doesn't mean being authoritarian. Authority works best when it's infused with respect and love" (p. 144).

To create a moral discipline system for your classroom, Lickona (2004) suggests involving your students in establishing the rules in a cooperative, mutually respectful manner. He describes how Hal Urban, an award-winning high school history and psychology teacher develops rules with his students.

Hal arranges his classroom into groups of five or six students because he believes it is important for students to have a support group. He asks each group to work as a team to brainstorm rules about what students should not be allowed to do and what students should be encouraged to do. Urban then posts signs in the classroom with the rules that the students have generated. He uses the signs when he sees a student doing something *not* allowed but also when he sees a student doing something that should be *encouraged*. He doesn't make a big production of using the signs but may simply point to one and give verbal encouragement along with the acknowledgment of the desirable or undesirable behavior.

Lickona (2004) proposes a system of moral discipline that focuses on the specific needs of each class and uses logical consequences that help students understand what they have done and what they must do to improve their moral conduct. For example, with a rule such as "Use respectful language in this classroom," the consequences (designed by the students in cooperation with their teacher) might be as follows:

First occasion: Take a timeout of 5 minutes and state or write the language you used that was disrespectful. Tell why it was disrespectful and to whom.

Second occasion: Write a letter of apology to the person or class to whom you were disrespectful.

Third occasion: Bring up your own behavior at a class meeting; ask for feedback on how you can stop using this type of language. Write a plan for improving your language and present it to the class.

Cheating by Students and Teachers

One important element of character development is demonstrating an awareness of right and wrong concerning cheating on schoolwork. Cheating is easier than ever before because of material available to students on the Internet. In earlier eras, children might copy word for word from an encyclopedia. Today, they can go online and buy a term paper or essay to turn in as their own. Confounding this trend is the fact that teachers and school administrators have shown an increasing tendency to cheat. Principals feel driven to show high test scores on standardized tests. Teachers may want their students to look good so that they, in turn, look good. Because it has become common practice to publish school-by-school test results in the media, and to grade and fund schools based on their scores, pressure is added for students, teachers, and administrators to do well. This added pressure causes concern.

In Walker County, Georgia, the Naomi Elementary School participated in a National Study of School Evaluation (NSSE) parent and student opinion survey on honesty and cheating. The survey indicated that cheating was a possible problem area for Naomi. An alarming 33.9% of students and 29.4% of parents felt that cheating occurred frequently at Naomi, while 61% of students admitted that they were only somewhat honest, fair, and responsible.

To tackle this issue, the school community established a goal (with performance indicators) that students would make a commitment to creating quality work and striving for excellence, while demonstrating that they are self-motivated to act with honesty and put forth their best effort in the pursuit of learning goals and tasks. The Naomi School community then created a series of "action steps" to reach their goal. They established a Project Action Team (PAT), consisting of school staff, parents, community members, and students, to establish an academic integrity policy that includes a clearly defined honor code for students and a verifiable contract to be utilized during the 2003–2004 school year. They implemented a curriculum that focuses on the ethical traits of honesty, responsibility, self-discipline, citizenship, integrity, honor, and determination. They commissioned students to create and present drama skits for parent-teacher organization (PTO) programs to be presented throughout the year on themes of fairness, integrity, responsibility, and work ethics. They conducted seminars for parents and community members to introduce the goal and to open dialogue concerning cheating. They developed a program to assist students, parents, and staff in the recognition and demonstration of character and ethical traits with emphasis on honesty, fairness, and integrity.

Naomi School set up an assessment plan that includes the use of surveys that will be distributed yearly to teachers, students, and parents. The surveys will be used to determine the perception of progress toward improvement in student demonstration of honesty, integrity, and fairness. Grade-level and school wide reviews and evaluations of student progress in relation to work study habits will be recorded on student progress reports and permanent records. Administration will review discipline referrals to determine any existing or developing trends in relation to honesty, integrity, and fairness.

Establishing Two-Way Communication with Parents

Discipline problems are less likely when teachers communicate their expectations to students and parents so that everyone is working with the same set of expectations. Communication with parents needs to occur early in the school year and continue on a regular basis. Teachers should clearly explain the policies, procedures, and rules that govern the classroom and should establish procedures for parents to ask questions and voice their concerns.

Susan McCloskey, a first-grade teacher at Greenberg Elementary School in Fresno, California, invites her parents to a parent meeting at the beginning of the year. She reviews the class rules and expectations for behavior and academics with the parents with the help of bilingual assistants in Spanish and Hmong. She also invites the parents to come into the classroom to work as volunteers or to do at-home support in areas such as collecting materials (egg cartons, milk jug caps, etc.). She sends home periodic newsletters (in three languages) with suggestions for ways to help at home. Susan makes frequent phone calls to parents to inform them of outstanding behavior or work being done by the students as well as expressing concerns when needed. Although Susan teaches in a very low-income neighborhood, she makes the parents feel as if they are part of a learning team.

Jody Salazar teaches seventh- and eighth-grade remedial reading at Martin Luther King Middle School in Madera, California. Jody also invites parents to school for a meeting at the beginning of the year. She explains her program and her expectations, and invites the parents to volunteer by sharing their vocations, hobbies, or interests with her classes. When a parent volunteers to talk to a class, Jody has the class read books about the topic to be presented and prepare questions for the speaker (or demonstrator). She also has the class practice the proper way to listen politely, introduce speakers, and thank them for their time. After the visits, the students write letters describing the parts of the presentation they found interesting.

Ron Clark (2003) taught in Harlem, New York City, and in his initial communication with parents, he stressed the importance of parents becoming part of the educational team. He asked for their cooperation in five important ways:

1. If there's a problem, call *me*, not the principal. Call me first and give me a chance to discuss the problem with you.
2. If you need to talk with me, send a note with your child. I will write back and we can set up a time to meet.
3. Don't allow your children to be late or absent for insignificant reasons. Let them know that school is important.
4. Realize that your child is one of many that I teach every day. I need your help to meet their needs. It's a team effort.
5. Trust that I know what I'm doing. If you don't understand, ask me, not someone else.

Confronting School Bullies

"Most children know when there's bullying," say Pepler and Craig (1997) of the LaMarsh Centre for Research on Violence and Conflict Resolution, "but they don't report it." Pepler and Craig have found that bullying problems tend to fester under the surface.

A study of Toronto schools found that a bullying act occurred every 7 seconds, but teachers were aware of only 4% of the incidents. Teachers may believe that they are with-it enough to be aware of bullying behavior in their classroom, but Pepler and Craig (1997) found that, while 7 of 10 teachers reported that they always intervene, their students disagree. Only one in four students says that teachers almost always intervene, and 75% of the students believe that teachers are either unaware or unwilling to get involved in the situation. Parents are not always seen as mediators either. Close to 40% of victims say that they have not talked to their parents about the problem. They suffer in silence on the playground or in the classroom, observed only by their peers, who are also reluctant to report the behavior.

Lack of intervention implies that bullying is acceptable and can be done without fear of consequences. Bullies and their accomplices need to understand the harm they cause and that their behavior will not be tolerated at school. They can change.

Ask any child what a bully looks like, and he or she is likely to describe someone who is bigger and stronger. While bullies certainly are known for their ability to overpower others physically, mental bullying can be just as damaging to children. When bullies are allowed to torment other students, physically or mentally, many feel the need to suffer in silence for fear that speaking up will provoke further torture. Bullying is not a problem that usually just takes care of itself. Action needs to be taken.

myeducationlab
The Power of Classroom Practice

For an example of a class discussion on bullying, go to the Video Examples section of Topic #3: Classroom Management in the MyEducationLab for your course and view the video entitled Eliminating Bullying in Schools.

As a reflective teacher using withitness to prevent bullying, you can take the following steps:

Use withitness to respond to bullying. Tell your students that you want to know when they feel bullied. When a bullying act is reported, have a frank discussion with the bully. Try to connect with him or her and find out what he or she wants or needs to feel happier and more successful without the need to bully other students.

Teach communication skills. If young, primary-age students are reluctant to discuss the subject, allow them to role-play bullying behavior with puppets or dolls. For intermediate and middle school students, hold a classroom meeting on the subject of bullying. Ask the class to suggest ways for children to express their feelings in a positive way. Practice methods that children can use to resolve problems firmly and fairly.

Identify ways to distinguish between teasing and bullying. Teach children how to ignore routine teasing. Not all provocative behavior must be acknowledged. Help children identify acts of aggression, bossiness, or discrimination. Encourage children not to give up objects or territory to bullies. This discourages bullying behavior.

In March 2004, Federal Health and Human Services Secretary Tommy G. Thompson announced a national campaign to educate Americans about bullying and youth violence, both of which have an extremely negative impact on children's success in school and their overall well-being.

"Bullying is something we cannot ignore . . . . "From the schoolrooms to the schoolyards we must nurture a healthy environment for our children. By engaging the entire community in preventing bullying we can promote a more peaceful and safe place for children to grow."

According to the U.S. Department of Education, one in four children who act as bullies will have a criminal record by the age of 30. These same students are much more likely to smoke, drink alcohol, and have lower grades in school. While we tend to think of the impact of bullying on the victims, we must not ignore the bully. These students are also our responsibility.

The U.S. Health and Human Services campaign against bullying is called "Take a Stand, Lend a Hand. Stop Bullying Now!" The campaign includes a Web-based, animated story and many other resources for teachers, administrators, and parents. See their website at www.stopbullyingnow.hrsa.gov.

Teaching Students How to Resolve Conflicts

In many schools, conflicts have escalated to violent confrontations. Students bicker, threaten, and harass one another. Conflicts among racial and ethnic groups are on the rise. Truancy is epidemic in some areas. Traditional discipline programs involving scolding, and suspensions do not appear to improve such situations. What can we do? What will you do when you are confronted with these situations? In some learning communities, teachers are instructing students how to be peacemakers and to resolve conflicts for themselves and their peers. Johnson and Johnson (1995) provide a curriculum for such programs in their book, *Teaching Students to Be Peacemakers.* Through the use of role plays and other learning opportunities to practice conflict resolution skills, students learn how to negotiate and mediate when conflicts arise.

Lisa Richardson, an eighth-grade teacher at Martin Luther King, Jr. Middle School in Modesto, California, teaches her students the communication skills they need to resolve conflicts peacefully. Based on the belief that conflict is inevitable and can even be healthy if dealt with in an honest and caring manner, Lisa sponsors the Peer Mediator program at her school.

PRAXIS
Strategies for conflict resolution are tested in PRAXIS™ Exam Section 1c: Students as Learners.

myeducationlab
For an example of ways to teach students to resolve conflicts, go to the Video Examples section of Topic #3: Classroom Management in the MyEducationLab for your course and view the video entitled Empowering Students to Resolve Conflicts.

✳ REFLECTIVE ACTION CASE STUDY ✳

Teaching Students How to Resolve Conflicts

Lisa Richardson, eighth-grade language arts teacher at Martin Luther King, Jr. Middle School in Modesto, California.

Teacher Begins to Plan

I was very troubled by the apparent lack of concern my students felt for other people. Instead of treating one another with respect, many of my students were involved in behaviors such as fighting, tattling, putting each other down, and interrupting when others were talking.

Teacher Considers What Students Already Know

My original belief was that the students were behaving as they behaved outside of school. They didn't seem to have the verbal skills to express themselves in a socially acceptable manner.

Reflective Teacher Uses Withitness and Reflects on the Event

Not willing to accept or perpetuate these behaviors, I asked myself: "How can I help these children to understand that people are different and have different ideas and perceptions, but that they are still very important? How can I help them learn to resolve their own conflicts? How can I teach them to make better choices for themselves?"

Teacher Does Research and Invites Feedback

I went to see mentor teachers in my district who were investigating a new peace education curriculum and asked them what programs or methods were helpful in building self-esteem. I gained an enormous amount of insight and information from these people as well as an enthusiasm to continue my search.

I did a literature search at a university library on the topic of peace education. I found from the articles that I read that this topic is a major concern to teachers across the country and that a number of programs are designed to address this issue. This search took about 2 months. I became so interested in the topic that I wrote my master's thesis on the subject as well. I also discovered a professor a Fresno State, Dr. Pamela Lane-Garon who was implementing peer mediattion programs at several local schools. I scheduled an appointment with Dr. Lane-Garon and discussed ways to begin peace and mediation programs at the middle school level.

Teacher Reflects Again, Using Feedback, Research, and Creativity

I decided that this problem was larger than my own classroom. My students would benefit most if the whole school became involved. This decision was a direct reflection of my values because I believe that each individual is important and must be shown respect and value, even if you don't agree with them. I also believe that there are alternatives to violence and that we need to teach these alternatives to our students.

PRAXIS
Techniques for planning instruction are tested in PRAXIS™ Exam Section 2b: Instruction and Assessment.

Teacher Creates a New Action Plan

I began my new effort by teaching my students to be more attentive listeners and how to solve problems among themselves without telling the teacher. We also began to practice sharing our feelings using "I" messages (e.g., "It hurts my feelings when you call me that name. I don't like it.")

Then I began to use role playing three to four times a week to involve my students in sharing feelings and practicing conflict resolution by listening to each other with respect. The students were very receptive to the curriculum. They loved being treated with respect by their peers. The class as a whole became cohesive and helpful toward one another.

After implementing these strategies in my classroom, I selected 30 students from classes throughout the school to become part of a peer mentoring program for the entire school. I taught them the same communication and conflict management skills that I had used in my classroom. These skills were all part of the Peer Mentoring Program designed by Dr. Lane-Garon (1997). I meet with the peer mentors twice a month for continued training. Each day they wear their blue jackets out on the playground and in the halls between classes and assist other students to resolve their conflicts peacefully.

Now, in our school, when a conflict occurs between students, a conflict manager takes the students involved in the conflict to a quiet corner or passageway to discuss the event. The patroller listens to students involved in a conflict and then asks them to suggest solutions. If a solution can be found by the students themselves, the conflict manager writes a brief report about the conflict and the solution. Copies of the report are given to the students, their teachers, and the principal.

I was concerned that not all teachers would take seriously the reports written by student peace patrollers, so I brought up this problem at a staff meeting. As a faculty, we have agreed that when we receive a peer mentor report, we show our respect for these successful conflict management encounters by congratulating the students for resolving their conflicts peacefully. I feel very proud of the role I took in developing this program for my school community.

Effective communication between teacher and student is based on mutual trust that grows from the basic moral principles of caring, consideration, and honesty. Reflective teachers who are guided by these moral principles express them in the classroom by listening empathetically or, as in the case of the Peer Mentoring Program at Lisa's school, by teaching students to listen empathetically. Listening is one of the most important ways of gathering information about students' needs in order to make informed judgments about why students behave the way they do.

Discussions between teacher and student must be guided by consideration for the child's feelings and fragile, developing self-concept. There is also a great need for honest, open exchanges of feelings and information among all members of a classroom. A sense of community and shared purpose grows from a realistic understanding of each other's perceptions and needs.

SCHEDULING TIME FOR ACTIVE LEARNING

Daily and Weekly Schedules

Teachers at all levels believe they cannot fit everything they want to teach into the school day. Charles (2002) cites "dealing with the trivial" as one of teachers' greatest time robbers (p. 243). When teachers simply try to fit everything into the day, they are as likely to include trivial matters as important ones. A reflective teacher weighs the relative importance of each element of the school program and allocates time accordingly. This may mean eliminating certain items entirely and carefully scheduling the minutes of the day to meet students' most important needs.

Schedules differ from grade to grade, depending on the relative importance of the subject at that grade level and the way the school is structured and organized. The most frequently used structure in elementary schools is to place students into grade-level, self-contained classrooms in which one teacher has the responsibility for teaching all academic subjects. In other cases, students may have a homeroom, but their academic subjects are departmentalized, meaning that teachers specialize in one academic area and students move from class to class during the day.

For example, the primary grades are usually structured as self-contained classrooms, and primary teachers often schedule reading and language arts activities for up to one-half of the school day. The intermediate grades may be self-contained or departmentalized, but in either case, math, science, and social studies activities are usually given more time than they are at the primary grades. In junior high school, the schedules are likely to be departmentalized, meaning that each teacher specializes in one subject and teaches it to several classes of students during the day.

No two schedules are alike. Teachers in self-contained classrooms are usually allowed great discretion in how they allocate time. Typically, state requirements mandate how many minutes per week are to be allocated to each of several subjects, but teachers make varied plans within those prescriptions. For example, the state may require a minimum of 150 minutes of math per week. Teacher A may schedule 30 minutes per day; teacher B may schedule 40 minutes for 4 days; teacher C may schedule 45 minutes on Mondays, Wednesdays, and Fridays, with brief review periods on other days.

Elementary class schedules may be rigid or flexible. They may be the same every day or they may vary greatly. They may be governed by bells or by the teacher's own inner clock. Charles (2002) recommends that, regardless of how it is determined, "the daily classroom schedule should be explained in such a manner that students know what activities are to occur at each part of the day and how they are to work and behave during those activities" (p. 10). When students know the schedule, they can learn to manage their own time more efficiently. A teacher who uses a consistent schedule may create a permanent display of the schedule on a bulletin board; a teacher who varies the schedule from day to day can write the current schedule on the chalkboard each morning.

The conventional wisdom of teachers is that the most difficult subjects should be scheduled early in the day, when students are most likely to be attentive. Reading and language arts are often the first subject of the day in a self-contained classroom, followed by math. Science, social studies, art, computers, and music compose the afternoons. This may be the preferred schedule, but often school constraints make it difficult to achieve. Physical education, art, computers, and music may be taught by other teachers in separate classrooms. The schedule for these special classes may affect the classroom teacher's schedule. Some groups must be scheduled for special classes in the morning, causing classroom teachers to adjust their plans.

Planning Time

Teachers may be annoyed when special classes interrupt their scheduled lessons, but they appreciate one important side effect: When the class leaves for art, computers, music, or physical education, the classroom teacher often has a planning period. Planning time is generally part of the teacher's contract and is designed to provide opportunities for individual or collegial planning. Teachers of self-contained classrooms usually have complete discretion over their planning time, but departmentalized teachers frequently hold meetings during their planning time to discuss how they will plan and deliver their shared curricula.

Teachers use planning time in various ways, some productive and others less so. Charles (2002) recommends that teachers use this time as efficiently as possible by "prioritizing tasks, giving attention to those that are absolutely necessary, such as planning, scoring papers, preparing for conferences, and preparing instructional materials and activities. Also high on the list should come those tasks that are difficult or boring, leaving for later those that are most enjoyable" (p. 244). Less efficient teachers may use the time for socializing, complaining, smoking, eating, reading magazines, or making personal telephone calls. Later they complain that the school day is too short and that they have too much work to do at home.

Charles (2002) recommends that routine tasks such as watering plants, cleaning the room, feeding animals, and distributing materials should not be done during planning time or by the teacher at all. The teacher who is an efficient time manager delegates as many of these routine tasks as possible to student helpers. This has two effects that contribute to a healthy classroom environment: (1) It reduces the stress teachers feel about time, and (2) it provides a sense of responsibility and meaningful accomplishment for the student helpers.

Most reflective teachers want to create a classroom in which students can meet their basic human needs for belonging and achievement. To accomplish this, they consider every aspect of the environment as it relates to children's needs. They arrange the furniture to meet students' needs for a sense of belonging; they create rules and schedule time to meet students' needs for security; they provide opportunities for students to write about and discuss their other feelings and needs. They do this because they want to create a nurturing sense of community in their classroom as a means of enhancing successful achievement.

Communicating with Parents

In Chapter 1, we emphasized the importance of sharing your philosophy of education with parents and helping them to understand the reasons why things were being done in your classroom. This communication is especially vital when it comes to classroom management and the rules and expectations of your classroom. Once you and the students have mutually established the classroom rules and procedures, these should be shared with the parents. This can be done through a class newsletter, via a website, or verbally at back-to-school night.

Parents should always feel that they are kept up to date with what is happening in the classroom. If a student is having adjustment difficulties or is having problems following the classroom rules, parents need to be aware of these problems. If you are able to communicate regularly with parents and give them updates, they will feel more a part of the learning team. When you and the parents can begin to align the expectations at home and at school, students will find the rules and expectations easier to understand and meet.

GUIDED GROUP EXPLORATION

1. Divide the class into groups.

2. Have each group match room arrangements (Figures 2.1, 2.2, 2.3, and 2.4) with the scenarios of the first day of school found in Figure 2.5 or 2.6 (high school).

3. Each group will then read the excerpts from the Philosophies of Education (Figure 2.7) and decide which of the teachers in the scenarios from the first day of school (Figure 2.5 or 2.6 high school) wrote each of the excerpts.

4. Bring the class back together to discuss how their group made their decisions.

Room 205

Mr. Evans is waiting at the front door, welcoming his students. The students enter the classroom and can be heard saying, "Hello, Mr. E." Mr. Evans says hello and that he's glad to have each student in class. He tells them to locate their seats by looking at the overhead in the front of the room. He has a seating chart shown on the overhead. Students begin to sit down and talk about their summer experiences.

After the bell rings, Mr. Evans walks to the center of the room and waits for quiet. The students look up and begin to prepare themselves for Mr. Evans's beginning remarks. One bulletin board in the front of the room is completed in the school colors and includes a picture of the school mascot, a pennant, and words from the fight song. The other bulletin board is filled with mathematical symbols and sayings by famous mathematicians. Along the top of the chalkboard is a set of very colorful geometric designs.

A set of rules is posted conspicuously on one of the walls of the room:

Rule 1: Respect each other.
Rule 2: Participate in class.
Rule 3: Help one another.
Rule 4: Everyone tries 100%.

Mr. Evans begins by saying, "Welcome to the best high school in the city. I hope each student has found his or her seat using the chart on the overhead. I believe that it is important that you know how to use such items as charts and graphs. I like to take every opportunity to use mathematics in my classroom. In addition, I would like to review the rules of this classroom. If you have any questions related to the rules, we should discuss them immediately. If you have suggestions for any additional rules, we may want to include them in the initial set of rules I've listed."

Room 206

Mr. Green leaves the teacher's lounge about 30 seconds before class starts. When he arrives at his classroom, the bell rings. Some students are still outside talking with friends. Mr. Green yells at the students to "get inside or I'll begin writing detention slips on the first day." The students begin to take seats or lean against the side shelves.

As you look around the classroom, there is nothing on any of the bulletin boards. Student books are stacked on the side shelves. They are obviously ready to be distributed to the class.

Mr. Green tells the students to "shut up" so that he can call the roll and tell students where their seats are going to be. He stands behind a podium and begins to call names and assign seats. As students go to their seats, they continue talking among themselves. Frequently, Mr. Green calls for silence, but the noise level does not diminish very much.

After the students are seated, Mr. Green complains that this is a bad beginning to the school year and warns the students again that he is not afraid to send them to detention if they don't know how to behave. He has used this tactic in the past, and he will use it with this class if necessary.

With no discussion of goals, rules, or expectations, Mr. Green appoints some of the boys to pass out the textbooks and writes "Read Chapter 1" on the chalkboard. Some students begin to read, while others continue to talk with each other. Mr. Green gets out his detention slips and begins to write names on them.

Figure 2.6 First day of a High School scenario.

I believe that teaching consists of making students aware of the responsibilities of a member of a free society. An effective classroom runs by having everyone be aware of the rules and expecting everyone to do their part. Cooperative learning has a place in my classroom, but I believe that I, the teacher, am the person responsible for planning instruction that meets the needs of each child.

I believe in discipline and hard work. I believe that students need to view school as their place of work. As a student, I was motivated and dedicated, and I want to pass that work ethic along to my students. I feel that most of today's children are given entirely too much freedom and are not learning any self-discipline. Teaching these attitudes and skills are a major part of my responsibility as a teacher.

I believe that it is my responsibility as a teacher to help each child discover the wonders of learning. I want my students to be an active part of all decisions in the classroom. Of course, I am ultimately responsible for the major decisions, but I want my students to learn to make good decisions and I feel that they won't be able to do that without practice in weighing the possibilities.

I believe that teaching consists of presenting material in an interesting way and then getting out of the way so that students can experiment and discover learning. I want my students to display their individual interests and strengths. I, the teacher, should not impose my preferences on them. I encourage my students to read widely and respond to their writing through their preferred intelligence. That may be writing, or drawing, or discussion, but that is their choice.

Figure 2.7   Excerpts from the educational philosophies of teachers.

REFLECTIVE ACTION ACTIVITY FOR YOUR PROFESSIONAL PORTFOLIO

What can teachers do to demonstrate concern about their students' self-concept? What actions can teachers take to demonstrate their willingness to help students develop good character and civic virtues?

I. Observing Classroom Management

1. Visit a classroom and focus on the classroom management strategies of the teacher you observe. Ask the classroom teacher if you can lead a 30-minute discussion with the students on the classroom rules and the consequences for breaking or following the rules. Retell what happened during your discussion. For example, describe the rules of the classroom and tell how they are documented. Are they clearly written for all students to see or are they simply "understood" to be the rules? Do the rules seem to be constant, or do they change from situation to situation? What are the consequences of breaking rules? Are the consequences clearly documented or are they merely "understood"? You must be able to describe all important elements and features of how the rules were created, how the teacher presents the rules to the students, and how the students respond. Include enough detail in your description that would allow an outsider to see what you saw as you observed the situation.

2. The next step is to write an *analysis* of this classroom teacher's rules and consequences. Analysis deals with reasons, motives, and interpretation and is grounded in the concrete evidence of the situation. What are the reasons the teacher gives for choosing these rules? What are the reasons for the teacher's selection of consequences? What do you think motivated the teacher to choose how to present and document these rules to the students? How do the students' responses to these rules and consequences give evidence of their effectiveness?

3. Finally, it is time for *reflection* on the entire process you observed. How would you approach the rule making and presentation process if this were your classroom? What would you do the same way as you observed this classroom teacher do, and why? What would you do differently, and why? Provide enough detail in your reflection to show assessors what you have learned from this experience, and how it will inform and improve your own teaching and classroom management practices in the future.

II. Connections Between Your Teaching Philosophy and Your Teaching Environment

1. Revisit the draft of the philosophy of education you began in the previous chapter.

2. Reflect on your philosophy and relate it to the type of classroom environment you will need to set up in order to implement your philosophy of teaching.

3. Using the blank classroom format activity sheet found on page 47, design a classroom furniture arrangement that would support the types of groupings and activities you may choose to implement in your approach to teaching.

References

Charles, C. (2002). *Elementary classroom management* (3rd ed.). Boston: Allyn & Bacon.

Evertson, C., & Harris, A. (2002). *Classroom management for elementary teachers* (6th ed.). Allyn & Bacon.

Gibbs, J. (2001). *Tribes*. Windsor, CA: CenterSource Systems, LLC.

Glasser, W. (2001). *Every student can succeed*. Los Angeles: William Glasser Institute.

Glasser, W.(1969). *Schools Without Failure*. NY: Harper and Row C.

Good, T., & Brophy, J. (2002). *Looking in classrooms* (9th ed.). Boston: Allyn & Bacon.

Goodman, J. (1995). *Laffirmations: 1001 ways to add humor to your life and work*. Sarasota Springs, NY: The Humor Project.

Herrell, A., & Jordan, M. (2007). *Thirty-five classroom management strategies: promoting learning and building community*, Upper Saddle River, NJ: Pearson Prentice Hall.

Johnson, D., & Johnson, R. (1995). *Teaching students to be peacemakers*. Minneapolis, MN: Burgess Publishing Co.

Jones, F. (2000). *Tools for teaching*. Washington, DC: Frederic H. Jones and Associates.

Kavalik, S. (1994). *Integrating thematic instruction: The model* (3rd ed.). Kent, WA: Books for Educators.

Lane-Garon, P., Nelson, E. & McWhirter, J. (1997) *Building a peaceful community: A handbook for implementing a comprehensive, school-based conflict resolution program*. Tempe: Arizona Educational Information System, Inc. (AEIS).

Lickona, T. (2004). *Character matters*. New York: Touchstone Books.

Loomans, D., & Kolberg, K. (2002). *The laughing classroom*. Tiburon, CA: HJ Kramer.

Marzano, R. (2003). *What works in schools*. Alexandria, VA: Association for Supervision and Curriculum Development.

Maslow, A. (1954). *Motivation and personality*. New York: Harper & Row.

Noddings, N. (2005). *The challenge to care in schools* (2nd ed.) New York: Teachers College Press.

Pepler, D., & Craig, W. (1997). *Bullying: Research and interventions*. Toronto, Canada: Institute for the Study of Antisocial Youth.

 Now go to Topics #3 and 15: Classroom Management and Collaborating with Colleagues and Families in the MyEducationLab (www.myeducationlab.com) for your course, where you can:

- Find learning outcomes for these topics along with the national standards that connect to these outcomes.
- Complete Assignments and Activities that can help you more deeply understand the chapter content.
- Apply and practice your understanding of the core teaching skills identified in the chapter with the Building Teaching Skills and Dispositions learning units.

Figure 2.8 Blank classroom Activity Sheet.

Lesson Planning and Sequencing

PRAXIS
Chapters 3 and 4
prepare you for
PRAXIS™ Exam
Section 2b:
Instruction and
Assessment.

W hen you think of *lesson plans*, what comes to mind? Perhaps you think of a piece of paper containing detailed directions that describe how to teach something to a class of students. Or perhaps you envision a weekly plan book with brief notations that serve to remind experienced teachers what they have planned to accomplish each period in the school day.

Beginning teachers often want to find examples of excellent lesson plans so that they can see how other, more experienced teachers have organized their teaching. How do they write meaningful learning objectives? How do they think of every detailed instruction? How do they write out a way to assess what students have gained from the lesson? It can seem like a mystery to many new teachers.

PRAXIS
Important
theorists in
education are
tested in
PRAXIS™ Exam
Section 1a:
Students as
Learners.

This chapter is designed to further demystify the process of writing your first lesson plans. We will describe ways to use the reflective action processes to envision and then describe on paper the goals and objectives you want to achieve, the materials you will need to gather, the step-by-step procedures you will use to teach your lesson, and the assessment devices you will employ to measure what your students have achieved.

Two major leaders in the process of developing meaningful lesson plans and curriculum are Ralph Tyler and Benjamin Bloom. You will see references to their research and methodology throughout the next two chapters. Ralph Tyler's (1949) basic principles on curriculum development were extended by Benjamin Bloom in a most useful way. A full discussion of Tyler's groundbreaking curriculum planning method follows in Chapter 4. A notable student of Tyler, Bloom and his colleagues (1956) attempted to respond to Tyler's first question of "determining the educational purposes that a school should seek to attain" as completely as possible. In meetings with other teachers, they brainstormed and listed all the possible purposes of education—all the possible educational objectives that they could think of or had observed during many years of classroom experience. Then they attempted to organize and classify all of these possible objectives into what is now known as the *taxonomy of educational objectives*. Their intent was to provide teachers with a ready source of possible objectives so that they could select the ones that fit the needs of their own students and circumstances. They also intended to help teachers clarify for themselves how to achieve their educational goals. A third purpose for the taxonomy was to help teachers communicate more precisely with one another. Bloom's taxonomy has been widely used in education for more than 50 years now. During the 1990s, a former student of Bloom's, Lorin Anderson led an assembly that met for the purpose of updating the taxonomy, hoping to add relevance for the 21st century. Representatives of three groups—cognitive psychologists, curriculum theorists, and instructional researchers—worked together to revise the taxonomy (Anderson & Krathwohl, 2001.)

Bloom's taxonomy first subdivides educational purposes into three domains of learning: cognitive, affective, and psychomotor. The *cognitive domain* deals with "the recall or recognition of knowledge and the development of intellectual abilities and skills"; the *affective domain* deals with "interests, attitudes, and values"; and the *psychomotor domain* concerns the development of manipulative and motor skills (Bloom et al., 1956, p. 7). The revised taxonomy (Anderson et al, 2001) updates the cognitive domain, the main focus of educational objectives, and further divides this domain into *factual knowledge, conceptual knowledge, procedural knowledge,* and *metacognitive knowledge.* "These categories are assumed to lie along a continuum from concrete *(factual)* to abstract *(metacognitive)*. The *conceptual* and *procedural* categories overlap in terms of abstractness, with some procedural knowledge being more concrete than the most abstract conceptual knowledge" (Anderson et al., 2001, p. 5). The definitions of the four categories are as follows:

Factual knowledge—The basic elements students must know to be familiar with a discipline or to solve problems within a discipline.

Conceptual knowledge—The interrelationships among the basic elements that enable them to work together.

Procedural knowledge—How to do something. Methods of inquiry, criteria for using skills, algorithms, techniques, and methods.

Metacognitive knowledge—Knowledge of learning in general as well as knowledge of a person's own learning.

(Adapted from Anderson et al., 2001)

CLARIFYING EDUCATIONAL GOALS AND OUTCOMES

Bloom's (1956) three domains (cognitive, affective, and psycomotor) are considered to be important in the curriculum because together they support the growth and development of the whole student. Educators used to begin writing curriculum documents by carefully wording their educational goals. An educational *goal* is a general, long-term statement of an important aim or purpose of an educational program. For example, most schools have a goal of teaching students how to read and write; other goals are to ensure that they understand the cultural heritage of the United States and to help them develop attitudes and habits of good citizenship.

Although standards-based education is relatively recent, it is based on an approach that has been in place for a number of years. In the past, the translation of goals into operational plans were specified as *outcomes*. Teachers thought about what outcomes were expected as a consequence of being in school and taking part in the planned curriculum. Educators need to be aware that goals express intentions, but that other factors may occur that alter the expectations in the educational process. Standards and outcomes are statements that describe what students will demonstrate as a culmination of their learning. Spady (1994) proposes that outcomes must specify "high quality, culminating demonstrations of significant learning in context" (p.18). A high-quality demonstration means one that is thorough and complete, showing the important new learning the student has gained or demonstrating the mastery of a new skill or process. Outcomes are designed to be assessed at or near the end of a learning period.

Written outcome statements are used to translate goals into actions. They describe what students will be able to do as a result of their educational program. If educators can envision what they want students to be able to do or know after a series of learning experiences, then they can plan with that outcome in mind. Learning outcomes generally describe actions, processes, and products that the student will accomplish or produce in a given period.

Cognitive outcomes are expressed in terms of students' mastery of content or subject-matter knowledge. For example, kindergartners are expected to master the alphabet; third-graders are expected to master multiplication facts; sixth-graders are expected to show knowledge of the history of ancient civilizations; while secondary students explore the history of ancient and modern civilizations, their ramifications, and their history-making interactions.

Educators also write many psychomotor outcomes, including strategies, processes, and skills that involve both the mind and the body in the psychomotor domain. You might note that some of these psychomotor outcomes might also be categorized as *procedural knowledge*. For example, elementary students are expected to learn how to decode symbols to read; write; calculate; solve problems; observe; experiment; research; interpret; make maps; and create works of art, music, and other crafts. These skills are successfully honed and practiced using similar methods at the secondary level.

Most teachers view affective outcome statements as being related to the development of character. Typically, schools highlight the affective outcomes emphasizing good citizenship; self-esteem; respect for individual and racial differences; and an appreciation of art, music, and other aspects of our cultural heritage. Positive affective outcomes are major goals in character education programs and have been shown to improve academic achievement, as noted in Chapter 2.

Individual teachers may write outcome statements for their own classes, but when they work collectively to clarify a set of schoolwide outcome statements, the effect on students is likely to be much more powerful and result in greater growth and change. This enhanced growth is a result of the consistency of experiences that students have in every classroom and with every adult in the school. Many school districts have statements of philosophy (often called mission statements) and outcome statements written in policy documents, but they may or may not be articulated and applied in the schools themselves. For effective change to take place, the school faculty must consider its educational purposes each year, articulate them together, and communicate them to the students through words and deeds.

In a classroom, each teacher has the right and the responsibility to articulate a set of educational outcomes for his or her students. Working alone or with teammates at the same grade level or subject area, the classroom teacher may want to articulate approximately two to four yearly outcome statements in each of the three domains. Tyler (1949) encourages teachers to select a small number of highly important goals "since time is required to change the behavior patterns of human beings. An educational program is not effective if so much is attempted that little is accomplished" (p. 33).

WRITING USEFUL AND APPROPRIATE OUTCOME STATEMENTS

The wording of standards or outcome statements must be general but not vague. This is a subtle but important distinction. Some school documents contain goals such as "to develop the full potential of each individual." What does this mean to you? Can you interpret it in a meaningful way in your classroom? Can you translate it into programs? Probably not.

PRAXIS

Learner objectives and outcomes are addressed in PRAXIS™ Exam Section 2b: Instruction and Assessment.

This goal statement is so general and vague that it cannot be put into operation, and it would be difficult to determine whether it is being attained.

An outcome statement should be general, in keeping with its long-term effects. It should also describe, clearly and precisely, how you want your students to change and what you want them to be able to do at the end of the term of study. Following are examples of useful *cognitive* outcome statements:

> Kindergarten students will recognize and name all the counting numbers from 1 to 20.
>
> Fifth-grade students will demonstrate that they understand how technology has changed the world by creating a timeline, graph, chart, or set of models to show the effects of technology on human experience.

Following are examples of *psychomotor* (sometimes referred to as skill or process) outcome statements:

> Third-grade students will measure and compare a variety of common objects using metric units of measurement of length, weight, and volume.
>
> Sixth-grade students will compose and edit written works using a word-processing program on a computer.
>
> High school students will demonstrate the ability to search the Internet to locate appropriate resources to support their hypothesis in written papers.

Following are examples of *affective* outcome statements:

> Second-grade students will demonstrate that they enjoy reading by selecting books and other reading materials and spending time reading in class and at home.
>
> Students at all grade levels will demonstrate that they tolerate, accept, and prize cultural, ethnic, and other individual differences in human beings by working cooperatively and productively with students of various ethnic groups.

In many school programs, outcome statements are intended to be accomplished over the course of a school year. Yearly outcome statements can be written for one subject or across several disciplines. Outcome statements can also be written for a shorter period, such as a term or a month. They are used as guides for planning curriculum and learning experiences for that length of time. At the end of a given time, the teacher assesses whether students have successfully demonstrated the outcome. If they have not, the teacher may need to repeat or restate the outcome statement to ensure that it can be met.

Some outcome statements may need to be modified because they are too vague. In the following examples, compare the first vague statement with the improved second statement:

> *Original outcome statement:* Students will demonstrate that they understand the U.S. Constitution.
>
> *Improved outcome statement:* Students will describe the key concepts in the articles of the U.S. Constitution and give examples of how they are applied in American life today.

Other outcome statements may need to be modified because they are too difficult for the students. Compare the following examples:

> *Original outcome statement:* Fourth-grade students will demonstrate that they know the key concepts of the Bill of Rights by creating a timeline showing how each has evolved over the past 200 years.
>
> *Improved outcome statement:* Fourth-grade students will create an illustrated mural showing pictorial representations of each of the articles in the Bill of Rights.

Some outcome statements may need to be improved by adding learning opportunities that will stimulate student interest and motivation to learn the material. Consider the following examples:

Original outcome statement: Students will recite the Bill of Rights.

Improved outcome statement: Students will work in cooperative groups to plan and perform skits comparing how life in the United States would differ with and without the constitutional amendments known as the Bill of Rights.

Standards and outcome statements are useful guides for educational planning, but they must be adapted to fit the needs of a particular teacher and class. For this reason, curriculum planning is an evolving process. A curriculum is never a finished product; it is constantly being changed and improved from day to day and year to year.

Standards might appear in one of three formats. Some standards are *procedural*; they refer to what procedures the students will be able to perform. Others are *declarative*; they state what broad concepts students will be able to understand. Still others are *contextual*; they refer to the ways and contexts in which the knowledge will be used. For example, a procedural standard might state that "students will locate mountain ranges and rivers on a state map." A declarative standard might state that "students will explain the concept of regional weather conditions." The contextual standard might state that "students will determine when to use a map and when to use a globe to locate needed information" (Kendall & Marzano, 2000).

Here is an obvious contrast between a more-reflective teacher and a less-reflective one. After teaching for 20 years, a reflective teacher has accumulated 20 years of experience and uses that experience to shape and improve curricular decisions. A less-reflective teacher is likely to have simply repeated one year of experience 20 times. Reflective teachers want to have an active role in the decision-making processes in their schools, and curricular decisions are the ones that count the most. They also display a strong sense of responsibility for making good curriculum choices and decisions, ones that will ultimately result in valuable growth and learning for their students.

WRITING OBJECTIVES TO FIT GOALS AND OUTCOME STATEMENTS

Goals are the broad, long-term descriptions of how you want your students to grow and develop; *outcome statements* refer to what you want students to know, understand, and be able to do during a given time. As you try to visualize your students accomplishing these goals and outcomes, it is useful to envision a sequence of events that will lead to successful accomplishment of the goal. Teachers often find it useful to write these sequential steps as a series of objectives that work together to accomplish the goal or outcome. Reflective teachers rarely plan a lesson in isolation. Rather, they consider each lesson in relation to what students already know as well as what they hope students will be able to do at a later time. This big-picture thinking characterizes reflective teachers, who realize that larger goals guide the selection of small daily tasks.

Educational Objectives

Educational objectives are short-term, specific descriptions of what teachers are expected to teach and/or what students are expected to learn. As described by Bloom and colleagues (1956) in the *Taxonomy of Educational Objectives*, they are intended to be used as an organizational framework for selecting and sequencing learning experiences. Embedded in any large goal (such as teaching children to read) are hundreds of possible specific objectives. One teacher may have an objective of teaching students how to decode an unfamiliar word using phonics and another objective of teaching students how to decode an unfamiliar word using context clues. Another teacher may select and emphasize the objectives of decoding unfamiliar words by using syllabification or linguistic patterns to meet the same overall goal.

The most commonly used model for writing behavioral objectives was based on the work of Ralph Tyler (1949). Tyler's model for writing objectives required the statement of a *behavior* and the *content* to be addressed, thus the term *behavioral objective*. Anderson and colleagues(2001) have revised these elements slightly, calling them *cognitive processes* instead of *behavior*s and addressing *knowledge* in place of *content*. Part of the reasoning behind these changes is to align the writing of behavioral objectives with current knowledge in cognitive psychology rather than the assumed, but not intended, alignment with behaviorism that was popular in Tyler's time (Anderson et al., 2001).

Objectives are also used to describe the sequence of learning events a teacher believes will help students achieve a given outcome. They also allow teachers to assess and chart group or individual progress. Teachers can ascertain students' needs more accurately if they have established a guideline of normal progress with which to compare each student's achievement.

Teachers who prefer to be specific about their lesson planning choose to write *behavioral objectives*. These include (1) the conditions under which the learning will take place; (2) the action, behavior, or cognitive process that will provide evidence of the learning; and (3) the criteria for success (how well a task must be completed or how often the behavior will occur). For example, a behavioral objective could be written as follows:

> After building words using initial consonants added to the word *at*, students will insert the correct "at" words in 8 of 10 cloze sentences.

This statement includes a description of the conditions for learning ("after building words using initial consonants added to the word *at*"), the behavior or cognitive process ("students will insert the correct 'at' words"), and the criterion for success ("in 8 of 10 cloze sentences").

Behavioral objectives can have a positive effect on teaching effectiveness; teachers who use them become better organized and more efficient in teaching and in measuring the growth of students' basic skills. When following a planned sequence of behavioral objectives, the teacher knows what to do and how to judge students' success. This system of planning also allows the teacher to better explain to students exactly what is expected of them and how to succeed.

Anderson et al (2001) identify three levels of objectives that can be used for different purposes in educational planning. **Global objectives** are broad and cover one or more years. They provide vision for successful planning and can be used to plan multiyear curriculum such as reading. **Educational objectives** have a more moderate scope, covering weeks or months. They can be used to design curriculum and plan units of instruction. **Instructional objectives** have a very narrow scope, covering just hours or days. They are used to prepare lesson plans and daily activities and experiences. All three of these types of objectives are vital in planning and implementing curriculum and instruction to meet the needs of all students. This use of multiple levels of objectives helps to overcome some of the problems and criticisms of the use of behavioral objectives.

Critics of behavioral objectives believe that when curriculum planning is reduced to rigid behavioral prescriptions, much of what is important to teaching and learning can be overlooked or lost. Thus, reflective teachers use behavioral objectives in their lesson planning for those learning events and activities that warrant them and rely on other, less-rigid objectives when appropriate.

As an alternative form for learning that cannot be predicted and calibrated, Eisner (1985) suggests the *problem-solving objective*.

> In a problem-solving objective, students are given a problem to solve—say, to find out how deterrents to smoking might be made more effective, how to design a paper structure that will hold two bricks 16 inches above a table, or how the variety and quality of the food served in

the cafeteria could be increased within the existing budget. In each of these examples, the problem is posed and the criteria necessary to resolve the problem are clear. But the forms of its solution are virtually infinite. (pp. 117–118)

Eisner (1985) points out that behavioral objectives have "both the form and the content defined in advance. There is, after all, only one way to spell aardvark." The teacher using behavioral objectives is successful if all the children display identical behavior at the end of the instructional period. "This is not the case with problem-solving objectives. The solutions individual students or groups of students reach may be just as much a surprise for the teacher as they are for the students who created them" (p. 119).

As an example, a problem-solving objective might be written:

> When given a battery, a lightbulb, and a piece of copper wire, the student will figure out how to make the bulb light.

This objective describes the conditions and the problem that is to be solved but does not specify the actual behaviors the student is to use. The criterion for success is straight-forward but is not quantifiable and, in fact, some of the most important results of this experience are only implied. The teacher's primary aim is to cause the student to experiment, hypothesize, and test methods of solving the problem. This cannot be quantified and reported as a percentage. Thus, problem-solving objectives, then, are appropriate when teachers are planning learning events that allow and encourage students to think, make decisions, and create solutions. For that reason, they are frequently employed when teachers plan lessons that are designed to develop critical, creative thinking. They are especially valuable when teachers are planning learning events at the higher levels of the revised Bloom's taxonomy (2001).

Planning for Higher-Level Thinking

Many teachers now use the revised *Taxonomy for Learning, Teaching, and Assessing* (Anderson et al., 2001) as the basis for organizing instructional objectives into coherent, connected learning experiences. The term *Bloom's revised taxonomy* (as commonly used by teachers) refers to the six levels of the cognitive domain described here. Any curriculum project, such as a year-long plan, a unit, or a lesson plan, can be enriched by a conscious planning of learning events at all six levels of the taxonomy.

Higher-level objectives.	Level 6: Creating
	Level 5: Evaluating
	Level 4: Analyzing
	Level 3: Applying
Lower-level objectives.	Level 2: Understanding
	Level 1: Remembering

Remembering-level objectives can be planned to ensure that students have the ability to retrieve, recognize, and recall relevant knowledge from long-term memory. *Understanding-level objectives* support students as they construct meaning from oral, written, and graphic messages through interpretation. Behavioral objectives are very useful and appropriate at the remembering and understanding levels.

At the *applying level*, problem-solving objectives or expressive outcomes can be written that ask students to apply what they have learned to other cases or to their own lives, thereby causing them to transfer what they have learned in the classroom to other arenas. *Analyzing-level* objectives and outcomes call on students to look for motives, assumptions, and relationships such as cause and effect, differences and similarities, hypotheses and conclusions. When analysis outcomes are planned, the students are likely to be engaged in critical thinking about the subject matter. Because the *evaluating level* requires students to make judgments based on criteria and standards, activities that involve research and critiquing are appropriate. *Creating-level* activities require that students use their knowledge and skills to put elements together to form a functional whole. These activities offer students opportunities to use creative thinking as they combine elements in new ways, plan original experiments, and create original solutions to problems. At the *evaluation level*, students engage again in critical thinking as they make judgments using internal or external criteria and evidence. For these levels, problem-solving objectives or expressive outcomes are likely to be the most appropriate planning devices.

For example, in planning a series of learning events on metric measurement, the teacher may formulate the following objectives and outcome statements:

Remembering-level behavioral objective: When given a meter stick, students will point to the length of a meter, a decimeter, and a centimeter with no errors.

Understanding-level behavioral objective: When asked to state a purpose or use for each of the following units of measure, the student will write a short response for meter, centimeter, liter, milliliter, gram, and kilogram, with no more than one error.

Applying-level problem-solving objective: Using a unit of measure of their choice, students will measure the length and width of the classroom and compute the area.

Analyzing-level problem-solving objective: Students will create a chart showing five logical uses or purposes for each measuring unit in the metric family.

Evaluating-level judgment-making objective: A group of four students will work together to judge the effectiveness of written arguments for the adoption of the metric system in the United States.

Creating-level expressive objective: Students will create a reader's theatre performance to illustrate ways in which the United States would be more globally viable if we changed to the metric system.

When we review the six objectives and outcomes for metric measurement, we see clearly that the first two differ from the others in that they specify exactly what students will do or write to get a correct answer. In addition, the criteria for success are not ambiguous. These two qualities are useful to ensure successful teaching and learning at the knowledge and comprehension levels. After successfully completing these first two objectives, students will have developed a knowledge base for metric measurement that they will need to do the higher-level activities. In the problem-solving objectives, students are given greater discretion in determining the methods they use and the form of their final product. In the expressive outcome statements, discretionary power is necessary if students are to be empowered to think critically and creatively to solve problems for themselves.

Although the taxonomy was originally envisioned as a hierarchy, and although it was believed that students should be introduced to a topic beginning with level 1 and working upward through level 6, most educators have found that the objectives and learning experiences can be successfully taught in any order. For example, a teacher may introduce the topic of nutrition and health by asking students to discuss their opinions or attitudes about smoking (an evaluation-level objective). The teacher may then provide the students with knowledge-level data about the contents of tobacco smoke and work back up to the evaluation level. When students are asked their opinions again, at the end of the lesson, their judgments are likely to be stronger and better informed.

As in the example about smoking and health, it is often desirable to begin with objectives that call on students to do, think, find, question, or create something and thereby instill in them a desire to know more about the topic. Knowledge- and comprehension-level objectives can then be designed to provide the students with the facts, data, and main ideas they need to know to further apply, analyze, synthesize, and evaluate the ideas that interest them. Figure 3.1 shows a planning device that offers teachers ideas for learning events that correspond to each level of the taxonomy.

Learning objectives can be planned at all levels of the revised Bloom's taxonomy. Behavioral objectives are best suited for remembering and understanding levels; problem-solving and expressive objectives are best suited for higher-level objectives.

Examples of objectives	Appropriate action verbs
Remembering Level	**Remembering Level**
Students will recognize and recall specific terms, facts, and symbols.	Find, locate, identify, list, memorize, recognize, name, repeat, point to, match, pick, choose, state, select, record, spell, say, show, circle, underline
Understanding Level	**Understanding Level**
Students will demonstrate understanding of the main idea of material heard, viewed, or read and interpret or summarize in their own words.	Explain, define, translate, relate, demonstrate, calculate, discuss, express in own words, write, review, paraphrase, summarize, classify, give examples
Applying Level	**Applying Level**
Students will apply an abstract idea in a concrete situation to solve a problem or relate it to prior experiences.	Change, adapt, employ, use, make, construct, demonstrate, compute, calculate, illustrate, modify, prepare, put into action, solve, do
Analyzing Level	**Analyzing Level**
Students will break down a concept or idea into its constituent parts; identify relationships among elements; distinguish cause-and-effect relationships, similarities and differences.	Distinguish, categorize, deduce, dissect, examine, compare, contrast, divide, catalog, inventory, question, outline, chart, survey, differentiate, organize, determine point of view
Evaluating Level	**Evaluating Level**
Students will make informed decisions about the value of ideas or materials, using standards and criteria to support	Appraise, critique, consider, judge, editorialize, give opinions, grade, rank, prioritize, value opinions and views.
Creating Level	**Creating Level**
Students will put together elements in new and original ways, create patterns or structures that are unique.	Combine, create, develop, design, build, arrange, assemble, collect, concoct, connect, devise, hypothesize, invent, imagine, plan, generate, revise, organize, produce.

Figure 3.1 Curriculum planning using the revised Bloom's taxonomy.

Source: Adapted from: Anderson et al. (2001). *A taxonomy for learning, teaching, and assessing: A revision of Bloom's taxonomy of educational objectives.*

PLANNING LESSONS FOR ACTIVE LEARNING

Teachers can use their reflective actions to ensure a high-quality learning experience for their students. They begin by using withitness when they write the first draft of their lesson plan. Reflective teachers try to picture in their minds what a lesson will look like in real life. They try to anticipate what their students need, what they can do easily, and where they will need the most guidance and positive feedback. Reflective teachers recognize that students are more motivated to learn when they understand why this learning is important. For this reason, they explain the reason for each lesson.

When describing your objectives, use words and examples that are easily understood by the students at your grade level. For example, during a science lesson, a reflective teacher might say:

> We are doing this experiment today to help you see for yourselves how solids can literally disappear in a liquid. The procedures we are going to use are the same type of procedures that real scientists use when they want to discover something new about the laws of science.

After this initial explanation, students are likely to be eager to begin. They want to get on with the experiment and see for themselves what happens. They enjoy acting as scientists during the process.

To make learning tasks even more inviting, reflective teachers know that it is important to model the physical behaviors or mental processes needed to do the work. Kindergarten teachers model how to write a capital letter *A*. Elementary teachers demonstrate how to divide a pizza into equal fractions. Middle school teachers show students how to place their hands on the keyboard of the computer. High school teachers do a sample algebra problem on the chalkboard. After modeling, reflective teachers stay just as active on the sidelines, encouraging and guiding students as they begin the active process of finding out how things work.

Another role that the most effective teachers take while teaching a new skill is to model internal behaviors (such as problem solving) by thinking aloud while they model the first example for their students. By telling the students verbally what they are thinking when they work on a problem, teachers provide real-life examples of how learning occurs. Thinking aloud is particularly helpful when asking students to comprehend an unfamiliar skill or a difficult concept.

At all stages of lesson planning and presentation, reflective teachers carefully observe and interact with their students—learning what students already know and where they need extra help. This observation and assessment is critical to the success of any given lesson, as well as to the planning and sequencing of future lessons. It also helps to think again about this three-step process when things happen during a lesson that surprise you or upset your plans.

Planning Assessments That Fit Your Lesson's Objectives

How does a teacher measure success? Chapter 10 covers in detail the topic of assessing students' needs and accomplishments, with a focus on creating authentic assessment systems that describe students' progress over time. In designing lesson plans, however, it is useful to consider some options for assessing students' accomplishments on a single lesson.

Traditionally, the methods used to assess individual achievement are either written or oral quizzes, tests, and essays. When elementary teachers want to determine whether the class as a whole has understood what was taught in a lesson, they frequently use oral responses to questions that usually begin with "Who can tell me . . . ?" These are useful and efficient ways to assess student achievement at the knowledge and comprehension levels of Bloom's taxonomy, but reflective teachers are seldom satisfied with these measures alone. They seek out other methods that are less frequently used but more appropriate in evaluating learning at the higher levels.

Remembering-level objectives are tested by determining if the student can remember or recognize accurate statements or facts. Multiple-choice and matching tests are the most frequently used measuring devices.

Understanding-level objectives are often tested by asking students to define terms in their own words. (Only memory would be tested if the students were asked to write a definition from memory.) Another frequently used testing device is a question requiring a short-answer response, either oral or written, showing that the student understands the main idea. Essays that ask students to summarize or interpret are also appropriate. Multiple-choice tests are also used as a test of comprehension, but the questions call on the students to do more than recall a fact from memory; they ask students to read a selection and choose the best response from among several choices.

At the applying level, students are usually asked to apply what was learned in a classroom to a new situation. For that reason, application-level objectives are usually assessed by presenting an unfamiliar problem that requires the student to transfer what has been learned to the unfamiliar situation. Essays in which the students describe what they would do to solve an unfamiliar problem can be used. In classrooms where students are encouraged to use manipulative materials and experiment with methods to solve problems, teachers assess the processes used by the student and the end-product, such as a hand-drawn or

PRAXIS
Assessment strategies are tested in PRAXIS™ Exam Section 2c: Instruction and Assessment.

computer-generated design of a new device, a written plan for solving a problem, or a model of a new product. These products may or may not be graded, depending on the teacher's need to quantify or qualify students' success.

Analyzing-level objectives may also require that the teacher present unfamiliar material and ask the student to analyze it according to some specified criteria. In these situations, students may be asked to analyze various elements, relationships, or organizational principles, such as the way in which elements are categorized, differences and similarities, cause and effect, logical conclusions, or relevant and irrelevant data.

Again, essays may be used to assess analytical behavior, but the essays must do more than tell the main idea (comprehension) and describe how the student would apply previously learned knowledge. Analytical essays must clarify relationships, compare and contrast, show cause and effect, and provide evidence for conclusions. Other student products that are appropriate for assessing analysis are timelines; charts that compare, contrast, or categorize data; and a variety of graphs that show relationships.

The types of student products that demonstrate *evaluating* are infinitely variable. They might include activities to create and use an evaluation standard or use one to compare and contrast the relative worth of products, written analysis, or practical applications. Products to demonstrate *creating* might include creative essays, stories, poems, plays, books, and articles. All of these are certainly appropriate for assessing language arts objectives. Performances, including original speeches, drama, poems, and musical compositions, are just as useful. Student-created products may include original plans, blueprints, artwork, computer programs, and models of proposed inventions. Student work may be collected in portfolios to demonstrate growth and achievement in a subject area.

Evaluating the relative success of higher-level products is difficult. No objective criteria may exist for judging the value or worth of a student's original product. When student products are entered in a contest or submitted for publication, outside judges with expertise in the subject area provide feedback and may even make judgments that the classroom teacher cannot make. Many elementary teachers simply record whether a finished product was turned in by the student rather than attempt to evaluate or grade it.

Evaluating-level objectives call on students to make a judgment. To test a student's ability to make a judgment, the teacher must provide all of the needed data, perhaps in the form of charts or graphs, and ask the student to draw certain conclusions from these data. Another form of evaluation is to ask students to state their opinions on a work of art or to judge the validity of a political theory, offering evidence to support their opinions. The types of products that students create at this level are critical essays, discussions, speeches, letters to the editor, debates, drama, videos, and other forms that allow them to express their points of view.

Evaluation outcomes and objectives are difficult to grade. A teacher who offers students an opportunity to express their own views usually places high value on independent thinking and freedom of expression. Therefore, the teacher cannot grade a student response as right or wrong. The teacher can, however, assess whether the student has used accurate, sufficient, and appropriate criteria in defending a personal opinion. Student work that has cited inaccurate, insufficient, or inappropriate evidence should probably be returned to the student with suggestions for revision.

In summary, evaluation of student accomplishment should be directly linked to the lesson's objectives. To assess basic knowledge and skills, behavioral objectives are useful because they state exactly what the student will be able to do and specify the criteria for success. For higher-level objectives, problem-solving objectives may be less precise, but they still should describe the type of student behavior or product expected and give some general criteria for success.

When teachers plan by writing clear behavioral, problem-solving, and expressive objectives for their lessons, they are, in effect, clarifying their expectations regarding what students will gain from the lesson and their criteria for success. The evaluation section of a lesson plan is then usually a restatement of the criteria expressed in the objectives. You will see an example of this in the sample lesson plans in this chapter.

Predicting Possible Outcomes of Your Lesson Plans

Imagine that you have written your first lesson plan, and decide to show it to some experienced teachers and ask them what they think about it. Congratulations! You are using this very important reflective action of inviting feedback. Now you hope that the veteran teachers will read your plan and look up with huge smiles to tell you that you have done a great job.

What is more likely is that one of the teachers will begin the discussion with "What if . . . ?" Another will say, "Have you thought about . . . ?" One might even laugh and tell a story about the "perfect lesson plan" that turned into a disaster in the classroom. When Judy Eby was a student teacher at the University of Illinois in Urbana, she planned just such a perfect lesson. Within a unit on animal behavior, she planned a series of lessons in which students were allowed to conduct experiments on live animals. Following her written lesson plan, she asked students to bring in small animal cages from home to house the animals. The students brought in leftover gerbil cages, bird cages, and other small containers. On the first day of the new unit, Judy went to the university and got one white mouse per student and put the mice into the students' cages. The mice were smaller and more agile than expected, however, and they quickly squeezed out of the cages and began running around the classroom. Chaos ensued. She asked the students to help catch the mice and put them all into a glass-walled aquarium. Although planned objectives were not met that day, there were certainly many opportunities for problem solving and "unintended" outcomes.

Judy and her master teacher spent the afternoon rethinking the entire lesson plan without separate cages. They decided to identify individual mice by using different colors and patterns of ink dots so that students could tell their mice apart. Having done this, they went home for the night. When they returned the next morning, the mice had disrupted the plan again. Baby mice had been born during the night, and some of the adult mice were dead or wounded by attacks from their own species. The third revision of this lesson plan called for mealworms instead of mice to be used as the experimental animals.

Most veteran teachers have experienced this type of scenario more than once. Even the best plans can go wrong. Indeed, part of the nervousness many teachers feel before teaching a lesson comes from this very realization. It is hard to prepare for the unexpected.

Even when the basic lesson plan runs smoothly, it is almost a given that in any lesson, some students will require different experiences or explanations to understand the new concept or skill being taught. Some teachers can think on their feet and address student confusion on the spot, but this can be a challenge for a new teacher. We suggest that you consistently plan a second way of introducing or extending any given concept just in case you need it. We think you'll often be glad you did. Relational teachers are aware that students learn differently and that some may need a second strategy to achieve the lesson objective.

As we observe new teachers presenting lessons, one thing we have noticed is that discipline and management problems rarely occur when the lesson content is focused slightly above students' current knowledge base. This is probably due to the fact that students feel challenged, but not overwhelmed, by the experience, so they are engaged in learning and feel happy to cooperate. In contrast, problems seem to arise when a teacher prepares a lesson that covers content the students already know. They act restless and may become disruptive when they feel that the teacher is babying them or talking down to them. What should you do when you arrive in a setting, materials in hand, and find out the students have already mastered the content you have planned to teach? Should you press bravely on, working your way through the lesson because it is what you worked so hard to prepare? To do so is to ignore the learning needs of your students. We have often seen this and believe that the biggest reason for this choice is a simple one—the teacher has nothing else prepared and has yet to think through the next steps in the learning sequence.

Varying Objectives for Students with Special Needs

Often teachers plan their lessons with a set of objectives for the students in their class whose knowledge and skills are at grade level. The term *at grade level* means the average or typical level of understanding or skill that most children are able to achieve at that age and in that

> **PRAXIS**
> Approaches for teaching students with special needs and/or varying learning styles are tested in PRAXIS™ Exam Section 1b: Students as Learners.

grade. As teachers gain experience teaching at a grade level, they are able to describe what the typical learner at that grade level can accomplish. Because most children in the class will have skills and knowledge near the average, it makes sense for teachers to plan lessons with difficulty levels conforming to that average.

Reflective teachers realize that in any classroom, there is likely to be a wide range of student achievement and experience. There are bound to be students who have already learned and mastered the concepts being taught. Many kindergarten students come to school knowing the entire alphabet and how to count to 100. Some secondary students could teach the teacher a thing or two about computer usage. Planning for ways to extend the knowledge of these students is just as important to the success of your lesson as is planning for ways to help students who do not understand the concept right away. When you enter a classroom with a plan for extending a lesson's concepts and content, you will feel more confident and will enhance the learning experiences of more of your students.

There are also likely to be students who appear to be completely bewildered during a lesson. Others give no readable cues for you to tell whether they understand or do not understand the lesson concepts. Some students may sit quietly but refuse to try the learning task you have assigned to them. Reflective teachers accept that there are many reasons students may fail to respond in the ways we hope and plan for. For example, a student may be hungry, tired, or preoccupied with a concern (outside or inside of school) that is more compelling than this lesson (Maslow, 1954). Students may doubt their ability to succeed at the task and avoid it in an attempt to save face or feel that the task is far too easy and therefore not worth the effort to complete. Students may also need more experience with new or unfamiliar vocabulary.

If you consider reasons a student may not respond appropriately to your lesson, you can begin to write variations in your lesson plan to accommodate these students. For example, if you realize that some students may feel threatened by a particular task, such as reading aloud to the entire class from their book report, you can plan an alternate task, such as allowing students to work in pairs and discuss their book reports with a peer. By having a backup plan, you will know what to do when a student stares blankly instead of working. By visualizing and trying to predict the possible outcomes of your lesson plan, you can avoid these uncomfortable situations, maintain the flow of the lesson, and involve all your students more productively.

WRITING A WELL-ORGANIZED LESSON PLAN

When teachers plan for day-to-day learning experiences, they are creating lesson plans. Usually a lesson plan is created for a single subject or topic for one day, although some experiential, hands-on lessons may be continued for several days in a row. Teachers in self-contained classrooms must devise several different lesson plans each day, one for each subject they teach, unless they choose to use multidisciplinary units. Teachers in the upper grades who work in departmentalized settings, where students travel from class to class for various subjects, must still create different lesson plans for each grade or group of students they teach.

In university or college courses designed to prepare teachers, the lesson plan is an important teaching or learning device. The professor and experienced classroom teachers can provide the aspiring teacher with models of good lesson plans. Students can search the Internet or purchase books that contain well-written lesson plans. However, it is only by actively creating their own plans that they are able to demonstrate the extent to which they understand and can apply the theories and principles they have learned about reflective thinking and planning.

For that reason, many university and college programs require students to create a number of precise and detailed lesson plans. Sometimes students observe that the classroom teachers they know do not write such extensive plans for every lesson. Instead, these teachers write their lesson plans in large weekly planning books, and a single lesson plan may consist of cryptic notations such as "Math: p. 108"; "Social Studies: Review Ch. 7"; "Science: Continue Nutrition." Although experienced teachers may record their lesson plans with such brief notes, novice teachers need to write lessons in great detail. They need to develop the mental skills and facilities to see each lesson in its entirety and in its attention to detail prior to presenting it to their students. This ability to think ahead and predict the lesson design related to expected outcomes comes after years of practice and lesson planning. Every good teacher has gone through this same process and recognizes the importance of good, clear planning in order to provide the greatest benefit for students. Writing detailed lesson plans also enables novice teachers to communicate their plans to the professor or mentor teacher, who can provide feedback on the plan before the lesson is taught. Experienced mentor teachers can easily see how the lesson is organized and may be able to offer suggestions for improving the presentation or, at the least, how to avoid predictable pitfalls.

Well-written lesson plans have additional value in that they can be shared. A teacher's shorthand notes that serve as a personal reminder can rarely be interpreted by an outsider. If a substitute teacher is called to replace a classroom teacher for a day or longer, the substitute needs to see the daily plans in language he can understand and use. Teams of teachers often write lesson plans together or for one another. In this case, they need to have a common understanding of the lesson objectives, procedures, evaluation, and resources.

The form may vary, but most lesson plans share a number of common elements. Three essential features of a complete, well-organized lesson plan are the objectives, procedures, and evaluation. These correspond to the four questions of curriculum planning formulated by Tyler (1949). Lesson objectives specify the "educational purposes" of the lesson. The procedures section describes both "what educational experiences can be provided" and the way they can be "effectively organized." The evaluation section describes the way the teacher has planned in advance to determine "whether these purposes are being attained" (Tyler, 1949, p. 1).

The description, another feature in a lesson plan, is used to identify it and give the reader a quick overview of its purpose or description. A lesson plan also often contains information about the resources teachers need as background preparation for teaching the lesson, as well as any materials necessary for actual execution of the lesson.

A suggestion for teachers in this age of computers is to create a basic outline of a lesson plan with a word-processing program and save it on a CD. Then, when you wish to write a lesson plan, you can put the outline on the screen and fill in the spaces. You may also want to take some time to access the Internet and look at various lesson plans posted there. Many sites are available through commercial publishers, as well as through groups of teachers at local and state levels.

The Internet also provides some new clues and models that can inform and enliven your teaching. Almost any search engine on the World Wide Web has a category called *education* and a subcategory called *K–12 education*. Type "K–12 Lesson Plans" into Google© to find webpages filled with real-life examples of teachers' lesson plans in every subject and at every grade level. Other exciting materials and suggestions can be found at http://k6educators.about.com/.

For example, Ask Eric Virtual Library can be accessed at http://ericir.syr.edu. This webpage contains a library of lesson plans created by teachers and submitted to the Educational Resources International Clearinghouse (ERIC). The Gateway to Educational Materials is another source of ready-to-use lesson plans at http://www.thegateway.org. Once you have located these webpages, you can bookmark them and refer to them frequently. When you have mastered the art of writing your own lesson plans, you can submit one of your best to these types of organizations for others to see.

A Lesson Plan Model

Including all of the ideas discussed in this chapter in one lesson plan can sound pretty daunting, but it is something that will become second nature to you with experience. To help you remember the important aspects of a lesson, we offer you a model of a lesson plan format in Figure 3.2. Take some time to review it now, and see if you can explain why each part has

Title of Lesson:

Subject Area: **Lesson Duration (estimate of time):**

Standards Addressed (state or national standards addressed):

Materials and Resources:
Teacher Materials: (What materials will you need to teach the lesson?)

Student Materials: (What materials will the students need to use to complete the lesson?)

Objective: (What will the students be able to do at the conclusion of the lesson?)

Reflective Action Procedures:
Pretesting: (How will you assess students' prior knowledge and skills related to this lesson?)

Adaptations for Students with Special Needs: (What adjustments will you make for English learners or special needs students?)

Motivation: (What will you say or do to get the students interested in the lesson?)

Teacher Explanation: (How will you explain what they will be learning and why learning it is important?)

Teacher Modeling: (How will you demonstrate what they will do?)

Guided Practice: (How will you take them step by step through the lesson?)

Check for Understanding: (How will you determine if they are ready to practice on their own?)

Independent Practice: (What will they do to practice what you have taught them?)

Closure: (How will you review or celebrate the learning that has taken place?)

Assessment: (How will you know that your objective has been met? How will you determine which students need further instruction?)

Plan for Further Instruction for Students Who Need It: (How will you provide additional instruction for the students who did not meet the objective?)

Figure 3.2 Annotated reflective action lesson plan format.

been included. This outline can be copied on your computer disk for use in college and the rest of your teaching career.

After you have put in the title, subject, grade level, and lesson duration, we suggest using clear and specific objectives for each lesson to help you maintain focus and avoid overwhelming students with too many ideas at once. Once you have established your basic objectives for the lesson, think about some of the students in your class who have special needs. Write notes to yourself to describe how you will scaffold the lesson for students who do not understand or who are learning to speak English. Write notes about enriching the lesson for students who have mastered the concept you are teaching and need a more challenging curriculum.

By listing the materials you need ahead of time, you avoid getting halfway through the lesson and missing something that you need. Each step of the procedures in our model may help you to think through what you will do to prepare for and teach the lesson. The pre-assessment step refers to the process of finding out what your students already know prior to teaching a new lesson. Reflective teachers use this strategy to avoid behavior problems from bored students as well as from those who do not have a clue what you are talking about. This strategy also helps you to build the background for the day's lesson. For example, if you were preassessing students' knowledge of metric measurement, you might want to show a meter stick to your students and ask if they know what it is and what it is used for.

After you have written a draft of your lesson plan, imagine yourself teaching it and consider the possible outcomes that may result. Think through what you will do if students do not understand or appear to be bored because they have already mastered the concept. What can you predict about the reaction of students in your classroom who are learning English? What will they need from you and their classmates to be successful in this lesson? You can see that the outcome prediction is a vital aspect of withitness and reflective action in teaching.

In the active learning experience example, the teacher can aid the students in comprehending what they have learned by having them share what they did that worked and what they did that did not work. Concepts can be developed by articulating and generalizing what they learned about electricity, for example. Such a teacher-led discussion is an essential part of active, hands-on learning. It provides a sense of closure.

Every lesson or presentation can benefit from some thoughtful consideration to its ending. It is important to allow time for closure. You may use this time to ask questions that check for understanding so that you will know what to plan for the lesson that follows. You may allow the students to close the lesson with their own conclusions and new insights. A few moments spent summarizing what was learned is valuable in any form. If insight is to occur, it will probably occur in this period. At the close of one lesson, you can also indicate what will follow in the next lesson so that your students know what to expect and how to prepare for it.

SEQUENCING OBJECTIVES IN SCHOOL SUBJECTS
Sequencing Objectives in Mathematics

Some subjects are very sequential in nature. Mathematics is the best example in the elementary curriculum because its concepts and operations can be readily ordered from simple to complex. Teachers can effectively organize the teaching of computational skills in the basic operations of addition, subtraction, multiplication, and division very easily. For example, outcome statement 1 describes a possible sequence for teaching an essential understanding about the concept of numbers.

> *Mathematics outcome statement 1:* Primary students will show how addition and subtraction are related to one another.

To accomplish this outcome, primary teachers will introduce students to the concept of numbers and give them concrete, manipulative experiences in adding and subtracting one-digit numbers. Students may act out stories in which children are added and subtracted from a group. They may make up stories about animals or objects that are taken away and then brought back to demonstrate subtraction and addition.

Math textbooks offer a sequence of learning activities and practice of math facts, but reflective teachers find that the math textbook must be used flexibly and supplemented with other learning experiences. Before planning math lessons for a particular group of students, the teacher must pretest their entry-level knowledge and skills. Pretests will reveal that some children have already mastered some of the skills in the sequence and do not need to spend valuable time redoing what they already know. They need enriched math activities to allow them to progress. Other children may not have the conceptual understanding of number relationships to succeed on the first step. For them, preliminary concrete experiences with manipulative materials are essential for success.

These are sample math objectives to fit outcome statement 1:

Students will be able to:

1. Use blocks to show addition of two single-digit integers.
2. Use blocks to show subtraction of two single-digit integers.
3. Use pennies and dimes to show place value of 1s and 10s.
4. Subtract pennies without regrouping.
5. Add pennies and exchange 10 pennies for a dime.
6. Subtract pennies by making change for a dime to show regrouping.
7. Tell how subtraction is related to addition using coins as an example.

These sample objectives are representative of the basic knowledge- and comprehension-level skills needed to accomplish the outcome statement. They can be written in the behavioral objective form, specifying what percentage of correct answers must be attained to demonstrate mastery.

These objectives emphasize basic computational skills that all students need to learn. However, in keeping with the National Council of Teachers of Mathematics' recommendations to emphasize problem solving over computation, reflective teachers are likely to plan lessons that allow students to explore the relationships between addition and subtraction. They are also likely to include many additional math outcomes and objectives at the higher levels of Bloom's revised taxonomy (Anderson et al., 2001) to teach students how to apply the math facts and computation skills they are learning to actual problem-solving situations. However, this example does illustrate the importance of matching objectives to outcome statements in a logical sequence. Each of the objectives builds on the one before it. As students master each objective, they are continually progressing toward mastering the outcome statement.

Sequencing Objectives in Language Arts

Not all subjects in the elementary curriculum are as sequential as mathematics. Language arts consist of knowledge, skills, and abilities that develop children's understanding and use of language. Reading, writing, speaking, listening, visually representing, and interpreting visual information are all part of the language arts curriculum, and each one can and should have its own outcome statement(s). Outcome statement 2 suggests one illustration of how the language arts curriculum is designed.

> *Language arts outcome statement 2:* Students will write standard English sentences with correct spelling, accurate grammar, and well-organized meaning and form.

Again, this outcome statement will take years to accomplish, but teachers at every grade level are responsible for providing learning experiences that build toward the ultimate goal. The objectives to reach this goal may be similar each year for several years but written in increasing levels of difficulty. This is known as a *spiral curriculum.*

These are sample language arts objectives to fit outcome statement 2:

By the end of grade 2, students will be able to:

1. Write a sentence containing a subject and a verb.
2. Use a capital letter at the beginning of a sentence.
3. Use a period or question mark at the end of a sentence.
4. Review and edit sentences for complete meaning.

By the end of grade 4, students will be able to:

1. Write a paragraph that focuses on one central idea.
2. Spell common words correctly in writing samples.
3. Use capitalization and sentence-end punctuation correctly.
4. Review and edit a paragraph to improve the organization of ideas.

By the end of grade 6, students will be able to:

1. Write several paragraphs that explain one concept or theme.
2. Use a dictionary to spell all words in a paper correctly.
3. Use correct punctuation, including end marks, commas, apostrophes, quotation marks, and colons.
4. Review and edit papers to correct spelling, punctuation, grammar, and organization of ideas.

By the end of grade 8, students will be able to:

1. Write papers with an introductory paragraph, logical reasons, data to support the main idea, and a closing statement.
2. Use a dictionary to spell all words in a paper correctly; use a thesaurus to add to vocabulary of the paper.
3. Eliminate fragments and run-on sentences.
4. Review and edit papers to correct spelling, punctuation, grammar, organization of ideas, and appropriateness for the purpose.

When teachers have curriculum guidelines such as these, they must still translate the outcome statements and objectives into actual learning experiences that are appropriate and motivating for their students. To pretest how well your students can use written language when they enter your classroom, plan a writing experience in the first week. Analyzing these writing samples will allow you to plan suitably challenging activities for your students. In this example, the second-grade teacher must decide on topics students should write about and when to limit students to copying teacher-made examples or allow them to begin to write their own sentences. The fourth-grade teacher knows that students will not learn all of these skills in just one writing lesson. It is necessary to provide many interesting classroom experiences so that students will have ideas to express in their writing. The sixth-grade teacher has to plan a series of research and writing experiences so that students will have ample opportunities to synthesize all of the skills required at that grade level.

Curriculum planning of subjects such as language arts is a complex undertaking because it contains so many varied outcomes and objectives. The previous example illustrates only a single outcome for teaching students how to write. Teachers must also plan outcome statements and objectives for reading, listening, speaking, visually representing, and interpreting visual methods.

Sequencing Objectives in Science

The science curriculum should inform students of the basic facts and concepts of science topics, but it should also allow students opportunities to experience how scientists work. These dual goals of the science curriculum are often expressed as *teaching both content and process*. An example of an outcome statement in science that covers both content and process follows:

> *Science outcome statement 3*: Students will demonstrate the properties of electricity and magnetism and show how their energy can be used to benefit humankind.

If Judy were planning a series of lesson plans to accomplish this outcome, she would use a sequence of process-oriented learning experiences that allow students to discover some important properties of electricity and magnetism, followed by a few content-oriented lessons to review and articulate what they discovered. As a culmination, she would allow students to apply what they have learned and synthesize their own inventions using the energy from batteries and magnets.

These sample science objectives to meet outcome statement 3:

By the end of the unit on electricity and magnetism, students will be able to:

1. Demonstrate how electricity travels in a closed circuit.
2. Demonstrate how magnetism attracts and repels certain metals.
3. Investigate the basic properties of electricity and magnetism.
4. Be able to compare and contrast electricity and magnetism and identify key properties of each.
5. Invent some beneficial ways to use electricity and magnetism.

Using this approach, the first lesson plan would involve hands-on experiences using batteries, copper wire, and lightbulbs so that students can demonstrate to themselves how electricity travels in a closed circuit. On subsequent days, lessons would be planned to allow students to investigate the properties of magnets and electricity. Then, Judy would plan a lesson for which students created charts comparing the two, and there would be a lesson in which students discussed the properties and learned to use terminology correctly. She might then have a written, individual test on these properties and terms. Finally, there would be several days for students to work on their inventions and present them to classmates and parents.

Sequencing Objectives in Social Studies

Reflective elementary teachers can also see the need for both content and process in their social studies curriculum. They attempt to help their students build a knowledge base in history and geography, but they also give attention and time to teaching students how to acquire information on their own. An example of an outcome statement in social studies that covers both content and process follows:

> *Social studies outcome statement 4:* Students will use a map and a globe to find place names and locations. They will then create a chart listing the countries, major cities, rivers, and mountain ranges in each continent.

These are sample social studies objectives to meet outcome statement 4:

At the end of the map and globe unit, students will be able to:

1. Identify the seven continents on a world map and a globe.
2. Interpret the country boundaries with a map legend.
3. List the countries in each continent.

4. Interpret the symbol for rivers on the map legend.
5. List the major rivers in each continent.
6. Interpret the symbol for mountain ranges on the map legend.
7. List the mountain ranges in each continent.
8. Create a chart showing the countries, cities, rivers, and mountain ranges in each continent.

In this example, the teacher has planned a set of learning activities that will add to the students' knowledge base about world geography. This set of activities also equips the student to be able to find and interpret information on maps and globes. This social studies curriculum demonstrates that by employing hands-on learning experiences, students are able to learn both content and processes simultaneously and that they are active rather than passive learners throughout the entire set of activities. An oral or written pretest might consist of having students name or point to certain geographical locations and read and interpret a map legend. The information from the pretest is valuable in planning lessons that use students' existing knowledge and add to it.

SAMPLE LESSON PLANS

Lesson plans are organized written that teachers to present a well-organized set of learning experiences for their students. The objectives of the lesson specify the teacher's expectations for what the students will learn or be able to do as a result of the lesson. When teachers plan objectives that specify the criteria for success, they are clarifying for themselves what the students must be able to do to demonstrate mastery of the skill or understanding of the lesson's concepts.

To plan the procedures of a lesson in advance, many reflective teachers visualize themselves teaching the lesson. They write what they must do to teach the lesson successfully and what the students must do to learn the material. Teachers who can visualize the entire process of teaching and learning can write richly detailed lesson plans. When they begin to teach the lesson, they have a supportive script to follow.

As teachers become more proficient and experienced at planning and teaching, their written lesson plans are likely to become less detailed. For beginning teachers, however, a thorough, richly detailed plan is an essential element for a successful lesson.

Sample First-Grade Writing Lesson Plan

Diane Leonard teaches in a first-grade classroom in Fresno, California. To support her students, many of whom are learning English as a second language, Diane does a lot of modeling before she asks her students to work independently. She also plans guided practice activities to help her students understand exactly what she expects them to do. When she has her students work independently, Diane often uses the time to teach an additional guided practice lesson with students who need extra help in order to be successful.

Diane begins the lesson with all of the children sitting in front of a chart. They sing a song about a turkey, which will be the topic of their writing. Diane then reads an informational book about turkeys, which helps the students to gain information about their topic. Diane then leads the class in labeling the parts of a turkey and adding descriptive words to their labels. This exercise provides a model for each student to use as they return to their desks to complete the prewriting activity, drawing and labeling a picture of a turkey. See Diane's lesson plan for this prewriting activity in Figure 3.3, and then view the lesson by going to MyEducationLab.

Diane will follow up this prewriting lesson with a lesson on drafting the story, following the same approach: explaining, modeling, providing guided practice, and supporting the students who need it with additional instruction while the majority of the class work independently. See Figure 3.4 for an example of one of the stories the children wrote.

Title of Lesson: Writing about Turkeys

Subject Area: Language Arts   **Lesson Duration:** 30 minutes

Standards Addressed: Writing: Students will write short descriptive paragraphs.

Materials and Resources:

Teacher materials: Chart paper, markers, informational book about turkeys.

Student materials: Writing paper, with room for a drawing at the top; pencils; crayons

Objective: After teacher explanation, modeling, and guided practice, students will draw and label a picture of a turkey and add a descriptive word for each of the labels in preparation for writing a descriptive paragraph.

Adaptations for Students with Special Needs: While other students are working independently, I will provide additional guided practice for the students who are not ready to work on their own as the others are working independently.

Reflective Action Procedures:

Pretesting: I will show a picture of a turkey and ask the children to identify its parts (feathers, tail, wattle, beak, legs, claws).

Motivation: "We have been talking about turkeys and today we are going to learn some more about them so we can write a story about them." We will sing a song about turkeys (to the tune of Bingo). I will write the word TURKEY on the chart paper as we sing the song.

Teacher Explanation: We are going to learn a good prewriting strategy. After I read a story about turkeys, we will draw a picture of a turkey, and then we will label the parts so that we will have the words we need to write our own story. (I will then read the book *Turkeys on the Farm* (*Shug, 2006*) and show the students the labeled picture in the book.)

Teacher Modeling: I will show the students how to use their hands to form the outline of the turkey by modeling (using my hand and the chart paper), and we will label each part on the chart.

Guided Practice: I will ask the students to help me write a descriptive word for each part of the turkey that we labeled. As the students suggest descriptive words, we will spell them together as I write the words on the chart.

Check for Understanding: I will go back through the process we have used: (1) drawing the turkey, (2) labeling the turkey, and (3) writing a descriptive word for each label. I will then ask the students to read each of the labels and descriptive words we have written on the chart.

Independent Practice: The students will go back to their seats to draw and label their turkeys.

Closure: The students will bring their labeled drawings to the celebration circle and share what they have done.

Assessment: During the circle time, I will observe the work the students have done and keep a list of those who will need additional instruction before they are ready to continue the writing.

Plan for Further Instruction for Students Who Need It: I will work with the students who need help in getting their drawings completed with labels and descriptive words, while the other students work in learning centers later in the morning.

Figure 3.3 Sample first-grade writing lesson plan.

Figure 3.4 First-grade writing sample.

Source: From Eby, Herrell, and Jordan, *Teaching in the Elementary School*, 5e, Figure 3.4, p. 69.

Title of Lesson: Sixth-Grade Cupcake Geology

Subject Area: Science   **Lesson Duration:** 1 hour

Standards Addressed: Montana Science 1 and 4

Materials and Resources:

Teacher Materials: 1 frosted cupcake and 1 straw, overhead transparency

Student Materials: 1 frosted cupcake each, iced with several different colors of icing; straws and paper towels; science notebooks; and pencils

Objective: Given an iced cupcake, students will use their straws to take core samples of the cupcake, from which they will make inferences about various strata found in the core sample.

Reflective Action Procedures:

Pretesting: During my opening discussion, I will ask how scientists find out about the Earth below its surface.

Adaptations for Students with Special Needs: Entries in the science notebooks may be adapted according to the performance needs of individual students; for example, drawing, labeling.

Motivation: I will use our classroom fish tank to remind students how we sometimes need assistance in imagining or picturing those parts of the world that we cannot easily see.

Teacher Explanation: Simulation helps us understand what we couldn't otherwise experience. Scientists use simulation to create models of natural phenomena. Today we will take the role of scientists who are taking core samples of the geology of the Earth.

Teacher Modeling: I will demonstrate, using my cupcake and my straw, how to take several core samples. I will show how to gently blow the samples onto my paper towel for further exploration.

Guided Practice: I will give one cupcake to each student. Then each student will take one core sample from his or her cupcake and gently place it on a paper towel. We will have a short discussion about what they see in the sample and how samples differ from each other. On an overhead transparency, I will have the students assist me in writing a lab report model based on the sampling process and the content of their sample. I will leave this on display for the students to use in completing their own lab report. During the process I will walk around the classroom, monitoring appropriate behaviors and sampling processes.

Check for Understanding: After observing that students have taken an appropriate sample, I will lead a discussion on the variability of samples and the need for possibly taking multiple samples.

Independent Practice: Students will continue taking several samples and enter their observations into their science notebooks.

Closure: We will discuss worldwide uses of core sampling and focus especially on the use of this technique in Montana, in the mining industry, and in paleontology research. I will also encourage students to come up with other uses for sampling, both real and imagined.

Assessment: I will collect and read the students' science notebooks. If a student is not clear in his or her description of the process and outcome, I will confer with that student to assess his or her understanding of the process and procedures.

Plan for Further Instruction for Students Who Need It: For students who had difficulty with the process or concept, I will work with them in small-group instruction, taking core samples and discussing the process together.

Figure 3.5 Science lesson plan.

Sample Science Lesson Plan

Judy's son, Alex Eby, recently completed a master's level teacher education program at Montana State University in Bozeman, Montana. During his program, he visited John Graves's classroom to teach a science lesson that would fit in Mr. Graves's geologic history unit. Alex found a lesson plan online entitled "Cupcake Geology." He referred to the Montana state standards to see whether this lesson plan was compatible and found that it fit Science Content Standards 1 and 4 very well.

The Montana Science Standard 1 states that students will design, conduct, evaluate, and communicate scientific investigations. Alex's plan was designed with student investigation as a major goal and with communication of findings as an important element. He also found that Montana State Science Standard 4 expects that students will demonstrate knowledge of the composition, processes, and interactions of the earth's systems and other objects in space. Alex's lesson plan would give students an opportunity to see for themselves how the composition of the Earth varies.

To prepare for his lesson, Alex baked 30 cupcakes. He divided the cupcake batter into three portions and used food color to distinguish them. He swirled together the chocolate, yellow, and green batters before baking them. After they were baked, he covered them with chocolate frosting.

The next morning he arrived at Mr. Graves's class and passed out paper towels to each student as he introduced himself and described his goals for the lesson. He tried to create a bond by saying, "Just like you, I am a student of Mr. Graves's in a science methods course at the university." He told the class that in the next hour, they would talk for a minute, do an activity, have a discussion, and write their observations. To describe the content goals for the lesson, he told the class that scientists often cannot see things that they want to study, so they create models and study those instead. He asked students to give examples of other scientific models and pointed out that the fish tank in the back of their room was a model of the unseen depths of a lake or ocean. He told the students that simulation is a powerful way to learn new and unfamiliar material. For Alex's lesson plan, see Figure 3.5.

Soon you will be a student teacher responsible for planning lessons in a classroom. Take your sense of humor with you, and especially your ability to laugh at your own mistakes. Your written lesson plans are great guides or scripts, but a reflective teacher is always willing to ad-lib if necessary. The art of teaching is a balance between careful planning and improvisation.

LONG-TERM CURRICULUM PLANNING

An Example of a Middle School Plan for Mathematics

We will use the subject of mathematics in order to provide an example of how curriculum plans are designed at the middle school level. The teaching of mathematics has changed over the years at every grade level. No longer a time for drill and practice, mathematics is often one of the most highly interactive parts of the K–12 school curriculum. Manipulatives that primary students use to demonstrate their understanding of number concepts include beans, beads, and number lines. But many teachers also use motivating materials such as pretzels, fish-shaped crackers, jelly beans, or coated chocolate candies. Recently, a little girl was asked how she knew it was math time and she answered, "That's easy! Math is when we have our snacks."

Kendall and Marzano (1995) provide a summary of recommendations made by the National Council of Teachers of Mathematics (NCTM) and the Mathematics Assessment Framework of the National Assessment of Educational Progress NAEP. These groups stress the importance of teaching mathematics in the context of real-life situations, and they recommend that school curricula be designed so that the student

1. Effectively uses a variety of strategies in the problem-solving process.
2. Understands and applies properties of the concept of number.

3. Uses a variety of procedures while performing computation.
4. Understands and applies the concept of measurement.
5. Understands and applies the concept of geometry.
6. Understands and applies concepts of data analysis and distributions.
7. Understands and applies concepts of probability and statistics.
8. Understands and applies properties of functions and algebra.
9. Understands the relationship between mathematics and other disciplines, particularly science and computer technology. (Kendall & Marzano, pp. 88–89)

With this emphasis on problem solving and application of mathematical concepts to real-life situations, the curriculum in many K–12 schools has changed dramatically from drill and practice to mathematical explorations and investigations. Teachers who try to incorporate these recommendations into their mathematics curricula find that the best way to do it is through the use of projects and multidisciplinary units. A year-long plan in mathematics will be divided into several strands or concepts, with opportunities for reviewing previously learned material from time to time.

Collaborative Long-Term Planning

Long-term planning, either individually or collectively, is an important job for teachers. If you are teaching in a self-contained classroom, you have the freedom to write your own curriculum as long as it relates to the district and state standards and responds to the learning needs of your students. If you are working in a team-teaching school, you will need to articulate your vision of the curriculum to your teammates and adjust yours to include their ideas as well as your own. In either case, the curriculum you create will improve with experience. As you see the effects of your original planning and assess your students' mastery of the standards, you will reflect on your planning and find ways to improve it with each succeeding year. If you work in a school where teachers teach individual subjects, you may have to team-teach in order to provide students with an integrated experience.

High School Teachers Collaborate in Long-Term Planning

Dr. Colin Bateman, chemistry teacher, Dr. Peter Gay, biology teacher, Jeannette Arn, English teacher, and Jeff Landers, mathematics teacher, all teach at Astronaut High School in Titusville, Florida. Dr Bateman and Dr Gay also teach a science research class in which their joint students design and implement science research projects to be entered in the local science fair, with the hope of moving on to the regional, state and national fairs. Because their science research students must also employ mathematics and writing skills in order to prepare their science research projects, these four teachers have developed a team-teaching approach to working with the science research students who come to school an hour early, during 0 block, to be involved in the science research project.

The local science fair is held in February each year; the teachers have worked together to plan a series of experiences to keep their students on track and armed with the skills they need to research their topics, design their projects, analyze their data, write their reports, and prepare their science project display boards.

The teachers work collaboratively to design a program that demonstrates effective research, science, mathematics, and writing skills to the students, who are ninth-, tenth-, eleventh-, and twelfth-graders. The long-term, collaborative plan they design looks like this:

September

Week 1	Using research skills to find interesting topics and learn what research has already been done on those topics (Bateman, Gay, and Arn).
Week 2	Narrowing down the research topic and writing research proposals (Bateman, Gay, and Arn).
Week 3	Writing hypotheses statements and continuing to do in-depth background research on the chosen topics (Bateman, Gay, and Arn).
Week 4	Designing the research studies (Bateman, Gay, and Math teacher). Designing the display board (local graphic artist).

October

Weeks 1 and 2	Conducting the research, designing the analysis methods, research journaling (all four teachers).
Weeks 3 and 4	Conducting the research, research journaling (Bateman and Gay).

November and December, January weeks 1 and 2

Weeks 1 to 4	Conducting the research, research journaling (Bateman and Gay).

January

Weeks 3 and 4	Analyzing the data, running statistical programs (Landers), preparing the research report, designing and preparing the display board (all four teachers).

February

Weeks 1 and 2	Analyzing the data, preparing the research report, completing the display board (all four teachers).
Week of the science fair	Practicing oral reports, fielding questions (all four teachers).

March, April, and May

Using the feedback from the judges to:
Prepare multiyear projects and continue to gather data.
Prepare for regional, state, and national level fairs as qualified.
(This may include gathering additional data, adding different statistical applications, rewriting written reports, etc.).

Source: Dr. Colin Bateman, personal communication, June 20, 2009.

Communicating with Parents

It is important that you communicate with parents about the state standards for the grade you are teaching. This should be done early in the school year through a newsletter or a parent meeting. This doesn't have to be a lengthy or in-depth discussion, but it is vital that parents understand how the standards change as their children move along in the grades.

The first requirement for this responsibility is that you understand exactly what is required at your grade level. Review the standards carefully and compare them to the standards from the year before. You can use a few key standards to help parents understand the way student requirements will be different in this new school year and ways that you will be supporting their child's growth.

This is also a good opportunity to involve the parents as members of the learning team. Provide them with ways in which they can support their children, such as:

- Providing a set time and place for homework to be done each night.
- Encouraging their children when they get discouraged.
- Providing their children with reading and writing materials at home.
- Providing their children with an example by reading and having time to interact, with the television turned off.
- Limiting television time and engaging in family conversation, game time, and reading.

Playing Catch Up

You may discover that some of your students have not met the grade-level standards during their previous schooling. You are, of course, responsible for teaching the grade-level standards for the grade you are assigned. The students who are behind will need support so that they can move forward and catch up. You have several responsibilities to these children:

1. You must assess their skills and determine exactly what they know and can do.
2. You must plan lessons, based on their present levels, that are designed to move them forward.
3. You must provide additional instruction to help them achieve the missing skills.
4. You must continue to include them in the activities of the class and provide support so that they can be as successful as possible while they are catching up.
5. You must provide all this support in a way that encourages them, motivates them, and validates their efforts.

If this sounds like a lot of responsibility, it is. This is one of the most challenging of a teacher's assignments. You are responsible for all your students, and you must take them where they are and move them forward. This requires careful planning. In order to have time to play catch up with the students who require it, you have to have some time during the day when the majority of your students are working independently so that you can provide additional instruction to those who need it.

One natural way of providing this type of differentiated instruction is to work with small groups. By grouping your students for instruction, you can provide expanded opportunities for students who are ready to move more quickly and also provide catch up instruction for those who are behind. Grouping also keeps the catch up groups from feeling that they are being singled out or punished.

When providing whole-group instruction, consider using the following four-step instructional model:

1. Teacher explanation, where you present the material to be learned and the reason for learning it.
2. Teacher modeling, where you demonstrate what is to be done.
3. Guided practice, where you walk the students through the task to be performed with guidance.
4. Independent practice, where the students practice the skill or task independently.

The beauty of this model is that it provides a natural time to provide additional guided practice for those who need it. The majority of the class will be ready to go to independent practice after some limited guided practice. While they work independently, the teacher can gather the students who need additional instruction and engage in additional guided practice.

GUIDED GROUP EXPLORATION

I. Place students in groups and ask them to identify the missing parts in each of these objectives in Figure 3.6. Each group should then rewrite the objectives to include all necessary elements.

What's Missing?

Identify the three elements of a learning objective in each of the following examples. If an element is missing, rewrite the objective to include all necessary elements. The three required elements are:

1. The conditions under which the learning will take place (ask yourself, "Do I identify the instruction or condition under which the students will be working?").
2. The action, behavior, or cognitive process that will provide evidence of the learning (ask yourself, "Do I identify what the student will do to demonstrate the learning that has taken place?").
3. The criteria for success (ask yourself, "What level of mastery do I expect in order to determine the success of the lesson?").

The Objectives:

After teacher explanation, modeling, and guided practice, students will alphabetize a list of ten words.

Given a set of 20 math problems, students will score at least 80%.

Students will write complete sentences with 90% accuracy.

Given a list of 20 prepositions, students will demonstrate their meaning.

Students will define their spelling words.

After guided practice, students will learn the names of the continents.

Students will complete a timed multiplication worksheet.

After reading Chapter 10 in their social studies books, students will know the contents of the chapter.

Students will write a descriptive paragraph.

After playing a game of opposites, students will identify the opposites of ten words by correctly matching them.

Figure 3.6 Incomplete objectives.

II. Bring the class back together and have them share their discussions and rewrites.

III. Have the students return to their groups to sort a group of objectives into the revised Bloom's Levels of the Cognitive Domain. See Figure 3.7.

Read these learning objectives, and sort them into levels according to Bloom's revised taxonomy. After they are sorted, refer to Figure 3.1 to check for accuracy.

Level 6:   Creating

Level 5:   Evaluating

Level 4:   Analyzing

Level 3:   Applying

Level 2:   Understanding

Level 1:   Remembering

1. Given a list of similes, students will generate a list of alternate examples they could use to complete each simile with 80% accuracy.

2. Given five descriptive paragraphs, students will rank them according to their use of description and verbally defend their ranking with examples.

3. After reading an essay promoting recycling, the students will develop a visual to represent the author's ideas with at least 80% of the essay's points demonstrated.

4. After reading poems by Shel Silverstein, students will memorize and recite one poem with 100% accuracy.

5. After reading Martin Luther King, Jr.'s "I Have a Dream" speech, students will paraphrase his ideas with 80% accuracy.

Figure 3.7 Sorting objectives.

IV. Bring the group back together to explain and defend their sorting.

REFLECTIVE ACTION ACTIVITY FOR YOUR PROFESSIONAL PORTFOLIO

Using the reflective action lesson plan format found in Figure 3.8, write a lesson plan that you might teach in your own classroom. Be sure to include all the required elements, and assume that you have one student with auditory deficits (learning disability) and another student who is just beginning to speak English for whom you need to plan adaptations.

Title of Lesson:

Subject Area: **Lesson Duration:**

Standards Addressed:

Materials and Resources:

Teacher Materials:

Student Materials:

Objective:

Reflective Action Procedures:

Pretesting:

Adaptations for Students with Special Needs:

Motivation:

Teacher Explanation:

Teacher Modeling:

Guided Practice:

Check for Understanding:

Independent Practice:

Closure:

Assessment:

Plan for Further Instruction for Students Who Need It:

Figure 3.8 Reflective action lesson plan format.

References

Anderson, L., Kratwohl, D., Airasian, P., Cruikshank, K., Mayer, R., Pintrich, P., Raths, J., & Wittrock, M. (Eds.) *A taxonomy for learning, teaching, and assessing: A revision of Bloom's taxonomy of educational objectives.* New York: Longman Publishers.

Bloom, B., Engelhart, M., Furst, E., Hill, W., & Krathwohl, D. (1956). *Taxonomy of educational objectives: Cognitive domain.* New York: Longman.

Eisner, E. (1985). *Educational imagination* (2nd ed.). Upper Saddle River, NJ: Merrill/Prentice Hall.

Kendall, J., & Marzano, R. (2000). *Content knowledge: A compendium of standards and benchmarks for K–12 education.* Aurora, CO: Mid-Continent Regional Educational Laboratory.

Maslow, A. (1954). *Motivation and personality.* New York: Harper & Row.

Schug, M. (2006). *Turkeys on the farm.* Mandato, MN: Capstone Press.

Spady, W. (1994). Choosing outcomes of significance. *Educational Leadership, 51*(6), 18–22.

Tyler, R. (1949). *Basic principles of curriculum and instruction.* Chicago: University of Chicago Press.

Now go to Topic #5: Instructional Planning in the MyEducationLab (www.myeducationlab.com) for your course, where you can:

- Find learning outcomes for this topic along with the national standards that connect to these outcomes.
- Complete Assignments and Activities that can help you more deeply understand the chapter content.
- Apply and practice your understanding of the core teaching skills identified in the chapter with the Building Teaching Skills and Dispositions learning units.

CHAPTER 4

Planning Curriculum Units

■■■■■■■■■■■■■■■■■■■■■■■■■■■■■■■■

PLANNING CURRICULUM UNITS

Do you have a vision of yourself teaching a roomful of students who are excitedly investigating, experimenting, discussing, and reporting on what they are learning? Beginning teachers and student teachers often report that their vision is to create a learning environment that motivates their students to want to come to school and learn as much as they can about important matters.

PRAXIS
Chapter 4 prepares you to address Section 2b on the PRAXIS™ Exam: Instruction and Assessment.

Current national standards and state curriculum guides are also the products of the vision of experienced teachers, working in collaboration to provide teachers, especially beginning teachers, with guidelines for what to teach and how to teach it. These documents encourage teachers to create programs that develop students' deeper understandings of a few important subjects rather than provide them with superficial surveys of data. At the local school district level, teachers are responsible for translating the curricular visions described in national and state standards into practical classroom learning experiences. The word *vision* is carefully chosen in this discussion because, at the local level, teachers and principals are often encouraged to develop a common vision and create a mental image of what they want to accomplish with students.

One of the most natural and authentic ways to translate a vision of core curriculum goals into practical classroom experiences is by planning thematic units of study that engage students in actively seeking information on a topic that has meaning in their lives. Many teachers use a series of thematic units for their long-term planning. There is something refreshing and inherently motivating for both teachers and students using this plan. A unit of study lasts a specified number of days or weeks, during which everyone is motivated to investigate and find out everything they can about the topic. Then, during an exciting culmination, the students proudly display what they have learned. After a brief period devoted to assessment, the unit ends, and a new one begins. When this rhythm is established in a classroom, complaints of boredom or repetition are rare from students or the teacher. The pace is quick, the goals are clear, and the expectations are high when everyone is involved in a thematic unit on an interesting and challenging topic.

One of classroom teachers' most important responsibilities is to plan the *curriculum*, the course of events and learning experiences for their students. To illustrate the complexity of the planning process, here is a brief account of some issues that Diane Leonard faced during her first 3 months at Balderas Elementary School in Fresno, California.

DIANE LEONARD'S FIRST 3 MONTHS AT SCHOOL

When I first walked into my second-grade classroom in July, I encountered a large, empty room with piles of textbooks on every counter. I knew that I had the freedom to create my own curriculum using the texts. But I also knew that I had to address the state-mandated standards in reading, writing, math, science, social studies, visual and performing arts, and physical education. I also knew that most of my second-graders were just learning English and I would also have to address the English language development standards with them.

I didn't know my students yet, so I didn't want to presume to plan an entire year's curriculum until I had met them and determined their needs. I knew I wanted to plan integrated units and collaboratively build the group into a learning community. I found my answer in the state history/social science standards. Standard 2.1 reads, "Students differentiate between things that happened long ago and things that happened yesterday." The standard suggests activities such as tracing family histories, conducting family interviews, timelines, and mapping family travel and relocations. I thought, "What a perfect way to get to know my students while addressing the social studies standards." I began to think of all the other grade-level standards that could be addressed in the process of a family history study. We will be practicing oral English as we interview our parents and grandparents. We will be addressing writing standards as we write the stories that we learned from our families.

I began to collect family-related literature to read to the students. I found stories about families doing things together, stories of grandparents and how they had lived long ago, and folktales from the different ethnic backgrounds represented by my students. I looked through the soft-back leveled readers I would be using for my guided reading groups to find family stories. I found short poems about families that I printed onto charts for daily choral reading. I also made copies of the poems so the children could illustrate them and practice reading them as their homework.

Because we were housed in a brand-new school, none of the children had attended our school the previous year, so we began the year with a short map-making activity where we created a map of our new school. We took walks around the school and practiced our oral English by interviewing the secretary, cafeteria manager, librarian, custodian, and principal. We placed their offices on our school map and used shared writing to create their stories. We learned how to ask questions and how to transfer our newfound knowledge into stories about our school. We talked about the new school becoming a community and wrote a class-book about our school. I used the big book I Went Walking *(Williams, 1990) for a shared reading, which I read aloud and we reread the repetitive text together and related the story to our walk around the school. We re-created the book, writing our own big book using our newfound school friends in place of the animals seen in the original story.*

During this same time, we were generating questions to ask our parents and grandparents. We were preparing for our family history unit. The students began to interview their parents and grandparents. They focused on questions about what life and school were like a long time ago when the parents and grandparents were 7 years old. The students brought their stories back to the classroom, and we began to write our family history books. Some of the children brought in photographs and crafts to add to the discussion. We used roll-type fax paper and created family timelines and, when possible, we invited parents and grandparents in to demonstrate the art, crafts, cooking, dances, or music of their cultures. Whenever we had guests, we asked questions about how things had changed since the guests were children.

Our culminating activity was a family covered-dish dinner where we shared the family books, timelines, and oral reports. Since my students come from many different cultures, we couldn't always communicate in English, but the older siblings served as translators. There were many tears shed as the students shared their family history books that evening. We had electronically scanned some of the photos so we could include them in the family books, and the parents were excited about the new family treasures created by the children.

We were able to incorporate math into our study as we created the timelines and determined the number of years between events. We also used math in creating the maps showing the travels of the families and the great numbers of miles they traveled to come to Fresno. We incorporated science as we compared the way things were done in the past, for example, the types of machines used to get work done when our parents and grandparents were young. We even discovered simple levers and pulleys in some of the modern machines we use today. We learned a lot about the visual and performing arts as we examined the various arts and crafts work done by the different cultural groups. We even practiced several types of dances, taught by our fellow students or their parents. One grandfather came to school and taught Tai Chi as a physical exercise. Some of the boys thought it rather silly until they tried it for a 20-minute period. We also learned a number of new playground games from the different cultures.

The morning after the family history dinner, the children were very excited about how well the families had received their books. They had discovered a number of new foods they liked, and they were ready to plan a new unit of study. Many of them had been very interested in the folktales we had read and wanted to do more of that. Several of them had been told traditional folktales by their parents and grandparents in the course of the family history interviews and wanted to write and illustrate the stories to create story books for their younger brothers and sisters. So began our second unit, writing and telling folktales. I immediately began to find ways to integrate other content areas into the study so I could address multiple-content standards.

As Diane's account shows, teachers face a multitude of complex issues and judgments in their own classrooms regarding curriculum. As a teacher, Diane has a great deal of freedom (and responsibility) to decide what to teach and when to teach it; but her decisions are influenced by many forces, both past and present. We all tend to focus on the way federal, state, and local standards are being used as the basis for educational decision making, but we should also be aware of how history and tradition exert powerful influences over what is taught in schools. The three R's have served as the basis for planning in U.S. schools for more than a century, and there are active and vocal groups of citizens who believe that the primary goal of K–12 schools should be to instill these basic skills in their students.

Some groups believe that schools are the custodians of culture and that the primary goal of education should be to develop good citizenship and understanding of the great ideas and literature produced by Western civilization. Others believe strongly that the primary goal of a modern education is to teach students how to use reasoning, problem solving, and communication skills as a means of learning "how to learn" so that they are able to gather the information they will need in their lives.

Others hold that the new wave of computer technology available to future generations make older forms of learning obsolete. They call for an emphasis on the use of technology in K–12 schools to prepare students for a future that will be vastly different from the present. There is also a growing trend toward creating school programs that are multidisciplinary and multicultural by design, with a new emphasis on investigation, inquiry, research, experimentation, and conflict resolution, especially through the use of the new technologies currently available.

Diane discovered how difficult it is to plan so many different types of school programs all at once. Like many beginning teachers, she wanted to incorporate the best ideas from all of the influential groups she had read about during her teacher education program. At times the responsibility seemed so overwhelming that she might have wished that there was just one standard curriculum for all teachers to follow. Her task was made easier, however, because she could refer to the content standards for which she was responsible and choose activities that would help move her students toward meeting those standards through exciting learning experiences.

HOW SCHOOL CURRICULA ARE PLANNED
National Standards and Federal Mandates

Many nations have uniform standards for school curricula. Where these standards exist, individual teachers plan their daily programs to coincide precisely with national expectations. In some countries, if you were able to visit several schools in various cities at the same time of the school year, you could find the students using the same textbooks and even working on the same chapter as students in other cities and rural areas of that country. Periodically, all children attending these schools take national examinations as a means of testing whether they have learned the requisite material and, at the same time, whether schools are accomplishing their mission of teaching the national curriculum.

Some countries, including the United States, have no such tradition of a uniform mandated curriculum. Historically, the regulation and supervision of K–12 curriculum in the United States has resided with the states. Although many states have established curriculum guidelines and examinations, there has also been a strong public sense that the best curriculum is the one planned at the local level based on local interests, values, resources, and the needs of a particular group of students in each school district.

Recently, however, some school districts have been criticized by the media or by citizen watchdog groups because their students have performed poorly on a variety of tests and measurements of academic progress. As a result of the public's perception that some school districts prepare students for the world much better than other school districts, a debate is growing over the value of establishing national standards for student performance. Recently, several movements to establish national standards for the preparation of teachers and for teaching effectiveness have entered the debate.

The first step in improving the quality of teaching and learning has recently been implemented with the passage of federally legislated mandates in the No Child Left Behind Act (http://en.wikipedia.org/wiki/No Child Left Behind), which requires that any school receiving federal education funding must employ "highly qualified teachers." The federal definition of a highly qualified teacher does not simply mean that the teacher holds a professional teaching credential but that the teacher also has passed a standardized test that documents the mastery of all the subject matter he or she will teach. For elementary school teachers, this means they must demonstrate mastery of reading, writing, science, social studies, and health and physical education. Secondary-level teachers must pass area-specific exams to validate their knowledge and understanding of subject areas they desire to teach. A variety of nationally standardized assessments are being used across the states to document credential candidates' subject-matter competency.

In addition to the testing of teacher candidates, and in response to the public's desire to be able to measure and compare the progress of students across the nation, Congress mandated the U.S. Department of Education to provide a set of assessment tools to measure K–12 students' subject-matter knowledge in five areas. They produced a document known as the National Assessment of Educational Progress (NAEP), which is commonly referred to as the nation's report card. NAEP provides *benchmarks* for each subject area, describing what students should be able to do or demonstrate at various grade levels.

As is often the case in a vigorous, multicultural democracy such as the United States, there is little agreement about the form that educational standards should take or how they should be used. Subject-area specialists, for example, argue that their disciplines are so different from each other that standardizing performance expectations across the disciplines would be impossible (Viadero, 1993 pp. 14–17).

Many other philosophical debates concern the purpose of national standards in education. Before establishing one set of universally accepted standards, educators will need to agree on issues such as whether the national standards and benchmarks ought to describe basic or minimal competency in each subject area or whether they ought to describe higher-level expectations. A national debate remains over the value of emphasizing content or process knowledge in most subject areas, and this causes the authors of standards and benchmarks to disagree about whether to assess content knowledge or performance standards.

State Standards Are the Basis for Curriculum Planning

In the United States, each state has a department of education that has traditionally taken responsibility for establishing guidelines for curriculum development. Recently, these state departments of education have become highly interested in measuring achievement as well.

Currently, 49 of the 50 states have adopted content standards in K–12 programs. This movement is not without its critics, however. Brooks and Brooks (1999) observe that most standards-based reform efforts are illogical because they ignore the differences in the way students learn and the diversity of experiences that students bring from their multicultural backgrounds. Assessing state standards for many states depends on constructing or buying standardized assessments that equate test results with student learning. These types of systems tend to reward schools whose students score well on the assessments and sanction against schools whose students do not. Brooks and Brooks (1999) decry the "un-deviating, one-size-fits-all approach to teaching and assessment in states that have crowned accountablility king. Requiring all students to take the same courses and pass the same tests may hold political capital for legislators and state-level educational policymakers, but it contravenes what years of painstaking research tells us about student learning" (p. 20).

Constructivists such as Brooks and Brooks (1999) believe that only by analyzing students' understandings and ways of learning, and then customizing our teaching approaches to each student's cognitive processes, can we hope to increase student achievement. This constructivist approach to learning and assessment of learning is closely aligned with the concept of *reflective action* in teaching that we propose in this textbook. Reflective action in teaching calls for teachers to use their withitness to perceive students' needs—individual student needs, in this case, that vary widely depending on background experiences, multiple intelligences, and physical development of the brain and nervous system. Diane Leonard's approach to the planning of units based on content standards, described in the beginning of this chapter, takes into account the needs and functioning levels of her students and is a reasonable way of addressing both sides of the debate.

Another role of state departments of education is to publish curriculum guidelines for all of the subject areas in public K–12 education. Many states revise their curriculum guidelines by inviting representative teachers and administrators from all areas of the state to form a committee responsible for considering ways to incorporate both state and subject-matter standards into meaningful curriculum outlines. The resulting documents are then published as "curriculum frameworks" and distributed to all of the school districts they serve.

Curriculum frameworks at the state level change frequently based on the latest research in education. They are also heavily influenced by political pressure and interest groups within the state. As a beginning teacher, you will be expected to become familiar with the latest curriculum frameworks for your state and implement them in your classroom.

Other Influences That Affect Curriculum Development

The notion that the learner's needs must be satisfied in order to be a successful teacher is not a new idea. Ralph Tyler (1949) observed this in his earliest work. Since then, there has been consistent support for Tyler's elegant (simple but not simplistic) curriculum planning method. He proposed four fundamental questions that should be considered in planning any curriculum (1949, p. 1):

1. What educational purposes should the school seek to attain?
2. What educational experiences are likely to attain these purposes?
3. How can these educational experiences be effectively organized?
4. How can we determine whether these purposes are being attained?

Reflective educators are likely to use Tyler's basic principles in planning, organizing, and evaluating their programs because they are remarkably similar to the process of reflective thinking. Essentially, he suggests that teachers begin curriculum planning by perceiving the needs of students, gathering information, making a judgment about an educational purpose, selecting and organizing the strategies to be used, and then evaluating the effectiveness of their curriculum plan by perceiving its effects on their students. These are very similar processes to those outlined in the model of reflective action presented in Chapter 1.

Although reflective teachers are not likely to memorize Tyler's four questions word for word, they are likely to carry with them the fundamental notion of each:

1. What shall we teach?
2. How shall we teach it?
3. How can we organize it?
4. How can we evaluate it?

It is interesting to note that Tyler's questions, stated in 1949, bear a remarkable resemblance to four questions identified and addressed by Anderson and his colleagues in the revised Bloom's taxonomy (Anderson et al., 2001):

1. What is important for students to learn?
2. How do we plan and deliver instruction?
3. How do we select or design appropriate assessment instruments?
4. How do we align objectives, instruction, and assessment?
(Adapted from Anderson et al., 2001)

With the adoption of state-mandated standards, question 1 is often answered for us. However, reflective teachers must still address questions 2 through 4 with respect to the needs and functioning levels of their students. Reflective teachers ask themselves these questions each year because they have probably noticed subtle or dramatic changes in their communities, subject-matter materials, students, or themselves from year to year that cause them to reexamine their curricula. On reexamination, they may confirm that they want to continue to teach the same curriculum in the same way or that they want to modify some aspects of it. As teachers grow in experience and skills, most greet each new year as an opportunity to improve on what they accomplished the previous year. Rather than continue to teach the same subjects in the same ways year after year, reflective teachers often experiment with new ways of teaching and organizing the curriculum.

An obvious contrast between more-reflective and less-reflective teachers is that reflective teachers want to have an active role in the decision-making processes in their schools, and curricular decisions are the ones that count the most. They also display a strong sense of responsibility for making good curriculum choices and decisions, ones that will ultimately result in valuable growth and learning for their students.

Evaluation and Use of Textbooks

School textbooks have an enormous impact on the curriculum. Elementary school textbooks are undergoing major revisions to meet the demand for updated, student-centered, active learning rather than the older emphasis on receptive, rote learning. Many of these changes are controversial, reflecting the often divisive issues that are hot topics among adults in our society.

One of the greatest controversies regarding textbooks today is the rewriting of social studies textbooks to include multiple perspectives on history. Critics of traditional textbooks suggest that they are written solely from the perspective of the white European male. They believe students should learn history from multiple perspectives. Traditionalists believe that eliminating or ignoring content in the traditional textbooks will misrepresent history and that the subject will become diluted in an effort to please every interest group. Reflective teachers attempt to clarify their own values and their own curriculum orientations and beliefs as they make decisions about the curriculum they teach.

When first-year teachers move into their classrooms, the textbooks are already there, in formidable rows or piled in cumbersome stacks. Novice teachers have been told about the importance of individualizing education and meeting the needs of all students in their professional preparation programs. When reality sets in, they realize that many of the materials they need to plan a highly creative program that meets the students' individual needs are not in the classroom. A less-reflective teacher will, without thinking, distribute the textbooks and begin teaching from page 1, perhaps emulating former teachers, with the intent of plowing through the entire book by the end of the year.

Reflective teachers, however, are more inquisitive and more independent in their use of textbooks. They ask questions of other teachers: "How long have you been using these textbooks? How were they chosen? Which parts match the school or district curriculum guides? Which parts are most interesting to the students? What other resources are available? Where do you go to get your ideas to supplement the textbook? In your first year of teaching, how did you meet the individual needs of your students when you had only textbooks available to you?"

Less-reflective teachers tend to assume without question that the "approved" or "correct" curriculum is the one found in textbooks because it is written by "experts." They attempt to deliver the curriculum as written, without questioning its effects or adapting it to the students' needs and interests.

More-reflective teachers consider decisions about curriculum planning to be within their jurisdiction, their domain of decision making. They consult with others, but they take responsibility for deciding which parts of a textbook to use to meet the needs of their own particular class and to match the goals and learning outcomes their state and local curriculum committees establish.

Reflective teachers are seldom satisfied to use textbooks alone. They know that students must have a motivation to search for meaning and create their own understanding of the world of ideas. "When students want to know more about an idea, a topic, or an entire discipline, they put more cognitive energy into classroom investigations and discussions and study more on their own," state Brooks and Brooks (1999, p. 22). Fortunately, there are many *trade books*, books not written to be used as textbooks, now available on many topics related to science, social studies, mathematics, and literature that are written at a variety of reading levels. Many of these are beautifully illustrated, sometimes with full-color photographs, and add much depth to any study in the classroom. Some schools have a fund that can be used for the purchase of these types of books. Teachers often collect *text sets*, sets of books on one topic or by one author, that can be used to add multiple perspectives to the unit studies. All of these can be supplemented in great depth, of course, through the use of multiple venues available through computer programs and Internet research.

PLANNING THEMATIC UNITS TO FIT YOUR CURRICULUM

No other model of curriculum development involves teachers in a more active and professional capacity than the planning, teaching, and evaluation of thematic curriculum units. They appeal greatly to reflective teachers who want to be part of the decision-making process that employs the use of their own creative ideas and methods. However, planning thematic curriculum units also adds greatly to the responsibility of classroom teachers. To create a successful unit, teachers must be willing to explore the state-mandated standards, gather a wide variety of information, and create an excellent knowledge base about the topics they have chosen so that the learning experiences they plan will be based on accurate and interesting information. They must also be willing to work with their colleagues to make sure that their curriculum units do not repeat or skip over important material in the elementary curriculum. Care must be taken to articulate their units with what was covered in earlier grades and what their students will learn in subsequent years.

Even when teachers decide to create their own thematic curriculum units to translate curricular visions into actual classroom experiences, many are not certain how to do that or what can or should be covered in each unit. In this chapter, we examine how teachers decide what units to teach and how they organize the learning experiences in a curriculum unit to ensure that students acquire the knowledge, skills, and processes that are intended.

Deciding on Unit Topics

A single teacher can work alone or with colleagues to translate state and local curriculum standards into units of study. Working alone, a single teacher analyzes state and local standards to be implemented at that grade level in math, science, social studies, language arts, and fine arts. The teacher also examines the curriculum materials supplied by the school district, looking for a theme. The teacher may choose to look for unit topics within a subject, such as a math unit on fractions or a science unit on magnets and electricity or a social studies unit on the electoral process. Other units may be *interdisciplinary*, that is, designed to include information and material from several subjects at one time. For example, a theme of "change" may include learning experiences in science, math, social studies, and literature.

Although many teachers choose to work alone, some teachers at the same grade level frequently work together to create units of study. When this occurs, their combined knowledge and ideas are likely to result in a much more comprehensive set of units and greater variety of learning experiences. Whether a teacher works alone or with a team, the first step is to decide on a series of curriculum units that corresponds to the major educational goals for that grade level.

When a unit topic comes to mind, you need to reflect on whether it is appropriate according to several criteria. Roberts and Kellough (2006) suggest that you consider the following questions: Is this theme one that has a proper length, not too short or too long? Will I be able to find good materials and resources on this subject? Does the theme have a broad real-life application? Does the theme have substance? Is it worth spending time on this topic? Will the students be interested in this topic and be motivated to learn about it?

Wiggins and McTighe (2005) recommend using a **backward design** for unit planning. What are the goals or standards that you want to accomplish, and how can your unit plan achieve these goals and meet these standards? This approach also requires you to think about the evidence that will prove that your students have met the standards. Evidence of achievement is usually gathered through some type of assessment of learning or understanding. Therefore, using the backward design approach for your unit plan, you will want to (1) identify the desired results, (2) determine what evidence can measure or assess the accomplishment of these results by your students, and (3) plan the learning experiences and methods of instruction that you will use in your unit plan.

When teachers select unit topics, Wiggins and McTighe (2005) recommend that the focus be on a topic that will result in students gaining "enduring big ideas that have lasting value beyond the classroom" of the subject rather than students simply learning facts or skills (p. 78). For example, if you want to plan a unit on nutrition, they suggest that you create a unit that will result in students learning that a balanced diet contributes to both physical and mental health throughout one's lifetime. This "enduring understanding" is more important than simply having students learn which foods fit into the various food groups.

Creating a Curriculum Unit Using Reflective Actions

First, consult your state standards for the subjects that you want to include in your unit. When reflective teachers approach the development of a curriculum unit, they consider their long-term goals for that subject or subjects. By consulting the state standards for the subjects to be included in the unit, you can be confident that your long-term goals and those in the standards are congruent. Your may begin with the questions, "What are my major social studies goals for this year? What are the state standards in social studies that support and coincide with my goals? What should I include in this unit of study to accomplish these goals?" Or you may begin by considering the core outcomes your students are expected to achieve during the year, and you may plan curriculum units that will encourage your students to learn the content and enhance the skills that make up those outcomes.

Considering What Students Already Know.   Consider and reflect on the skills and knowledge the students will need to bring to the unit to be successful in learning new material. Pretest your students to assess prior knowledge and skills they bring to the new unit. Some may have already mastered most of the content you intend to teach. Consider ways to challenge them by *compacting* the curriculum so that they can go on to more challenging material. Other students may have serious gaps in their knowledge or may lack background experiences or language structures necessary to participate successfully in the planned activities. Consider how you will scaffold the new material to make it accessible to them.

Teachers who think and plan using the reflective actions described in Chapter 1 are likely to consider the cues they perceive from their students' interests and talents when planning thematic units. As they plan curriculum, teachers tend to ask themselves, "What do my students need to learn? How do they enjoy working? What learning experiences will motivate my students to become actively engaged in the learning process? What language skills and vocabulary will need to be taught so that students can express their newly acquired knowledge?"

Creating an Initial Plan for the Unit.   Once they have decided on a topic, teachers who use reflective actions then sketch out a preliminary draft of a unit and begin to consider some interesting ways to teach it. The first draft may resemble a concept web or something they have read in a curriculum guide or seen online. It might even resemble the type of unit plan they recall from their own school experiences.

Reflecting on the Initial Plan and Working to Make It Fit the Needs of Your Students.   Reflective teachers are likely to begin to establish some criteria for selecting certain content or methods while omitting others. As reflective teachers consider what to include and what to exclude, they ask, "What knowledge and skills am I responsible for teaching at my grade level, and how can I help my students understand the application of this content to their success in school or in life? How can this curriculum assist them in developing what they need most? What attitudes do I want to instill in my students? How can this unit help them to attain those attitudes? What values do I want to model for my students during this curriculum unit? How can I best model those values for them?"

Researching or Conferring with Colleagues.   At many points along the way, reflective teachers are likely to do additional research on the subject or on teaching methods they can include in their new unit. They are also likely to talk with other trusted colleagues about how they have taught the subject. Many teachers share their unit plans with others, but most agree that sharing a unit plan is very much like sharing their recipes for making spaghetti sauce. No two sauces, or units, are identical. Still, a trusted colleague can point out things for the beginning teacher to consider, share strategies for motivating student interest, and suggest new materials to include in the unit.

Revising the Unit.   What changes have occurred to you as a result of your interaction with colleagues? Do you have a new and original way to approach the topic? Have your basic goals changed? Teachers who use reflective action tend to enjoy the process of combining all the content materials and methods they have learned during planning into an original set of learning experiences that fit their own teaching style and the needs of their students. No two thematic units are ever alike. Even when teachers plan together up to this point, they are likely to interpret the materials they have gathered differently and add their own unique spin to the way they teach the unit.

Throughout the process of planning and teaching the unit, teachers who use reflective action are likely to be asking themselves, "How can I adapt the materials I have available to meet my goals? What new instructional materials shall I create to teach this material effectively? What risks are possible if I try to teach this unit in my own way? Which risks am I willing to take? What gains are possible if I take risks? Do the possible gains outweigh the risks?"

During a thematic unit, teachers create original bulletin boards, group activities, work or activity sheets, processes for promoting student interaction, methods for assessing student accomplishments, and ways to allow their students to perform or display what they have learned. Teachers are also carefully examining standards across disciplines. In planning a social studies unit, for example, many standards in reading and writing, science and mathematics, visual and performing arts, and so on can be infused in the planned unit activities. If there are English language learners in the class, then language objectives must be included in each of the activities to ensure their full participation and success. For many reflective teachers, these opportunities for creativity are some of the most important sources of pride and are often cited as some of the most significant perks of their careers.

Considering Alternate Plans

All teachers encounter challenges in teaching and managing their classrooms. Teachers who use reflective action are able to prevent some of these challenges because they try to imagine the consequences of their plans before putting them into action. For example, if you are planning to introduce innovative learning materials to motivate students, you will want to consider what types of management procedures will be needed for distributing and using these materials. The introduction of new and interesting materials may need to include time for the students to explore the materials before they are asked to implement their use in activities.

Teachers who use reflective actions in their thinking and planning anticipate the students' need to explore. Making your expectations very clear will assist in arriving at a positive outcome in student interaction with materials. If unexpected problems arise, teachers use withitness in the midst of the problem to observe what is happening and to respond appropriately. Afterward, they talk with the students themselves and with their colleagues to reframe the problem, and create a new plan, if necessary.

Putting the Plan into Action and Getting Student Feedback

The day you present your new unit plan to your students is usually an exciting day for you and your class. There is a sense of heightened expectations as you reveal the plan. Students may have a lot of questions. You may be able to answer some but not all of their questions right away. You will use withitness during the initial presentation to get feedback from your most important critics: your students. They will give you cues as they react to the plan with excitement, confusion, fear, or increased motivation to learn. You can also discuss the first day's presentation with your colleagues and get ideas about how to reframe the plan for yourself or for your students. After the first day, you will be even better equipped to rethink and adjust certain parts of the plan. If your students react with fear or confusion, you can make changes now, before it is too late. If they react with excitement, you can consider adding even more challenging material to the plan.

Reflective teachers are also able to laugh at their own mistakes and learn from their errors in judgment without an overwhelming fear of the consequences or feelings of guilt. As they plan their thematic units, they are likely to encounter difficulties in locating suitable materials. When this happens, they become very good at scrounging for the materials they need, or they substitute and go on anyway.

When they begin to teach their units, some of the lessons they planned are likely to turn out quite differently than they expected, but they simply assess, regroup, and reteach as needed. As the unit nears completion, they may discover that, due to their students' choices and actions, some unplanned effects occur. These are simply accounted for and evaluated along with the outcomes that were planned.

Throughout the process of planning, organizing, teaching, and evaluating a thematic unit, good communication skills are necessary. Reflective teachers must often convince or persuade their colleagues or administrators to allow them to take the time, spend money, take certain risks, and establish certain priorities necessary to teach their thematic units the way they want. Assertiveness is a very important trait in curriculum development, especially considering the different curriculum orientations that various members of the faculty adopt. The ability to clearly connect the unit and its outcomes to established and mandated standards continues to be a powerful influence on these types of decisions.

Conflicts may arise with students as well. When reflective teachers introduce a creative new way to learn a difficult subject, some students may react by stating their own preferences. When this occurs, teachers who use reflective actions simply explore new ideas with the students and attempt to address the needs of the students and the possibility of working those needs into revised approaches and activities within the unit plan.

SEQUENCING LEARNING EXPERIENCES

Practically speaking, the process of developing a curriculum unit includes the following:

1. Defining the topics and subject matter to be covered in the unit.
2. Defining the cognitive process and affective goals or outcomes that tell what students will gain and be able to do as a result.
3. Outlining the major concepts that will be covered.
4. Gathering resources that can be used in planning and teaching.
5. Brainstorming learning activities and experiences that can be used in the unit.
6. Organizing the ideas and activities into a meaningful sequence.
7. Planning lesson plans that follow the sequence.
8. Planning evaluation processes that will be used to measure student achievement and satisfaction.

PRAXIS
Scope and sequence in planning is tested in PRAXIS™ Exam Section 2b: Instruction and Assessment.

Analysis reveals that these statements correspond to Tyler's (1949) four questions. Items 1, 2, and 3 pertain to his question, "What shall we teach?" Items 4 and 5 relate to the question, "How shall we teach it?" Items 6 and 7 respond to the question, "How shall we organize it?" Item 8 answers the question, "How will we know if we are successful?"

When seen in print, as they are here, these steps appear to depict an orderly process, but curriculum planning is rarely such a linear activity. Instead, teachers find themselves starting at various points in this process. They skip or go back and forth between these steps as ideas occur to them. For example, a team member may begin a discussion by sharing a resource book with a particular learning activity that could be taught as part of the new unit. Discussions may skip from activities to goals, to concepts, to evaluation, to organization. Nothing is wrong with this nonlinear process as long as teachers are responsible enough to reflect on the overall plan to determine if all of Tyler's questions have been addressed fully and adequately. When the plan is complete, it is important to review it and ask yourself: "What are the outcomes I expect from this unit? Are the learning experiences directly related to the outcomes? Is my organization of activities going to make it possible for my students to achieve my outcomes? Are the assessment systems I've established going to measure the extent to which the students have accomplished the outcomes?"

Thematic units vary in types of learning experiences and in organization. Some subjects, such as math, are organized sequentially, but others are not. The type of learning experiences also vary greatly depending on the subject, the resources available, and the creativity or risk taking of the teacher.

Most teachers use the textbook or a district curriculum guide as the basis for planning and as an important resource. *Do not limit yourself, however, to a single textbook as the source of all information in planning your unit or in teaching it.* A good textbook can be a valuable resource for you as you plan and for your students as they learn about the topic, but a rich and motivating unit plan will contain many other elements.

Supplemental reading materials from libraries or bookstores might include biographies, histories, novels, short stories, plays, poems, newspapers, magazines, how-to books, and a myriad of other printed materials. Other resources to consider are videos , audiotapes, and computer programs on topics that relate to your unit. Many interesting student-centered computer programs allow your students to have simulated experiences, solve problems, and make decisions as if they were involved in the event themselves. A good example is the computer game, Oregon Trail, distributed by the Minnesota Educational Computer Consortium (MECC), in which the student travels along the Oregon Trail, making decisions about what supplies to buy, when and where to stop along the way, and how to handle emergencies. This program can enrich a unit on westward expansion by providing more problem-solving and critical-thinking experiences than reading and discussion can ever yield.

Many educational games also provide students with simulated experiences. Some are board games that can be purchased in a good toy store or bookstore. Others are more specialized learning games sold by educational publishers or distributors. Your school district probably receives hundreds of catalogs from educational publishers. What better lessons on "economics" than those that might be found in a good game of Monopoly©, especially if it has been refocused to depict the local area. Locate these resources and find out about the many manipulative and simulation games available on your topic.

Consider field trips that will provide your students with experiences beyond the four walls of the classroom. Which museums have exhibits related to your topic? A simple walk through a neighborhood to look for evidence of pollution or to view variations in architecture can add depth to your unit. If you cannot travel, consider inviting a guest to speak to your students about the topic. Sometimes parents are excellent resources and are willing to talk about their careers or other interests.

In thinking about how to organize a unit, many reflective teachers prefer to begin with a highly motivating activity such as a field trip, a guest speaker, a simulation game, a hands-on experiment, or a film. They know that when the students' initial experience with a topic is stimulating and involving, interest and curiosity are aroused. The next several lessons in the unit are frequently planned at the remembering and understanding levels involved in the revised Bloom's taxonomy (Anderson et al., 2001) to provide students with basic facts and concepts so that they can build a substantial knowledge base and understanding of the topic. After establishing the knowledge base, further learning experiences can be designed at the application, analysis, synthesis, and evaluation levels to ensure that the students are able to think critically and creatively about the subject. This model of unit planning is not universal, nor is it the only logical sequence, but it can be adapted to fit many topics and subjects with excellent results.

Designing the Curriculum to Reflect Multicultural Values

One of the enduring controversies in curriculum planning is how to design curriculum that accurately reflects and honors the wide variety of cultural values represented by students in our schools and communities. James Banks, director of the Center for Multicultural Education at the University of Washington, has similar goals when he advises teachers to redesign their curricula to promote "cultural excellence."

Banks (2007) believes that the redesigned curriculum should describe the needs and contributions of all Americans, including their struggles, hopes, and dreams. It should not be an add-on to the existing curriculum but should become an integral part of every subject we teach. Ask students to reflect, discuss and write about questions such as "Who am I?" "Where have I been?" "What do I hope for?" Banks believes that when students can answer these questions, they will be better equipped to function in their own world, as well as in the larger community that may be populated by people who answer the same questions very differently.

To develop a multicultural curriculum for your classroom, no matter what subject you teach, plan learning experiences that reflect the concerns of the diverse cultural groups that make up the class. Reflective teachers believe that the school and the community offer a variety of possibilities for including diverse perspectives in educational processes. Encourage students to share their different views and opinions, and show that you value the special ways that they solve problems and view the world around them.

Reissman (1994) recommends that you, as you assign learning tasks, consider how each assignment can be used to strengthen intergroup understandings; respect for each other's cultures; and the development of skills that will later be needed in community, national, and global citizenship. Her book entitled *The Evolving Multicultural Classroom* may be a valuable resource in your curriculum planning. Students "develop knowledge by interacting mentally and to some extent physically with people and objects around them. This interaction requires active involvement. Knowledge that is poured into a passive mind is quickly forgotten" (Sleeter & Grant, 2007, p. 218).

One side benefit of the multidisciplinary curriculum is that it has led teachers to share what they are doing and work together to plan learning experiences. Teachers who come to school, close the doors of their classrooms, and teach in isolation are becoming a thing of the past. For example, in curriculum planning, many districts team beginning teachers with experienced teachers to develop and share curriculum materials. This new trend has created an environment in which teachers do not structure their curricula into separate blocks of time. As Beane (1991) points out, when confronted with a problem, individuals do not say, "Now which part of this is science and which part of this is language arts?" Instead, people address problems with a multidisciplinary approach and use whatever resources and content they need to resolve them. This has become as commonplace in secondary classrooms as it is in elementary settings.

In his analysis of subject-matter teaching, Brophy (1992) emphasizes the importance of teaching fewer topics with more depth. This practice allows students to have a greater understanding of the topics and lets teachers emphasize higher-order applications. Brophy indicates that state curriculum guides and textbooks should be modified to accomplish this task and, in many cases, they are being revised to include a greater emphasis on integrated curricula.

Planning Curriculum for a Multicultural, Bilingual Classroom

Ruth Reyes teaches sixth grade at Washington School in downtown San Diego, California. This school follows a special policy of developing biliteracy among all its students. All classes are taught in both Spanish and English. In her class, Ruth teaches one day in Spanish and the next day in English. Her curriculum is designed to allow students to move from one language to another very flexibly. When she designs a unit of study, she selects resources in both English and Spanish. The students use both or select the ones that fit their own level of language development.

Ruth has chosen to use a year-long theme that she calls "environment/survival." This theme grows out of her own special interest in biology. It also ties in with social studies curriculum and grows out of her belief that sixth-grade students need to be aware of the concept of environment and the relationship between humans and their environment. She wants her students to leave her class with a commitment to saving our natural environment. She also wants them to begin to develop survival skills and strategies to improve their own environment.

Ruth describes how she translates this important goal into daily learning experiences that cover the state- and district-mandated curricula for math, science, social studies, and language arts. She describes the process in this way:

I looked through the course of study provided by the school district and the curriculum guides from the state and the school district. Then I opened up all the teacher's manuals for the textbooks we use in sixth grade. As I looked for a way to organize all this material into meaningful chunks, it was clear to me that I should use the social studies standards as the basis for planning. At sixth grade, we focus on the study of world history and geography. That's a perfect fit with my interest in the environment and its relationship to mankind. I can teach the historic material and at the same time bring in contemporary issues and show how they relate to each other.

But before I plunge into the year-long thematic curriculum, I spend the first week of school assessing students' interests and needs. My goals are to get to know my students and learn their strengths and interests. For that week, I use a short literature book that really interests me. This year, I used Kurusa's (1981) The Streets Are Free *and the Spanish edition,* Las Calles son Libres. *This book about the rainforests fits my theme and allows me to introduce the major ideas we'll be studying all year long. The students do a lot of reading, writing, discussion, and group assignments so that I can observe them as they work together. I spend most of my time during that week observing and taking notes on students as they are working in various groupings. I try to identify what each student enjoys, what is easy, and what is a challenge for each of them. As I walk around with my clipboard, I take notes on computer labels (one label per student), which I can then transfer to their portfolios without rewriting. I look for as many positives as possible and also jot down what appears to be challenging for each student. Everyone in my class is learning a new language so I have to be alert when I hear students speak in the unfamiliar language, so that I can encourage them and plan activities that will allow them to be successful.*

During the second week of school, we begin our study of the first social studies/literature unit for the year. The topics that are covered in the social studies curriculum include early man, the beginning of civilization, ancient Hebrews and Greeks, India, China, and Rome. For language arts, I locate several literature books that are related in some way to each of these topics. We spend about 3 weeks on each novel. For example, with the study of early man, I use a book about a girl who lived during the Ice Age who has to help her family survive by moving to a winter cave. See, it fits my theme in every way. For math and science, we study the timelines and the ages of prehistoric Earth. We also write word problems for math involving the characters in the novel.

I am not rigid in my organization of the whole year, but we spend about 3 weeks per book. For some historical eras, we read two or three books. I try to get each book in Spanish and in English. When this isn't possible, then I get similar books on the topic so that my students can choose to read in English for one book, Spanish for another.

We begin a new unit by brainstorming what we already know about rainforests. We make a chart of what we know and put it up in the classroom. Then we make another chart of what we want to learn about rainforests. Based on what we want to know, I create five categories and divide the class into five groups. Each group focuses on researching one of the categories, such as animals or trees. Each group researches their topic for about 3 days and then they begin to organize their material into a book. They use the computer to write, edit, and illustrate their books. When they are completed, they teach what they have learned to the rest of their classmates. The books they write become part of the school library's collection for the rest of the year.

When I think of what my students experience during the entire year, I want them to see that every subject is related to each other. When they see the connections between subject matter, I feel that I have been successful. Some children come to school believing that in order to do math, they have to use a math book. I want them to learn that we do math every day of our lives. I also want them to see the relationships between different authors and their style. We concentrate a lot on comparing and analyzing in my room. Whenever we read a new book, we are constantly looking for ways that this book compares to other books we've read or to the social studies book or to some idea in math or science. When I hear my students making these analyses, I feel that my methods of teaching are validated.

Timelines That Fit Your Goals and Outcome Statements

Time is the scarcest resource in school. Reflective teachers who organize time wisely are more successful in delivering the curriculum they have planned than are teachers who fail to consider it. Teachers who simply start each subject from page 1 of every textbook and hope to finish the text by June are frequently surprised by the lack of time. In some cases, they finish a text early in the year, but more often the school year ends and students never get to the subjects at the back of the textbook. In mathematics, some classes never get to geometry year after year. In social studies, history after the Civil War is often crammed into a few short lessons at the end of the year.

Will you be satisfied if this happens in your classroom? If not, you can prevent it by preplanning the time you will give to each element or subtopic of each subject area you are going to teach. This may seem like an overwhelming task at first, but it can be less threatening if you understand that you are not required to plan every outcome and objective for every subject before the year begins. You need to give the entire curriculum an overview and determine the number of days or weeks you will allot to each element.

Begin by examining the standards for your grade level and comparing them to the textbooks in your classroom, looking at the way in which they are organized. Most books are divided into units, each covering a single topic or collection of related topics within the academic subject. Mathematics books are likely to contain units such as place value, operations, measuring, and geometry. History books are divided into units on exploration, settling the new frontier, creating government, and others. English books contain units such as listening, writing, and speaking.

Curriculum units are excellent planning devices because they show students how facts, skills, concepts, and application of ideas are related. The alternative to planning with units is planning a single, continuous, year-long sequence of experiences or planning unconnected and unrelated daily experiences. Units will be used as the basis for planning throughout the rest of this book.

Decide if the units in your school's textbooks are valuable and important as well as whether you agree with the way in which they are organized and the quality of learning experiences they contain. Consider whether using the textbook will result in achieving the state-mandated standards. Will it result in achieving the goals and outcomes you have for your class? If the textbook learning experiences match your outcomes and the state standards, you can plan the year to coincide with the sequence of units in the book. If the textbook does not coincide with your planned outcomes or if you disagree with the quality or the organizational pattern of the book, you have several options. In reviewing the textbooks, you must also decide if the textbooks fit your students and if they respond to the learning needs of your students. You can plan to use the book but present the units in a different order. You can delete units, or you can use some units in the book as they are written, but supplement with other materials for additional units not covered or inadequately covered in the book. The most adventuresome and creative teachers may even decide to use the textbook only as a resource and plan original teaching units for the subject. They search bookstores and the Internet for resources.

In any case, you should carefully consider the amount of time you want to allot to each unit you plan to teach. Use your computer to create a timeline, chart, or calendar for each subject, and use it as you judge how much time to spend on each subtopic. For timeline planning, you can divide the school year into weeks, months, or quarters. For a subject such as mathematics, you may think about the year as a total of 36 weeks and allot varying numbers of weeks to each math topic you want to cover during the year. For a subject such as language arts, you might think of the school year as 8 months long and create eight different units that involve students in listening, speaking, writing, and reading activities. You may divide the year into four quarters for subjects such as science or social studies, with four major units planned for the year. These examples are only suggestions. Each subject can be subdivided into any time segment, or you may combine subjects into interdisciplinary units that involve students in mathematics, science, and language arts activities under one combined topic for a longer period of time.

Making reasonable and professional judgments about timeline planning depends on having information about your students' prior knowledge and their history of success or failure before the year begins. The pace of your curriculum depends to some degree on the skills and knowledge your students have acquired before you meet them. But your own expectation for their success is also important. You want to avoid, the trap many teachers fall into, reviewing basic skills all year because a majority of your students have been unsuccessful in the past. If you expect them to succeed in your curriculum and be ready to move on to new material, then you should provide them with new challenges. They are much more likely to respond to your positive expectations.

The timelines you create at the beginning of the year need not be rigid and unchanging. They are guidelines based on the best knowledge you have at the time. As the year progresses, you will undoubtedly have reasons to change your original timeline. Students' needs, interests, and success will cause you to alter the pace of the original plan. Current events in the country, your classroom, or your local community may cause you to add a new unit to your plan. Interaction with other faculty members may bring you fresh insights about how you want to organize the way you allocate time in your classroom.

Collaborative Long-Term Planning

Long-term planning, either individually or collectively, is an important job for teachers. If you are teaching in a self-contained classroom, you often have the freedom to write your own curriculum as long as it relates to the district and state standards and responds to the learning needs of your students. If you are working in a team-teaching school, you will need to articulate your vision of curriculum to your teammates and adjust yours to include their ideas as well as your own. Secondary teachers often plan "big idea" units in which individual subjects intertwine and overlap across the curiculum, demonstrating the interrelatedness of learning. In either case, the curriculum you create will improve with experience. As you see the effects of your original planning and assess your students' mastery of the standards, you will reflect on your planning and find ways to improve it with each succeeding year.

Hayes-Jacobs (2004) recommends that faculty members in a school work together to map the curriculum so that everyone on the staff knows what is actually going on in classrooms. This strategy requires teachers to meet and create "maps" for each subject area or grade level. The maps include a brief description of the content to be covered, a description of the processes and skills that will be emphasized, and the type of assessments that will be used to demonstrate that students have achieved the goals and met the standards that apply.

When you begin teaching, you may be assigned to a curriculum task force or planning committee. In discussions with your colleagues, you are likely to gain new insights and information, but you may also experience frustration with points of view that differ from your own ideas that come from a different perspective. Be prepared to speak assertively about your own ideas and beliefs. You may be the one to suggest innovative ways of dividing the curriculum into units. Although your ideas may be met with skepticism or resistance from some teachers, it is quite appropriate for you to articulate them because schools rely on fresh ideas from faculty members with the most recent college or university training to enhance the curriculum and create positive innovations and change.

EXAMPLES OF THEMATIC UNITS

The following subsections illustrate the processes teachers use as they select, order, and create unit plans in several subjects from the curriculum. Because each teacher has a personal curriculum orientation and philosophy, the process of decision making is more complex when teachers plan together than when they plan alone. The following examples demonstrate how teachers create their own curriculum units and what they put down on paper to record their plans for teaching. You will notice many variations in the way units are created and what they contain, depending on their purposes and the philosophies and values of the teachers who create them.

A Multidisciplinary Primary Unit

Adams (1999) suggests that multidisciplinary units are the way to develop literacy across the curriculum. Literacy is much more than reading in today's educational environment. We are equally concerned with promoting mathematical, historical, social, and scientific literacy.

To create such units, teachers frequently choose themes or topics and plan learning experiences that involve students in reading, writing, speaking, science investigations, mathematical problem solving, music, and art. A single teacher can certainly plan and teach a multidisciplinary unit, but we have found that the units planned by two to four teachers are often more exciting because they incorporate each teacher's different perspectives and strengths. For example, at Woodland School in Carpentersville, Illinois, three first-grade teachers often plan their whole language thematic units together. Ginny Bailey, Judy Yount, and Sandra Krakow recently planned an interdisciplinary unit on "change," highlighting the changes of caterpillars and butterflies.

They begin with State of Illinois language arts standards, such as the reading standard for primary grades that reads, "Apply reading strategies to improve understanding and fluency." Section 1.B.1a requires teachers to "establish purposes for reading, make predictions, connect important ideas, and link text to previous experiences and knowledge." Section 1.C.2b calls on teachers to create opportunities for students to "make and support inferences and form interpretations about main themes and topics."

Bailey, Yount, and Krakow also know that teachers often have difficulty fitting all the subjects into their busy curricula. They find that, by using a thematic unit, they can teach several subjects simultaneously. To plan a unit, these teachers use a graphic organizer known as a *planning web*. They sit down with a large piece of paper and write the thematic topic in the middle of the page. They write the various disciplines they want to cover at different positions on the paper and then brainstorm learning experiences that fit the topic under the appropriate subject areas. One of their planning webs is shown in Figure 4.1.

Through their observations of the students they teach, the three teachers learned that, in the minds of first-grade students, reading and writing are closely related. Their interdisciplinary thematic units allow students to read, write, and investigate interesting topics such as

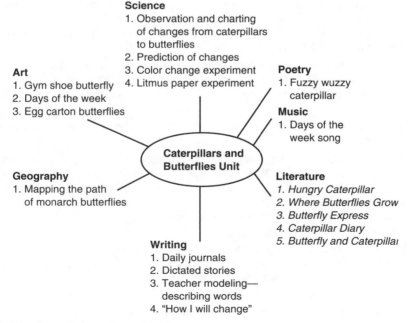

Figure 4.1 Planning web for a thematic unit.

Source: Virginia Bailey, Judy Yount, and Sandra Krakow, Woodland School, Carpentersville, Illinois.

caterpillars, cookies, and planets. In each unit, they select appropriate topic-specific children's books of fiction, nonfiction, and poetry. They locate songs on the topics when possible. Skill teaching is embedded in the unit, within the context of the literature, poetry, or music. The science and social studies facts and concepts are easily mastered by students when they are presented in the context of hands-on experiments and are reinforced by illustrated stories, poems, and songs. Math concepts are introduced by counting, measuring, sequencing, and patterning games and activities appropriate to each unit. Figure 4.2 shows a written plan for the unit on changes; it describes some of the specific learning experiences and how the unit is evaluated.

Description

This primary learning unit was planned to provide students with a set of varied learning experiences to understand the concept of change, with an emphasis on changes in the life cycle of living things.

- **Cognitive goal:** Students will understand that all living things change over time.
- **Affective goal:** Students will accept change as a natural part of their own lives and environment.
- **Psychomotor goals:** Students will use observation skills to identify changes. They will use writing and speaking skills to report what they have learned through observation.

Activities

Nature Walk: Before the nature walk, students are asked to imagine what they might find out about caterpillars and butterflies on their walk. During the walk, they look especially for cocoons. When they return to the classroom, they discuss their findings. They predict whether the cocoons they found will become butterflies or moths. Then they write about what they saw on their nature walk.

Observing Caterpillars: Caterpillars ordered from a science supply dealer arrive in plastic jars. Students observe them climb to the top of the jar preparing to form a chrysalis. In just a few days, they begin to spin their chrysalis. They remain in this form for three or four days and then emerge as butterflies or moths.

As a follow-up activity, students are asked to illustrate the various changes they observe. A strip of 18-inch by 6-inch paper is prepared for each child. Children fold the paper into fourths and draw each stage of a butterfly's development: (1) egg on a leaf, (2) caterpillar, (3) chrysalis or cocoon, and (4) butterfly or moth.

In groups of four, children evaluate their products and check the proper sequence. Each child can then tell the other children a story about his or her butterfly.

Color Changes: In a learning center, students experiment to discover how colors change. Working with diluted red, blue, and yellow food color, the children use an empty cup and an eye dropper to mix colors and experiment on their own to create new colors from the original primary colors.

Children's Literature: The teacher collects a variety of picture books for use in this unit. Some books will be read aloud by the teacher and used as a focus for discussion. Others will be selected by the children to read on their own.

Caterpillar/Butterfly Art Activity: Students create a wiggly caterpillar by cutting 12 cups from an egg carton and turning them upside down. They make a small hole in the bottom of each cup, tie a knot at one end of a piece of yarn, and string the 12 cups together. Then they add paper eyes and decorate the caterpillars with crayons or paint.

They create a butterfly by cutting out 3 of the 12 cups from an egg carton for the body. Then they add wings and pipe-cleaner antennae.

Gym Shoe Butterfly: Each child places his or her gym shoes on a large piece of pastel paper (arches facing out) and traces the shoes into a butterfly shape. The child then cuts out the shape and adds antennae. The child can write a poem inside the butterfly shape.

Figure 4.2 A multidisciplinary primary unit on "Changes: Butterflies and Moths."

Source: This first-grade unit plan was created by Virginia Bailey, Judy Yount, and Sandra Krakow, Woodland School, Carpentersville, Illinois.

Days of the Week: Students create a caterpillar with seven circles cut from construction paper. They then copy the name of a different day of the week on each circle and glue them onto a background paper in the correct order. Afterward, they add a face, legs, and antennae. Students learn a song about the days of the week.

How People Change: Students bring in pictures of themselves as babies and put them on a bulletin board. Current school pictures are also arranged on the bulletin board. Students have to try to match the baby pictures with the current pictures of their classmates. Discussions focus on how people change (observing differences in size, hair, and other physical features) and what people are able to do at different ages. As a follow-up, students write in their journals about how they have changed.

Growth Charts: Charts on the students' current heights and weights are initiated during this unit. Each student measures and weighs a partner. The data are recorded on a wall graph. The charts are updated three times during the year.

Poetry about Change: Poems about caterpillars and butterflies, seasons, and other changes are distributed frequently during the unit. Students read them, memorize and recite them, discuss them, and illustrate them. The poems are also used to teach language structure and vocabulary skills. A poem is projected onto a screen using an overhead projector. Students also have copies of the poem on their desks. We teach skills such as these:

1. Reading from left to right
2. Finding and reading individual words
3. Using the context of the poem to decode words
4. Learning specific phonics skills (such as beginning sounds, endings, rhyming words)

Art/Nutrition: Create a caterpillar out of fruit, vegetables, and peanut butter. Eat it for a snack and discuss its nutritional value.

Unit Evaluation Activity

Provide students with a paper that has the beginning of three paragraphs (shown below). Use a copy on the overhead projector and clarify for students how to begin and what is expected.

Because primary students are unable to write all that they know and have observed, this evaluation can be extended by asking children from an upper elementary grade to interview the primary children and write the younger students' responses for them.

This week, I learned about butterflies and moths. First, I learned _____

_____

_____

Next, I learned _____

_____

_____

Finally, I learned _____

_____

_____

Figure 4.2 (Continued)

Fourth-Grade Social Studies/Literature Unit

Janet Gengosian, a fourth-grade teacher at Greenberg Elementary School in Fresno, California, begins her exploration of the westward movement with a series of books related to the gold rush era in California. The first of the books, *Nine for California* (Levitin, 1996), describes a family's trip across the broad expanse of middle and western America on a stagecoach to join their father, who was already working in the goldfields of California. The second in the series, *Boom Town* (Levitin, 1998), looks at the growth of a small town around the mining activities and takes into account the ideas of supply and demand and a variety of economic interests. The third book in the series, *Taking Charge* (Levitin, 1999), gives us an account of the responsibilities of maintaining a family in the early days of a boom town. It gives provides an opportunity to contrast children's lives of the past with those of today. Janet chose this series of books because she can use them to explore a great variety of the content contained in the history/social studies standards in the context of high-interest stories. They will also provide opportunities for active learning strategies for the children through simulations, active vocabulary role play, reader's theatre, and so forth.

Janet's planning starts with reviewing both the history/social science standards and the reading/language arts standards for the fourth grade. She then begins to gather support materials for her California history unit, which will begin with a simulation based on *Nine for California*. She plans to come dressed as the character of the mother in the book. The students will begin a "simulation journal" by writing a daily entry as the story unfolds day by day, during the 21-day stagecoach trip to California. She also includes activities such as mapping the family's route across the country. These maps will include topographic features encountered in their journey. Janet plans to integrate a number of history/social science standards related to the westward movement, the gold rush, and basic economics into this study.

Under the reading/language arts standards, Janet will address a number of standards related to comparing and contrasting information from several sources and writing narratives based on experiences and simulations, with a focus on descriptive writing. Because her students are second-language learners, she plans to focus on vocabulary development and comprehension through writing and multiple readings of reader's theatre scripts.

Janet begins the unit with reading and simulation activities. She quickly grabs the students' interest and creates a heightened level of excitement by using *Nine for California*, a book which tells the story through the eyes of children who are relatively the same age as her students. In talking about the gold rush, it becomes evident to Janet that there are some gaping misconceptions about certain terms (for example, "gold fever") related to the study. The students, based on their understanding of what a fever means, relate this to an "illness" that the miners had. Janet sees the need for an activity to help clarify this term. She paints some rocks with gold paint and plans a simulated "gold fever" activity. While the students are out of the room, Janet hides the gold rocks throughout the room. She greets her students at the door and explains that the room has been turned into a goldfield. Before she allows them to enter the room, she gives them each a length of yarn with which to mark their "claim" area. Janet has set up a video camera to capture the actions of the children as they search for gold and "stake their claims" around the room. Once started, the activity is quite frenzied as the children rush from place to place within the room, discovering gold and staking their claims. The video camera captures all the action, and when Janet reviews the tape with the students at the end of the activity, they are quite surprised at how frantic their actions appeared. The discussion following the viewing of the videotape allows Janet to clarify the term "gold fever." She follows this activity with a writing prompt, leading the children to write descriptive entries in their simulation journals telling how they felt when they suffered from "gold fever".

In the exploration of *Boom Town*, they will set up a mock frontier town, including needed businesses to stimulate discussion of economy and concepts of supply and demand. As students begin to choose businesses to open, they will deliver an oral presentation to the "town council" with supporting reasons as to why they should be allowed to bring their business to the town. They will continue adding to their simulation journals, describing how the town is growing and developing.

Taking Charge, the third book in the series, leads the class into a study of the way of life in the boom town and the responsibilities of adults and children. It gives Janet an opportunity to engage her students in a comparative analysis of life in the gold rush days versus life today. She also takes this opportunity to challenge the students to investigate the differences in the types of information that might be gained from different types of texts, that is, narrative text versus informational or expository text.

Janet's culminating activity for the unit is the writing of a class poem using a format called "I used to think, but now I know." She starts the poem off for the children with the line, "I used

To plan her California History Unit, Janet identified the following standards and then put them into a sequence of learning experiences as described in the text:

California Fourth Grade History/Social Science Standards

Identify physical geographic features.

Use maps, charts, and pictures to describe how communities vary.

Compare how and why people traveled to California and the routes they traveled.

Analyze the effects of the gold rush on settlements, daily life, politics, and the physical environment.

Study the lives of women who helped build California.

Explain how the gold rush transformed the economy of California.

Discuss immigration and migration to California and its effects on diversity.

Describe the daily lives of the people.

California Reading/Language Arts Content Standards

Read and understand grade-level-appropriate material using predictions and compare information from several sources.

Identify sequential and chronological order to strengthen comprehension.

Compare and contrast information on the same topic from several sources.

Create multiple paragraph compositions.

Write compositions that describe and explain events and experiences using concrete sensory details.

Ask thoughtful questions and respond to relevant questions with appropriate elaboration in oral settings.

Summarize major ideas and supporting evidence in effective oral presentations.

Figure 4.3 Integrating standards into a history/social studies unit plan.

to think gold fever was a disease, but now I know it describes the way the miners rushed to search for gold and stake their claims." The students then continue adding their own verses to the poem, stating new things they had learned or correcting misconceptions they had prior to the unit study.

Janet also includes a variety of activities in the unit that address other content standards. Math is included through mapping, documenting distances traveled, computing economic transactions in the mock village, taking measurements for the creation of products to be sold, and so forth. Visual and performing arts standards are addressed in the simulations and dramatic representations, illustrations, and songs produced by the students during their "travels" across the country. Science standards are included in investigations of machines, geology, and navigation. Physical education standards are incorporated in a variety of games and dances the children re-create from the period.

Janet used the California standards in history/social science and language arts to prepare her unit plan. She used the set of procedures shown in Figure 4.3 as a guide for making certain that the standards were addressed adequately. Then she used her imagination and creativity to make sure the unit engaged her students in active learning.

A Middle School Mathematics Unit

Mathematics is generally thought of as a subject that does not lend itself to multidisciplinary planning, but recently many teachers have been experimenting with ways to connect mathematics to other subject areas and life experiences. As Piaget demonstrated (Wadsworth, 2005), mathematics is a subject that requires early experiences with concrete examples and hands-on experiences that allow students to manipulate materials to understand mathematical relationships. Later, upper intermediate grade and secondary students can be expected to understand these same relationships at a more abstract level without the need to "see" them in a concrete way. Many teachers like to plan their mathematics curriculum using thematic units so that students have many opportunities to experience and investigate the mathematical relationships they are learning.

Mathematics is also a subject that requires lateral thinking, reasoning, and problem-solving strategies that cannot be taught in a sequential series of lessons. Current mathematics units encourage students to explore mathematical relationships and select from a variety of strategies to set up and solve problems. Skillful computation is no longer sufficient as an outcome or performance expectation; it is also important that students be able to apply mathematical operations to real-life problems and tasks.

Based on these organizational principles, an effective curriculum unit in math is likely to (1) present new skills and concepts in order of difficulty; (2) initiate new learning with concrete, manipulative experiences so that students can understand the concepts involved; (3) teach students a variety of problem-solving strategies; and (4) provide examples, tasks, and problems that call on students to apply their newly learned skills and strategies in lifelike situations and to problems they can relate to and want to solve.

Mathematics is an example of a spiral curriculum. This means that certain concepts and skills are taught and repeated every year but in an upward spiral of difficulty. Each year begins with a review of skills from previous years, then an introduction of new skills and concepts. For this reason, the topics of mathematics units are likely to be similar from year to year, but the way these topics are addressed and the complexity of the concepts vary greatly. Mathematics education now emphasizes problem solving and investigation as a means of developing mathematical power. When possible, real situations and problems are becoming the basis for the curriculum.

California State Mathematics Standards for the upper elementary and middle school grades ask teachers to provide learning experiences that will challenge students to "use data samples of a population and describe the characteristics and limitations of the samples." A good example of a mathematics unit that involves students in realistic data collection and interpretation is presented in Figure 4.4. Pam Knight created this unit, entitled Television Viewing Habits, for her middle school students. She uses it during the first week of school to engage her students' interest in mathematics, to help them develop a sense of confidence in their mathematical power, and to show the students how useful and important mathematics can be in their everyday lives.

A Science Unit at Yellowstone National Park

John Graves is a middle school teacher at Montforton School, in Bozeman, Montana. Living near Yellowstone National Park gives him the opportunity to make geology and Earth science come alive for his students. Each year, John plans a 3-day outdoor education experience as the culmination of his unit on geologic history. Before going to Yellowstone, he provides his students with many hands-on experiences in the classroom that will get them thinking like scientists. They examine rock specimens and test for geologically distinguishing features. They simulate the examination of rock layers using three-dimensional cut-and-fold papers colored differently for different layers.

Then, when they arrive at the national park, they are ready to think and act like scientists. They have a different focus on each of their 3 days in the park. On day 1, they visit Mammoth Hot Springs to learn about geothermal phenomena. On day 2, they take a 4-mile hike to Specimen Ridge, where they discover petrified trees still standing where they grew eons ago. John asks students to observe and take field notes. The students list, describe, and draw what they can see from Specimen Ridge. By the time they leave the ridge, their notebooks contain information about kettle lakes, U-shaped valleys, lateral moraines, glacial erratics, and other geologic features of the region. (For more on the Yellowstone petrified trees, go to http://www.grisda.org/origins/24002.htm.) Day 3 finds John and his students climbing

Bunsen Peak, the core of an old volcanic mountain. From the top of this mountain, they can see the effects of ancient glaciers and modern erosion on the land below them.

John developed this unit of study several years ago, but now, in the era of state and national standards, he is happy to find that his goals are very much in synch with these guidelines. The National Science Education Content Standard D states that, as a result of their activities in grades 5 through 8, all students should develop an understanding of the structure of the Earth system and the history of the Earth.

Description

This unit functions both as a personal exploration of how students use their free time and as a mathematics investigation. Students keep a log of all the time they spend watching TV every day for a week. With parental permission, students may also log the TV viewing habits of their parents. After a week of data gathering, students carry out a variety of mathematical calculations and interpret the data they collected.

Cognitive and Skill Outcome Statements

* Students will be able to collect and record data accurately and efficiently.

* Students will be able to calculate percentages of time spent watching television and compare those with percentages of time spent doing other activities.

* Students will be able to create bar and circle graphs based on the data they collected and the percentages they calculated.

* Individually, students will interpret the data they collected about their own television-viewing habits.

* As a class, students will combine their data with that collected by other members of the class to make interpretations and generalizations regarding TV-viewing habits of their age group.

* Individually, students will write articles describing the conclusions and generalizations they reached from this study.

* In small groups, students will make oral presentations on the findings of their group.

Affective Outcome Statement

Students will become aware of the amount of time they and their classmates spend watching television and will make value judgments about whether they want to continue spending their time in this way.

Calendar of Events

I plan this investigation for the first week of school. It gives me insight into the students' incoming work habits and mathematical power.

First Week of School

Friday: Introduce unit and distribute data collection materials. Assign students the task of collecting data, beginning Sunday, on the amount of time they watch television. Because video games are played on a TV screen, my students also decided to count the time spent playing video games. I ask students to be as honest as possible and to keep track to the nearest quarter of an hour.

Second Week of School

Monday–Friday: Data collection continues. Discussions in class focus on data-collection problems and techniques.

Third Week of School

Monday: Bar Graphs. Individually, students create bar graphs demonstrating the amount of time they watched TV each day of the preceding week.

Figure 4.4 A mathematics unit called Television Viewing Habits.

Source: Created by Pam Knight, Garden Road Elementary School, Poway, California.

Tuesday: Calculating Percentages and Circle Graphs. Individually, students calculate the amount and percentage of time they spent sleeping, in school, in after-school or weekend activities, and watching television, as well as extra time not spent watching television. They create circle graphs showing these percentages.

Wednesday–Friday: Group Data Interpretation. Cooperative groups combine class data in order to answer these questions:

1. Which grade level watches more television? Explain how you came to this conclusion.

2. Which day of the week do people watch the most television? Explain how you came to this conclusion.

3. Who watches more television in general—boys or girls? Does any particular age group watch more television? How did you come to your conclusions?

4. By using data about parent viewing habits, have you discovered any relationship between the television-viewing habits of a parent and the habits of a child?

Fourth Week of School

Monday: Writing Articles. Individuals are assigned to write an article about their conclusions about the television-viewing habits of fifth and sixth graders. They must answer the questions "Who? What? When? Where? and Why?" in the articles.

Tuesday–Wednesday: Oral Presentation Planning. Cooperative groups plan presentations on the findings of their groups. They create visual displays to show the data they collected.

Thursday: Oral Presentations. Cooperative groups present their findings to the rest of the class.

Friday: Unit Evaluation. Students evaluate their accomplishments in this unit. Individuals participate in a teacher–student conference to discuss the points each student earned in the unit. Cooperative groups discuss the processes they used in their group planning sessions, the visual displays they made, and the effectiveness of their oral presentations.

Figure 4.4 (Continued)

A major goal of science in the middle grades is for students to develop an understanding of the Earth and the solar system as a set of closely coupled systems. The idea of systems provides a framework in which students can investigate the four major interacting components of the Earth system—geosphere (crust, mantle, and core), hydrosphere (water), atmosphere (air), and biosphere (the realm of all living things). In this holistic approach, students investigate the physical, chemical, and biological processes of the planet. Students investigate the water and rock cycles as introductory examples of geophysical and geochemical cycles. Their study of Earth's history provides some evidence about the co-evolution of the planet's main features—the distribution of land and sea, features of the crust, the composition of the atmosphere, global climate, and populations of living organisms in the biosphere.

By plotting the locations of volcanoes and earthquakes, students can see a pattern of geological activity. Planet Earth has an outermost rigid shell called the lithosphere. It is made up of the crust and part of the upper mantle. It is broken into about a dozen rigid plates that move without deforming, except at boundaries where they collide. Those plates range in thickness from a few kilometers to more than 100 kilometers. Ocean floors are the tops of thin oceanic plates that spread outward from mid-ocean rift zones; land surfaces are the tops of thicker, less-dense continental plates.

Closer to home, there are the Montana Standards for Science to consider. John finds his unit to be in close congruence with Montana's educational requirements. Montana Science

Content Standard 4 states that students should be able to demonstrate knowledge of the composition, structures, processes, and interactions of the Earth's systems and other objects in space. His science program also coincides with the state benchmarks for students to achieve by the end of eighth grade. They should be able to (1) model and explain the internal structure of the Earth and describe the formation and composition of the Earth's external features in terms of the rock cycle and plate tectonics, (2) differentiate between rocks and classify rocks by how they are formed, and (3) explain scientific theories about the origin and evolution of the Earth and solar system by describing how fossils are used as evidence of climatic change over time.

John takes his students to the top of the world to learn about the Earth and its history. He believes that by providing his students with these real-life, hands-on experiences, they will learn to care deeply about the Earth and will also learn to think and act like scientists in the classroom. It is after these experiences that classroom discussions get interesting, and students show much greater interest in reading textbooks, doing online research about Earth's history, or even listening to the occasional lecture on the topic. By providing these science explorations, John believes that he gives his students a reason to learn. They want to know more and are motivated to find out as much as they can about our world as a result of their science investigations in class and their field trip to the national park.

We hope that these unit plans will inspire you to think outside the box when you have your own classroom and are able to plan curriculum. The state standards that you must meet are easily incorporated into highly creative and motivating thematic units. Your students will experience the thrill of researching and investigating topics of high interest, and you will experience the pride and success that comes when the whole class is engaged in active learning for a real-life purpose.

Communicating with Parents

When you plan to spend an extended amount of time on a study area such as in a thematic unit, it is important to convey your plans to the parents of your students. Explain the purpose of the unit and the goals and standards to be addressed. Let them know what will be expected of the students, especially if you will be requiring long-term projects. Keep parents informed of the timelines, due dates, and any special events that they will want to attend. Let them know how you will be communicating their child's progress to them. You may find that you have parents with expertise or access to resources that will be very helpful in your planning. Make sure that the parents know that you welcome any help, support, or resources they can provide.

Playing Catch Up

Thematic units provide a unique opportunity to build background knowledge for students who may not be working at grade level. As you collect books and materials for your thematic units, keep these students in mind. Gather materials at appropriate reading levels that will allow your students to read and gain information at their reading levels. so that they will be able to contribute to the unit. Recognize special talents, like art, music, or physical skills, that your students have and that provide ways for them to be an integral part of the unit study. When designing presentations, remember that some of your students may need additional scaffolding. For instance, be sure to include live links in electronic presentations that point to additional background information for those students who may need it. Thematic units provide a great opportunity to expand learning in your classroom.

GUIDED GROUP EXPLORATION

1. Divide the class into groups, one group for each grade level.

2. Search the appropriate Department of Education Web site for a list of state standards, and choose one overarching concept that is taught at all grade levels (for example, government, American symbols, heroes, mechanics of writing, etc.). For an example from the California Social Studies Standards, see Figure 3.3.

3. On a large piece of chart paper, each group writes the grade-level standard related to the selected overarching concept.

4. Each group then generates a list of grade-level appropriate activities related to the overarching concept. Write the suggested activities on the chart below the standard. They might be added in different colors.

5. Each group posts its chart around the classroom in grade-level sequence and makes a short oral presentation briefly discussing the standard and explaining how their suggested activities relate to the standard.

6. Each group should also point out how their grade-level standard expands on and/or adds to knowledge gained in the previous grade level.

This activity points out the viability of a spiralling curriculum in which knowledge is built on previous knowledge in an additive process of reviewing and expanding learning.

Mapping skills

Kindergarten—Distinguish between land and water on maps and globes, and locate general area references in legends and stories.

First Grade—Locate on maps and globes the students' local community, their state, the United States, the seven continents, and the four oceans.

Second Grade—Locate on a simple letter-number grid system the specific locations and geographic features in their neighborhood or community.

Third Grade—Identify and locate on a map the geographical features (deserts, mountains, valleys, hills, coastal areas, oceans, and lakes) in their local region.

Fourth Grade—Explain and use the coordinate grid system, of latitude and longitude to determine the absolute location of places in their state and on the Earth.

Fifth Grade— Trace the routes of the major land explorers of the United States; the distances traveled by explorers; Atlantic trade routes that linked Africa, the West Indies, the British colonies, and Europe.

Sixth Grade—Locate and describe the major river systems, and discuss the physical settings that supported permanent settlement and early civilizations in Mesopotamia, Egypt, and Kush.

Seventh Grade—Map the spread of the bubonic plague from Central Asia to China, the Middle East, and Europe and describe its impact on global population.

Eighth Grade—Map the changing boundaries of the United States from the time of the founding of the nation until now.

Tenth Grade—Map the important battles of World War II, noting important factors such as topography, waterways, distance, and climate.

Eleventh Grade—Map the changing landscape during the rise of industrialization in the United States, noting the cities involved and how they are linked by industry and trade.

Figure 4.5 Overarching concepts for guided exploration.

Source: Adapted from CA History-Social Science Standards.

REFLECTIVE ACTION ACTIVITY FOR YOUR PROFESSIONAL PORTFOLIO

Give Evidence of Your Reflection on Long-Term Curriculum Planning

1. Choose one state standard that you will be expected to use in your curriculum planning for student teaching.
2. Write the standard.
3. Write a brief paragraph on what you think are the reasons and motives that resulted in this state standard being adopted. What is this standard going to accomplish? Why do you think it was adopted by your state?
4. How will this standard affect the way you create curriculum in this subject area? How will this standard make your planning easier than if you had no standards to follow? How will it make your planning more difficult?
5. Imagine that you are beginning to plan a year-long curriculum for this subject area. How would you use this state standard to begin planning? Write a general long-term plan to achieve this standard. Will you teach it continuously for a period of time or come back to this subject matter every week or so during the year?
6. How will you assess your students' accomplishment of this standard? How will you prove to yourself that your students have successfully mastered this standard? How will you prove this to your school administrators?
7. Reflection always requires self-analysis. Reflect on the difficulties you had in planning this simple curriculum. How will you improve this process when you are called upon to plan a real curriculum?

References

Adams, D. (1999). *Literacy today: New standards across the curriculum*. New York: Garland Publishing.

Anderson, L., Kratwohl, D., Airasian, P., Cruikshank, K., Mayer, R., Pintrich, P., Raths, J., & Wittrock, M. (Eds.) (2001). *A taxonomy for learning, teaching, and assessing: A revision of Bloom's taxonomy of educational objectives*. New York: Longman Publishers.

Banks, J. (2007). *Educating citizens in a multiculural society* (2nd ed.). New York: Teachers College Press.

Beane, J. (1991). Middle school: The natural home of the integrated curriculum. *Educational Leadership*, *49*(2), 9–13.

Brooks, J., & Brooks, M. G. (1999). In search of understanding: The case for constructivist classrooms. *Educational Leadership*, *57*(3), 18–24. Alexandria, VA: Association of Supervision and Curriculum Development.

Brophy, J. (1992). Probing the subtleties of subject-matter teaching. *Educational Leadership*, *49*(7), 4–8.

California State Department of Education (1998). History-Social Science Content Standards for California Public Schools. Sacramento, CA: California State Department of Education.

Hayes-Jacobs, H. (2004). *Mapping the big picture* (2nd ed.). Alexandria, VA: Association of Supervision and Curriculum Development.

Kendall, J., & Marzano, R. (1995). *The systematic identification and articulation of content standards and benchmarks*. Aurora, CO: Mid-Continent Regional Educational Laboratory.

Kurusa, D. (1981). *The streets are free (Las calles son libras)*. New York: Annick Firefly Books (English version); Caracas: Ekara-Banco del Libro (Spanish version).

Levitin, S. (1996). *Nine for California*. New York: Orchard Books.

Levitin, S. (1998). *Boom town*. New York: Orchard Books.

Levitin, S. (1999). *Taking charge*. New York: Orchard Books.

Reissman, R. (1994). *The evolving multicultural classroom*. Alexandria, VA: Association for Supervision and Curriculum Development.

Roberts, P., & Kellough, R. (2006). *A guide for developing interdisciplinary thematic units* (4th ed.). Upper Saddle River, NJ: Merrill/Prentice Hall.

Sleeter, C., & Grant, C. (2007). *Making choices for multicultural education* (6th ed.). Upper Saddle River, NJ: Merrill/Prentice Hall.

Tyler, R. *(1949)*. *Basic principles of curriculum and instruction*. Chicago: University of Chicago Press.

Viadero, D. (1993). Standards deviation: Benchmark-setting is marked by diversity. *Education Week*, June 16, 14–17.

Wadsworth, B. (2003) *Piaget's theory of cognition and affective development*. New York: Allyn and Bacon.

Wiggins, J., & McTighe, G. (2005). *Understanding by design handbook* (2nd ed.). Alexandria, VA: Association of Supervision and Curriculum Development.

Williams, S. (1990). *I went walking*. Boston: Red Wagon Books.

Now go to Topics #5: Instructional Planning in the MyEducationLab (www.myeducationlab.com) for your course, where you can:

- Find learning outcomes for this topic along with the national standards that connect to these outcomes.
- Complete Assignments and Activities that can help you more deeply understand the chapter content.
- Apply and practice your understanding of the core teaching skills identified in the chapter with the Building Teaching Skills and Dispositions learning units.

CHAPTER

5

Assessing and Meeting Students' Diverse Needs

■ ■

As soon as teachers succeed in getting a teaching position, most of them are eager to get into their classrooms to arrange furniture, establish schedules, put up bulletin boards, consider rules and consequences, and plan major units of study. However, surprises are inevitable when school starts and the classroom is filled with students from many different backgrounds who have a variety of abilities, talents, and needs.

PRAXIS
This section prepares you for PRAXIS™ Exam Section 1a: Student Development and the Learning Process.

The first day of school can be a daunting experience for a teacher who has spent a lot of time and energy planning the perfect beginning for the school year. Some students may appear to be totally disinterested, while others appear to be intent on disrupting the teacher's plans. In most classrooms today, there are likely to be some students who are struggling to understand and speak English. Many new teachers find themselves sitting at their desks thinking, "What ever made me think I could do this?" Even experienced teachers often find themselves comparing their new class to last year's class, thinking, "These students have so many more needs than last year's group!" They may be forgetting that last year's class had made a whole school year's worth of progress when they parted at the end of the school year.

Teaching today's diverse student population is definitely a challenge. Students bring a wealth of different perspectives to the classroom, whether they are from mainstream American homes or culturally diverse homes where multiple languages are spoken. We believe that all students are teachable, and we hope you agree. Teachers who have faith in their students' abilities to learn are the ones who are able to make the most significant and positive differences in their students' lives.

Stephanie Collom is a resource teacher in Fresno, California, at Hidalgo Elementary School, where native English speakers are rare. She observed: "All the children come to school with faith in me, as their teacher. I have to find ways to support their learning so that their faith is justified. I also have to have faith in their abilities as learners and find a way to make sure that they succeed."

Many teachers begin their teaching careers expecting the students in their classes and the curriculum they teach to resemble the students and curriculum they experienced when they were in school. It is sometimes a big shock to realize how much has changed in education in a very short time. The students in today's classrooms come to school from diverse backgrounds, not only in experiences but also in language exposure and perceptions of what school is all about. To add complexity to the issue, it seems that at the same time as our student body becomes more diverse, the state-mandated curricula are becoming more focused on meeting a single set of standards for all.

Teachers in today's schools are often expected to be able to teach the traditional skills to a very nontraditional group of students. In addition, teachers are also expected to diversify their instructional methods in ways that support students' self-esteem, knowledge of technology, and ethnic and language backgrounds. An added challenge in working with diverse populations is the different expectations that parents from different cultures bring to the school.

Celebrating diversity is vastly different than tolerating diversity. At the end of the 20th century, the goal for teachers in multicultural settings seemed to be to show acceptance of students' differences. In the present and (we hope) more enlightened century, teachers have the goal of finding ways to encourage all students to value their own cultural heritage and appreciate the contributions of their classmates from other backgrounds.

One major difference that affects learning is that of language. To teach effectively, teachers must understand how language is acquired and know how to adjust their assessment, curriculum, and planning to take advantage of the multiple language-centered perspectives contained within almost every classroom.

LANGUAGE ACQUISITION AND THE CLASSROOM TEACHER

PRAXIS
This section prepares you for PRAXIS™ Exam Section 1b: Students as Diverse Learners, and Section 3b: Cultural and Gender Differences.

The research into language acquisition issues has become rich and productive. Linguists and educators working together have discovered effective ways to support students in their acquisition of new languages and content knowledge. It is vital that classroom teachers understand the implication of language acquisition theory so that they can provide the scaffolding necessary for their students to be successful in the classroom (Krashen, 1996).

In his study of language acquisition, Krashen makes a distinction between language acquisition and language learning that is vital to the support of students in the classroom in their gradual acquisition of fluency in a new language. Krashen's research demonstrates that language acquisition is a natural process. He observes how easily and readily young children acquire their home language without formal teaching and drill and practice! Natural language acquisition is a gradual, interactive process based on receiving and understanding messages, building a listening (receptive) vocabulary, and slowly attempting verbal production of the language in a highly supportive, nonstressful environment.

Krashen (1996) recommends to teachers that it is necessary to duplicate these conditions as much as possible in a classroom to foster the acquisition of a second language. According to this theory, teachers will be most successful in teaching English if they plan interactive learning activities and speak or write words selected carefully to match their students' level of understanding. This concept is termed *understandable language* or *comprehensible input*, and it is to be used with props, gestures, pictures, and other strategies that contribute to each child's acquisition and eventually to the production of the language.

Language Scaffolding

Scaffolding is a term used in teaching that involves modeling and demonstrating a new skill. It requires a highly interactive relationship between the teacher and the student while the new learning occurs. Bruner's (1997) work with mothers and children led him to recommend that.

As a mother reads aloud to a toddler, she may simplify the book to meet the attention span and interests of her child, calling the child's attention to material that is appropriate and eliminating material that is beyond the child's present capacity. She is also likely to allow the child to interact with her as they read and discuss the words and pictures on each page. This flexible and simplified interaction between child and parent allows the child to connect new ideas to existing schemata at his or her own level.

Teachers can apply scaffolding in the classroom by reducing complex tasks to manageable steps; helping students concentrate on one task at a time; being explicit about what is expected and interpreting the task for the student; and coaching the student using familiar, supportive words and actions. When a teacher coaches the student through a difficult task, he or she must provide sufficient scaffolding through the use of hints and cues so that the student can succeed. As students become more skillful, scaffolding can be reduced and finally eliminated.

Scaffolding is an especially valuable technique for the primary teacher because most young students require supportive interaction and accommodation to their existing vocabularies to learn new skills. Scaffolding is also appropriate for upper-level students when the tasks are complex or the students have difficulty with the language.

For some beginning teachers, scaffolding may not come naturally because they may not have experienced its use during their own learning in their personal school experiences. This technique can be learned only by reflecting on the needs of students, gathering the latest information on such techniques from reading, talking with experienced teachers who have used the techniques successfully, and gradually adding such strategies to personal repertoires.

Scaffolding academic language supports students' successful participation in content area instruction. Academic language is associated with school subjects such as mathematics, science, and social studies. It places a higher cognitive demand on the listener or speaker.

Cummins (1986) identified two types of language that students acquire. The first, basic interpersonal communication skills (BICS)—or social language—is learned more quickly and easily than the second, cognitive academic language proficiency (CALP)—or academic language. Academic language scaffolding supports the student in CALP, the language necessary for the student to participate successfully in classroom learning opportunities.

For students to participate successfully in academic lessons in the classroom, teachers use a series of scaffolding strategies that include modeling academic language; contextualizing academic language using visuals, gestures, and demonstrations; and supporting the students in the use of academic language through active learning activities.

Susan McCloskey, a kindergarten and first-grade teacher at Viking Elementary School in Fresno, California, provides a perfect example of language scaffolding as she teaches her students the concepts of same and different. She begins her lesson by modeling. She takes two large teddy bears and holds them up for the students to see: "These are the same," she says. She puts one bear down and picks up a stuffed bunny: "These are different," she repeats. She asks students to come to the front of the class and hold two stuffed animals. The other students repeat the words *same* and *different*, depending on the animals the child is holding. Susan then has the students draw pictures of their favorite foods. They show their pictures and talk about the fact that some children like the same foods and others like different foods. During recess, she photocopies some of their pictures onto a large sheet of copy paper and when they return to the classroom, she arranges the students into pairs, carefully placing them together so that each pair has a relatively proficient English speaker. All of her students are English language learners, so she does not have the advantage of strong English models, other than herself and classroom volunteers and aides.

As she gives the instructions for the activity, Susan demonstrates. She tells the students to cut out the pictures as she models cutting out the pictures. She tells them to paste the pictures together that are the same. As she says this, she models choosing two pictures of hamburgers and placing them together on a large sheet of construction paper. She repeats, "These are the same," as she points to the two hamburgers she has pasted onto the construction paper. The students work together, some talking in English, some in Hmong, their native language. Susan moves around the room supporting the students, asking questions about the concepts of same and different. To anyone observing, the lesson is obviously a success.

However, it is at the end of the lesson that Susan adds the piece that scaffolds the students into new levels of language. As each pair completes the task, they bring the paper to Susan. She points to one group of pictures on the construction paper and asks, "Why did you put these together?"

The first child says, "Same." "Yes," confirms Susan. "They are all the same. This is a hamburger. This is a hamburger. This is a hamburger. This is a hamburger. They are all the same," she says as she points to each hamburger on the page. She then continues to ask the same child, "Why did you put these together?" as she points to the hot dogs. The child responds, "This is hot dog. This is hot dog. This is hot dog. This is hot dog," as he points to each one. "They all same." Susan then asks the other child in the pair the same questions. Because this child has been watching and listening, she responds in phrases just as Susan has modeled. In just a few minutes, these two children have moved from one-word responses to simple-sentence responses with the teacher's language scaffolding. Many teachers would have been pleased that the students had completed the task correctly and would have put a smiley face or star at the top of the page without utilizing the "teachable moment" and providing the vital language scaffolding as part of the lesson. Knowing how children acquire language is a necessary part of effective teaching with English language learners.

The Stages in Language Acquisition

When students are acquiring a new language, they go through predictable stages. The stages begin with students listening to language. They are taking in or "receiving" language at this stage, often called *the silent period*. Teachers should be aware that students are processing the language they are hearing, and it is important that the language be contextualized so that it is understandable. After this silent or preproduction period, students move into the *early production stage* where they can give one- or two-word responses. They then move into *speech emergence*, where they are attempting to speak phrases and short sentences but are still making grammatical errors. They then move gradually into *intermediate fluency*, where their sentences lengthen and their errors are fewer. Finally, over time, they become *fluent* in English.

Teachers need to be aware of these stages so that they can adapt their questioning strategies and expectations to support students' progress into higher language stages. It is especially important that teachers actively seek ways to keep English language learners involved in the classroom community. Allowing students to sit idly, not engaged in processing the instruction that is going on in a classroom, is never acceptable, but teachers must be armed with strategies to use in engaging students.

Leveled questions are used when teachers adapt the way they ask questions so that students can answer or respond to them according to their language acquisition stage. The use of leveled questions enables a teacher to include English language learners in the classroom activities and support their active engagement, which in turn supports their language acquisition. To level the questions, the teacher must observe the students while they are interacting in English. Once the teacher knows the level at which the students interact in English, the questions the teacher poses to the students can be adjusted to ensure their success in answering. This may involve the teacher using gestures or visuals or slowing the speech slightly while asking the questions. The teacher asks the questions in a way that encourages each student to answer by pointing to a visual or giving a one-word response, complete sentence, or explanation, depending on the level of language acquisition. The teacher's role in using this strategy involves knowing the students' level of English acquisition and providing enough context in the question so that the students can respond, either verbally or nonverbally, with understanding and confidence.

Optimal Levels of Instruction

Reflective teachers who want to encourage each student to function at the highest level of achievement monitor each student's level of understanding closely to see what interventions are needed. Lev Vygotsky, a Russian cognitive psychologist, identified the optimal level of instruction for each student as the zone of proximal development (ZPD). The ZPD for each student is based on the level at which the student can no longer solve problems on his or her own but must be supported by a teacher or more knowledgeable peer (Dixon-Kraus, 1996). For the

Level	Description	Appropriate Questions	Ways to Adapt Instruction
Pre-production	The child is not yet producing English words or phrases (also called the silent period). They *are* developing receptive language.	Show me . . . . Is this the ____ one? (Using a picture or graph)	1. Add pictures or realia (real objects) to develop vocabulary. 2. Give multiple examples. 3. Always accompany verbalizations with gestures, visuals, or realia. 4. Keep sentences short. 5. Smile and nod a lot to give encouragement.
Early production	The child is beginning to say a few words or short phrases.	Is it ____ or ____? (Giving choices so the child just has to repeat one of the words or phrases)	1. Labeling things with both English and native language labels. 2. Show, don't just tell. 3. Always accompany verbalizations with gestures, visuals, or realia.
Speech emergence	The child is beginning to produce simple sentences (still making a lot of pronunciation and grammar errors).	Did this happen at the beginning or the end? Where did you find this answer? (Can now ask questions that require short sentences in response)	1. Written assignments may still need to be shortened. 2. Students may need a little more time to complete assignments. 3. Reading texts may still need to be simplified. (Just rewrite science and social studies text using shorter sentences and simpler words.) 4. Will need vocabulary instruction especially in science and social studies.
Intermediate fluency	The child is producing longer sentences and is less reluctant to speak English, but he or she is still making some errors in pronunciation and grammar.	How did you . . . ? What was the character trying to do?	1. Should be able to participate in regular lesson with success as long as you add visuals, gestures, and realia. 2. May still need direct instruction related to higher-level vocabulary.

Figure 5.1 Adapting instruction for different language development levels.

Source: Adapted from Herrell & Jordan 2007.

teacher to be able to provide instruction for each student at an optimal learning level, or ZPD, the teacher must use reflective actions to gain an understanding of the student's needs. This is especially vital for students who have special needs or who are learning English as a second language. For suggestions on identifying language levels and adapting instruction for the different levels, see Figure 5.1.

FIVE FACTORS IN MEETING THE NEEDS OF DIVERSE STUDENTS

Whether a student is learning English as a second (or third) language or having difficulty absorbing academic content, there are five factors that reflective teachers consider when planning and implementing instruction.

PRAXIS
This section prepares you for PRAXIS™ Exam Section 1c: Student Motivation and the Learning Environment.

The first factor is *comprehensible input.* The teacher looks at the lesson and asks, "Is the instruction I am giving understandable to my students?" If the students are experiencing confusion or simply not "getting it," the teacher must consider ways in which the instruction can be made more understandable. It is important to consider how to give explanations while demonstrating something. The teacher may want to ask, "Am I just talking or am I modeling, using pictures, gestures, real objects to demonstrate the concepts I am trying to get across? Am I using words that I have defined and demonstrated? Am I relating new concepts to past experiences, giving examples, showing instead of telling?"

Good explanations require a lot of thought. Giving multiple examples supports understanding. Giving nonexamples is also very helpful. For example, when teaching about the characteristics of mammals, a teacher might say, "A zebra and an elephant are both examples of mammals; fish and birds are not examples of mammals."

The second factor is *quality of the verbal interactions* with and among your students. Ask yourself, "Am I providing opportunities for the students to interact with one another? Do the students have an opportunity to use hands-on materials? Are they given a chance to see the practical importance of what they are being asked to learn?"

The third factor is the *contextualization* of the language experiences you provide for your students. In other words, are new words and ideas presented within a context so the students have an opportunity to link the vocabulary and concepts to a bigger picture? One of the biggest factors in a student's ability to comprehend language is how well that language is supported by context. The direction, "Take out your science book," when spoken while holding up the science book is easily understood even by a student who knows no English or a student who cannot hear well. Just getting in the habit of supporting instruction with the use of gestures, visuals, and showing while telling is highly supportive of language acquisition and student understanding.

The fourth factor is *selecting teaching and grouping strategies that serve to reduce student anxiety* rather than aggravate it. Students who are anxious about being called on to speak aloud in front of their peers often have difficulty processing information or even listening attentively. Krashen (1996) calls this the **affective filter**, an emotional process that prevents the learner from hearing or processing new information. Teachers who want to be able to diminish or eliminate the likelihood of triggering a student's affective filter must find ways to create a classroom climate that encourages and motivates students while at the same time reducing their anxiety. One important consideration for you to reflect on is the way you ask questions and respond to errors. If students know that making an error is not going to cause them to be ridiculed in front of the class, they are much freer to answer questions and take risks. It is not enough to refrain from embarrassing students, however. There should be a consistent monitoring of the verbal interactions among students as well. A "no tolerance rule" related to student ridicule proves a healthy classroom climate conducive to learning. This happens only when the teacher models it, discusses it openly, and tolerates no negative verbal interactions among the students.

The fifth factor to be considered is how to *increase the level of active involvement* of students within the classroom. Opportunities to actively engage in classroom activities designed to practice and gradually master the skills being taught is as vital to language acquisition as it is to other aspects of student learning. Activities that provide students with opportunities to work in small groups on a project that requires the use of new skills and problem-solving strategies also require the students to engage in verbal interactions, contextualize the language they are using, and generally serve to reduce anxiety.

When all five of these factors are considered in scheduling the school day and planning individual lessons and activities, the classroom becomes a *community of learners*. The reflective teacher observes the classroom climate and uses withitness to perceive any indications of discord or anxiety that may be standing in the way of learning. Planning time for purposeful student interaction is a vital building block for developing a strong sense of community. Students need time to interact and get to know one another. As they know more about each other, they will begin to value the diversity and uniqueness of the individuals who make up the community.

Two of these important goals can be achieved by using cooperative group activities as a strategy for teaching in your classroom. Language acquisition for English language learners is enhanced by taking part in a cooperative group effort where communication skills are required to complete an assigned task, and increased understanding and appreciation of diversity occurs as well.

Slavin (1995) reports that cooperative groups may actually improve race relations within a classroom. When students participate in multiracial teams, studies show that they choose one another for friends more often than do students in control groups. Researchers attribute this effect to the fact that working together in a group as part of a team causes students to promote more differentiated, dynamic, and realistic views (and therefore less stereotyped and static views) of other students (including peers with special needs or from different ethnic groups) than do competitive and individualistic learning experiences (Johnson & Johnson, 1993).

You must remember that it is you, the teacher, who is responsible for providing comprehensible instruction for all of your students and adjusting that instruction for their individual needs. Do not rely on students to provide the adjustments for you. It is tempting to seat English learners or students who need additional attention next to stronger students and ask them to provide scaffolding for the English learners. Although this is sometimes helpful, it should never take the place of adapted instruction by the teacher. Try to add visuals, gestures, realia, and multiple examples to your instruction to support those students who need a little extra help. You may even have to rewrite some of the more difficult text using shorter sentences and less complex vocabulary. This is not as difficult as it sounds and may benefit many of your students.

The Forgotten Minority

You may have students in your classroom who are very bright or working at a higher level than the others. These students are often overlooked and not challenged because they are able to participate with success, or even find other activities to fill their time, like reading library books or drawing pictures. Make it a habit to plan some extension activities for those students who appear to be just filling time once their work is done. These students can become the class experts or be given the task of using the Internet to find additional information about topics the class is studying.

Using learning centers in your classroom provides a unique opportunity to provide assignments on several levels so that your struggling students can do a basic task and others can complete a "challenge" task. You may even be surprised at the students who choose to attempt the challenge task. The results of their challenges will enhance everyone's understanding if you give them a chance to share their research with the class in some way. We will explore additional ways of challenging your most able students in Chapter 9.

Interactive Goal Setting

Teachers can support the growth of their students' levels of performance by using interactive goal setting as a natural forum for celebrating growth and setting goals for the future. Vince Workman, a fifth-grade teacher in Fresno, California, sets aside time to discuss his students' accomplishments with them during each of the six grading periods in the school year. He schedules these student conferences throughout the year, recycling back through his class in approximately the same order so that students can expect to meet with him for goal setting every 6 weeks. Since Vince and his students work together to select work samples for student portfolios, he begins the conferences by asking the students to talk about the work they have accomplished since their last student–teacher conference. Students talk about the work they have chosen to share and then, together, the teacher and student look at the grade-level standards and decide which of the standards have been met or are in the process of being met. They decide together on an appropriate challenge for the next week.

ALBERTO'S VOCABULARY JOURNAL

WEEK 1 — GOAL: Learn two new words each day.

Day 1: Words from *Stellaluna*

clutched   I told my mom that I clutched my bookbag so I would not lose it.

clambered   I clambered onto the school bus after school.

Day 2: Words from science class

explored   We explored drops of water. We looked at them very closely.

process   When water changes from water to steam, that is called a process of evaporation.

Figure 5.2 Alberto's vocabulary journal.

For example, Alberto, a student who is reading at approximately the third-grade level, has set a goal of reading two library books a week. He is keeping a reading journal and a vocabulary notebook to monitor his own understanding of the books he is reading and to focus on building his English vocabulary. Vince encourages Alberto to use the new words he is learning every day and often calls on Alberto in class to share some of the new words he is practicing. Because vocabulary study is one of Alberto's self-selected goals, he is much more motivated to keep working on his vocabulary journal. Vince talks to him briefly almost every day about new words he is exploring and celebrates Alberto's growing word knowledge with him frequently by simple responses such as, "That's a great word for that, Alberto. Explain where you first found that word and some of the ways you have found to use it." Alberto's first vocabulary goal was to learn two new words a day. He has increased his goal every 6 weeks so that he is now focusing on six new words each day. His vocabulary journal helps both Alberto and Vince track the progress he is making. A sample page from Alberto's vocabulary journal might look like the one in Figure 5.2.

BUILDING SELF-ESTEEM AND INTRINSIC MOTIVATION

A student's ability to learn is greatly enhanced when self-esteem and self-perception are strong and the student has a high degree of motivation. Krashen (1996) suggests that students who feel valued, who feel like the tasks they are being asked to accomplish are "doable," and who feel they can make mistakes without recrimination are more open to instructional processes. When students think the work is too difficult, or they are afraid to ask questions and to seek help, their "affective filter" is raised once again, impeding the educational processes. This means that students' emotional needs are screening out any information being presented by the task or the text being read so that they are unable to absorb or thoroughly understand educational input.

Raths (1998) also identified eight emotional needs that people strive to satisfy. These are the need for love, achievement, belonging, self-respect, freedom from guilt, freedom from fear, economic security, and self-understanding. Raths believes that children whose needs are not satisfied exhibit negative, self-defeating behaviors such as aggressiveness, withdrawal, submissiveness, regressiveness, or psychosomatic illness.

Raths (1998) recognizes that teachers cannot expect to satisfy the many unmet needs experienced by all the students in their classrooms. However, he does believe that "children cannot check their emotions at the door and we should not expect them to. If unmet needs are getting in the way of a child's growth and development, his learning and his maturing, I insist that it is your obligation *to try* to meet his needs" (p. 141). Raths's (1998) book, *Meeting the*

Needs of Children, contains many pages of specific suggestions about what teachers can do to help meet children's emotional needs so that they are free to learn.

The Enhancing Effects of Success

All individuals want to win or succeed. Virtually all students who walk into a classroom on the first day of school hope that this year will be *the* year, that this grade will be *the* grade, and that this teacher will be *the* teacher who will make it possible for them to succeed. Some enter secure in the knowledge that they have succeeded before, but they are still anxious to determine whether they can duplicate that success in this new situation. Others enter with a history of failure and harbor no more than a dim, hidden hope that maybe they can succeed if only they can overcome their bad habits and learn how to succeed.

Winning and success are two powerful motivators for future effort and achievement. Dr. William Glasser (1969) noted:

> As a psychiatrist, I have worked many years with people who are failing. I have struggled with them as they try to find a way to a more successful life. From these struggles I have discovered an important fact: regardless of his background, his culture, his color, or his economic level, *he will not succeed in general until he can in some way first experience success in one important part of his life*. Given the first success to build upon, the negative factors . . . mean little. (p. 5)

It is possible to restate Glasser's message as a significant principle of teaching and learning: When an individual experiences success in one important part of life, that person can succeed in life regardless of background, culture, color, or economic level. Glasser's (1998) *Choice Theory in the Classroom* is a practical guide to assist teachers as they reflect on the fundamental goals of education and begin to establish an environment where students can learn to make positive, productive choices that lead to success.

It is especially important for children who may have been raised in culturally different settings to experience success in their new school environments. Caring, reflective teachers are quick to perceive that children who are new to the school or the community need to experience success quickly to be able to adjust well to their new surroundings. Assign new students a task that you are sure is well within their capability and then show your acceptance and satisfaction with the work they accomplish.

The same is true for students who may appear indifferent or even resentful of school and teachers. Try to understand that they may have a history of being unfairly treated by other, less caring teachers. Students who have faced failure again and again often develop very negative attitudes toward schoolwork and frequently mask their need for approval with defensive and disruptive behaviors in an effort to hide their hurt and shame. Glasser (2000) points out that students' history of ongoing educational failure leads them to give up on the idea that it's even possible for them to succeed in school. This puts a great burden on the educational system, and teachers in particular, to provide them with a variety of opportunities for success, providing them with the opportunity to see themselves and their relationship with schools in a more positive light. You can be a teacher who helps them change their behavior by perceiving their need for success and structuring some tasks to fit their unique talents and abilities so that they can experience the true and lasting joy of succeeding and being productive.

Classrooms as Communities

How does a class of strangers or competitive individuals develop into a community? As with all other important classroom effects discussed in this chapter, the teacher has the power to create a positive, healthy, mutually supportive, and productive classroom environment from the first day of school. Through furniture arrangement, schedules, body language, words of welcome, rules, consequences, and interaction with the class, the teacher demonstrates a unique leadership or teaching style to the students. A sense of community is also achieved through honest, open communication of needs and feelings among students and their teachers.

It takes more than talk to create a classroom community, though. Students need to be taught to work together in obtaining mutually agreed upon goals. These goals can be related to content standards such as supporting one another in learning multiplication tables, working together to complete a community-based project, or writing a collaborative reader's theater script to present at back-to-school night.

Communities of learners grow throughout the school year. They grow from roots established at the very beginning by a classroom teacher who accepts children's suggestions and builds on these ideas, integrating content into related studies based on students' unique interests. Communities recognize that diversity among its members is a positive factor. Cultural diversity tends to enrich the classroom communities when reflective teachers choose to celebrate differences among students rather than seek to make all students adapt to one standard.

In Jody Salazar's middle school classroom in Madera, California, the feeling of community is evident, although her students change classes every 50 minutes. The students enter the classroom and begin writing in their journals immediately. Three students a day sign up to share their journal entries each day. Jody is aware of the importance of building student confidence. None of her students are native English speakers, but they recognize Jody's support as she leans forward and encourages their verbal participation by saying "Go on, I'm getting it" as they communicate in English. Jody often forms cooperative groups in her classroom and encourages English interaction in discussing the reading of text and the writing of responses.

A typical lesson in Jody's classroom might involve a collaborative listing of words that describe feelings while viewing a photograph of a sinking ship with a lifeboat loaded with passengers in the foreground and writing a description of the feelings being experienced by the people in the lifeboat. During the writing activity, the musical theme from *The Titanic* is played softly in the background. The students are then given the opportunity to share their writing within the relative safety of the small group seated at the table together. At the end of the period, Jody recognizes students who have used many of the feeling words from the chart and asks some to read their writing aloud. An amazing number of students volunteer to read. They are obviously confident in their ability to succeed in this activity, even though they are assigned to this class because of their below-grade-level reading abilities.

Glasser (1998) believes that students need to feel safe, happy, and proud of themselves in a classroom if they are going to become convinced that schoolwork is worth their time and effort. To enlist their support, he recommends that you allow your students to know you as a human being, not just as an authority figure. Isn't it true that the better you know someone and the more you like them, the harder you will work for that person? Glasser suggests that you use this same principle when establishing the expectations and procedures for your classroom. He suggests that, during the first few months you are with your students, look for natural occasions to tell them:

1. Who you are.
2. What you stand for.
3. What you will ask them to do.
4. What you will do for them.
5. What you will not do for them.

Jane Speidel, language arts teacher at Astronaut High School in Titusville, Florida, starts her year off by sharing a small bit of information about herself. Because Jane is an avid reader and writer, she talks about the types of books she likes to read and shares a brief piece she has written. She also brings some pictures of her family and talks briefly about them. Jane reserves a bulletin board in her classroom for photos and other memorabilia her students bring to class. She refers to this as their "Wall of Fame." If the student wants to talk about the pictures or pieces of writing, Jane gives them time to do so. By the end of the year, Jane usually has a complete wall of student photos and writing. She has found that the memorabilia help her students build a sense of community. It also provides support for her writing program because she knows more about her students and can suggest writing topics, and the students themselves find ideas in the pictures and writings of the other students.

Jane also sponsors the school newspaper, and her students often write articles for the newspaper about the accomplishments of their colleagues. Sometimes the articles are about out-of-school activities that students might never know about except for Mrs. Speidel's Wall of Fame.

Reforming Schools to Provide Multicultural Equity

Did the schools that you attended favor one group of students over others? Do you see remnants of racial, ethnic, or gender discrimination in the schools you are observing today? Banks and Banks (2002) seek to create a truly color-, gender-, and race-blind environment where students who are members of diverse racial, ethnic, language, and cultural groups will have an equal chance to achieve academically in school. They believe that we must be vigilant in our examination of every aspect of school life in order to root out the effects of discrimination. Every variable in a school, such as its culture, its power relationships, the curriculum and materials, and the attitudes and beliefs of the staff must promote educational equality for students from diverse groups.

But even teachers who carefully structure their classroom lessons to ensure success are frequently baffled by the tendency of some students to fail to succeed even under optimal conditions. Rimm (2008) observes that there is no single cause for underachievement, nor is there a single cure. Also, no consistent characteristics are associated with underachievement. Some underachievers are bossy and aggressive; others are lonely and withdrawn. Some are slow and perfectionists; others are hurried and disorganized. A few have adopted a behavior pattern of learned helplessness because of previous experiences in school, overly high expectations at home, or even because of their position in the family as the youngest child. These students perceive that they are certain to fail at whatever they try, so they have learned not to try. They may also have learned to manipulate others to do things for them by acting helpless.

Students from culturally diverse backgrounds or those raised in poverty may underachieve because of low self-esteem or a lack of experiences such as family trips or exposure to English reading materials in the home. Marc Elrich, a sixth-grade teacher in Washington, D.C., was frustrated to find that, even though he and his colleagues had created a curriculum celebrating diversity and talking about it as a source of strength, he was unable to change his students' own preconceptions about their self-worth. One year, 27 members of his class of 29 students were either African American or Hispanic and had been raised in academically disadvantaged neighborhoods. Marc observed that even at age 10 or 11, most students showed very low self-esteem and had low expectations for their future. He enriched his curriculum with many examples of African American and Hispanic literature and other contributions to art and music. Still, the stereotype within the students did not seem to change.

In a discussion with his students exploring the issues of race, Marc heard his African American students attribute negative racial stereotypes to themselves. "Blacks are poor and stay poor because they're dumber than whites (and Asians). Black people don't like to work hard. White people are smart and have money. Hispanics are poor and don't try hard because, like blacks, they know it doesn't matter, they said."

Teachers like Marc are not willing to accept the status quo. They keep trying to create a therapeutic classroom environment that will encourage their culturally diverse students to raise their own hopes and expectations to appropriate levels. He reflected on how to teach them to like themselves. He considered the frequently used strategy of setting aside a month for studying black history but decided that this was not an adequate remedy. He pondered, "These students aren't naïve. What are the other eleven months? White history months?"

Marc is still trying to solve this problem, as is our society. You as teachers will have an opportunity to confront this difficult issue as well; and create new educational opportunities to improve your students' view of themselves and encourage the people of our nation to grow together rather than apart. The good news on this topic is the recent increase in the resources available to teachers in the form of multicultural literature that they can read and discuss in the classroom. Many of the new publications focus on the things all cultures share in common, and they celebrate the differences as variety and uniqueness. Teachers can begin discussions in the classroom by reading one of these books and not only supporting students in their acceptance of the variety in our American culture but also in understanding the many similarities among the wealth of cultures in the nation. Books like the series by Ann Morris include titles such as *Bread, Bread, Bread* (1989a), *Hats, Hats, Hats* (1989b), and *Shoes, Shoes, Shoes* (1995). Other titles that focus on similarities among cultures are *Everybody Cooks Rice* (Dooley, 1991) and *Everybody Bakes Bread* (Dooley, 1996). Even though these are primary picture books, teachers in upper elementary grades and even middle and high school have found them to be successful discussion starters. Some teachers have even encouraged students to find other elements of society shared by all cultures and write their own books with titles such as *Money, Money, Money* or *Work, Work, Work*.

Herrell and Jordan (2007), in their studies of effective teachers of English language learners, found common attributes and behaviors in their classrooms. The most effective teachers display the following characteristics:

- They truly believe in the ability of all their students to be academically successful.
- They convey this belief to the students on a regular and ongoing basis.
- They find time to celebrate student achievements and successes in the classroom.

These same effective teachers employed active learning strategies in their classrooms on a regular basis. They also provided daily opportunities for oral and written English practice. Herrell and Jordan's (2007) book, *Fifty Strategies for Teaching English Language Learners*, Third Edition, is a valuable resource for teachers at any grade level who have multilingual students in their class. The strategies include step-by-step instructions and real-life examples from classrooms. These 50 strategies can be a valuable resource for reflective teachers who want to widen their perspective and create new action plans to meet the needs of their diverse student body. Refer to Herrell and Jordan's book for a complete discussion.

USING ASSESSMENT DEVICES TO IDENTIFY STUDENT NEEDS

In many ways, the teacher's role in diagnosing students' needs is quite similar to the role of the medical doctor in diagnosing disease. Doctors get information from observing and talking with patients about their medical histories. Similarly, teachers observe and talk with their students to assess their learning histories. But some important information needed for an accurate diagnosis cannot be observed or discussed. Just as doctors may find that laboratory tests provide them with valuable information about the patient, teachers may find that achievement tests and other assessment procedures can provide them with valuable data about their students.

Many school districts use nationally normed standardized tests to assess the academic achievement their students make from year to year. The typical standardized test consists of reading, spelling, English, mathematics, science, and social studies exams given over a period of several days. The teacher does not write the questions or establish the criteria to fit a particular classroom. Instead, the tests are created by nationally recognized testing companies, and the items are written to approximate what is taught across the nation in each subject area at each grade level.

Statistical calculations of test scores provide information about a student's performance. The score may be translated into a percentile or a grade-equivalent score. These interpretations are done by comparing the student's raw score with the raw scores of the sample population. A *percentile rank* tells you what percentage of the people tested scored below a given score. For example, if Joe receives a percentile rank of 78, this means that 78% of the students at Joe's grade level scored lower than he did.

Grade-equivalent scores were created by test publishers especially for use in schools. The results are reported as a function of grade level. For example, if Sally receives a grade-equivalent score of 4.2, this means that her performance is similar to students who are in the second month of fourth grade. If Sally is in the fourth grade, her score tells the teacher that Sally is doing about as well as she is supposed to be doing. If Sally is in the second grade, the score tells the teacher that Sally is capable of functioning like students who are 2 years above her present grade level. If Sally is in sixth grade, however, her score alerts the teacher that Sally is functioning like students who are 2 years below her present grade level. When used well to inform teachers about students' academic needs, standardized tests provide numerical scores that can be used to document the growth of students in their abilities to read; work math problems; and answer questions about academic subjects such as science, social studies, English grammar, and spelling.

Because standardized tests are written by English speakers and assume that students are fluent in the English language, the potential exists for misinformation to occur when the tests are given to students who are learning English as a second language. Standardized tests also require that standardized procedures be used for administering the exams. All students must hear the same instructions, work under the same time limitations, and have access to the same tools and materials during the test (Tanner, 2001).

English language learners often have difficulty in demonstrating their true abilities on standardized tests because of the inability of the teacher to vary the instructions that are part of the standardization of the test. For a student with a limited English vocabulary, the instructions may not be clear, and the students may not be able to understand what is expected of them. They may be able to perform the tasks if they could understand the directions but are unable to demonstrate their true abilities when the instructions are a mystery to them.

Teachers must create a variety of ways for English learners to demonstrate their understanding. It is important that teachers provide ways to document the learning of English learners so that appropriate lessons can be planned for continued growth. It is also vital that English language learners be able to show what they are learning and for them to be included in the classroom interaction. Because much assessment can be extremely language based, assessment strategies must be adjusted to find out how well the students understand the concept being taught. Less-formal assessment also provides an opportunity for teachers to learn more about the English language learners' understanding of English vocabulary and use of sentence structure.

Assessment strategies appropriate for English language learners include the use of observation and anecdotal records (Rhodes & Nathenson-Mejia, 1993) by the classroom teacher and paraprofessionals, watching these students' reactions and responses, and documenting their growth. In addition, performance sampling, where students are asked to perform certain tasks, and teachers observe and document their responses, is effective in monitoring and documenting student growth. The third assessment strategy, portfolio assessment, is a way of maintaining records of observations, performance sampling, and ongoing growth. These three assessment strategies, when combined, provide a rich store of information about English language learners and give a more complete picture of their individual growth and learning development (Herrell & Jordan, 2007).

The use of standardized tests varies widely from district to district. In some schools, they are used to diagnose learning difficulties of individuals so that corrective measures can be taken. In some school systems, the test results are published in local newspapers to compare how well students from different schools are doing in the basic skills. This practice is a controversial issue among educators. The tests were not designed to be used as a measure of excellence among schools, but the public and the press have come to believe that they can be used that way.

Interpreting Data from Students' Cumulative Files

Standardized test scores are recorded in a permanent record for each student. This record of information, called the *cumulative file* (often referred to as a *cume file*), is kept on each student in a school. Each year, the classroom teacher records in the students' files data such as information about the student's family, standardized test scores, reading levels, samples of written work, grades, and notes on parent–teacher conferences. At the end of a school year, the cume files are stored in the school or district office until the next year when they are redistributed to the students' new teachers.

Obviously, these files contain much useful information for teachers to use in preliminary planning. By studying them, the teacher can make judgments about placement in reading, math, or other study groups before meeting the students. Alert teachers may discover information about a student's home environment, such as a recent divorce or remarriage, that can help in communicating with the student. Some files may reveal little about the students; others may be overflowing with records of conferences and staff interactions signaling that the student has exhibited a special need or difficulty.

Many teachers resist looking at their students' cume files before meeting the class. This approach has both positive and negative aspects. It is extremely important to learn about special needs, special programs, and health concerns of a student. If teachers in your school write written remarks about students and if you've read about problems a child experienced or discipline issues from former teachers, it is difficult to give the student a fresh start.

Susan McCloskey, first-grade teacher in Fresno, California, recently shared the following experience with Adrienne, one of the authors of this book:

> I received a new student, Mario, from another state. It took several weeks for his cume folder to arrive. He was quiet and his English was limited, but I found him to be motivated and respectful. When I received his cume folder, I was shocked by the comments written by his former teacher. She stated that he was unmotivated and rarely completed his work. She also stated that he did not get along with others well and suggested that he be referred for testing as a possible candidate for special education. I was so concerned that I called the former teacher long distance to talk to her more about the types of problems Mario had experienced in her classroom. I found that he was the only non-English speaker in the class and that all the other students had been together through preschool and kindergarten. In my class he was one of thirteen native Spanish speakers and I speak enough Spanish to clarify directions, with the help of my students. Mario had helped me with Spanish pronunciation several times, with a big grin. I think I discovered Mario's need. He needed to be valued and accepted. I'm so glad I didn't see that teacher's comments before I met Mario. I like to think I draw my own conclusions, but that teacher had written some strong remarks that might have colored my thinking. (McCloskey, 2009)

Although data and observations about students made by former teachers may be a valuable resource for planning, many reflective teachers, like Susan McCloskey, are aware of the power of the self-fulfilling prophecy, in which their own expectations may influence the way their students behave or achieve in school. What you expect from a student may actually interfere with your ability to make objective observations. If you expect Janie to fail, you may see only the mistakes or misbehaviors she displays. You may overlook or discount her attempts to show improvement. In this way, your expectations can discourage Janie from trying very hard because you fail to notice when she does her work well, and she may give up her efforts and live "down" to your expectations.

When cume files contain data and descriptions of low academic achievement or misbehavior, nonreflective teachers may assume that the students are "not teachable or unmanageable." On the first day of school, the teacher may place such students at desks set apart from the rest of the class or hand them textbooks from a lower grade. These teacher behaviors tell the students how the teacher expects them to behave and perform in this class. If these expectations are consistent over time, they are likely to affect the students' self-concept and motivation in such a way that they achieve poorly and behave badly. In contrast, consider the possible effects of warm and encouraging teacher behavior on these students. If the teacher builds rapport with the students, includes them in all classroom activities from the first day, and works with them to establish their achievement levels and needs, it is likely that their behavior and achievement will improve during the year.

Reflective teachers who understand the great influence of their expectations on their students prefer to assess the strengths and needs of each student independently in the first few weeks of class. They may read the cume folders at the end of September to see how their assessments fit with those of the students' previous teachers.

A good case can be made for either point of view: using cume folders for preliminary planning or waiting to read them until the students are well known to you. This is an issue that you will need to consider and decide for yourself. Perhaps if you understand the power of teacher expectations, you can find a way to use the information in the files to establish positive expectations and resist the tendency to establish negative ones.

Avoid Labeling Students

Tests and other recorded information about a student can sometimes cause teachers and parents to think about students in oversimplified terms or labels. Whether you gain information about your students through formal assessments or informal interactions, it is important to avoid the temptation to categorize or stereotype particular students. You can probably recall a time in your own life when you were burdened with a label you resented. Perhaps you dealt with a nickname you detested or with an academic designation that failed to capture your real potential. Being able to learn about your students and act in their best interests without labeling requires a great deal of care and reflection. A quick perusal of a cumulative file, a glance at a standardized test score, or a few days of observation in the classroom have often led a teacher to label a student as a *slow learner, behavior disordered*, or *an underachiever*. These labels can stick for life! When communicated to a student and his or her family (whether directly or indirectly), such labels can have disabling effects all by themselves. Many labels imply that a student is deficient in some way and contribute to a self-fulfilling prophecy, where further erosion of self-concept and self-confidence causes even more severe learning difficulties.

Students with excellent school performance can also suffer from labeling. Some teachers refer to their most capable and willing students as *overachievers*. This pseudo-scientific term is attached to students whose tests scores are only moderate but whose grades and work habits are excellent. The implication is that these students are working beyond their capacity, and this is somehow seen as a negative characteristic by some teachers (and some peers).

Students with high test scores on standardized tests, especially IQ or achievement tests, are frequently labeled as *gifted students*. At first glance, this label may appear very positive; certainly many parents seek it for their children. Careful reflection, however, reveals that this label can be as damaging as any other. Rimm (2008) notes that "any label that unrealistically narrows prospects for performance by a student may be damaging" (p. 84). Being labeled a gifted student tends to narrow the expectations for performance for that student to a constant state of excellence. Any performance less than excellent can be interpreted by the student and/or the parent as unacceptable.

The *gifted* label also has other negative implications. Eby & Smutny (1990) ask the following questions: "If 2% to 5% of the students in a given school are labeled as gifted, then what are the other 95% to 98% of the students? Not gifted? What is the hidden consequence for a sibling or a very good friend of a so-called gifted student? Or what about the student who scores a few percentage points below the cutoff score for a particular gifted program? What do we call him, *almost gifted*?"

Broader labels also carry damaging consequences. The term *minority* carries a connotation of being somehow less than other groups with respect to power, status, and treatment. Terms such as *economically disadvantaged*, *culturally deprived*, and *underprivileged* may also create stress and anxiety among those to whom they are applied. These may be especially insidious because they fail to acknowledge the value and unique contributions of various individuals or groups.

As you become aware of the various strengths and needs among your students, you can work to address them without relying on labels. Students who are learning English can be joyfully released to work with a special tutor and be warmly welcomed back to the classroom. Children who encounter difficulty working in large-group settings can spend part of their day in small groups and build interaction skills in larger groups under carefully designed conditions. Children who learn more quickly can be challenged to extend their thinking through engaging inquiry projects. No matter what their unique need, our students can be welcomed to our classrooms as unique and valued individuals—labeled only as *important*, *cared for*, and *wanted*.

Authentic Assessments for a Diverse Student Body

In this textbook, we use the term *authentic assessment* to evaluate procedures that take into account each student's unique and various needs for clarity and support and to demonstrate what they are truly capable of doing. Most authentic assessments are designed by teachers in their own classrooms to match what has just been taught. Authentic assessment tasks are similar or identical to actual tasks that students routinely accomplish in the classroom setting, unlike standardized assessment tasks, which tend to differ from everyday classroom activities.

It is vital for the teacher to have a good understanding of English language learners' levels of English development. This assessment can be done through observation in a classroom setting where students are free to interact verbally. Beginning English learners may signal their understanding of verbal interactions with nodding, pointing, or physically responding, but they may not be comfortable giving oral English responses. Remember, we call these students *preproductive* because they are not yet producing English responses, although they may comprehend a lot of what is being said. *Early production* English speakers will respond verbally but usually with one or two words. They are much more comfortable responding verbally when given a model to follow or a choice to make. *Speech emergence* English learners begin to verbalize in phrases or short sentences but still make a number of pronunciation and grammatical errors in their English production. *Intermediate fluency* English learners produce longer sentences with fewer pronunciation and grammar errors (Herrell & Jordan, 2007).

To fully engage English learners in classroom activities, teachers must recognize the level of verbal production that is comfortable for each student and adjust their own questions to provide opportunities for these students to become full participants (Herrell & Jordan, 2004). Adjusting the types of questions asked to fit the English language development of the student during a lesson is called *leveling* questions. A student at the preproduction stage can be asked to show something. A student at the early production stage can be asked to choose between two alternatives. Speech emergence and intermediate fluency students can be expected to respond in phrases or short sentences, but this is a good stage at which to model the use of the question as a "stem" to the response. For example, if you ask the question "What is the capital of Florida?" the student can use the question to create a complete response: "The capital of Florida is Tallahassee."

It is often helpful to keep anecdotal records of the verbal responses of the English learners in your classroom for the purpose of noting their English language development; any pronunciation, grammar, or sentence structure errors they are making; and their willingness to participate in verbal interactions in English. Examining these types of records is helpful in planning mini-lessons for groups of students at the same level or groups of students making similar types of errors.

In Chapter 10, we provide a much more expanded discussion of assessment issues and examples of authentic assessment tasks and procedures. We raise the issue in this chapter because assessment procedures have become such a controversial issue in relation to student diversity.

Using Pretests to Diagnose Student Needs

Pretests are assessment devices designed to gather useful information to plan what students need to learn and what teachers need to teach. At the beginning of a term or a unit of study, teachers use pretests to determine what skills and knowledge pertaining to the subject their students have already mastered. Pretests can take the form of brief short-answer quizzes, or teachers may ask students to write a paragraph or two telling what they already know about a topic to be studied. They may also describe any prior study they have done on the topic, in another year or another class, on family trips or through other experiences they have had that relate to the study about to be explored.

The best use of pretests occurs when the teacher and the student discuss the results together and share their insights about what the student needs to do next. For example, a pretest may reveal a pattern of correctable mistakes in a mathematics operation. The teacher may be able to reteach the process quickly, and the student will be able to proceed successfully. In another instance, a pretest may reveal that the student has mastered the material already, and the conference may then focus on an enriched or accelerated learning opportunity for that student while the others are learning the material.

Placement and Grouping Decisions

Standardized tests are frequently used to qualify students for special programs such as special education, classes for the gifted, or bilingual education. In most cases, these types of placements are no longer made solely on the basis of test results but also include opportunities for the parents and teachers involved in the student's education to provide information and share in the decision.

For many years, teachers used pretests and standardized test scores to determine students' placement in reading groups for instructional purposes. In recent years, teachers are using more authentic types of reading assessments, such as Clay's (2002) observation survey and reading observations called *running records*, to document students' reading abilities, use of strategies, and cueing systems. In kindergarten and first-grade classes, students are grouped in flexible reading groups for guided reading instruction. They read short paperback books for this instruction so that the groups can remain flexible. The short books can be read in one reading group period, and then students can be regrouped when they show the need. This practice helps to eliminate the old, traditional "speedboats," "sailboats," and "rowboats" reading groups. These groups served to convince students that they were poor readers because they were always placed in the low (rowboats) reading group and, once there, they stayed in that group for their entire elementary school careers. Teachers today are finding that grouping can help students to learn if the grouping is done with careful reflection. Heterogeneous groups, where each student has a special function, are being used frequently in classrooms because students get more opportunities to interact, work together to solve problems, and discuss the task to be done.

Teachers may also use data from pretests, observations, and running records to create cooperative groups and partners for peer tutoring. To strengthen student motivation and interaction, many teachers employ the cooperative team concept. Cooperative groups typically consist of three to five students who are assigned a set of tasks to complete by cooperating with and assisting one another. Each student in the group has an assigned function, and the group must work together to complete the assignment. Cooperative groups are extremely effective when they are given instruction on working together to achieve their goals. In some classrooms, teachers use pretest data to decide which students to assign to each team. Often teachers use cooperative groups to promote peer coaching and interactive assistance among their students. In this case, a team of four students may consist of one student with very strong performance, two with moderate performance, and one with relatively weak performance in the subject area. Similarly, peer tutoring dyads may consist of one skilled and one less-skilled student, or one student with little English vocabulary and another student who speaks the same home language but can speak English at a higher level. These are simply examples; other types of cooperative group placement decisions, for different purposes, are also possible.

Performance Sampling

Performance sampling is a form of authentic assessment where a student is observed in the process of accomplishing academic tasks and is evaluated on the way in which the tasks are done. Performance samples are well named because the teacher observes a sample of the student's performance in given academic tasks. Following are examples of the types of tasks used in performance sampling:

- Working math problems.
- Responding to a writing prompt by creating a prewriting activity, writing a draft paper, and then revising the paper.
- Researching a topic in science or social studies and creating a poster or overhead transparency to demonstrate the main concepts that were researched.

Performance sampling is particularly appropriate for assessing English language learners because the degree of achievement they can demonstrate is based on their ability to perform the task rather than their fluency in English (Hernandez, 1997).

Portfolio assessment is a term that refers to a system for gathering observations, performance samples, and work samples in a folder or portfolio; analyzing the contents of the portfolio on a regular basis; and summarizing the students' progress as documented by the contents of the portfolio (Herrell & Jordan, 2007). Often, students are involved in making selections of work to be kept in the portfolio. Students are also involved in reviewing and summarizing the work, setting goals for future work, and sharing the contents of the portfolio with parents (Farr & Tone, 1994).

This approach to assessment is particularly appropriate for English language learners and special education students because it allows assessment based on actual sampling of the students' work and the growth they are making; it depends less on scores from standardized tests, which are often difficult for these students to understand (Hernandez, 1997). Portfolio assessment allows students to demonstrate their content knowledge without being so dependent on English fluency or reading ability. The focus in this approach to assessment is celebration of progress rather than focus on weaknesses.

myeducationlab
The Power of Classroom Practice

To see an example of a how one teacher involves students in selecting work for their portfolios, go to the Video Examples section of Topic #6: Assessment in the MyEducationLab for your course and view the video entitled Documenting Learning.

Communicating with Parents

Communicating with parents sometimes becomes challenging when the parents don't speak or read English fluently. It is important to make sure that all your parents are receiving information in a form that they can use. Most schools have someone on staff who can translate notes and newsletters so that parents can be aware of the needs of their children or the important events taking place at the school. Using these services requires some advance planning, however. Translation takes time. If there is no one available to provide this important service, you can find several reliable translation sites online. Before you use these online services for translation, though, it is very helpful to have a native speaker read through the translation to make sure you are saying what you want to say. Go to http://www.world.altavista.com/ to try the translation service.

The American Federation of Teachers has produced a valuable packet of information for Spanish-speaking parents that you can order for a nominal fee. This packet includes an informational video in both English and Spanish and a number of parent letters in both languages. For information about ordering this information, go to http://www.colorincolorado.org/.

Playing Catch Up

Learning English doesn't happen overnight. Students take 1 to 2 years to acquire social English and may take as long as 7 to 10 years to be fully proficient in academic English (Krashen 1983). Because of this, English learners often need additional support in order to be successful in the classroom. By using a teaching procedure where you go through four steps—teacher explanation, teacher modeling, guided practice, and independent practice—you are providing several important supports for your students who need additional instruction. First, by demonstrating what the students are supposed to do instead of just explaining it verbally, you are reducing the dependence on language alone. Second, when the majority of the class is ready to practice independently, you have time to pull a small group together and provide more guided practice. You will find this valuable for your English learners but also for other students who need a little more direct instruction. If you follow your lessons with learning centers where students can continue to practice their new-found skills or extend them with challenging activities, you will provide more opportunities to differentiate instruction, added practice on basics for those who need it, and ways to expand knowledge for those who are ready for a challenge.

One model that is being used in many schools with great success is entitled the Continuous Improvement Model (CIM). In their book *Closing the Achievement Gap: No Excuses*, Davenport and Anderson (2002) describe a process of using testing to identify students who need additional instruction and forming tutorial groups to ensure that every child experiences success. This model also includes the use of enrichment activities to meet the needs of students ready to engage in more challenging activities. This model will be explored in more depth in future chapters.

Another technique that provides scaffolding for students who need it is called preview/review (Lesson-Hurley, 1990). Preview/review was originally designed for bilingual classrooms where the lesson was previewed in the students' first language, taught in English, and then reviewed in the first language. In an adaptation of this technique for an English-only classroom, teachers can preview the material to be taught using realia, visuals, gestures, and vocabulary instruction as part of the preview; refer to these support materials during the lesson; and then review vital concepts and vocabulary using the support materials again. See Figure 5.3 for suggestions of support materials that can be used for this activity.

Realia	Visuals	Activities
Foods	Transparencies made from photos	Role playing
Household objects	Magazine pictures	Illustrating
Animals	Line drawings	Sorting and labeling
Costumes of the period	Art prints	Lesson word walls
Music of the period	Maps	Reader's theatre
		Creating display boards
		Creating board games

Figure 5.3 Support materials for preview/review lessons.

Source: Herrell & Jordan (2007) Used with permission.

GUIDED GROUP EXPLORATION

This exercise provides practice in recognizing the different levels of English language development.

1. Divide the class into small groups. Ask one student in each group to serve as the recorder and another student to serve as the reader.
2. Ask each group reader to read each of the scenarios provided in Figure 5.4.
3. Using Figure 5.1 as a resource, ask each group to identify the English language development level for each student described in the scenarios. They should also explain how they determined the language development level for each student. The recorder will be taking notes so that the groups can report back to the class.
4. Bring the groups back together to share, compare notes, and discuss their findings.

---

1. Juan is 8 years old, and his family speaks Spanish at home. He seems to be fluent in English on the playground. He has an accent and makes grammatical errors but has no problem making himself understood. In the classroom, however, he has great difficulty reading the textbooks. He can read the third-grade reading text with some mispronunciations. He is not able to answer questions about what he has read and also has difficulty understanding the meanings of the words he reads.

2. Maria is a quiet 5-year old with big brown eyes. She doesn't speak at all but watches everything that is going on around her. She seems to understand what is being said to her because she lines up with the other students, comes to circle time when the signal is given, and follows oral directions. On the playground, she plays with the other girls, but they always converse in Spanish.

3. Chan is the most popular fellow on the playground. He is a great soccer player and shouts instructions to his teammates in English. In the classroom, he is fairly successful and can complete most assignments, although he sometimes needs extra guidance in following directions. He often asks "What's that word mean, teacher?" when class discussion involve science or social studies concepts. His pronunciation is fairly accurate, but he often omits articles in both reading, speaking, and writing.

4. Ivan is one of the most verbal students in the classroom. His oral delivery is rapid, although he often mispronounces words. He leaves off plurals and other endings, but it doesn't seem to slow him down. He has a wealth of background knowledge in his native language, Russian. He's eager to share this information and wants the teacher to help him perfect his English.

5. Ming is just beginning to put together English sentences. She listens attentively and tries to imitate English pronunciation. She gets confused when you give her more than one direction at a time, but she always tries to do what she is asked. She has developed a habit of watching the other students before she responds to directions because she doesn't want to do the wrong thing. She is most comfortable in activities where she can reply with a formula sentence like "I would like red one, please."

Figure 5.4 Scenarios for the guided practice activity.

REFLECTIVE ACTION ACTIVITY FOR YOUR PROFESSIONAL PORTFOLIO

Show Evidence of Your Ability to Use Analysis in a Student Needs Assessment Plan

Providing appropriate instruction requires that you have a plan for truly getting to know your students. To practice ways of gaining knowledge about your students, we suggest that you interview a student to determine the student's academic needs at this point in time. Select a student whose culture is different from yours. Talk with the student about what is important and valued in his or her family. Ask questions to learn about how this student prefers to learn. Sample questions are provided here, but you may want to make up your own as well.

Do you learn easily by reading about something?

Do you learn well by listening to a teacher explain something?

Do you need the teacher to write examples on the board?

Do you learn best by having somebody show you something or by working alone?

Do you need a quiet room, or can you work when others are talking or when the television is on?

Does it bother you when there is movement around you?

After your interview, write an initial description of what conditions this student needs in order to learn and feel safe and comfortable in your classroom. Ask yourself what else you need to know in order to make a thorough assessment of this student's needs.

What can you find on the Internet that relates to needs assessment? Talk to an experienced teacher, or try a chat with other teachers on the Merrill Methods Cluster page or on Schoolnotes.com.

If possible, try to meet the student's family and learn what the parents' hopes and expectations are for their child.

Now write an analysis of this student's academic and social/emotional needs in the classroom. What do you think motivates this student to learn? Why does the student have certain strengths and weaknesses? Give evidence to support your analysis and conclusions. Then write a brief action plan describing the classroom conditions that you believe to be important for this student to learn effectively. Include in your plan ideas for encouraging this student to feel safe and comfortable in your classroom.

References

Banks, J., & Banks, C. (Eds.). (2006). *Multicultural education: Issues and perspectives* (6th ed.). San Francisco: Jossey-Bass.

Bruner, J. (1997). *The culture of education*. Cambridge, MA: Harvard Press.

Clay, M. (2002). *An observation survey: Of early literacy abilities* (2nd ed.). Portsmouth, NH: Heinemann.

Cummins, J. (1986). Empowering minority students: A framework for interaction. *Harvard Review*, 56, 18–36.

Davenport, P. & Anderson, G. (2002). *Closing the achievement gap: N o excuses*. Houston, Texas: American Productivity & Quality Center.

Dixon-Kraus, L. (1996). *Vygotsky in the classroom: Mediated literacy instruction and assessment*. White Plains, NY: Longman.

Dooley, N. (1991). *Everybody Cooks Rice*. Minneapolis: Carolrhoda Books.

Dooley, N. (1996). *Everybody Bakes Bread*. Minneapolis: Carolrhoda Books.

Eby, J., & Smutny, J. (1990). *A thoughtful overview of gifted education*. White Plains, NY: Longman.

Farr, R., & Tone, B. (1998). *Portfolio and performance assessments*. New York: Wadsworth Publishing.

Glasser, W. (1969). *Schools without failure*. New York: Harper & Row.

Glasser, W. (1998). *Choice theory in the classroom*. New York: Perennial.

Glasser, W. (2000). *Every Student Can Succeed*. Mosheim, TN: Black Forest Press.

Hernandez, H. (1997). *Teaching in multilingual classrooms*. Upper Saddle River, NJ: Merrill/Prentice Hall.

Herrell, A., & Jordan, M. (2007). *Fifty strategies for teaching English language learners* (3rd ed.). Upper Saddle River, NJ: Merrill/Prentice Hall/Pearson.

Johnson, D., & Johnson, R. (1993). *Circles of learning: Cooperation in the classroom*. Alexandria, VA: Association for Supervision and Curriculum Development.

Krashen, S. (1996). *The natural approach: Language acquisition in the classroom*. Upper Saddle River, NJ: Prentice Hall.

Lesson-Hurley, J. (2004). *The foundations of dual language instruction* (2nd ed.). White Plains, NY: Longman/Pearson.

McCloskey, S. (2009). Personal communication. March 25, 2009.

Morris, A. (1989a). *Bread, Bread, Bread*. NY: Lothrop, Lee, & Shepard Books.

Morris, A. (1989b). *Hats, Hats, Hats*. NY: Lothrop, Lee, & Shepard Books.

Morris, A. (1995). *Shoes, Shoes, Shoes*. NY: Lothrop, Lee, & Shepard Books.

Raths, L. (1998). *Meeting the needs of children*. Educator's International Press, Inc.

Rhodes, L., & Nathenson-Mejia, S. (1993). Anecdotal records: A powerful tool for ongoing literacy assessment. *The Reading Teacher, 15*, 503–509.

Rimm, S. (2008). *Why bright children get poor grades* (3rd ed.). Scottsdale, AZ: Great Potential Press.

Slavin, R. (1995). *Cooperative learning* (2nd ed.). Boston: Allyn & Bacon.

Tanner, D. E. (2001). *Assessing academic achievement*. Boston: Allyn & Bacon.

myeducationlab The Power of Classroom Practice

Now go to Topics # 6 and 12: Assessment and Diversity: Cultural and Linguistic in the MyEducationLab (www.myeducationlab. com) for your course, where you can:

- Find learning outcomes for these topics along with the national standards that connect to these outcomes.
- Complete Assignments and Activities that can help you more deeply understand the chapter content.
- Apply and practice your understanding of the core teaching skills identified in the chapter with the Building Teaching Skills and Dispositions learning units.
- Examine challenging situations and cases presented in the IRIS Center Resources.

CHAPTER
6

Establishing a Basis for Active, Authentic Learning

■■■■■■■■■■■■■■■■■■■■■■■■■■■■■■■■■■■

The mission of teachers is to be knowledgeable about the subjects they teach and about how to teach those subjects to students. They need to demonstrate that they have attained specialized knowledge about how to convey a subject to students. The knowledge of subject matter, while essential, is not enough to become a master teacher. Certified teachers must also be able to demonstrate knowledge and skills needed to present the subject matter to students effectively. Teachers need to employ a variety of teaching methods, including analogies, metaphors, experiments, demonstrations, and illustrations. In this chapter, we describe these methods and many more that you can learn how to use in your classroom.

Teachers are also responsible for managing and monitoring student learning. They should place a premium on student engagement. Our model of *reflective action in teaching* also makes active student engagement a priority. Facilitating student learning is not simply a matter of placing young people in educative environments; teachers must also motivate them, capturing their minds and hearts and engaging them actively in learning.

Teachers need to use multiple methods to meet their goals. Accomplished teachers should know how to employ a variety of instructional skills: how to conduct Socratic dialogues, how to lecture, and how to oversee small cooperative learning groups. The sections of this chapter will provide you with the basic ideas of these and many other teaching strategies. As a reflective teacher, you know that the information in this textbook is just a starting place. You will need to do more research on each strategy to become proficient in it.

The term *authentic learning* is used to distinguish between the achievement of significant, meaningful, and useful knowledge and skills from that which is trivial and unrelated to students' lives. The Wisconsin Center on Organizing and Restructuring of Schools has concentrated on defining standards of authentic instruction. Its studies have led to the

PRAXIS
Chapters 6, 7, and 8 prepare you for PRAXIS™ Exam Section 2a: Instructional Strategies.

conclusion that many conventional instructional methods do not allow students to use their minds well and result in learning that has little or no intrinsic meaning or value to them beyond achieving success in school.

These studies recommend establishing standards for teachers to use as guidelines in selecting and learning to use teaching strategies that promote authentic learning. According to their research, the standards for authentic instructional methods should emphasize higher-order thinking, depth of knowledge, connectedness to the world, and substantive conversation and should provide social support for student achievement (Newman & Wehlage, 1993).

As a learner, you may have had teachers who used teaching strategies that stimulated you to use your higher-level thinking and problem-solving skills. You may recall learning experiences that encouraged you to delve deeply into a subject that had real meaning to your life. You may recall class discussions that sparkled with enthusiastic exchanges of ideas and opinions within a social system that encouraged you to challenge yourself to make more and more meaningful accomplishments. If you recall school experiences such as these, you have experienced authentic learning.

You may have had other teachers who relied on conventional methods that required rote memorization of facts and dates or other content. You may recall learning a lot about a little or participating in boring recitations in which students were expected to parrot what they had memorized. You may recall competitive social systems that rewarded those students who were able to memorize and recite quickly and those who were able to figure out what the teacher wanted to hear. If you recall school experiences such as these, you will need to overcome the natural tendency to repeat learned patterns and challenge yourself to learn to use many new and exciting instructional strategies.

Your personal conception of the teaching/learning process is drawn from your own experiences as a learner, but for reflective teachers, it is also drawn from the values and beliefs they hold about what students need to know and how students ought to behave and from perceptions and reflections about the theories and practices of other classroom teachers they observe. To become a reflective teacher, you must make yourself aware of the emerging research and knowledge base about teaching and learning. Gathering information from research is an important attribute of a reflective thinker and teacher.

PRAXIS Your knowledge of important educational theorists is tested in PRAXIS™ Exam Section 1a: Students as Learners.

RETRIEVAL PROCESS
Schema Theory

The retrieval process is obviously a critical factor in being able to use stored information. Knowledge, concepts, and skills that are learned must be stored in the brain until they are needed. According to Piaget's *schema theory* (1970), each subset of knowledge is stored in a *schema*, an outline or organized network of knowledge about a single concept or subject. It is believed that young children develop *schemata* (the plural form of *schema*) made up of visual or other sensory images and, as language increases, verbal imagery replaces the sensory images.

For example, an infant stores sensual images in the schemata for *mother*, *bottle*, *bed*, and *bath*. Later the verbal labels are added. A schema grows, expands, or otherwise changes due to new experiences. If the infant sees and touches a large, round, blue ball, he or she can store sensory images of its size, color, rubbery feel, and softness. At a later encounter, the infant may experience it bounce, and he or she can store these images in the same schema. A year later, when the child learns to say the word *ball*, the label is acted on in working memory and stored in long-term memory within the schema for *ball*.

Students come to school with varied schemata. Some students who have had many experiences at home, in parks, at zoos, in museums, and in other circumstances may enter kindergarten with complex schemata for hundreds of topics and experiences. Other students, whose experiences have been severely limited by poverty or other circumstances, are likely to have very different schemata, and some of these may not match the prevailing culture's values or verbal labels. Similarly, if students come from highly verbal homes where parents talk with them frequently, their schemata are likely to contain accurate verbal labels for stored sensory experiences and phenomena. Students who are raised in less-verbal homes, however, will have fewer verbal components to their schemata. This theory complements Piaget's observations of stages of development and helps us to understand how a child's vocabulary develops.

Schemata also vary according to their organizational patterns. As children mature, each schema expands to include many more facts, ideas, and examples. In cases of healthy development, the schemata are frequently clarified and reorganized. Learning new information or observing unfamiliar examples often causes a schema to be renamed or otherwise altered. For example, very young children might have a schema labeled *doggy* that includes all four-legged, furry creatures. As they see new examples of animals and hear the appropriate labels for each type, the original schema of *doggy* is reorganized to become simply a subset of the schema *animal*. New patterns and relationships among schemata are forming every day of a child's life when the environment is full of unfamiliar concepts and experiences.

Schema theory helps to explain why some students are able to retrieve knowledge better than others. Students who have many accurately labeled schemata are more likely to have the background knowledge needed to learn an unfamiliar concept. Students whose schemata are richly detailed and well organized into patterns and hierarchies are much more likely to be able to retrieve useful information on request than are students whose schemata are vague and sparse.

Reflective teachers who believe that it is in their power to help their students improve their cognitive processing recognize that one of the best ways to do this is to stimulate students to actively create more well-developed, accurately labeled, and better-organized schemata. At the elementary grade levels, teachers recognize that one of their most important responsibilities is to aid students in schema development with accurate verbal labels. In the earliest grades (especially kindergarten), teachers emphasize spoken labels, teaching students to recognize and be able to name objects and concepts such as numbers, letters of the alphabet, and colors. In the primary grades, teachers emphasize the recognition and decoding of written labels as an integral part of the reading program. When students exhibit difficulties in learning to read, the reflective teacher is likely to plan learning experiences that assist the students in developing schemata that are prerequisites for reading.

Students who have been raised in environments characterized by few experiences with books are likely to have an underdeveloped schema for reading and books. This may also prove true for English language learners, who may not have access to text material at home or whose parents are reluctant to read books to them, even in the first language. Reflective teachers who consider the needs of the whole individual are likely to provide their students with many opportunities to hear stories read aloud, to choose from a tempting array of books, and to write their own stories as a means of developing a rich and positive schema for the concept of reading.

Advance Organizers

When teachers want to assist students in retrieving information from their schemata, they provide verbal cues that help the students access the appropriate information efficiently. In the case of English language learners, this may require multisensory cues, gestures, and visual cues as well. Teachers can also provide cues to assist students in accurately and efficiently processing and storing what they read, see, or hear. Ausubel (1960) proposed that learners can comprehend new material better when, in advance of the lesson, the teacher

lead with purpose

provides a clear statement about the purpose of the lesson and the type of information that learners should look or listen for. This introductory statement is known as an *advance organizer.* English language learners benefit from a similar teaching strategy called *preview/review*, in which the students are given an advance organizer prior to the lesson and a review following the lesson, both in the native language. This allows them to be prepared for the information they are about to receive and to clear up any questions or misunderstandings following the lesson.

When we relate this theory to the information processing theory, it is apparent that the advance organizer provides the learner with an important cue about which schema will incorporate this new knowledge. The learner can be more efficient in processing the information in working memory and transferring it to the appropriate schema in long-term memory than if no advance information was presented. For example, consider what is likely to happen when a third-grade teacher introduces a lesson on long division with no advance organizer. Some students will simply reject the new knowledge as incomprehensible. Using an advance organizer, the teacher might begin by writing, as an example, on the board a large number such as 100 and then ask students to subtract 10 from that number. Students will compute the subtraction problem 100 - 10 and get 90. Then, they will compute 90 - 10, 80 - 10, and so on, until they reach zero. In this way, students can use the previously learned skill of subtraction to organize their thoughts and make division more comprehensible. When the teacher asks how many 10s are in 100, the students can look at their subtraction problems and count the number of 10s they subtracted from 100. When the teacher then tells the students that division is a short way to solve this problem, it provides students with the cues they need to retrieve their subtraction schema in advance of the new learning.

In Chapter 3, we read about Alex's geology lesson plan on the methods and uses of core sampling to determine what is hidden beneath the surface of the earth. If Alex had just begun lecturing on this topic, many students might have been bewildered by the concept. Instead, Alex used cupcakes—something every child can understand—as an advance organizer for his lesson. Students were motivated by their desire to learn what was hidden beneath the surface of the cupcake. As they performed their experiments, they were able to organize their thoughts about how scientists discover hidden geological phenomena as well.

In follow-up studies of Ausubel's hypothesis, many educational researchers designed experiments that showed the same effects. Therefore, this knowledge has been added to our growing common knowledge base about teaching and learning. In fact, this particular study demonstrates the way in which the knowledge base grows. The original hypothesis and study conducted by Ausubel (1960) led others to apply the principle to different types of students and environments. As the hypothesis was confirmed in subsequent studies, the knowledge was gradually accepted as a reliable principle of effective teaching. You probably experience the beneficial effects of advance organizers when your teachers tell you in advance what to listen for in a lecture or what to study for on an exam. Now you can learn how to use this principle in your teaching career for the benefit of your students.

PRAXIS
Strategies for increasing student motivation to learn are tested in PRAXIS™ Exam Section 1c: Students as Learners.

Differentiated Instructional Strategies

One size does not fit all when it comes to education. This commonsense idea is used as a metaphor for learning by Gregory and Chapman (2002) as they describe methods teachers can use to respond to students' individual differences. It is possible to differentiate your school program in four important ways: content, assessment tools, performance tasks, and instructional strategies.

The first requirement for a differentiated curriculum is the creation of a safe and nurturing classroom environment, much as we described in Chapter 2. For students to be able to express needs and acknowledge differences, there needs to be a climate of warmth, safety, and nurturance. Students need to be encouraged to take risks and to recognize that what is a safe

Safe, warm classroom environment

and easy task for one student may pose a risk for others. The classroom environment must be collaborative and inclusive of all ranges of ability, talents, interests, and special needs without making a big point about it or without calling attention to it. This can frequently be accomplished by the creation of cooperative groups, or tribes, as described in Gibbs (2001). Tribes are communities, and communities tend to be inclusive and collaborative. In addition, there needs to be a sense of heightened interest, challenge, and stimulation in the classroom so that all students feel suitably challenged.

In every class and for almost every assignment, there are likely to be students who have great difficulty achieving the objective of the lesson. They are not likely to succeed unless the teacher modifies the initial lesson plan to provide them with individual or small-group lessons to reteach the skills they lack. For some children to achieve successful growth of skills and understanding, the teacher must be willing to alter the pace of the lessons, the difficulty of the material, and the criteria for success.

For students who learn more slowly, one modification that is needed is to reduce the volume of material in a lesson. If the grade-level lesson calls for the students to complete 20 problems in one class period, the teacher may reduce this requirement to 10 or 15 problems for a student who works slowly. If 20 problems were expected of this child, there would be little chance for success, resulting in frustration for both the teacher and student. When the pace is lowered, the student has an opportunity to succeed and is likely to show an increase in motivation that accompanies success.

A child may have missed or not learned some important basic skills in previous grades for a variety of reasons. Illness, family problems, emotional difficulties, inferior teaching, or frequent moves may have prevented a child from learning the skills that most students his or her age have attained. For students who have not attained the basic skills necessary for a grade-level task, the modification needed is to teach the prerequisite skills before introducing the new material. When these prerequisite skills have been successfully mastered, the student may proceed at the pace of the rest of the class.

Some children in your classroom may have been identified as having *learning disabilities*. This may mean that a child has one or more of a variety of learning disorders, some physical and others social or emotional in origin. When a student has been designated as learning disabled, a teacher who specializes in working with such students will be called on to create an individualized educational plan (IEP) for that student. The classroom teacher will receive some guidance from the IEP on how to modify lessons for that student.

Many of the students in some schools come from backgrounds where the primary language of the home is not English. This has implications for instruction and lesson planning. Although these students may be able to understand the content of the lessons, the teacher may need to vary the delivery of the content in order to make it comprehensible to them. English as a second language (ESL), or sheltered English programs, may be available for students learning this new language. When this is the case, the ESL teacher can assist teachers in assigning appropriate materials, adjusting teaching styles, and helping students acquire language skills that will help them to succeed. For students learning the language, it is necessary to offer contextualized learning experiences—lessons that provide context clues using props, visuals, graphs, and real objects. Teachers may need to speak more slowly and enunciate more clearly while encouraging the ESL student's classmates to do so as well.

Children with hearing impairments need lessons that are modified to provide directions and instruction using visual aids. Similarly, children who have sight impairments may require extra auditory learning aids. Less obviously, some children in your classroom may have strong auditory, visual, or kinesthetic learning style preferences. To meet the needs of these children, teachers must modify their lessons to accommodate all three types of learning styles. This is usually accomplished by providing instructions and examples using visual aids to learn, such as the chalkboard, books, and written handouts. For auditory learners, the teacher may allow them to use recorders to record the instructions and examples given in class. Kinesthetic learners require manipulative materials and hands-on experience to make sense of unfamiliar material. When a teacher provides visual, auditory, and kinesthetic learning aids and experiences, students may modify their own lessons by taking in the needed information in the form that fits their own learning style preferences.

For students who work unusually rapidly and accurately on grade-level material, the task is to provide appropriately challenging learning experiences so that these students are able to continue to make gains even though they have mastered the grade-level requirements. Two standard methods serve the needs of highly able learners: *acceleration* and *enrichment.* Although both strategies are valuable modifications, acceleration is appropriate for sequential subjects such as math, and enrichment is appropriate for other subject areas. An inappropriate modification is to give the child more work at the same level. For example, if 20 math problems are required of the students working at grade level, an inappropriate modification is to require the highly able learner to do 40 problems. This practice is common, but it does not serve the student's real need to be challenged to gain new skills and understanding.

Some acceleration strategies that teachers can choose from include ability grouping, curriculum compacting, and mastery learning. *Ability grouping* requires the teacher to modify the curriculum to correspond to three different groups in the classroom. High, middle, and low groups are created, with variations in material and expectations for success. Reflective teachers must consider the possible negative consequences of lowered self-esteem and the possible positive benefits of academic fit and organizational efficiency when deciding whether or how to use ability grouping in the classroom. In some schools, ability grouping may be organized across several grade levels. Subjects such as math and language arts may be scheduled at the same time of day, allowing students who work above or below grade level to leave their own classrooms and travel to other classrooms where the instruction is geared to their learning level.

Curriculum compacting can occur in a single classroom. This strategy requires the teacher to pretest students in various subject areas. Those children who demonstrate mastery at the time of the pretest are allowed to skip the subsequent lessons altogether. This strategy compacts the grade-level curriculum for them. Teachers then provide materials at a higher level of depth and difficulty for these students, who typically work on their own through the more-challenging material with little assistance from the teacher, who is busy instructing the students at grade level.

Mastery learning is a highly individualized teaching strategy designed to allow students to work at their own pace on material at their own difficulty level. Pretests are used to place students at the appropriate difficulty level. As each new skill is learned, a posttest demonstrates mastery. This technique is described in detail in Chapter 7.

Enrichment strategies vary according to the imagination of the teacher who creates them. The teacher provides students who demonstrate mastery of a basic skill with a challenging application of that skill. Objectives and learning experiences at the higher levels of Bloom's taxonomy are often used as the basis for enrichment activities. A child who easily masters grade-level material is frequently allowed to investigate or research the topic in greater depth. For outcomes of enriched activities, students typically create an original product, perform an original skit, or teach the class something that they have learned from research.

Modification of lessons is a continuing challenge to teachers. It is not easy to decide whether a student needs a modified lesson. Reflective teachers struggle with this decision because they know that when they lower their expectations for a student, one of the effects may be lower self-esteem, creating the conditions for a self-fulfilling prophecy that the student cannot achieve at grade level. But they also know that when adult expectations are too high, students experience little or no success, leading to a similar downward spiral. For beginning teachers, it is wise to consult with other teachers in the school, especially teachers who specialize in working with children who have special needs in some way. Discuss your concerns with these specialists, and make informed decisions about lesson modifications.

PRESENTATION SKILLS THAT INCREASE CLARITY AND MOTIVATION

Teaching is more than telling. You have been on the receiving end of teachers' lectures, discussions, and other forms of lessons for many years. You know from your own experience that the way teachers teach or present material has an effect on student interest and motivation, which are both integral aspects of the classroom climate. You may have been unable to understand the beginning of a lesson taught by a teacher who failed to get the full attention of a class before speaking. You have probably experienced a sinking feeling when a teacher droned on in a monotonous voice during a lecture. You may have experienced frustration when a teacher explained a concept once and hurried on, ignoring questions or comments from the class. Reflective teachers are not likely to be satisfied with a dull, repetitive, or unresponsive presentation style. Most of them are anxious to improve their presentation skills to stimulate interest and motivate student achievement.

Getting Students' Attention

To consider systematically the way in which you present a lesson, think about the beginning. The introduction to a lesson is very important, whether it is the first lesson of the day or a transition from one lesson to another. As Kounin (1977) found in his study of well-functioning classrooms, transitions and lesson beginnings start with a clear, straightforward message or cue signaling that the teacher is ready to begin teaching and stating exactly what students should do to prepare themselves for the lesson. To accomplish this when you teach, you need to tell your students to get ready for a certain lesson and to give you their full attention. Some teachers use a visual cue for this purpose, such as a finger on the lips or a raised arm. Others may strike a chime or turn off the lights to cue the students that it is time to listen.

It is unlikely that students will become quiet instantly. It will probably take a few moments to get the attention of every student in the class. While you are waiting, stand up straight and make direct eye contact with those who are slow to respond. Watch quietly as the students get their desks, pencils, books, and other needed materials ready for the lesson. The waiting may seem uncomfortable at first. You will be tempted to begin before they are ready because you will think that time is being wasted. Do not give in to this feeling. Wait until every voice is quiet, every chair stops scraping, every desktop stops banging, and every pencil stops tapping. Wait for a moment of pure, undisturbed silence. Then quietly begin your lesson. You will have the attention of every student. The more often you are consistent with this behavior, the less time it will take in subsequent attempts.

[handwritten margin note: wait until everyone is quiet]

Some teachers use a bit of drama to begin a lesson. They may pose a question or describe a condition that will interest their students. Richard Klein, a teacher at the Ericson School on Chicago's West Side, begins teaching a unit on aviation by asking students what they know about the Wright brothers. The students' replies are seldom very enthusiastic, so he unexpectedly asks them, "Then what do you know about the Wrong brothers?" They show a bit more interest but are still unable to provide many informed responses. So Mr. Klein turns off the lights and turns on a videotape of the Three Stooges in a skit called "The Wrong Brothers." Afterward, partly in appreciation of Mr. Klein's humor, the students show a greater willingness to learn about the real historical events.

Often teachers begin with a statement of purpose, describing how this particular lesson will help their students to make an important gain in skills or knowledge. Still others begin by doing a demonstration or distributing some interesting manipulative materials. This technique, called providing an *anticipatory set*, is used both to gain attention and to motivate students to be interested in the lesson. Your presentation skills can benefit if you employ a variety of anticipatory sets appropriate to the lesson content and objective.

In contrast, less-reflective teachers begin almost every lesson with "Open your books to page 259. David, read the first paragraph aloud." This example employs no presentation skills. This "nonmethod" relies on the material itself to whet the students' interest in the topic.

Although some materials may be stimulating and appealing, most are not. The message the teacher gives to the students is "I don't care much about anything; let's just get through this." The students' motivation to learn drops to the same level as this message and can best be expressed as "Why bother?"

Teachers often display a greater degree of excitement and interest for material they themselves enjoyed learning, and they pass that excitement about learning on to the students. A teacher who reads aloud with enthusiasm conveys the message that reading is fun. A teacher who plunges into a science investigation with delight causes students to look forward to science.

After you gain your students' attention and inspire them to want to know more, move on to the lesson itself. Presentation skills that you can learn to use systematically in your lessons include the following:

Enthusiasm
Clarity
Smooth transitions
Timing
Variation
Interaction
Active learning
Closure

Enthusiasm

Animation is the outward sign of a teacher's interest in the students and the subject. Enthusiasm is the inner experience. There are at least two major aspects of enthusiasm. The first is conveying sincere interest in the subject. The other aspect is vigor and dynamics, and both are related to getting and maintaining student attention. Outwardly, the teacher displays enthusiasm by using a bright, lively voice; open, expansive gestures; and facial expressions that show interest and pleasure. Salespeople who use animated, enthusiastic behavior could sell beach umbrellas in the Yukon in January. Why shouldn't teachers employ these techniques as well? You can "sell" long division better with an enthusiastic voice. You can convince your students that re-cycling is important with a look of commitment on your own face. You can encourage students' participation in a discussion with welcoming gestures and a warm smile.

Is animation something you can control? Absolutely. You can practice presenting information on a topic with your classmates, using an animated voice and gestures. They can give you feedback, which you can use to improve your presentation. Have someone make a video of your presentation. When you view yourself, you can be your own best teacher. Redo your presentation with new gestures and a different voice. Repeat this procedure several times, if necessary. Gradually, you will notice a change in your presentation style. You will add these techniques to your growing repertoire of effective presentation skills.

Clarity

The clarity of the teacher's presentation of lesson directions and content is a critical factor in student success. Good and Brophy (2002) listed the importance of teacher clarity as a consistent finding in studies of teacher effectiveness. Their review of research on teacher clarity describes negative teacher behaviors that detract from clarity. These include using vague terms, mazes, discontinuity, and saying *uh* repeatedly.

As an example of vague terms, how would you expect students to respond to a lesson introduced in the following way?

See if you can find page 76 and look at this division problem. This example might help you to understand a little more about how this all works. Maybe, if you read this, you can even get some idea of how to do these problems.

The vague terms such as *might, maybe, some,* and *how this all works* in this example have the effect of making the teacher sound tentative and unsure of the content. As an introduction to a lesson, it is not likely to capture students' attention or interest. Clarity can be improved, in this example, by exchanging the vague terms for specific ones, resulting in a simple, straightforward statement.

> Turn to page 76 and look at the long division problem at the top of the page. We are going to work through this example together, until you are confident that you know how to do this type of problem.

Clarity also suffers from what Good and Brophy (2002) call *mazes,* which are false starts or halts in the teacher's speech, redundancy, and tangled words. See the following example.

> Okay now, let's turn to page . . . um, just a minute. Okay, I've got it now. This chapter, er, section in the book lesson *will hopefully, um, it better or we're both in trouble,* get you to understand multiplication, *uh,* facts . . . . I mean the patterns behind, underlying the facts.

Even when students attempt to pay attention, they may be unable to decipher the meaning of the teachers' words if the presentation is characterized by the false starts in this example. It is obvious that the way to improve this statement is to eliminate the redundant words. This example is a very simple one.

Clarity is also reduced when the teacher has begun to present a lesson, is interrupted by a student's misbehavior or a knock at the door, and then begins the lesson again. Kounin (1977) observed that the most effective teachers are able to *overlap* teaching with other classroom management actions. That is, they are able to continue with the primary task, presenting the lesson to the class, while at the same time opening the classroom door or stopping misbehavior with a glance or a touch on the shoulder. When teachers can overlap their presentations, the clarity of their lessons is greatly enhanced.

The third teacher behavior that detracts from clarity is discontinuity, in which the teacher interrupts the flow of the lesson by interjecting irrelevant content (Good & Brophy, 2002). This is why lesson planning is so important. Without a plan, teachers may simply begin a lesson by reading from a textbook. As they or the students are reading, the teachers (or a student) may be reminded of something they find interesting. They may discuss the related topic for quite some time before returning to the original lesson. This side discussion may or may not be interesting or important, but it is likely to detract from the clarity of the original lesson.

The fourth detractor from teacher clarity is repeatedly saying *uh.* It is also likely that other repetitive speech patterns are just as annoying, such as *you know?* or *okay?* For the beginning teacher, it is likely that some of these behaviors will occur simply as a result of nervousness or unfamiliarity with the content being taught. It is most likely that these detracting behaviors decrease as a result of teaching experience. In other words, as a teacher gains experience, detracting behaviors subside and clarity increases. Two other teacher behaviors found to enhance clarity are (1) an emphasis on key aspects of the content to be learned and (2) clear signaling of transitions between parts of lessons.

Smooth Transitions

Just as lesson introductions are important in gaining students' attention, smooth transitions are essential to maintaining that attention level and making the classroom a productive working environment. Transitions occur within a lesson as the teacher guides students from one activity to another. They also occur between lessons as students put away what they were working on in one lesson and get ready for a different subject.

Good and Brophy (2002) note that knowing when to terminate a lesson is an important element of teacher withitness. When the group is having difficulty maintaining attention, it is better to end the lesson early than to doggedly continue. This is especially important for younger students, whose attention span for even the best lesson is limited. When lessons continue after the point when they should have been terminated, more of the teacher's time is spent compelling attention and less of the students' time is spent thinking about the material.

myeducationlab
The Power of Classroom Practice

For an example of how one teacher transitions to a new activity, go to the Video Examples section of Topic #7: Strategies for Teaching in the MyEducationLab for your course and view the video entitled Making Transitions.

Similarly, transitions between activities and lessons may require that students move from place to place within a classroom, such as having one group come to the reading circle while another group returns to their seats. Usually students are required to exchange one set of books and materials for another. These movements and exchanges have high potential for noise in the form of banging desktops, scraping chairs, dropped equipment, and students' voices as they move from lesson to lesson.

Jerky, chaotic transitions result when the teacher gives incomplete directions or vague expectations about student behavior. For instance, "Take out your math books" is incomplete because the teacher does not first specify that the students should put away other materials they have been working with. The result may be that the students begin to work on desks cluttered with unnecessary materials.

Often, inexperienced teachers begin to give directions for a transition, and the students start to get up and move around while the teacher is speaking. When this happens, teachers may attempt to talk louder so that they can be heard over the din. A way to prevent this from occurring is to inform students clearly that they are to wait until all directions have been given before they begin to move.

Smooth transitions are characterized by clear directions from the teacher about what is to be put away and what is to be taken out, who is to move and where they are to go. Clear statements of behavioral expectations are also important. The same techniques for getting attention that were described previously apply to the beginning of each new lesson. After a noisy transition between lessons, it is essential for the teacher to have the students' complete attention before beginning the new lesson. The teacher should wait until all students move into their new positions and get all their materials ready before trying to introduce the lesson.

The teacher can use a signal to indicate that the new lesson is about to begin. As previously mentioned, a raised hand, lights turned off and on, or a simple verbal statement such as "I am ready to begin" signals to the students that they should be ready for the next lesson. After initiating the signal, the teacher should wait until the students have all complied and are silent before beginning the new lesson.

In considering strategies that result in smooth transitions, teachers do well to reflect on the students' needs for physical activity. In a junior high or high school, students generally move between periods. At the elementary school or in a block period of time in the middle school, it is unrealistic to expect students to be able to sit still through one lesson after another. Some teachers take 5 to 10 minutes to lead students in singing or movement games between two working periods. Other teachers allow students to have a few moments of free time in which they may talk to friends, go to the washroom, or get a drink of water. Some transitions are good opportunities for teachers to read aloud from a story book or to challenge students to solve a brain teaser or puzzling mathematics problem. Reflective teachers find that when they allow students a respite and a change of pace during a brief transition period, the work periods are more productive and motivation to learn is enhanced.

Timing

Actors, speakers, and comedians give considerable attention to improving the timing of their presentations. Good use of timing engages the attention of an audience, emphasizes major points, and sometimes creates a laugh. Teachers also work in front of an audience, and class presentations can be improved by considering timing and pacing as a means of getting attention and keeping it. Pausing for a moment of complete silence before you begin teaching is a good example of a way to incorporate timing into your presentation.

In most instances, students respond best to teachers who use a brisk pace of delivering information and instructions. Kounin's (1977) research on the most effective classroom managers demonstrates that students are best able to focus on the subject when the lesson has continuity and momentum. Interruptions result in confusion. When teachers forget to bring a prop, pause to consult a teacher's manual, or backtrack to present material that should have been presented earlier, inattention and disruptive behavior are likely to occur. Jones (1987) found that students' attention improved when teachers gave them efficient help, allocating

20 seconds or less to each request for individual help or reteaching. When this time was lengthened, the result was restlessness and dependency on the part of students.

At times, a pause in instruction can improve your presentation. Researchers have found that it is important to present new information in small steps, with a pause after the initial explanation to check for understanding. Students may not respond immediately during this pause because they need a moment to put their thoughts into words. Wait for them to do so. Encourage questions and comments. Ask for examples or illustrations of the fact or concept being discussed. This pause allows your students to reflect on the new material and allows you to test their understanding.

Variation

Lesson variation is an essential presentation skill for teachers who want to develop a healthy, vital classroom climate. In analyzing classroom videotapes, Kounin (1977) noticed that satiation results in boredom and inattentiveness. If presentations are monotonous, students will find a way to introduce their own variation by daydreaming, sleeping, fiddling with objects, doodling, or poking their neighbors.

Planning for variation is important when you plan a lesson of 30 minutes or longer. Divide your lesson into several segments. Use lecture for only part of the time. For example, include segments of discussion, independent practice, small-group interaction, and application activities. If you cannot break a single lesson into segments, plan to use a variety of strategies during the course of a day. Use quiet, independent work for one subject, group interaction for another, lecture for a third, and hands-on activities for a fourth. In this way, your students will always be expectant and eager for each new lesson of the day. They will feel fresh and highly motivated to learn because of the variations in the way you choose to present material. If teachers attempt to address different learning styles in each lesson, they cannot help but provide variation in the classroom. All lessons should be checked for activities that address the different learning modalities. This topic is discussed in detail later in the chapter.

Interaction

Students thrive on interaction with the teacher and with their classmates. Rather than employing a traditional teacher-to-student, student-to-teacher communication pattern, open up your classroom to a variety of interactive experiences. Pushing the desks into a large circle encourages open-ended discussion from all students. Arranging the desks in small groups encourages highly interactive problem solving. Moving the desks aside leaves a lot of space in the middle of the room for activities. Pairing the desks provides opportunities for peer teaching or partnerships of other kinds. Your presentations can include all these types of activities, and you will find that it is motivating not only to your students but to you as well. You will feel a sense of expectant excitement as you say, "All right, students, let's rearrange the desks."

The need for interaction derives from the powerful motivational need for belonging described by Maslow (1954) and Glasser (2001). When these needs are frustrated or denied, disruptive behavior is likely to occur as a means of satisfying them. When teachers consciously plan interactive learning experiences, they allow students to satisfy their important drive for belonging and thereby prevent unnecessary discipline problems.

Active, Authentic Learning Experiences

Teachers who value authentic learning present material in ways that engage their students in active rather than passive learning by including many verbal, visual, or hands-on activities. Consider a lecture on a topic such as the closed circuit in electricity. Ho-hum. Add a visual aid such as a poster or an overhead projection, and students sit up in their seats to see more clearly. Now add a demonstration. Turn off the lights. Hold up a battery, some copper wire, and a lightbulb. Your students watch expectantly with a new sense of interest.

Turn on the lights again. All these techniques are adequate to teach the students a concept, but none is as valuable as a hands-on experience for in-depth learning and understanding. Picture this scene instead. After lunch the students come into their classroom to find a battery, a flashlight bulb, and a piece of copper wire on each desk. After getting their attention, the teacher simply says, "Working independently, try to get your bulb to light up." Lights go on all over the room, as well as in children's eyes and in their minds as they struggle with this problem. The motivation to succeed is intense and intrinsic, not tied to any exterior reward. Each individual has a sense of power and a need to know.

The key to authentic learning is in allowing your students to encounter and master situations that resemble real life. Simulated experiences are often just as valuable as real life for elementary school students and are much safer and more manageable for the beginning teacher. While your students may never invent a marketable product, you can simulate this type of exploration by inventing products that are needed in your classroom. You can simulate the debate and communication skills necessary to solve international crises by creating a mini–United Nations in your room, in which each student studies one country in depth and engages in substantive conversations about the varied needs and strengths of each country.

Closure

At the end of most learning experiences, the teacher can ensure that students have mastered the objectives of the lesson or have integrated the new concepts into their existing schema by having them share what they did that worked and didn't work or by articulating and generalizing what they have learned about a new concept. For example, after a period of independent investigation about how batteries and lightbulbs work, the teacher may ask students, "What could you do to make your lightbulb give off *more* light?" Such a teacher-led discussion is an essential part of active, hands-on learning. It provides a sense of closure and allows the teacher to encourage students to an even higher plane of knowledge.

Every lesson or presentation can benefit from some thoughtful consideration to its ending. It is important to allow time for closure when you plan your lessons. You may use this time to ask questions that check for understanding so that you will know what to plan for the lesson that follows. You may allow the students to close the lesson with their own conclusions and new insights by asking them an open-ended question such as "What did you discover today?" If insight is to occur, it is likely to occur during this summary experience. At the close of one lesson, you can also indicate what will follow in the next lesson so that your students know what to expect and how elements of the lessons fit together to make a whole concept.

Michael and Adrienne were working recently as consultants at Hoover High School in San Diego, California. Hoover is a highly diverse school in an urban section of San Diego, which has been involved in a project in collaboration with San Diego State University to raise teacher effectiveness and student performance. As part of their work at Hoover, Michael and Adrienne were asked to plan and teach a 10th-grade lesson on *The Odyssey*, a required piece of literature in the 10th-grade English curriculum.

Michael taught the lesson in the classroom employing a sequence of activities that combined a number of the strategies discussed in this chapter. The lesson was planned to include an advance organizer—viewing a video clip of the film version—and a review of book nine of *The Odyssey*, which the students had read and discussed up to the point of the lesson. This video clip also served to introduce new characters that the students would be encountering and to set the stage for book ten.

Michael introduced the lesson with enthusiasm and involved the students in reviewing the events of book nine. He asked them to contribute to a graphic organizer in the form of a web drawn on the whiteboard, allowing them to visualize the connections between the characters and the sequence of events so far.

Because of the number of second-language learners in the class, Michael spent some time introducing new vocabulary, listing the words and short definitions on the whiteboard, and asking students to use the words in sentences related to the book to be read. By way of introduction, Michael also treated them to a fun activity by reciting a rather funky rendition of "The Odyssey Rap" from Hart and Mantell's (1999) book, *Ancient Greece!*—with the students taking on the role of the Greek chorus in appropriate places. The students took great delight in Michael's futile but animated attempt at being "Rapper O."

Michael then introduced the video clip he was about to show, saying that it would show scenes from book nine and then show the characters the students would meet in book ten. The students watched the 6-minute clip with interest, and Michael paused the tape at intervals to discuss the individual characters. One student said, "Bernadette Peters looks just like I thought the goddess would look." Another student added, "The part where the men are turned into pigs was funny. That's a good movie. Can we see the whole thing when we finish reading the book?" Their teacher promised them that this would be done.

A colorful pictographic map handout from Adrian Mitchell's (2000) book *The Odyssey*, showing the routes of Odysseus' journeys, allowed the students to trace the journey up to book ten. As they explored the maps, they were working in small groups writing summaries of the events encountered so far. The discussion that followed the mapping activity served as a closure to the lesson, making sure that all students had gained the needed information and leading the students up to the point of book ten. They ended the lesson with predictions about what might happen next. Michael was excited to hear one student's comment at the end of the period when Michael told the students they were to read the first part of book ten for the next day's activity. Yolanda said, "You can't leave now. We need to know what's going to happen next." Michael's response was, "Well, when you read the next book, you will find out for yourself. Then we'll discuss it." Michael and the students were all smiling as he left the class. They all felt successful.

SYSTEMATIC CLASSROOM INSTRUCTION
Direct Instruction of New Knowledge and Skills

The curriculum contains a high proportion of basic knowledge and skills that learners must master thoroughly to succeed in the upper grades. Basic language concepts such as letter recognition, phonics, decoding words, writing letters and words, and the conventions of sentence and paragraph construction must be mastered. Basic mathematical concepts such as number recognition, quantity, order, measurement, and the operations used in computation must be learned.

Several models of direct instruction are appropriate for teaching this type of material. One of the most common is known as the 7-Step lesson. It describes steps in a chronological sequence that capture and hold the students' attention. It reviews what has been learned up to the current lesson; systematically teaches, models, and practices the new material; then demonstrates individual and independent mastery of what was taught. The 7-Step instructional model includes the following:

1. Create an anticipatory set to interest your students in the lesson by asking a thought-provoking question, providing an interesting visual aid, or using a puzzling and intriguing opening statement about the topic.
2. Connect this lesson with what has come before by providing a short review of previous, prerequisite learning or otherwise describing relationships between the current lesson and other subjects being studied by the class.
3. A short statement of the purpose of learning this new information is likely to convince your students that this lesson has a meaning to their lives beyond just achieving well in school. Tell them what they are going to learn and why it is important.
4. Present new, unfamiliar, and complex material in small steps, modeling each step by doing an example yourself. Give clear and detailed instructions and explanations as you model each process.

PRAXIS
Appropriate uses of direct instruction are tested in PRAXIS™ Exam Section 2a: Instruction and Assessment.

PRAXIS
Modeling is addressed in PRAXIS™ Exam Section 2b: Instruction and Assessment.

5. Provide a high level of active practice for all students. After you model a step, allow every student to practice the example on his or her own or with a learning partner.

6. Monitor students as they practice each new step. Walk around and look at their work as they do their sample problems. Ask a large number of questions to check for student understanding. Try to obtain responses from many students so that you know the concept is being clearly understood by the class. Provide systematic feedback and corrections as the need arises.

7. At the end of each practice session, provide an opportunity for independent student work that synthesizes the many steps students have practiced during the lesson. This may be assigned as seatwork or homework. It is important to check this work and return it to students quickly and to provide assistance for those who have not demonstrated independent mastery of the new material.

When these seven strategies are reviewed quickly, many readers may respond with reactions such as "But isn't that what all teachers do? What is new about these methods?" It is true that many teachers have used these strategies throughout the history of education. Unfortunately, many other teachers have not. We have all observed classroom teachers who take a much less active role than these systematic procedures call for. They assign work, collect it, and have students exchange papers and correct the work.

On close examination, these seven steps describe methods that would be used by a teacher who takes an active role in helping students process the new information being taught. They are also highly compatible with the concept of authentic learning because students are encouraged to think about what they are learning, construct the new knowledge in a meaningful context, and respond to substantive discussion in a supportive environment for learning. Although direct instruction is frequently associated in peoples' minds with whole-class instruction, you can readily see that these systematic steps can be used during small-group instruction as well.

In selecting appropriate teaching methods and strategies, reflective teachers are likely to look for and discover relationships among various theories of learning and methods of teaching. One such relationship exists between this direct instruction model of systematic teaching and the process of thinking and learning known as *information processing*.

The first step in information processing is to begin a lesson with a short review of previous, prerequisite learning. This strategy is a signal to the learner to call up an existing schema that will be expanded and altered in the new lesson. Beginning a lesson with a short statement of goals provides the student with an advance organizer that allows more efficient processing. In practice, these first two steps are often presented together and can be interchanged, with no ill effects.

Current information processing theories suggest that there are limits to the amount of new information that a learner can process effectively at one time (Gagne, 1985). When too much information is presented at one time, the working memory becomes overloaded, causing the learner to become confused, to omit data, or to process new data incorrectly. This overload can be eliminated when teachers present new material in small steps, with student practice after each step. This allows learners to concentrate their somewhat limited attention on processing manageable pieces of information or skills. Teachers who model new skills and give clear and detailed instructions and explanations are likely to provide students with the support they need while they are processing new information in their working memories.

Providing students with a high level of active practice after each step, and again at the conclusion of a series of steps, is important because the practice enhances the likelihood that the new information will be transferred from working memory to long-term memory, where it can be stored for future use. Each time a new skill is practiced, its position in long-term memory is strengthened.

As teachers guide students during initial practice and ask a large number of questions to check for student understanding and obtain responses from all students, teachers are also encouraging their students to process the information accurately. Learning occurs when schemata stored in long-term memory are expanded, enriched, and reorganized. Effective teacher questions and checks for understanding cause students to think about new ideas from a variety of perspectives and to update their existing schemata accordingly. Providing systematic feedback and corrections and monitoring students during seatwork also increase the likelihood that students will process the important points and practice the new skills in the most efficient manner.

Teacher Modeling and Demonstration

When teachers present new information to students, they must carefully consider the method they will use to introduce it. For students, it is rarely sufficient for teachers simply to talk about a new idea or skill. A much more powerful method of instruction is to model or demonstrate it first and then give students an opportunity to practice the new learning themselves.

A simple example of this technique in the primary grades can be something simple, like teachers saying, "First, I will say the word; then you will say it with me." In the middle grades, the teacher may first demonstrate the procedures used in measuring with a metric ruler and then ask students to repeat the procedures. In the upper grades, teachers may write an outline of a paragraph and then ask students to outline the next one.

Teacher demonstration and modeling is an effective instructional technique for almost every area of the curriculum. It is useful in teaching music: "Clap the same rhythm that I clap." It is vital in teaching mathematics: "Watch as I do the first problem on the chalkboard." It can be easily applied to the teaching of creative writing: "I'll read you the poem that I wrote about this topic, and then you will write your own." When teachers circulate throughout the classroom to monitor students as they practice or create their own work, it is efficient to use modeling and demonstration on a one-to-one basis to assist students in getting started or in correcting mistakes.

Structuring Tasks for Success

Researchers have found that the degree of success that students have on school tasks correlates highly with achievement in the subject area. This supports the widely known maxim that success breeds success. Both formal research and informal discussions with students reveal that when students experience success on a given task, they are motivated to continue working at it or to tackle another one. The number and type of successful learning experiences that students have affect their self-knowledge, leading them to have expectations regarding probable success or failure in future tasks.

To structure tasks for success, a teacher must create a good fit among his or her expectations, student ability, and the difficulty of the task. Rimm (1995), who has specialized in assisting underachieving students reach their potential, believes that students must learn early that there is a relationship between their effort and the outcome. If their schoolwork is too hard, their efforts do not lead to successful outcomes but only to failures. If their work is too easy, they learn that it takes very little to succeed. Either is inappropriate and provides a pattern that fosters under-achievement.

When teachers select and present academic tasks to their students, they need to reflect continually on how well the task fits the students' present needs and capacities.

Glasser (1969) has been committed to improving schools throughout his career. As a psychiatrist, he strongly believes that a person cannot be successful in life "until he can in some way first experience success in one important part of his life" (p. 5). Glasser recognizes that children have only two places in which to experience success: home and school. If they are lucky enough to experience success in both settings, they are likely to be successful in their adult lives. If they achieve success at home, they succeed despite a lackluster school experience. But many students come from homes and neighborhoods where failure is pervasive. For these students especially, it is critical that they experience success in school. Glasser's (1969) book, *Schools Without Failure*, offers many realistic and practical methods for teachers to develop a classroom environment that breeds success. His newer book (2001), *Every Child Can Succeed*, updates this classic and valuable philosophy for your classroom.

The CIM Model (Continuous Improvement Model) is currently being used with great success in many states (Davenport and Anderson, 2002). In this model, the daily delivery of instruction follows a set sequence that includes:

- Warm-up – This is a review of previously taught material to support the students' use of background knowledge. It also supports maintenance of skills, concepts, and strategies.
- Lesson for the day – New material is introduced and guided practice provided. This may involve several cycles of instruction, modeling, and guided practice. Guided practice means the teachers are on their feet monitoring and guiding students as they work.
- Independent practice – Students are given the opportunity to use the material independently. The teachers are still monitoring but instruction and support are lessened.
- Daily quiz – The students are given a quick quiz to determine their understanding. From the results of this quiz, the teacher determines which students need additional instruction and which students are ready to move forward. If most students need more instruction, additional lessons are planned. If a small group of students need additional instruction, a tutorial is provided for them. If a small group of students is ready for enrichment activities, those are also provided.

This model is based on the premise that all students can learn and that additional instruction must be planned and provided for those who need it. Teachers work in teams to provide the tutorials and enrichment activities their students need. Time is scheduled for tutorials and enrichment activities during the last period of the school day (and sometimes after school) to make sure that each student experiences success and continuous improvement.

Matching Learning Styles and Teaching Styles

Each person has a particular pattern of needs or preferences that allow for optimal learning. Some students learn best in quiet rooms; others prefer a certain level of noise in the room. Students have individual preferences for degrees of light and dark, temperature, and seating arrangements.

Learning styles in enormous variety have been described, including preferences for the structure of tasks and the best time of day for learning. Although you cannot accommodate the needs of every student, you will want to become aware of some of the many variations in learning styles so that when a student with an unusual sensitivity or a severe impediment to learning appears in your classroom (and this will happen), you will be able to reflect on the student's particular needs and provide a learning environment or restructure your teaching style to better match the student's learning style. A set of learning styles based on sensory preferences is especially useful to reflective teachers. Eight studies in the 1980s examined preferences for visual, auditory, and kinesthetic learning. Most learners were found to prefer receiving information either visually (by viewing or reading), aurally (by hearing), or kinesthetically (by touching, working with, or otherwise manipulating materials). Teachers have a strong tendency to teach using their own preferred modality. Specifically, visual learners who rely on reading and viewing material to learn tend to rely on reading and other visual aids as teachers. Similarly, if you learn best by hearing, you may assume that others do also and, as a result, you may teach primarily using lecture and discussion. Kinesthetic learners who enjoy hands-on activities as students tend to provide many of these active learning materials in their own classrooms.

myeducationlab
The Power of Classroom Practice

For an example of a teacher using hands-on activities within the learning cycle model and fostering academic language development in his middle school science lessons, go to the Video Examples section of Topic #12: Diversity: Cultural and Linguistic in the MyEducationLab for your course and view the video entitled "Using the Learning Cycle to Enhance Academic Success."

Currently, two major approaches exist for solving this educational dilemma. One solution requires schoolwide cooperation. At each grade level, teachers may be identified as having visual, auditory, or kinesthetic preferences. Students are then tested and placed in the classroom with the teacher whose style matches their own. But this approach offers few opportunities for learners to improve their weaker learning modalities. Another approach is for each teacher to conscientiously plan to teach using all the three modalities. For example, when presenting a lesson, the teacher provides visual aids in the form of pictures and reading material; auditory aids in the form of lecture, a discussion, or recorded material; and kinesthetic aids in the form of models or other manipulative materials. Studies show that providing all three types of learning experiences to all students is likely to result in higher achievement than simply providing one style.

Learning Experiences Designed for Multiple Intelligences

For students to experience success in school, it is necessary for teachers to understand that each individual perceives the world differently and that there is not just one way to learn or one way to teach. Prior to the emergence of this theory, most people were convinced that there was just one type of intelligence and that all human beings had an intelligence quotient (IQ) that ranged from 0 to approximately 200, with the great majority of individuals in the average range near 100, plus or minus 16 points.

Gardner's (2000) theory of multiple intelligences disputes that old belief system. He proposed the alternate theory that humans have more than one type of intelligence. He originally described seven different intelligences: verbal/linguistic (word smart), logical-mathematical (logic and math smart), visual/spatial (art smart), musical (music smart), bodily-kinesthetic (body and movement smart), interpersonal (people smart), and intrapersonal (self-awareness smart). Later, he added an eighth intelligence known as the naturalist, describing people who are very smart about nature and natural phenomena, and a ninth intelligence called the existentialist. Other researchers have suggested additional intelligences. In her teaching and curriculum planning, Eby (1990) proposed an intelligence related to mechanical and technical inventiveness. Her curriculum projects encouraged students to be inventive and to expand their technical and mechanical skills.

> **PRAXIS**
> Approaches for diverse learning styles are tested in PRAXIS™ Exam Section 1b: Students as Learners.

Teachers who wish to acknowledge and support the varied intelligences of their students try to provide learning experiences that allow students to use their special strengths in learning a subject or skill. For example, when teachers present new material to a class, they are likely to describe it in words and ask for verbal feedback for linguistically talented students. They attempt to provide problem-solving activities related to the subject for logically and mathematically oriented students. They give spatially talented students visual cues and allow them to react to the new material with drawings or diagrams. They may encourage musically talented students to commit the new material to memory via a song or allow them to create a musical response to what they have learned. They set aside time and space for kinesthetically gifted students to learn with their bodies by modeling, acting out, or pantomiming the material they are learning. For students with a special facility for interpersonal communication, teachers plan stimulating classroom discussions; and for students who are especially good at intrapersonal examination, they provide opportunities for written and/or oral responses about how the new material relates to their own sense of self by encouraging journal writing activities related to the subject being taught. Interactive goal setting and evaluation conferences also promote the development of intrapersonal intelligence.

Kagan and Kagan (1998) provide a teacher's guide to using the multiple intelligences (MI) in the classroom in their book entitled *Multiple Intelligences: The Complete MI Book*. This resource suggests three MI visions: matching, stretching, and celebrating. The first vision describes methods that teachers can use to match instructional strategies with their students' varied intelligences. The second vision encourages teachers to stretch each student's capacities in their nondominant as well as their dominant intelligence. The third vision suggests ways of celebrating and respecting one another's differences and unique patterns of learning.

By incorporating the concept of multiple intelligences into your curriculum planning, you are taking a large, positive step toward accomplishing the goal of differentiated instruction. One size does not fit all when it comes to education, and neither does one teaching strategy. Lesson plans that take advantage of the various strengths, talents, and intelligences of your students are much richer and more interesting to everyone. Give visual/spatial learners the opportunity to do a visual presentation of what they learn. Ask kinesthetic learners to do an activity to demonstrate the concept. Let musicians create a musical response. Your classroom will hum with activity and enthusiasm.

Armstrong (2009) has explored ways that teachers can apply this concept to K–12 educational experiences. He describes these intelligences as follows:

Linguistic intelligence ("word smart")

Logical-mathematical intelligence ("number/reasoning smart")

Spatial intelligence ("picture smart")

Bodily-kinesthetic intelligence ("body smart")

Musical intelligence ("music smart")

Interpersonal intelligence ("people smart")

Intrapersonal intelligence ("self smart")

Naturalist intelligence ("nature smart")

Instead of a single IQ number, each individual has a different profile of strengths and talents among these eight domains. One child might have a very high spike in logical-mathematical intelligence and low levels on the seven other intelligences. Another student may have several high peaks on her profile. Some students may have relatively high levels for six or seven or more of the intelligences. In fact, it is our belief that people who choose elementary education as their field of study and career are often people who have relatively high levels of many intelligences. They are good, but not great, at math, language arts, sports, music, and art, for example. This profile may predispose a person to consider being a teacher at the elementary level, where they are able to use all their talents and interests in creating curriculum and teaching the many varied subjects in the elementary curriculum. Reflective teachers are those who also embody high levels of interpersonal and intrapersonal intelligence. They know themselves, and they want to know and understand others. These teachers are likely to acknowledge and support the varied intelligences of their students by providing learning experiences that allow students to access their special strengths in learning a subject or skill.

Armstrong (2003) also describes methods for using multiple intelligences to promote literacy. He retells the story of the blind men who touch various parts of an elephant and then report that an elephant is like a rope or a wall or a tree stump based on their individual experiences. Armstrong suggests that the concept of "literacy" is just as complex as an elephant and, hence, is not easily described by any single individual. If a king were to ask several blind educators in his village to examine the concept of literacy, one educator might respond that literacy is made up of words—whole words. The second educator might return to the king and say, "Literacy isn't made of whole words! It's made up of sounds! All kinds of sounds! Sounds like *thhhh* and *buh* and *ahhhhh* and *ayyyyy* and *juh* and many more. In fact, I counted all the sounds, and there are exactly 44!" A third educator might examine the concept and claim that it isn't made up of sounds or whole words at all. It's constructed out of stories, fables, songs, chants, poems, and books. A fourth educator might say, "They're all wrong! Literacy is made up of whole cultures. It's about understanding who we are and what we're capable of, and how each of us can speak, read, and write with our own voices, and in this way contribute to the good of all" (Armstrong, 2003, pp. 5–6).

Reflective, caring teachers are likely to confer with their colleagues and try to understand concepts as complex as literacy with open minds and hearts. They will try to see one perspective and then look for other perspectives or sides to each issue. They search and reflect, actively trying to improve their own understanding of educational dilemmas. They are not threatened by the complexity or ambiguities inherent in their chosen profession. Rather, they become excited by the opportunities to learn more about each student's learning style and preferred intelligence patterns. They can use this information to create original unit plans or lesson plan activities that encourage their students to become active searchers and interpreters of knowledge rather than passive recipients of knowledge. With this philosophy, reflective teachers attempt to plan varied and interesting lessons, which their students view as authentic, meaningful, and purposeful learning experiences.

Communicating with Parents

As you are making plans to involve your students in active, authentic learning experiences, it is important to include parents in the learning team. When you design class newsletters or parent meetings, explain the types of activities you will be exploring in the classroom, and help parents find ways to include activities at home that will reinforce some of the same learning. Parents can be very helpful in finding ways for their children to apply skills in real-life activities. Here are some examples:

- Doing the math involved in planning a party, measuring a room for paint or wallpaper, or doubling a recipe.
- Writing letters to friends or relatives.
- Reading to younger brothers, sisters, or cousins.
- Drawing plans for new flowerbeds.
- Designing a cake for a relative's birthday.
- Composing a poem or song for a special family occasion.
- Designing a crossword puzzle to help a sibling learn spelling words.
- Researching a family's genealogy and relating it to history.

GUIDED GROUP EXPLORATION

1. Divide the class into several groups.
2. Give each group a specific task to teach in a given subject area.
3. Each group designs three teaching activities for their task or concept using three different intelligences from Gardner's work on multiple intelligences.
4. Have each group discuss their task and activities.

Suggested tasks:

Introducing subtraction
Rhyming words
Irregular verbs
Introducing economics
The culmination of the Civil War
Condensation
The color wheel
Rules for a playground game
Rhythm

REFLECTIVE ACTION ACTIVITY FOR YOUR PROFESSIONAL PORTFOLIO

Teachers Command Specialized Knowledge of How to Convey a Subject to Students

Accomplished teachers possess knowledge of the most appropriate ways to present subject matter to students through analogies, metaphors, experiments, demonstrations, and illustrations. Teachers must be able to make well-reasoned and careful decisions about what aspects of the subject matter to emphasize, what type of presentation skill to employ, and how to pace their instruction.

In this chapter, we described many presentation skills that increase clarity and student motivation. To perceive your own teaching performance, it is important to see yourself in action. Videotape one of your teaching lessons. As you watch the video of your own teaching later, observe your presentation skills and rate your enthusiasm, clarity, smooth transitions, timing, variation, interaction, active learning, and closure. Allow yourself to see your own strengths and weaknesses. What does your body language say? How does your voice sound? Do you make false starts in your phrasing, such as "Here is an example . . . I mean . . . . Look at this . . . ." Do you have eye contact with your students? What facial expressions and gestures do you want to work on? Choose one of the presentation skills described in this chapter that you want to improve in your own teaching. For example, you may choose *enthusiasm* if you feel that your presentation style is low-key. On the next four occasions when you work with students, focus on the skill and attempt to improve it. Ask your mentor teacher for feedback, and work to refine and master this skill to your own satisfaction. If possible, teach the lesson again, making improvements according to your perceptions.

Record the lesson again to see if the presentation skill you worked on has improved. Decide what your strongest presentation skills are at this point in time. Write a one- to two-page description, analysis, and reflection of the recording to include in your portfolio, which will give evidence of your ability to learn from experience.

References

Armstrong, T. (2009). *Multiple intelligences in the classroom* (3nd ed.). Alexandria, VA: Association of Supervision and Curriculum Development.

Armstrong, T. (2003). *The multiple intelligences of reading and writing: Making the words come alive.* Alexandria, VA: Association of Supervision and Curriculum Development.

Ausubel, D. P. (1960). The use of advance organizers in the learning and retention of meaningful verbal material. *Journal of Educational Psychology, 51,* 267–272.

Davenport, P & Anderson, G. (2002). *Closing the achievement gap: No excuses.* Houston, Texas: American Productivity & Quality Center.

Eby, J. (1990). *Gifted behavior index.* Buffalo, NY: Dok Publications.

Gagne, E. (1985). *The cognitive psychology of school learning.* Boston: Little, Brown.

Gardner, H. (2000). *Intelligences reframed.* New York: Basic Books.

Gibbs, J. (2001). *Tribes.* Windsor, CA: CenterSource Systems, LLC.

Glasser, W. (1969). *Schools without failure.* New York: Harper & Row.

Glassser, W. (2001). *Every child can succeed.* Los Angeles: William Glasser Institute.

Good, T., & Brophy, J. (2002). *Looking in classrooms* (9th ed.). Boston: Allyn & Bacon.

Gregory, G., & Chapman, C. (2002*). Differentiated instructional strategies: One size doesn't fit all.* Thousand Oaks, CA: Corwin Press.

Hart, A., & Mantell, P. (1999). *Ancient Greece!* Charlotte, VT: Williamson.

Jones, F. (1987). *Positive classroom discipline.* New York: McGraw-Hill.

Kagan, S., & Kagan, M. (1998). *Multiple Intelligences: The complete MI book.* San Clemente, CA: Kagan Cooperative Learning.

Kounin, J. (1977). *Discipline and group management in classrooms.* New York: Kreiger.

Maslow, A. (1954). *Motivation and personality.* New York: Harper & Row.

Mitchell, A. (2000). *The odyssey.* New York: Dorling Kindersley.

Newman, F., & Wehlage, G. (1993). Five standards of authentic instruction. *Educational Leadership, 50*(7), 8–12.

Piaget, J. (1970). *Science of education and the psychology of the child.* New York: Viking Compass Book.

Rimm, S. (2008). *Why bright children get poor grades* (2nd ed.). Scottsdale, AZ: Great Potential Press.

---

myeducationlab PEARSON
The Power of Classroom Practice

Now go to Topics #7 and 12: Strategies for Teaching and Diversity: Cultural and Linguistic in the MyEducationLab (www.myeducationlab.com) for your course, where you can:

- Find learning outcomes for these topics along with the national standards that connect to these outcomes.
- Complete Assignments and Activities that can help you more deeply understand the chapter content.
- Apply and practice your understanding of the core teaching skills identified in the chapter with the Building Teaching Skills and Dispositions learning units.
- Examine challenging situations and cases presented in the IRIS Center Resources.

Teaching Strategies That Increase Authentic Learning

School experiences should be enjoyable for both teachers and students. One way of heightening the enjoyment is by using a variety of teaching strategies and activities. When learning experiences are varied and purposeful, students are more likely to become actively engaged in the learning process. Their intrinsic motivation to learn is also likely to improve if the skill or knowledge they are learning is presented in an interesting format. To promote the enjoyment of teaching and learning, many reflective teachers are continuously searching for new methods and strategies to motivate and engage their students in the learning process. Developing a repertoire of teaching strategies is also necessary because students' needs and learning styles are diverse. For this reason, teachers must be ready to modify lesson plans and present information in more than one way.

The purpose of this chapter is to introduce you to a variety of teaching strategies and to encourage you to plan engaging lessons and learning experiences for your students. As you consider each strategy, you will quickly recognize that the descriptions in this chapter are not sufficiently detailed for you to become proficient in using the new strategy. This book can provide only an overview of the descriptions, illustrations, and examples you will need to employ these methods successfully. For strategies that you wish to implement in your classroom, you will need to actively use the reflective action of initiating an active search for more detailed descriptions of these strategies in books and journal articles or through observations of experienced teachers.

As you read about or select a strategy to try in a laboratory setting or classroom, you will find that some strategies work for you while others may not. You will need to reflect about what works for you and your students and why. As you think about what works for you, it is quite acceptable for you to combine, adapt, modify, and add your own unique strategies to the ones you read about or observe. Through this process of practice and reflection, you will discover, create, and refine your own unique teaching style.

We described a lesson in Jody Salazar's middle school classroom in Chapter 2. Jody employs a variety of teaching strategies daily in her classroom. Most of her students are reading below grade level and are learning English as a second language, so she uses a simulation activity called *vocabulary role play* whenever she can because enacting new words helps her students to remember them. She also uses graphic organizers frequently to strengthen visual learning. She often has her students work in learning teams, ensuring that those who need it most have more verbal interaction in addressing the problems she poses to them.

Jody frequently integrates her reading/language arts lessons with social studies standards because her students find reading the social studies texts difficult. Her eighth-graders are experiencing difficulty understanding the social studies unit they are studying, so Jody designs a reading/writing/oral report project for them that integrates their social studies content with her reading class.

Jody begins the study with a K-W-L chart about Native Americans. It becomes evident in building the chart that the students know a lot about Native Americans, but they have many misconceptions. They express generalizations like "All Indians live in teepees" and "All Indians hunt buffalo." As they discuss what they want to know about Native Americans, Jody creates a data chart with their questions and makes individual copies for the students. See Figure 7.1 for a sample of the data chart.

She then places her students into learning teams and provides them with reading materials about Native Americans. These materials include a number of easy-to-read books about their assigned nation or tribe:

- The Picture the Past Series (*Life in a Sioux Village, Life in a Hopi Village*, etc.)
- The Scholastic Series (*. . . If You Le, . . . If You Lived with the Cherokee*, etc.)
- The Watts Library Series (*The Iroquois, The Crow*, etc.)
- The True Book Series (*The Apache, The Shawnee*, etc.)

Tribe or Nation _____ Learning Team _____

Tribal name (What does it mean?)	Where they lived	Dwellings	What they ate	What they wore	What tools they used	Kinds of celebrations
Hunters? Gatherers? Farmers?	Form of government	Other interesting facts				

Books used: _____

Unique information found: _____

Figure 7.1 Data chart for Native American project.

The students read the books together and answer questions about the Native American nation their learning team has been assigned. Once the team has found answers for the questions on their data chart, they are instructed to work together to create an oral report about their nation. As a part of the report, they create visuals and some type of "demonstration."

As a class, Jody and her students create a scoring rubric for the oral reports. The students contribute standards such as:

Talking loud enough to be heard.
Sharing a visual that adds to the report.
Providing a demonstration of something unique about the tribe or nation.
Answering all the questions on the data chart.

Each learning team then writes a chapter on their assigned tribe or nation for the class book about Native Americans. The book is published using a word processing program, illustrated by the team members, and bound with metal rings. This "class book" is then placed into the library in Jody's room; a second copy is contributed to the social studies teacher's class library, where it is eagerly read by other members of the social studies class.

After the completion of the Native American project, Jody teaches her students to write a poem using the "I used to think . . . but now I know . . ." format. The first line of their class poem says, "I used to think that all Indians lived in teepees, but now I know that they lived in many different types of houses, depending on the natural resources they found in their land."

In this study, Jody used several different types of teaching strategies. Her students addressed many different types of standards as well: reading for information, writing reports, preparing and giving oral reports, exploration of Native American tribes, using multiple research strategies, comparing and contrasting Native American tribes and nations.

EXAMPLES OF TEACHING STRATEGIES IN ACTION

Discovery Learning

PRAXIS
Discovery learning is a topic tested in PRAXIS™ Exam Section 2a: Instructional Strategies.

The philosophy underlying discovery learning is that students will become more active and responsible for their own learning in an environment that allows them to make choices and encourages them to take initiative. To accomplish this goal, many teachers like to arrange their classrooms to provide as much space as possible for activity and learning centers. They enjoy creating curriculum units and lessons that allow students to choose from among many alternatives. The main principle of discovery learning is that students learn best by doing rather than just by hearing or reading about a concept. Teachers may find this strategy an excellent addition to their repertoire. It can be used occasionally to provide real, rather than vicarious, experiences in a classroom.

In employing discovery learning, the teacher's role is to gather and provide equipment and materials related to a concept that the students are to learn. Sufficient materials should be available so that every student or pair of students has immediate access to them. Materials that are unfamiliar, interesting, and stimulating are especially important to a successful discovery learning experience. After providing the materials, the teacher may ask a question or offer a challenge that causes students to discover the properties of the materials. Then, as the students begin to work with the materials, the teacher's role is to monitor and observe as the students discover the properties and relationships inherent in the materials, asking occasional questions or making suggestions that will guide the students in seeing the relationships and understanding the concepts. The period of manipulation and discovery is then followed by a discussion in which students report on what they have observed and learned from the experience.

A simple example at the primary level is the use of discovery learning to teach the concept of colors and their relationships to one another. Rather than telling students that blue and yellow make green or demonstrating the combination of the colors while students watch, the strategy of discovery learning is to provide every student with a brush and two small puddles of blue and yellow paint on white paper and allow them to discover it for themselves. In this case, the opening question may simply be, "What happens when you mix blue and yellow together?" When this relationship becomes apparent and students verbalize it, the teacher can then provide additional puddles of red and white paint and challenge students to create as many different colors as they can. Experiences can be designed to allow students to discover how and why some things float, what makes a lightbulb light, how electricity travels in circuits, and the difference between solutions and mixtures.

Math relationships also can be discovered. Beans, buttons, coins, dice, straws, and tooth-picks can be sorted according to size, shape, color, and other attributes. Objects can be weighed, measured, and compared with one another. The concept of multiplication can be discovered when students make sets of objects in rows and columns. Many resources in the form of math curriculum projects involving discovery learning are presently being developed for schools because discovery is a part of the problem-solving process, currently a hot topic in education.

To view multiple examples of discovery lessons, go to http://edcommunity.apple.com/ali/. This site also offers a large collection of teacher demonstrations of a variety of active learning strategies discussed in this chapter, which you can find by choosing from among the alternative descriptors in the table of contents at the site.

Inquiry Training

Closely linked to the discovery method is a strategy known as inquiry training. Teachers who believe that their students must learn how to ask questions and carry out other types of investigations to become active learners often plan lessons that stimulate their students' curiosity. They train them in asking productive questions and using critical thinking, observation skills, and variations of the scientific method to gather information, make informed estimates or predictions, and then design investigations to test their hypotheses. See Figure 7.2 for a step-by-step model for inquiry learning.

As an example, a classroom teacher wanted to train her students to think like scientists; to use the skills of observation, inquiry, prediction, hypothesis testing, and experimental design to find out what they need to know. She grouped her students into pairs and distributed a clear

---

Model For Inquiry Learning

This model is designed to promote strategies of inquiry and the values and attitudes that are essential to an inquiring mind, including process skills (e.g., observing, collecting, and organizing data), active learning, verbal expression, tolerance of ambiguity, and logical thinking.

1. Confrontation with the Problem
    1. Explain inquiry procedures
    2. Present discrepant event
2. Data Gathering—Verification
    1. Verify nature of objects and the conditions
    2. Verify the occurrence of the problem situation
3. Data Gathering—Experimentation
    1. Isolate relevant variables
    2. Hypothesize (and test) casual relationships
4. Organizing, Formulating, and Explaining—Formulate rules or explanations
5. Analysis of inquiry process—Analyze inquiry strategy, and develop more, effective ones

Figure 7.2 Inquiry learning model

Source: Courtesy of Ginny Bailey adapted from Joyce, Weil, & Showers, (1992).

plastic glass and five raisins to each dyad. She asked them to predict what would happen to the raisins if they were dropped into a glass of water. Most students correctly guessed that the raisins would sink to the bottom of the glass. The teacher then discussed with her students the need to keep an open mind and not jump to easy conclusions based on prior knowledge. She poured a carbonated lemon-lime beverage into the students' glasses and asked them to predict whether the raisins would sink or float. Each pair of students wrote down their prediction. The teacher generated a chart on the board showing the class predictions.

After recording the predictions, the teacher allowed the students to drop the raisins into their glasses. At first it appeared that the students who predicted that the raisins would sink were correct because the raisins fell to the bottom of the glasses. But as the students watched, several raisins began to rise to the top. In the next few minutes, the students observed a puzzling phenomenon: Raisins moved up and down in the glasses, each at their own pace.

At this stage in the lesson, the teacher encouraged the students to ask questions of her and of each other as they all tried to make sense out of what they were observing. The teacher answered their questions with either yes or no, giving her students the responsibility of articulating the questions and gathering the information they needed to make meaning out of the situation. Soon they began to generate new investigations that they would have to undertake to discover why some raisins moved up and down more quickly and why some settled to the bottom.

To stimulate your own curiosity and encourage you to use the reflective actions of gathering information, being creative, and being persistent in solving problems, we will not disclose the reasons for the raisins' movement. Try the experiment yourself and try to think like a scientist. If you have opportunities to learn like this yourself, you will be better able to provide your students with the encouragement and support they need without rushing to provide them with answers. You will allow them to take the time they need to inquire and experiment so that they can succeed and fully experience the "aha" moment, just as scientists do when their inquiries lead them to new understandings.

Role Playing

When problems or issues involving human relationships are part of the curriculum, teachers may choose to use role playing to help students explore and understand the whole range of human feelings that surround any issue. This strategy is frequently used to resolve personal problems or dilemmas, but it can also be employed to gain understanding about the feelings and values of groups outside the classroom. For example, to help students understand the depth of emotions experienced by immigrants coming to a new and unfamiliar country, the teacher may ask students to role-play the interactions among family members who are separated, or the dilemmas of the Cubans who set off for the United States in a leaky boat, or others who want to immigrate to the United States but are stopped by immigration quotas.

Successful and meaningful role playing has two major phases: the role playing itself and the subsequent discussion and evaluation period. In the first phase, the teacher's responsibility is to give students an overview of both phases of role playing so that they know what to expect. The teacher then introduces and describes a problem or dilemma, identifies the roles to be taken, assigns the roles, and begins the action by setting the stage and describing the immediate problem the actors must confront. Roles must be assigned carefully. Usually teachers select students who are involved in the problem to play the role. In an academic dilemma, the roles may be assigned to students who most need to expand their experience with and understanding of the issue. Students who are not assigned roles are expected to be careful observers.

To set up the role-playing situation, the teacher can arrange some chairs to suggest the setting of the event to be played out. During the role play itself, the actors are expected to get inside the problem and "live" it spontaneously, responding realistically to one another. The role play may not flow smoothly; actors may experience uncertainty and be at a loss for words, just as they would in real life. The first time a role is played, the problem may not be solved at all. The action may simply establish the problem, which in later enactments can be probed and resolved.

To increase the effect of role playing, the actors may exchange roles after playing a scene once and play out the same scene so that they grow to understand the other characters' points of view. Actors may be allowed to select consultants to discuss and improve the roles they are playing.

In the second phase, the observers discuss the actions and words of the initial role players. The teacher helps the observers review what they have seen and heard, discuss the main events, and predict the consequences of actions taken by the role players. Following the initial discussion, the teacher will probably decide to have new class members replay the role to show an alternative way of handling the problem. The situation can be replayed a number of times if necessary. When a role-play situation generates a useful solution or suggests an effective way of handling a problem, the situation can be adapted and subsequent role plays can focus on communication skills that will enhance or improve the situation even further.

Role playing has many applications in both the cognitive and affective goals of the curriculum. Through role playing, students can experience history by researching the life of a public figure and taking the role in an historical interaction. Each student in the class, for example, can study the life of a U.S. president and be the president for a day. Frequently, teachers ask students to play the role of characters in books that they have read as a means of reporting their own reading and stimulating others in the class to read the book. Students can enact the feelings of slaves and slave traders, the roles of scientists as they are conducting experiments, or the interaction between an author and editor as they try to perfect a piece of writing.

Vocabulary role play is a simple yet effective tool for getting students involved in an active learning process of learning new words and applying their meanings. In this type of activity appropriate vocabulary words are physicalized with students acting out words to internalize their meanings. Primary children may participate with action words such as *jumping*, *squeezing*, and *shrugging*, words that require physical involvement and movement. Older students may use scenarios to demonstrate the meaning of more complex words and expressions such as *honesty*, *revolution*, *respect*, or *serenity*. The physicalization of these words and terms provides a different route of internalization and makes the vocabulary come alive for the students. This strategy has been found to be especially effective with English language learners (Herrell & Jordan, 2007).

Students can learn new behaviors and social skills that may help them win greater peer acceptance and enhance their own self-esteem. Interpersonal conflicts that arise in the classroom can be role-played as a means of helping students discover more productive and responsible ways of behaving. For example, when two students argue about taking turns with a toy in the kindergarten class, the teacher can ask the students to role-play the situation in an effort to learn new ways of speaking to one another, asserting their own desires, and creating a plan for sharing the scarce resource. In a classroom, the teacher may notice that one student is isolated and treated like a scapegoat by others in the class. The dilemma can be role-played, with the role of the isolated student assigned to some of the students who have been most critical and aggressive toward the student. Through this active, vicarious experience, students may learn to be more tolerant and accepting of one another.

myeducationlab)
The Power of Classroom Practice

To see an example of a vocabulary role-playing lesson, go to the Video Examples section of Topic #7: Strategies for Teaching in the MyEducationLab for your couse and view the video entitled Vocabulary Role Play.

Storytelling

Adrienne recently taught a graduate class in storytelling and story writing. In this course, the 25 students were all teachers in the public schools, grades pre-K all the way through high school. Using Hamilton and Weiss's wonderful book *Children Tell Stories* (Hamilton & Weiss, 2005), the graduate students viewed the DVD that comes with the book and then developed storytelling units tailored to the ages and needs of their students. The graduate students learned to tell stories themselves to stir enthusiasm for their students and to experience the nervousness of telling stories to their peers.

This course was taught during the spring semester, when all Florida students in grades 4, 8, and 10 are administered the Florida Writes examination. The graduate students who taught at these grade levels arrived at class the week after the writing scores came out, and they were raving about how well their students had done on the exam. The test is an actual writing sample scored by a team of teachers using a writing rubric. One fourth-grade teacher shared that her principal approached her, wanting to know how she had managed to prepare her students so well for the exam. The teacher's reply was, "We've been telling stories as prewriting." The graduate students were all amazed at the number of standards that were addressed in a storytelling unit: speaking and listening skills, writing stages, and editing skills, just to mention a few. The tenth-grade students did especially well on the persuasive writing because they had been writing and telling stories to attempt to convince their peers to change their minds about specially chosen topics as part of their storytelling unit.

Simulation

Student drivers drive simulated vehicles before they learn to drive a real car on the highway. Airplane simulators provide a realistic but safe way for student pilots to practice flying in which mistakes lead to realistic consequences without threatening lives. Simulations usually involve some type of role playing but also include other gamelike features, such as a set of rules, time limits, tokens, or other objects that are gained or lost through the action of the simulation, and a way of recording the results of the players' decisions and actions. Simulations almost always focus on dilemmas in which the players must make choices, take actions, and then experience feedback in the form of consequences for their actions. The purpose of simulations is primarily to allow young people to experience tough, real-life problems and learn from the consequences in the safe, controlled environment of the classroom.

Many valuable academic and social simulations can be used to enrich the classroom experience and prompt students to understand the relationships among their choices, actions, and the consequences. The teacher can purchase or create simulation games. A company named Interact publishes catalogs of simulations in all areas of the curriculum that can be purchased for a relatively small price. You can access their webpage at http://www.interact-simulations.com/. Their kits include teacher manuals describing the rules, time limits, and procedures to follow, and a set of student materials that may include fact sheets, game pieces, and record-keeping devices. Titles of some of the simulations they publish include *Goldrush*, *Egypt*, and *Underground Railroad*. In their Web-based simulation called *Internet Cruises*, students become members of six "advance teams," each sent by a cruise line to explore a different travel destination. They use the Internet to explore geographic locations (which can be tailored to your classroom needs); conduct focused Internet research on the history, geography, nature, foods, and culture of the region; and report back to the class with travel brochures they have created.

The role of the teacher during a simulation is to explain the conditions, the concepts to be covered, and the expectations at the outset of the event. A practice session may be held to further familiarize participants with the rules and procedures that govern the simulation. After assigning roles or creating groups that will interact, the teacher moderates, keeps time, clarifies misconceptions, and provides feedback and consequences in response to the participants' actions. At the conclusion of the simulation, the teacher leads a discussion of what occurred and what was learned by asking students to summarize events and problems and to share their perceptions and insights with one another. At the end of the discussion, the teacher may compare the simulation to its real-life counterpart and ask students to think critically about what they would do in real life as a result of having taken part in the simulation.

An example of a simulation in economics involves the creation of small companies or stores in which students decide on a product, create the product, set up the store, price and sell the product, and keep records on the transactions. The purpose, of course, is to learn about the principles of supply and demand, as well as the practical skills of exchanging money and making change. Along with the primary goals of the simulation are secondary learning experiences. Students are also likely to increase their capacity for critical thinking and to learn about their own actions and decisions regarding competition, cooperation, commitment to a goal, and communication.

Students may simulate the writing of the U.S. Constitution by writing a classroom constitution. After studying various countries of the world, sixth-grade students may take part in a mock United Nations simulation in which students are delegates and face daily world problems presented to them by the teacher.

In language arts, students may establish a class newspaper to learn how news is gathered and printed in the real world. They may even establish a number of competitive newspapers to add another dimension of reality to the simulation. Additionaly, students may simulate the writing, editing, and publishing processes as they write, print, and distribute their own original books.

Simulations may be used to introduce a unit or as the culminating activity of a unit. They may take a few minutes or the entire year. They may be continued from week to week but played for only a specified amount of time during each session. Some may take a full day or longer. Simulations are powerful learning experiences that may change the way students view themselves and the world.

Mastery Learning

Teaching strategies known as *mastery learning* derive from the philosophy that all students can learn if they have sufficient time to master the new skill or concept. Bloom (1984) proposed that students have different *learning rates* rather than different ability levels. He created a practical system for instruction using mastery learning based on the assumption that learners can achieve the educational objectives established for them, but because they learn at different rates, they need different amounts of time to complete the required work. Bloom points to cases in which students are tutored to prove his point. In a controlled experiment, he demonstrated that "the average tutored student outperformed 98% of the students in the control class" (p. 5). He attributes this finding to the fact that a tutor is able to determine what each student knows in a given subject and is then able to plan an educational program that begins instruction at the student's level and proceeds at the student's own pace.

The basic structure of the mastery learning model, including adaptations known as *individually prescribed instruction (IPI)* and *continuous progress*, lend themselves best to the learning of basic skills in sequentially structured subjects. Specific behavioral objectives are written for each unit of study. Pretests are used to assess students' prior knowledge, which then determines their placement or starting level. Working individually, each student is required to master each objective in the sequence of learning before moving on to the next. Periodically, unit tests covering several objectives are given to assess the mastery and retention of a whole range of knowledge and skills.

The teacher's role in this process is quite different from teaching skills with a whole-class approach. The teacher rarely instructs the entire class at one time. Instead, as students work independently, the teacher monitors their progress by walking around the classroom and responding to requests for assistance. This also frees the teacher to work with small groups of students rather than devoting all of the time responding to individual needs.

The value of mastery learning is that it allows students to actively learn new material and skills on a continuous basis. Motivation to achieve also presumably increases because students are working at their own pace and have the prerequisite skills necessary for success. Also, because testing is done individually and they have opportunities to repeat what they did not learn, students should suffer less embarrassment when they make mistakes. The effective goal of mastery learning programs is to help students become independent, self-directed, and confident learners.

Contracts for Independent Learning

Because mastery learning is appropriate for use primarily in sequential subjects that require a great deal of independent practice, many teachers are searching for methods of promoting independence and self-directed learning in other subjects as well. An alternative to direct, whole-class instruction is the use of independent or group academic learning contracts.

PRAXIS
Strategies for independent study are tested in PRAXIS™ Exam Section 2a: Instructional Strategies.

**Westward Expansion of the United States
Required Learning Activities**

Date	Approval	
_____	_____	Read Chapter 6 in the social studies textbook.
_____	_____	Write answers to the questions at the end of the unit.
_____	_____	Locate and read a book on the American West or Indians.
_____	_____	Write a 2–4 page summary of the book.
_____	_____	Play the computer game "Oregon Trail" until you successfully reach the state of Oregon alive.

Alternative Learning Activities

_____	_____	Imagine that you are a member of a wagon train heading west. Write a series of letters back "home" describing your journey.
_____	_____	Write a play about a meeting between Indians and settlers. Find a cast for your play and present it to the class assembly.
_____	_____	Draw or paint a large picture of a scene that you imagine took place during the westward expansion.
_____	_____	Create a song or ballad about life in the west. Be prepared to play and sing it for the assembly.
_____	_____	Create a diorama or a model of a Plains Indian village.
_____	_____	Research the lives of the Plains Indians today. Be prepared to give a speech about the conditions in which they live now and how this is related to the westward expansion.
_____	_____	Create an alternative plan for a learning experience on this topic.

_____

I, _____ , agree to complete the required learning activities by the date _____ . In addition, I select two to five alternative activities to pursue on my own. I will present my creative work to my classmates at our assembly on _____ .

_____   I have reviewed this contract and understand the work
           student signature   my child has agreed to do. I agree to support this effort.

_____   _____
          teacher signature   parent signature

Figure 7.3 Independent learning contract.

A learning contract, such as the one in Figure 7.3, is usually created by the teacher at the beginning of a unit of study. The contract specifies one list of required activities, such as reading a chapter in the textbook, finding a library resource and writing a summary of the topic, completing a fact sheet, and other necessary prerequisites for developing a knowledge base on the subject.

A second list of activities is offered as choices or alternatives for students to pursue. This list includes opportunities to do additional independent research or create plays, stories, songs, and artwork on the topic. When learning contracts are offered to develop independence, individuals usually select the activities they want to accomplish. A variation on this strategy would be to combine the concepts of cooperative groups and learning contracts and allow each group to sign a joint contract specifying the tasks and products they will complete.

Science investigations, social studies research projects, and creative language arts activities can be described in learning contracts. The primary advantage of this strategy is that it allows individuals at various ability levels to work on an appropriate amount and type of work during the unit of study. Students who work quickly and accurately can select the maximum number of tasks and projects, while other students select fewer tasks. Theoretically, both types of students can actively learn and experience success during the same amount of time.

Group Rotations Using Learning Centers

Learning centers or stations are areas of the classroom where students can go to do independent or group work on a given subject or topic. Learning centers vary enormously in appearance, usage, and the length of time for which they are set up. Teachers who use learning centers use them for a variety of purposes and with a variety of expectations.

PRAXIS
Strategies for using learning centers are tested in PRAXIS™ Exam Section 2a: Instructional Strategies.

Some centers may be informal and unstructured in their use. For example, a classroom may have a permanent science center containing a variety of science equipment and materials. Students may go to the center to do science experiments in their free time. The same classroom may have a permanent reading center furnished with a rug, comfortable chairs, and shelves or racks of books, where students can go to read quietly.

Other centers are set up for a limited amount of time and have highly structured expectations. For example, to accompany the unit on settling the western United States described in the learning contract, the teacher may have set up an area of the classroom as a research center. It would contain a computer, with the Minnesota Educational Computing Consortium (MECC) computer program called Oregon Trail turned on and ready for students to use. It would also contain posters and maps of the western United States and a variety of reading materials on the topic. When the unit is finished, the center will be redesigned, new learning materials will replace the ones from the finished unit, and the center will become the focus of a new unit of study.

In primary classrooms, learning centers are often an important adjunct to reading and language arts. Many teachers set up four or five learning centers or stations with different activities each week. Students in small groups travel from one station to another according to a pre-specified schedule. For example, Ginny Bailey uses a weekly theme as the basis for her first-grade language arts program. Each week, she sets up activities related to that theme in her five stations: art, math, writing, listening, and reading. To accompany her butterfly theme, students find books on butterflies to read at the reading station, paper and directions for a writing project at the writing center, paint and brushes to create a picture at the art station, a prerecorded tape to listen to at the listening station, and a math game involving butterflies and caterpillars at the math station. Ginny uses five centers—one for each day—and that means each group can visit each center once a week. Figure 7.4 shows the posted schedule of

Group	Monday	Tuesday	Wednesday	Thursday	Friday
Blue	Art	Math	Writing	Reading	Listening
Green	Math	Writing	Reading	Listening	Art
Red	Writing	Reading	Listening	Art	Math
Yellow	Reading	Listening	Art	Math	Writing
Orange	Listening	Art	Math	Writing	Reading

Figure 7.4 Learning station schedule.

groups and centers. In Ginny's classroom, students can go to their stations only after completing their daily work assignments. In her system, the stations not only extend the students' learning experiences on the weekly theme but are also used as an incentive system for students to complete their required work.

Teachers who work with students with limited English proficiency are finding that rotations from one learning center to another give the students many rich opportunities to use the English language with their peers as well as with adults. In a kindergarten classroom at Hamilton School in mid-city San Diego, Susan King recently completed her English Language Learners (ELL) teaching credential. In her classroom, she wants to create a learning environment that enables her English language learners to take risks with English so that they develop oral fluency in their new language. In the following case study, you can read about how she changed her entire system of teaching within a few months when she became aware that her students were becoming less proficient and quieter under the conventional teacher-centered system she had been using.

❋ REFLECTIVE ACTION CASE STUDY ❋

Establishing Learning Centers

Susan King, ELL Kindergarten, Hamilton School, San Diego, California

Teacher Begins to Plan

At the beginning of my first year as a kindergarten teacher, I organized my classroom for whole-group instruction in reading and language arts. I used conventional methods in which my students all worked at the same task at the same time, with a great deal of direct instruction from me.

Teacher Considers What the Students Already Know

Then I began to perceive that the room was too quiet. Students sat quietly, waiting passively for me to tell them what to do. There were very few opportunities for oral language development using this teacher-centered approach to teaching.

Teacher Has Expectations

One day after school, I was thinking about my classroom and I decided that I needed to take some risks and reorganize my entire classroom system to stimulate talking, problem solving, and cooperative learning.

Teacher Does Research and Invites Feedback

Our district has designated mentor teachers who are willing to share the teaching strategies they employ with beginning teachers. I arranged to visit a mentor teacher who uses a rotation schedule for her kindergarten–first-grade classroom and I learned more in that one day than I could imagine. I was able to see the physical arrangement of her classroom and watch her students travel from one learning center to another. I took pictures of the charts and schedules she used to direct traffic in her room. I also took pictures of the students working at the various centers she had established. From this visit, I was able to envision the changes that would need to be made in my classroom. Because many of my students are English language learners, I also decided to sign up for some courses to get my English Language Learners (ELL) credential.

Teacher Reflects Again Using Feedback, Research, and Creativity

The new knowledge I gained from these visits and my courses caused me to become aware of the needs of the students in my class. I became aware of how important it was to include parent volunteers or peer tutors who are familiar with the primary or first language (L1) of the English language learners in my program. In my classroom, these L1 languages include Spanish and Laotian.

Teacher Creates a New Action Plan

I recruited Spanish- and Laotian-speaking parents and upper-grade students to assist me in my classroom. I also decided to use the resources of my own students who are bilingual. I began to design the materials I would need to get started. In January, I plunged into the whole new system. I set up four different learning stations in my classroom: journal writing, a reading basket, a structured activity center, and the guided reading group. Peer tutors supervised the structured activity center to help children with science, math, and social studies. In all the centers, I encouraged my students to talk with each other, share ideas, help each other, and solve whatever problems were at hand. I instructed them to ask everyone in their group for help and then ask the peer tutor or group captain before coming to ask me for help. With this management system, I was free to work with the guided reading group without interruptions.

Unforeseen Problems Occur

It took about 2 weeks for the children to be accustomed to the movement from one area to the next. It took even longer for them to become independent learners. At first they would stand still, waiting for me to come and give them direct teaching or instruction about every little step. When I saw this response of stillness and waiting to be spoon-fed, I thought to myself, "What a disservice we are doing to children when we train them to be passive learners. I realized that the whole-group teaching I had done for the first 5 months had caused this response. I had trained them to wait for my every word and not to think for themselves."

Teacher Uses Withitness in Response to Problem

To be able to give my full attention to the students in the guided reading group, I had to find a way to organize the learning environment so that the other 25 students were busy and would not need to interrupt me. This felt like a real challenge to me because, even though I had recruited parent volunteers, they did not come consistently. So I went to my colleagues who teach the upper grades and asked them to send me some helpers who would like to help in the kindergarten. The response was overwhelmingly positive. Just as my students needed peer tutors, the older children need this type of responsibility to enhance their own self-image.

A resource teacher who visited recently looked around to see the children working so independently. As he left, he told me, "I can't believe this is a kindergarten class. The children are so responsible—so in charge of their own learning."

COOPERATIVE LEARNING STRATEGIES

Cooperative groups are a welcome change of pace for many students. They enjoy the opportunity to interact with their peers for part of the school day. Teachers may be hesitant to try this strategy, however, for fear that the students will play or talk about outside interests rather

> **PRAXIS**
> The use of cooperative learning is tested in PRAXIS™ Exam Section 2a: Instructional Strategies.

than work at the assigned task. Cooperative groups can degenerate into chaotic groups if they do not meet certain conditions.

Imagine that a teacher hears some general ideas about cooperative groups at a conference or reads the first few paragraphs of an article on the strategy. Thinking that it seems to be an intriguing idea, the teacher may hurry back to the classroom, divide the class into several small groups, and tell them to study the Civil War together for a test that will be held next Friday. After a few moments of discussing what they have (or have not) read about the Civil War, the groups are likely to dissolve into chaos or, at best, evolve into groups who sit near one another and talk to one another as each person studies the text in isolation.

When the group has a poor understanding of the goals of the task, the results may be unproductive and frustrating. To prevent this, the teacher must clearly state the goals and expectations of each group task and provide a copy of them in writing so the group can refer to them from time to time. This includes assigning specific duties to each group member that, when combined, result in a smoothly functioning interaction.

Cooperative learning is designed to encourage students to help and support their peers in a group rather than compete against them. This purpose assumes that the perceived value of academic achievement increases when students are all working toward the same goal. Cooperative groups emphasize the notion of pride in one's team in much the same way that sports teams do. A teacher using cooperative learning must be constantly vigilant to ensure that one or two students are not dominating the group to the educational detriment of the other children in the group. Quite often, dominant students will disregard the contributions of other members of the group based on a perception of educational "worthiness." Students who are not strong readers, for example, are often left out of discussions, their ideas minimized or disregarded altogether. Students are sometimes the objects of negative interactions simply because of their linguistic or ethnic backgrounds. It is the teacher's responsibility to monitor the groups' progress and intervene when necessary to make sure that all children are given the opportunity to participate in the group process (Cohen, 1994).

Another major purpose of cooperative learning is to boost the achievement of students of all ability levels. The assumption is that when high-achieving students work with low-achieving students, they both benefit. Compared to tracking systems that separate the high achievers from the low achievers, cooperative groups are composed of students at all levels so that the low-achieving students can benefit from the modeling and interaction with their more capable peers. It is also believed that high-achieving students can learn to be more tolerant and understanding of individual differences through this type of experience than if they are separated from low achievers.

Still another point is that cooperative teams are believed to be more motivating for the majority of students because they have a greater opportunity to experience the joy of winning and success. In a competitive environment, the same few high-achieving students are likely to win over and over again; but a classroom divided into cooperative teams, each with its own high- and low-achieving students, more evenly distributes the opportunity to succeed. To this end, the reward systems do not honor individuals but depend on a group effort. As in a sports team, individual performances are encouraged because they benefit the whole team.

Teachers may believe that they are using cooperative learning when, in reality, they are simply making physical changes in the classroom desk arrangement or allowing students who work rapidly and well to tutor or mentor their slower classmates. Johnson and Johnson (1993) provide us with a valuable perspective by telling us what cooperative learning is *not*:

Cooperation is *not* having students sit side by side at the same table to talk with one another as they do their individual assignments.

Cooperation is *not* having students do a task with the instruction that whoever finishes first is to help the slower students.

Cooperation is *not* assigning a report to a group of students wherein one student does all the work and the others put their names on the product, too.

Learning Teams Enhance Achievement

Slavin (1995) emphasizes the team concept in cooperative learning. For example, the teacher presents information to the entire class in the form of lectures, discussion, and/or readings. As a follow-up, students are formed into four- or five-member heterogeneous teams to learn the new material or practice the new skills.

These learning teams are designed to provide a way to encourage both individual accountability and group efforts at the same time. A baseline score is computed for each team by combining the data from individual pretests. Students then work together and assist each other in learning new material. At the conclusion of the study period, individual posttests are given to determine how well each member of the group has learned the material. Students are not allowed to help one another on the tests, only during the practice sessions. The individual test scores are then combined to produce a team score, but the winning team is not necessarily the team with the highest combined score. The results that count are the *improvement scores*, which are computed by determining the difference between each individual's original baseline pretest score and the final posttest results and adding these individual improvement scores together to create a final group improvement score.

For example, students may be pretested on 20-word spelling lists. High-scoring students are grouped with lower-scoring students to study and practice together, with the goal of having all students in the group earn improvement points for their team. One group's scores and points might look like this example:

Name	Pretest Score	Posttest Score	Difference = Improvement Points
John	13	15	+2
Mary	17	14	−3
Jorge	12	19	+7
Carla	8	18	+10

The teacher may use the total score of 16 or calculate an average improvement score for this group, which is 16 divided by 4, for an average group improvement score of 4. This group's score can then be compared with other groups in the class, and a competition among the study groups may be used to stimulate interest and motivation in working together to improve everyone's scores. If all groups do well and achieve impressive group improvement scores, then all groups can earn awards or extra privileges. Teachers can design award certificates or plan a menu of extra privileges to encourage students to work hard individually and in cooperation with each other.

Cooperative Learning of the Basic Skills

Cooperative learning can be used to assist students in the mastery of basic skills such as computing basic addition, subtraction, and multiplication facts. In a traditional classroom, teachers may prepare students for this assessment by providing them with daily worksheets for practicing and memorizing the math facts. Students may win rewards or recognition for being the fastest or the most accurate on these work assignments.

Although this type of competitive environment may please and motivate the high achievers, it is likely to encourage the remainder of the class. To modify the process of learning math facts from a competitive to a cooperative experience, teachers can adapt the student team achievement division model to fit the needs of their classrooms. Using a learning team approach, the teacher would begin by giving a pretest of 100 math facts to the entire class. By sorting the pretests into high, medium, and low scores, the teacher can divide the class into heterogeneous groups with equivalent ability in math facts. Each group would contain one of the top scorers, one of the lowest scorers, and two in the middle range.

How the teacher sets up the conditions and expectations for this cooperative learning experience is very important. The achievement goal and the behavioral expectations must be clearly explained at the outset. For example, the teacher may state that the groups are expected to practice math facts for a given time each day. Worksheets, flashcards, and other materials will be provided, and the teams are free to choose the means they use to practice. The goal, in this instance, is to raise all scores from pretest levels as much as possible. A posttest is given on a certain day, and each individual receives an improvement score, which is the difference between the correct responses on the posttest and the correct responses on the pretest. The group improvement score is computed by adding the individual improvement scores. This method of scoring encourages the group to give extra energy to raise the scores of the lowest scorers because they have the most to gain. Top scorers, in fact, may not gain many points at all because their pretests may already be near the total. Added incentives, such as a certain number of points for a perfect paper, may be devised for this group.

The incentives that will be awarded for success depend a great deal on the class itself. The teacher may choose to offer one reward for the group whose scores improve the most or reward each group, depending on their gains. For example, a single reward for the most improved group may be tangible, such as a certificate of success or temporary possession of a traveling math trophy. Less tangible incentives are also important to third-graders, such as the opportunity to be first in line for a week, go to the library together during a math class, or eat lunch with the teacher. To spread the incentives to all groups, the points that each group earns may be translated into an award, such as 1 minute of free time per point or the opportunity to "buy" special opportunities and materials.

Once students become accustomed to helping their classmates in one subject area, they are likely to take considerable interest in assisting and supporting their classmates in doing well in other subjects. Similar groups can operate to improve spelling, vocabulary, the mechanics of writing, or other basic skills. The membership of each group would be different because students are likely to score differently on pretests for various subjects.

Cooperative Learning in Science

In many classrooms, the conventional approach to teaching science once centered on textbook reading, discussion, an occasional demonstration by the teacher, and written tests of understanding. More recently, science curricula have been revised to include many more hands-on experiments and investigations. The current philosophy is that students need to learn how to *do* science rather than simply learn about it.

Hands-on science is an area that fits naturally with cooperative group strategies. By participating in cooperative science investigations, students learn how scientists themselves interact to share observations, hypotheses, and methods. Although many teachers value these current science goals, they may be reluctant to try them because they are unsure of how to manage the high level of activity in the classroom when science experiments are happening. Cooperative groups can provide the support and structure needed to manage successful science investigation in the classroom.

When you teach science using a topic or unit approach, each unit offers opportunities for cooperative learning. For example, jigsaw groups may study the topic of astronomy, with each group studying one planet, creating models and charts of information about their planet, and reporting their findings to others.

Investigations into the properties of simple machines, magnets, electricity, and other more advanced topics in physics can be designed by establishing a challenge or a complex goal for groups to meet by a given date. Groups may be given a set of identical materials and told to create a product that has certain characteristics and can perform a specific function. For example, given a supply of toothpicks and glue, groups are challenged to construct a bridge that can hold a pound of weight without breaking. Given a raw egg and an assortment of materials, groups may work together to create innovative ways to protect their eggs when they are dropped from a high window onto the pavement below.

Science groups can be mixed and matched frequently during the year, offering students an opportunity to work cooperatively with most other members of their class. This strategy is likely to reinforce the principles of social science as well. For example, during the astronomy unit, the emphasis could be on learning how to come together as a group quickly, quietly, and efficiently when getting started on the day's project. During the bridge-building unit, groups could practice encouraging everyone to participate, taking time to ask for opinions and suggestions from every member of the group before making an important decision. After completing each unit, the groups should participate in evaluating how they worked together and how well they demonstrated the interpersonal skill emphasized during that unit.

Literature Circles

Reading instruction may be conducted in a variety of formats. Primary teachers may teach small groups of students reading individual storybooks in flexible groupings that change almost weekly. These groups of students are often engaged in active learning experiences after each small book is completed. In some classrooms, more conventional methods of teaching reading, three homogeneous reading groups based on ability, may still be used at many grade levels. Each group reads stories, essays, poems, and plays collected in a basal reader geared for the group members' reading ability. The teacher leads discussions of reading materials and assigns seatwork to be done while he or she works with other groups.

Many upper elementary, middle, and high school teachers prefer to use literary materials in their own format rather than as collections in basal readers or anthologies. They believe that students' motivation to read will improve if they are encouraged to choose and read whole books, novels, poetry collections, and plays. A variety of paperback books in sets of six to eight books apiece are needed to carry out this type of reading program.

At Our Lady of Mercy School in Chicago, sixth-grade teacher Roxanne Farwick-Owens has developed a system that allows choice, maximizes cooperative efforts, and holds individuals accountable. To maximize student motivation and enjoyment of reading, Roxanne believes students must be allowed to choose their reading materials. Each month, she provides three or four reading selections, in the form of paperback books, to the class. Students are allowed to choose the book they want to read, and groups are formed according to interest rather than ability level. Roxanne may advise students about their selections and try to steer them toward appropriate selections, but in the end, she believes that they have the right to choose for themselves what they will read, especially because she has provided only books that have inherent value for sixth graders.

During initial group meetings, students decide for themselves how much to read at a time. They assign themselves due dates for each chapter. Periodically, each group meets with Roxanne to discuss what they are reading, but most discussions are held without her leadership. Usually, she holds the groups responsible for generating their own discussion on the book. To prepare for this discussion, all members are expected to prepare questions as they read. For example, each person in the group may be expected to contribute three "why" questions and two detail questions per session. Roxanne reviews the questions each day as a means of holding each individual accountable for reading the material and contributing to the group.

Another task is to plan a presentation about the books—using art, music, drama, and other media—to share with the rest of the class at the end of the month. This allows groups to introduce the books they have read to the other members of the class, who are then likely to choose them at a later date. One group made wooden puppets and a puppet stage to portray an event from Mark Twain's *Tom Sawyer*. After reading Judy Blume's *Superfudge*, a group created a radio commercial for the book, complete with sound effects and background music. Familiar television interview shows are sometimes used as a format, as are music videos.

About once per quarter, two teams are formed to compete in a game show–type tournament. Questions about the books are separated into categories such as characters, plot, setting, authors, and miscellaneous. Each person is responsible for writing five questions and answers on index cards to prepare for the tournament. One student acts as emcee, while another keeps track of the points. The team with the most points wins the tournament.

Roxanne finds that this cooperative group structure increases her students' social skills, especially their ability to work with others and to find effective ways to handle disagreements. The primary reason for the program is to help her students see that reading can be enjoyable and that it can have a social aspect instead of being a solitary pursuit. Roxanne believes many of her students may become lifelong readers from this year-long experience.

Peacemaking Groups

Some cooperative groups are formed for the social purpose of teaching students how to resolve conflicts, handle anger, and avoid violence in their lives. Many schools are taking an active role in training their students to incorporate conflict management skills in their daily lives. Johnson and Johnson (1991) have created a series of learning experiences that teachers can use for this purpose. Students are taught to recognize that conflict is inevitable, and that they can choose between entering into destructive or constructive conflicts. They learn how to recognize a constructive conflict through cooperative group experiences and simulations.

For example, a group of students may be told that they have just won an all-expense-paid field trip to the destination of their choice. Now comes the hard part: Where will the group choose to go? Students pair up to list their choices and create a rationale for them. Through negotiation, the group must resolve the dilemma and make a plan by consensus.

In other group sessions, students learn to identify how they personally react to conflicts and learn how to be assertive rather than aggressive or withdraw from arguments. For example, one session may be devoted to assisting students in dealing with insulting remarks and put-downs. In another, they may deal with a simulated situation in which one student refuses to do her part in a cooperative group assignment. Cooperative group activities such as these are designed to encourage students to seek peaceful solutions in their school environment. Teachers who use these methods are also likely to believe they may be useful to their students as adults and may lead to future generations seeking more peaceful solutions in business, politics, or other issues in their families and communities.

Creating Well-Balanced Cooperative Groups

Assigning students to cooperative groups can be the most difficult part of the process for teachers. The philosophy of heterogeneous grouping is excellent in theory, but it is difficult to achieve in a real-life classroom. A classroom is likely to have one or two superstars whose ability cannot be matched in some subject areas. Similarly, one or two students may have very unusual learning difficulties or behavior problems. For most types of learning situations, the teacher must simply make the best judgment about the combinations that are approximately equivalent in ability.

It is advisable to put non-task-oriented students into groups with highly task-oriented teammates so that peer pressure will work to keep them on task. This theory, however, does not always work out in the classroom. Angry or highly restless students may refuse to participate or otherwise prevent their team from succeeding. When this happens, the group itself should be encouraged to deal with the problem as a means of learning how to cope with and resolve such occurrences in real life.

In arranging the room during cooperative group activities, each group should have a comfortable space, and members should be able to face one another and have eye contact with every other member of the group. Separating the groups from one another is also necessary so they can each work undisturbed by the conversations and activities taking place in other groups.

Materials intended for cooperative groups may differ from those used in conventional teaching and learning situations. It is suggested that only one set of materials explaining the task and the expectations be distributed to each group. This causes students in the group to work together from the very beginning. In some cases, each member of the group may receive different information from other members. This promotes interdependence because each member has something important to share with the others. Interdependence can also be encouraged by the assignment of complementary and interconnected roles to group members. These roles will vary with the type of learning and task, but they might include discussion leader, recorder of ideas, runner for information, researcher, encourager, and observer.

Tasks that result in the creation of products, rather than participation in a test or tournament, are more likely to succeed if the group is limited to the production of one product. If more than one product is allowed, students may simply work independently on their own products. Members of the group should also be asked to sign a statement saying that they participated in the development of the group's product.

To ensure individual accountability, students must know that they will all be held responsible for learning and presenting what they learned. During the final presentations, the teacher may ask any member of the group to answer a question, describe an aspect of the group's final product, or present a rationale for a group decision.

The Effects of Cooperative Learning

In a school setting, students learn in classes made up of their age mates, for the most part. With conventional teaching methods, relationships among peers in a class are likely to become somewhat competitive because most students are aware of how well they are doing in relation to their classmates. Grading systems reinforce the competitive nature of school, as do standardized tests and entrance exams.

Individual competition can enhance the motivation for high-achieving students who perceive that they have a possibility of winning or being the best. However, the public nature of competitive rewards and incentives leads to embarrassment and anxiety for students who fail to succeed. When anxiety and embarrassment are intense, students who recognize that they are unlikely to win no matter how hard they work eventually drop out of the competition in one way or another. Even when anxiety over competition is less intense and under control for students with average or high-average achievement, they may become preoccupied with grades to the extent that they avoid complex or challenging tasks that will place their academic standing and grades at risk.

Despite these negative effects of competition, it is difficult to imagine a classroom without some type of competitive spirit or reward system, and despite its obvious flaws, competition does create an energetic response from many students. Slavin's (1995) models of cooperative group structures are designed to maintain the positive value of competition by adapting it in the form of team competition so that each student is equally capable of winning.

Reflective teachers who undertake some form of cooperative learning will need to be aware of all possible effects and observe for both positive and negative interactions among teammates. When using competitive teams, teachers should take steps to ensure that every team has an equal chance of winning and that attention is focused more on the learning task than on who wins and loses. When anger or conflict arises within groups, teachers must be ready to mediate and assist students as they learn the interpersonal and communication skills necessary to learn from their team losses.

Slavin (1995) and Sharan (1999) also report that cooperative groups may actually improve race relations within a classroom. When students participate in multiracial teams, studies show that they choose one another for friends more often than do students in control groups.

Researchers attribute this effect to the fact that working together in a group as part of a team causes students to promote more differentiated, dynamic, and realistic views (and therefore less stereotyped and static views) of other students (including peers who are handicapped and students from different ethnic groups) than do competitive and individualistic learning experiences (Johnson & Johnson, 1991).

Promoting dynamic interactions among your students and between you and your students is the likely effect if you choose to learn and master the use of cooperative learning strategies for your future classroom. All of the teaching strategies presented in this chapter have the potential of creating a stimulating, motivating, and highly interactive learning environment. They are all strategies that enhance the relational aspects of teaching. Simulations encourage interaction, role playing encourages self-awareness and understanding of others' points of view, discovery learning and learning centers foster independence and intrinsic motivation, and cooperative groups promote interdependence. By using many of these strategies in your classroom, you will be inviting your students to learn for the sake of learning while at the same time providing them with opportunities for becoming reflective and relational human beings.

Communicating with Parents

The use of active learning during the teaching of curriculum units provides a great opportunity for parent involvement during culmination exercises. Inviting parents back to school for displays of student projects, readers theatre performances, oral presentations, and the like, provides a clear connection between learning and stated outcomes. Allow the parents and significant others to share this learning with their children and to become co-participants in the educational processes that you have chosen to use in your classroom.

Some teachers like to invite parents to back-to-school night to explain the active learning approach that they use. They sometimes structure the room with learning centers that the parents can participate in to acquaint them with the active learning concepts. Often, they will use displays from the previous year to demonstrate some of the learning processes and to encourage the parents to get involved with their children's learning.

GUIDED GROUP EXPLORATION

myeducationlab
The Power of Classroom Practice

To see an example of middle school students learning cooperation, go to the Video Examples section of Topic #9: Group Interaction Model in the MyEducationLab for your couse and view the video entitled Puzzle Activity to Promote Cooperation in Groups.

1. Go to MyEducationLab and show the video on Cooperative Learning.
2. Divide the class into small groups.
3. Have each group discuss the video clip and respond to the following questions:
   a. Why did Ms. Salazar require the students to work without talking at the beginning of the exercise?
   b. How did she make her expectations clear?
   c. How did she use verbal and nonverbal language to encourage the students?
   d. How did this exercise help the students to cooperate within groups?

REFLECTIVE ACTION ACTIVITY FOR YOUR PROFESSIONAL PORTFOLIO

PRAXIS
This activity prepares you to write a constructed response similar to what you will be required to do on the PRAXIS™ Exam.

Visit www.interact-simulations.com and review a simulation that is appropriate for the grade level that you would like to teach. Explain how you could integrate it into a unit of study at your chosen grade level. Write a reflection on how the simulation would build the students' background knowledge, how the simulation would help address grade-level standards, and what learning outcomes you could expect through the use of the simulation.

References

Bloom, B. (1984). The search for methods of group instruction as effective as one-to-one tutoring. *Educational Leadership, 41*(8), 4–17.

Cohen, E. (1994). *Designing groupwork* (2nd ed.). New York: Teachers College Press.

Hamilton, M., & Weiss, M. (2005). *Children tell stories: Teaching and using storytelling in the classroom* (2nd ed.). Katonah, NY: Richard C. Owen Publishers.

Herrell, A., & Jordan, M. (2007). *50 strategies for teaching English language learners* (3rd ed.). Upper Saddle River, NJ: Merrill/Prentice Hall.

Johnson, D., & Johnson, R. (1991). *Teaching students to be peacemakers*. Edina, MN: Interaction Book Co.

Johnson, D., & Johnson, R. (1993). *Circles of learning*. Alexandria, VA: Association of Supervision and Curriculum Development.

Joyce, B., Weil, M., & Showers, B. (1992). *Models of teaching* (4th ed.). Boston: Allyn & Bacon

Sharan, S. (1999). *Cooperative learning methods*. Westport,CT: Praeger Publishers

Slavin, R. (1995). *Cooperative learning* (2nd ed.). Boston: Allyn & Bacon.

Now go to Topics #9 and 11: Group Interaction Models and Inquiry Models in the MyEducationLab (www.myeducationlab.com) for your course, where you can:

- Find learning outcomes for these topics along with the national standards that connect to these outcomes.
- Complete Assignments and Activities that can help you more deeply understand the chapter content.
- Apply and practice your understanding of the core teaching skills identified in the chapter with the Building Teaching Skills and Dispositions learning units.

Engaging Students in Classroom Discussions

![decorative dotted line]

In Chapter 6, Michael (MJ in the dialogue below) began teaching a lesson on *The Odyssey* with tenth-graders. As a follow up to this lesson, he conducted an interactive discussion about the book with the students.

MJ:	*We've been reading* The Odyssey. *Recently this book was listed as number one on a list of the 100 best books of all times. Why do you think it was ranked this high?*
Amanda:	*Well, it's really an old book and it's been read for many years.*
Jose:	*It's an action story with lots of strange twists.*
MJ:	*What are the things you think would need to be part of a book in order for it to make the list?*
Jose:	*Must have to be pretty interesting.*
Carlos:	*It would have to have "stood the test of time."*
MJ:	*What does that mean?*
Amanda:	*Like I said before, it's been around for a long time and people still want to read it.*
Maria:	*It also has to have something different about it. It can't be like a lot of other books.*
Jose:	*This book reminds me of some of the great action movies, too, like* The Matrix *or* Spiderman.
Carlos:	*I agree with Jose. It just has a lot of action and a lot of surprises, like men being turned into pigs and big monsters with one huge eye in the middle of his forehead.*
MJ:	*Well, those things certainly make it kind of weird and interesting to read, but what was special about having those kinds of characters in the story?*
Claudia:	*I was more about what he did with those characters, how he reacted to them.*

MJ:	*You're right, Claudia. We read a lot about how he interacted with the characters and situations he encountered. So, thinking about that, Jose, how did it remind you of* Spiderman *and* The Matrix?
Jose:	*Well, like, they had to deal with some bad dudes and situations, like this guy did.*
MJ:	*And did they have to be creative in solving problems, like Odysseus did?*
Jose:	*Yeah, they had to come up with special ways of taking care of every problem they came up on.*
Maria:	*And they were heroes, like he was, like always good defeating evil.*
Claudia:	*Yeah, that's kinda what makes this a great book. It's about a hero struggling against evil and winning. And that kinda story is still being used today, like in the movies Jose is talking about. It's still heroes taking on the bad guys and winning.*
Jose:	*And that what you mean when you say it "stood the test of time." It's like a story that's been around for a long time and it's still being talked about and copied.*

This introductory discussion then led to further discussions and writing activities based on the idea of "heroes"—who they are and what makes them a hero. Discussions usually centered around real-life, present-day heroes identified by the students themselves. Bringing these so-called old ideas into the present, into the real world of the students, made them more relevant and comprehensible to the students without distorting the ideals of the original story. When students become actively and enthusiastically interested in thinking about and discussing an idea, they are experiencing *cognitive engagement*, a powerful concept for teachers to aim for when they select teaching strategies for their classrooms.

Cognitive engagement results in the opposite of the sterile, passive classroom environment, where students attend listlessly to the lessons and carry out their seatwork and homework with little real effort or interest. When students are fully engaged in reading, listening, discussion, or creative activities, the classroom climate is more likely to be lively and stimulating. When teachers structure classroom discussions to engage their students fully in substantive, meaningful, and highly interactive exchanges of information and ideas, authentic learning is more likely to occur.

Can you recall a classroom learning experience so powerful that you have almost total recall of it many years later? When you recall the event, do you feel as if you are reliving it because the memory is still so vividly etched in your mind? Do you think of this event as life-changing? Perhaps it altered the way you think about an issue, caused you to change your career goal, or provoked you into making a lifestyle change. Bloom (1981) calls these relatively rare classroom events *peak experiences*.

For many students, peak learning experiences occur during especially stimulating classroom discussions, in which all members of the classroom community express their ideas, opinions, and points of view. Students experience these discussions as authentic, substantive, and valuable. Teachers also have a sense of exhilaration and pride when they are able to create the environment and structure needed for such powerful exchanges. In this chapter, we will examine some of the strategies you can use to stimulate and guide substantive and satisfying classroom discussions.

PRAXIS
This chapter prepares you for PRAXIS™ Exam Section 3c: Communication Techniques That Stimulate Discussion.

ASKING QUESTIONS THAT STIMULATE HIGHER-LEVEL THINKING

Imagine you are observing a classroom discussion after the students have read a biography of Dr. Martin Luther King, Jr. The teacher asks the following questions:

When and where was Dr. King born?

Who were the other members of his family?

How did King's father and mother earn a living?

What career did Dr. King choose?

What does the term *ghetto* mean?

What does *prejudice* mean?

What did Dr. King accomplish that earned him the Nobel Peace Prize?

As you watch and listen to this discussion, you might reflect on the way you would lead it and the questions you would like to ask the students. Perhaps you believe that there are other, very different types of questions that the teacher could use to stimulate higher-level thinking and engage the students in a discussion that connects what they have read to their own lives.

Many reflective teachers use the revised Bloom's taxonomy (Anderson et al., 2001)) to think of discussion questions that promote the use of higher-level thinking processes. Discussion questions can be readily planned at every level of the taxonomy, just as other learning experiences are planned. The term *higher-level* refers to the top four levels of the hierarchy.

Higher-Level Thinking Processes

> Creating
>
> Evaluating
>
> Analyzing
>
> Applying

Lower-Level Thinking Processes

> Understanding
>
> Remembering

In the previous example, the teacher has asked only lower-level (remembering and understanding) questions. But you can plan your discussions to highlight the thinking processes of applying, analyzing, evaluating, and creating. Although this system can be used at any grade level and with any topic, the following examples are taken from the discussion of Dr. King's biography.

Remembering Level.   At this level, the learners are asked to recall specific bits of information such as terminology, facts, and details.

> When and where was Dr. King born?
>
> Who were the other members of his family?
>
> How did King's father and mother earn a living?
>
> What career did Dr. King choose?

Understanding Level.   At this level, the learners are asked to summarize and describe the main ideas of the subject matter in their own words.

> What does the term *ghetto* mean?
>
> What does *prejudice* mean?
>
> What did Dr. King accomplish that earned him the Nobel Peace Prize?

While the teacher in the previous example stopped here, a reflective teacher is likely to use these questions only as a beginning to establish the basic facts and ideas so that the class can then begin to engage in a spirited discussion of how Dr. King's life and accomplishments have affected their own lives.

Applying Level.   At this level, the learners are asked to apply what they have learned to their own lives or to other situations.

Are there ghettos in this community? What are they and who is affected by them?
Give an example of prejudice that has affected you.
If Dr. King were alive today, what do you think he would be most concerned about?
What do you think he would do about it?

Analyzing Level.   At this level, the learners are asked to describe patterns, cause-and-effect relationships, comparisons, and contrasts.

How did Rosa Parks's decision to sit in the front of the bus change King's life? How did her decision change history?
In what ways did Dr. King exhibit the qualities of a minister, a politician, and a teacher?
If Dr. King had never been born, how would your life be different today?

Evaluating Level.   At this level, the learners are asked to express their own opinions or make judgments about some aspect of the topic.

What do you believe was Dr. King's greatest contribution?
Which promotes greater social change: nonviolence or violence? Give a rationale or example to defend your answer.
What social problem do you most want to change in your life?

Creating Level.   At this level, the learners are asked to contribute a new and original idea on the topic.

Complete this phrase: I have a dream that one day . . . .
If there were suddenly a strong new prejudice against people that look just like you, what would you do about it?
How can we, as a class, put some of Dr. King's dreams into action?

Some teachers find that the revised Bloom's taxonomy is a useful and comprehensive guide for planning classroom discussion questions as well as other classroom activities. Others find that the taxonomy is more complex than they desire and that it is difficult to discriminate among some of the levels, such as comprehension and analysis or application and synthesis. Other systems of classifying thinking processes are available. Doyle (1986) proposes that teachers plan classroom tasks in four categories that are readily applicable to classroom discussions: (1) memory tasks, (2) procedural or routine tasks, (3) comprehension tasks, and (4) opinion tasks.

Classroom questions and discussion starters can be created to fit these four task levels, as follows:

Memory questions. Learners are asked to reproduce information they have read or heard before.

When and where was Dr. King born?
Who were the other members of his family?

Procedural or routine questions. Learners are asked to supply simple answers with only one correct response.

How did King's father and mother earn a living?
What career did Dr. King choose?

Comprehension questions. Learners are asked to consider known data and apply them to a new and unfamiliar context.

What does the term *ghetto* mean?
What does *prejudice* mean?
What did Dr. King accomplish that earned him the Nobel Peace Prize?
How did Rosa Parks's decision to sit in the front of the bus change King's life? How did her decision change history?
In what ways did Dr. King exhibit the qualities of a minister, a politician, and a teacher?

Opinion questions. Learners are asked to express their own point of view on an issue, with no correct answer expected.

> Are there ghettos in this community? What are they and who is affected by them?
>
> Give an example of prejudice that has affected you.
>
> If Dr. King were alive today, what do you think he would be most concerned about? What do you think he would do about it?
>
> Complete this phrase: I have a dream that one day . . . .
>
> If there were suddenly a strong new prejudice against people who look just like you, what would you do about it?
>
> How can we, as a class, put some of Dr. King's dreams into action?
>
> Which promotes more social change: nonviolence or violence? Give a rationale or example to defend your answer.
>
> What social problem do you most want to change in your life?

You will notice that the questions in Doyle's four categories are the same as the ones listed in the taxonomy's six levels. Questions at the understanding and analyzing levels are both contained in Doyle's comprehension category, and questions at the applying, evaluating, and creating levels are contained in the opinion category. Both of these systems offer teachers a comprehensive framework for planning a range of thought-provoking questions. You may choose to write out the questions you ask ahead of time, or you may just remind yourself as you participate in a discussion that you need to include questions from the higher-level thinking categories.

STRATEGIES FOR INTERACTIVE DISCUSSIONS

In some classrooms, what pass for discussions are really dull and repetitive question-and-answer periods. Some teachers may simply read aloud a list of questions from the teachers' manual of the textbook and call on students to recite the answers. As you probably recall from your own school experiences, when this type of "discussion" occurs, many students disengage entirely. They read ahead, doodle, or do homework surreptitiously. They seldom listen to their classmates' responses, and when it is their turn to recite, they frequently cannot find their place in the list of questions.

Reflective teachers value the process of considering alternatives and debating opinions and ideas. That is how reflective teachers approach the world themselves, and they are likely to want to stimulate the same types of behavior among their students.

Authentic learning experiences depend heavily on the promotion of high-quality and actively engaged thinking. Teachers who are committed to creating authentic learning for their students do so by planning discussions that stimulate higher-level thinking processes, problem-solving skills, critical thinking, and creative thinking and that acknowledge the multiple intelligences of their students.

These terms and concepts can be confusing and overwhelming for the beginning teacher, who may think it is necessary to establish separate programs for each of them. That is not the case, however. It is possible to discover common attributes among them and plan classroom discussions and other experiences that promote higher-level thinking, problem-solving skills, and critical and creative thinking in all seven of the multiple intelligences at the same time. One question may pose a problem, another may call for a creative response, a third may be analytical, and a fourth may ask students to evaluate a situation and make a critical judgment. The best (which is to say, the most highly engaging) classroom discussions do all of these in a spontaneous, nonregimented way.

The following sections describe various thinking processes along with alternatives for planning classroom discussions to promote these processes. As you read these sections, reflect on the similarities and differences; look for patterns and sequences; and consider how you would use, modify, and adapt these systems in your classroom.

Although these processes can be applied to both academic and nonacademic areas of the curriculum, we will illustrate how classroom discussions are created and managed, using the topic of racial discrimination as a common theme. In this example, the operational goal is to promote understanding of how racial discrimination affects the lives of human beings and to generate a sense of respect for individuals who are different from oneself.

Problem-Solving Discussions

Much has been written about the need for developing students' problem-solving and decision-making abilities. This can be done by presenting students with a complex problem and providing adequate scaffolding for them to learn how to solve problems. Although some solutions require paper and pencil or a hands-on experimental approach, classroom discussion can solve other problems.

To create productive problem-solving discussions, the teacher must understand the processes involved in problem solving and then structure the questions to guide students through that process. A problem is said to exist when "one has a goal and has not yet identified a means for reaching that goal. The problem may be wanting to answer a question, to prove a theorem, to be accepted or to get a job" (Gagne, 1985, p. 138).

According to cognitive psychologists, the framework for solving a problem consists of identifying a goal, a starting place, and all possible solution paths from the starting place to the goal. Some individuals are efficient and productive problem solvers; others are not. An excellent classroom goal for the beginning teacher is to help students become more efficient and more productive problem solvers.

Nonproductive problem solvers are likely to have difficulty identifying or defining the problem. They may simply feel that a puzzling situation exists, but they may not be aware of the real nature of the problem. Students who are poor problem solvers need experience in facing puzzling situations and defining problems. They also need experience in identifying and selecting worthwhile goals.

When a problem has been defined and a goal established, it is still possible to be either efficient or inefficient in reaching the goal. Efficiency in problem solving can be increased when students learn how to identify the alternative strategies to reach a chosen goal and recognize which ones are likely to provide the best and quickest routes to success. This can be done by helping students visualize the probable effects of each alternative and applying criteria to help them choose the most valuable means of solving the problem they have defined.

As in the teaching of higher-level thinking processes, several useful systems are available to teachers who want to teach students to become better problem solvers. Many teachers enjoy using the technique known as *brainstorming*, which includes four basic steps.

1. Define the problem.
2. Generate, without criticism or evaluation, as many solutions as possible.
3. Decide on criteria for judging the solutions generated.
4. Use these criteria to select the best possible solution

Brainstorming is an excellent way to generate classroom discussion about a puzzling issue. Rather than formulating a series of questions, the teacher supplies a dilemma or a puzzle, teaches the students the steps involved in brainstorming, and then leads them through the process itself.

In discussing the life of Martin Luther King, Jr., and helping students to understand the effects of racial discrimination, the teacher might use a portion of the classroom discussion to brainstorm answers to one of the most perplexing questions. For example, the teacher might choose to use brainstorming to expand discussion of the following questions:

If Dr. King were alive today, what do you think he would be most concerned about? What do you think he would do about it?

The techniques of brainstorming call for the teacher to pose the question or problem so that it engages students' interest and motivates them to take it seriously. Because students may not be proficient at discussion of this sort, it is frequently necessary for the teacher to give additional cues and suggestions as a scaffold. In this instance, the teacher might need to pose the original question and then follow it up with prompts such as these:

> What do you think he'd be concerned about in our community?
> What has been in the news lately that might alarm him?
> Who are the people in the world who are presently in need?
> What about threats to our environment?

Open-ended questions such as these generate many more responses than if they were not used. After recording all of the student responses on the chalkboard or overhead or computer projector, the teacher leads the students through a process of selecting the most important items for further consideration. This may be done by a vote or general consensus. When the list has been narrowed to several important issues, the teacher must then lead the students through the process of establishing criteria for judging the items.

Because the question is related to King's values, one possible criterion is to judge whether King showed concern for the issue in his lifetime. Another criterion might be the number of people who are threatened or hurt by the problem. After judging the items by these criteria, the class makes a judgment about which items would most concern King. Then the process of brainstorming begins again, but this time the problem that the class is considering is what King would be likely to do to help solve the problem. Generating responses to the first question—"If Dr. King were alive today, what do you think he would be most concerned about?"—will help students understand the many aspects of racial discrimination that exist today. By selecting one of these as the main concern and generating responses to the question "What do you think he would do about it?" the students will reflect on their own responsibilities to other human beings and on ways to increase tolerance and build a sense of community in their neighborhoods.

To moderate a brainstorming discussion, the teacher faithfully records every response generated by the students, no matter how trivial or impossible it sounds. The teacher then leads students through the process of eliminating the least important items and finally works through a process of establishing criteria to use in evaluating the best possible solutions.

Brainstorming alone does not solve problems. It merely trains students to think productively about problems and to consider alternative solutions. In some classrooms, teachers may wish to extend the hypothetical discussion of possible solutions to an actual attempt to solve a problem or at least contribute to a solution.

Group Investigations

Occasionally, a crisis or an unusual event will excite students' interest and concern. When the topic is appropriate, and especially if it relates to the curriculum for that grade level, teachers allow students to participate in an investigation of the puzzling event to learn as much as they can about the subject and, in the process, learn research and communication skills. Often teachers create puzzling situations or present unusual stimuli as a means of causing students to become curious and learn how to inquire and investigate to gather information that leads to accurate assessments and judgments.

Perhaps there is a change in local government or a national election that students want to know more about. Perhaps a change occurs in the way their own school is managed, or a community event unfolds around them and affects their lives. The first hint of student interest may occur in a classroom discussion. To the extent that reflective teachers are sensitive to their students' concerns, they may wish to allow students time to talk about the event.

The first discussion of the event may simply be time to air students' early opinions and express their feelings about the event. If the teacher decides that the event is a worthwhile issue, the class may be encouraged to read about it, ask questions, or interview other members of the community and bring back their findings for more expanded discussions. These, in turn, may lead students to form small investigative groups that attempt to discover as much as they can about the event and even suggest solutions to the problems or issues under discussion.

The teacher's role in this type of investigative discussion is to encourage students to find out more about the subject and to allow them opportunities to express their opinions and share their findings. The discussion may continue for a few days or a few weeks, depending on the seriousness of the event and its impact on the students' lives. Under the guidance of a caring, reflective teacher, this type of discussion is authentic learning at its very best.

When teachers want to stimulate curiosity and discussion, they may present a social dilemma or demonstrate a strange event. For example, the teacher may drop a number of different fruits and vegetables into a large, clear bowl of water, asking students to predict and observe which will sink and which will float. Students are encouraged to ask the teacher questions and to formulate hypotheses about floating and sinking objects. As the discussion progresses, the large-group discussion may be adjourned to allow small groups to conduct investigations of their own, reaching their own conclusions. After small-group investigations are completed, class members reconvene to share their hypotheses, demonstrate their investigations, and present their conclusions.

Discussions That Promote Critical Thinking

The term *critical thinking* is not a separate and distinct concept that is different from higher-level thinking processes and problem solving. It overlaps both of them. It is presented here in a separate section because, during the past few years, it has become a field of study with its own research base and suggested classroom processes.

The field of study known as critical thinking grew out of the philosophical study of logic, which was designed to train people to think about a single hypothesis deductively to arrive at a rational conclusion. Logical thinkers are prepared to deal with a single issue in depth, but sometimes they are not prepared to deal with unexpected evidence or ideas. They may be stumped when they are asked to think "outside the box" or to deal with complex ideas that defy one right answer.

Critical thinking, then, is partially defined as a complex set of thinking skills and processes that are believed to lead to fair and useful judgments. Lipman (1988) points out the strong association between the words *criteria* and *critical thinking*. Through the use of problem-solving discussions, students learn the technique of brainstorming and applying criteria to select the best solution.

But critical thinking is a much more multifaceted concept than problem solving. Critical thinking involves more than simply training students to use a set of strategies or procedures. It also involves establishing some affective goals for students to support them in becoming more independent and open-minded. Paul (1988), director of the Center of Critical Thinking at Sonoma State University in Rohnert Park, California, proposes that some of the affective attributes of critical thinking include independence, avoidance of egocentricity and stereotyping, and suspension of judgment until appropriate evidence has been gathered.

Paul recommends that school curricula be designed to teach students cognitive strategies such as observation, focusing on a question, distinguishing facts from opinions, distinguishing relevant from irrelevant information, judging the credibility of sources, recognizing contradictions, making inferences, and drawing conclusions. Because almost every specialist in critical thinking proposes a slightly different set of thinking processes and skills that compose critical thinking, reflective teachers need to judge for themselves which of the strategies to stress in their own classrooms.

A more recent addition to the knowledge base on critical thinking is the topic of critical literacy. Vasquez (2003) describes critical literacy as an approach to reading that empowers the reader to ask questions about the origin of the reading material. The reader is encouraged to

PRAXIS
Strategies for encouraging critical thinking are tested in PRAXIS™ Exam Section 2a: Instruction and Assessment.

ask questions about the author's point of view, the purpose of the text, and who benefits from the knowledge that is being shared. The reader is also taught to ask questions such as "Is there another voice that should be heard in this discussion?"

Discussions That Improve Observation Skills

When possible, in your curriculum, bring in photos or objects related to the subject you are studying. Invite students to read their stories, essays, or poems aloud for other students to listen and respond to. You may even be able to stage an event to elicit student observation skills. For example, as you study the concept of community, ask some students to role-play a disagreement; then ask them to describe what they observed, using as many details as they can. Call on as many students as possible and encourage each of them to make their own response to the situation. If they seem to be making impetuous or repetitive observations, guide their thinking with questions that ask them to explain or support their observations.

Show your students that they can observe with all five senses, not just sight. As you study nutrition, for example, allow students to taste a variety of foods and describe their taste observations. During a study of sound waves, provide a variety of different sounds and ask students to identify the objects they have heard. The more students use their five senses and discuss what they observe, the more likely they are to develop accurate, detailed schemata for the subject matter they are studying.

Discussions That Enhance Comparison Skills

In classroom discussions, compare two or more objects, stories, characters, or events by asking students first to articulate ways that the two subjects are the same. Take as many responses as possible. Then ask students to tell how the two are different. This type of discussion can occur in any subject area. You may ask them to compare fractions with percentages in math, George Washington and Abraham Lincoln in history, Somalia and the United States in geography, electric- and gasoline-powered engines in science, or the wording and effects of two different versions of a classroom rule in a classroom meeting.

Discussions That Guide Classification Skills

Introduce a collection of words or, for young children, a set of manipulative materials appropriate to the grade level. For example, you may use a collection of buttons, small toys, pasta shapes, or shells. When possible, conduct this type of discussion using cooperative groups. Ask each group to examine the collection, look for distinguishing attributes, and create a system for classifying the objects into groups. During follow-up discussions, a spokesperson for each group can describe the attributes that the group observed and present a rationale for the classification system used.

Older children can classify the words on their spelling lists, books or stories they have read, foods, games, clothing, famous people, or television programs. The best results occur when the teacher has no preestablished criteria or notion of right or wrong classification systems. As children discuss the characteristics of, for example, the shells or television programs they are classifying, they may discover some of the same attributes that adults have already described, or they may discover a completely original rationale on which to base their categories. The object of the discussion is not to get the most right answers but to participate in the open-ended process of sharing observations and making critical judgments they can defend with evidence.

Discussions That Identify Assumptions

Use advertisements for products that your students want to buy as a means of stimulating a discussion to identify assumptions people make. Show a newspaper ad for a product, and ask students to describe what they believe the product will be like based on the advertisement alone. Then discuss the actual product, and compare the students' prior assumptions with the real item.

Talk about assumptions human beings make about each other. Ask students to examine the meaning of clothing fads in their lives. When a subject arises that illustrates the effects of making decisions based on assumptions, take the time to discuss these events with your class. For example, ask students to discuss what assumptions are being made when they hear someone say, "He's wrong" or "She's the smartest girl in the class."

Socratic Dialogues

One form of discussion that reveals individual assumptions to the speaker and the listeners at the same time is the technique known as Socratic dialogue, in which the teacher probes to stimulate in-depth thinking among students. Teachers who use this method believe that individuals have many legitimate differences in opinion and values. They want to encourage their students to listen to each other to learn different points of view.

To conduct a Socratic dialogue, the teacher presents an interesting issue to the class and asks an individual to state an opinion on the case. With each participant, the teacher probes by asking the student to identify the assumptions and values that led to this opinion. Further questions may be posed to the same student to encourage clarification of the consequences of the student's opinion or the relative importance it has in the student's priorities.

This type of exchange between the teacher and a student may take several minutes and from 3 to 10 questions. While the teacher conducts the discussion with one student, the others are expected to listen carefully, comparing what they believe to what is being said by their classmate. Another student with a different opinion is likely to be the next subject of the Socratic dialogue. When the teacher believes that the most important issues have been raised by the dialogues, then a general class discussion can be used to express how opinions may have been changed by listening or participating in the Socratic dialogues.

Discussions That Enhance Creative Thinking

Can individuals learn to be creative? Perhaps the more important question is, Do individuals learn to be uncreative? More than a century ago, William James (1890) stated his belief that education trains students to become "old fogies" in the early grades by training them to adopt habits of convergent, conformist thinking.

Divergent thinking is the opposite of convergent thinking because it deviates from common understanding and accepted patterns. Guilford (1967) contributed a definition of divergent thinking that is still well accepted and has become the basis for E. Paul Torrance's (1966) well-known tests for creativity. Guilford describes (and Torrance's test measures) four attributes of divergent thinking: *fluency*, *flexibility*, *originality*, and *elaboration*. In other words, a divergent thinker is one who generates many ideas (fluency), is able to break with conformist or set ideas (flexibility), suggests ideas that are new in the present context (originality), and contributes details that extend or support the idea beyond a single thought (elaboration).

Classroom discussions can be designed to help students develop these four attributes of creativity. In a technique similar to brainstorming, the teacher can ask students to generate many responses to a single question as a means of helping them to become more fluent in their thinking. For example, given our topic of King's "I Have a Dream" speech, the teacher may begin the process with the unfinished sentence, "I have a dream that one day . . . ."

Students may be asked to write their own responses for several minutes before the actual discussion begins. This allows each student to work for fluency individually. Then the ideas on the paper are shared, and other new ideas are created as a result of the discussion. To promote flexibility, the teacher may ask students to imagine making their dreams come true and suggest ways that they could do this, using flexible and original strategies rather than rigid and ordinary methods. Finally, to extend the students' elaborative thought, the teacher may select one

PRAXIS
Techniques for stimulating creative thinking are tested in PRAXIS™ Exam Section 2a: Instruction and Assessment.

dream and ask the entire class to focus on it and create a detailed vision and an in-depth plan to accomplish it.

Einstein and Infeld (1938) added an additional dimension to our understanding of creative thinking:

> The formulation of a problem is often more essential than its solution, which may be merely a matter of mathematical or experimental skill. To raise new questions, new possibilities, to regard old problems from a new angle, requires creative imagination and marks real advance in science. (p. 92)

Problem solving, then, is related to creative thinking. It is readily apparent that the methods described for improving problem solving involve critical thinking and that both involve the use of higher-level thinking processes. Whatever we call it, the goal of aiding students in developing better thinking skills is an integral part of any classroom discussion.

Just as we respect Einstein's ability to pose new problems, so should we respect and develop our own and our students' capacity to ask questions and suggest new ways of solving age-old problems. Certainly, the teaching profession needs people with the capability of regarding old educational problems from a new angle. Often it is the newest and youngest members of a faculty who see things from a helpful new perspective and suggest new ways of dealing with difficult school issues.

Another dimension of creativity involves the production of something useful, interesting, or otherwise valued by at least a small segment of society. In synthesis, a creative thinker is one who poses new problems; raises new questions; and then suggests solutions that are characterized by fluency, flexibility, originality, and elaboration. The solutions result in a unique product for that individual in those circumstances.

Discussions That Encourage Imagination and Inventiveness

In the process of discussing almost any type of subject, teachers always have opportunities to ask students to consider, "What if . . . ?" Imagine living on an island with no electricity. What would your life be like? How would it be different than it is now? What could we do to make our school a better place? What would you do if you were the main character in the story? How would your actions change the ending of the book? For many reflective teachers, these questions are as important as those that test student recall of information or understanding of the main idea. While it is seldom necessary to plan a discussion with the sole intent of stimulating children's imagination, it is a worthy goal to include these types of questions in any classroom discussion.

Another technique is to assign a group of students a certain task that requires them to discuss strategies and invent a method for carrying them out. For example, give students a single dollar bill and ask them to discover how high a stack of 1 million dollar bills would be. Give them a few pieces of cloth and some string and ask them to make an effective parachute. Have each group work together to design a map of the school property. These real-life and simulated tasks provide incentives for authentic discussions on substantive and meaningful topics.

Prewriting Discussions

Another method that teachers may use is to focus on images, analogies, and metaphors in creative discussions. These are very effective discussions before students begin writing because they encourage students to use these literary techniques in their writing. Gordon and Poze (1975) suggest that analogies allow us to make the strange familiar and the familiar strange. In discussions, teachers can present an unfamiliar idea or object and assist students in describing it using sensory images or comparing it with another, more familiar concept. For example, when presented with a rusty lawnmower engine, students may be led to describe it according to size, shape, imaginary sounds, or uses. They can compare it to other, more familiar objects. The teacher may ask students what the machine reminds them of.

Fluency	Explain the rules of brainstorming: (1) Go as fast as you can, (2) list all ideas, (3) a recorder writes *all* ideas, (4) no judging of ideas, (5) no negative comments. Divide the class into groups of four or five, and ask them to brainstorm about birds.
Flexibility	To illustrate flexibility, ask the groups to look at their lists and see how many different categories their answers fall into. (These might be athletic teams, musical groups, species of birds, food from birds, idiomatic expressions, etc.)
Originality	To illustrate originality or rarity, ask the groups to look at their lists and see which items are the most original, or are rare. They may have come up with "Larry Bird" or "Bird of Paradise." If an item is listed by only *one* group, it is original.
Elaboration	To illustrate elaboration, ask each student to draw a picture of one of the items on the group list. Ask them to draw with detail, and try to make their drawing unique. Once they have completed their drawings, ask them to pass it to a neighbor, who will add to, or elaborate on, the drawing.
Transformation	Ask the students to look at all the drawings in their group, and choose one that can be changed enough to transform it into something else.

Figure 8.1   An exercise in divergent production.
Source: Adapted from J. Piirto, (2004) Understanding Creativity.

This may generate responses such as "The machine is like my old shoes." Then the teacher probes by asking the child to tell why the machine and the old shoes are alike: "Because they are both old and muddy." Another child may see the machine in a whole different context: "The machine is like a kangaroo because it has a lot of secret compartments." Discussions like this can begin to have a life of their own and can lead to fresh new ways to express one's ideas.

Do schools enhance or undermine the conditions and processes that encourage creativity? Do textbooks, curriculum guides, rules, regulations, and expectations support the development of creative thinking and the processes needed to create a unique product? Caring and reflective teachers do. They work very hard to create stimulating classroom discussions that assist students in learning to become creative thinkers. Teachers may need to plan some creative activities to stimulate this type of thinking. See Figure 8.1 for an example of this type of activity.

Discussions That Address Multiple Intelligences

You have created a thematic unit plan that has an interesting topic and many opportunities for students to read, research, and report on their findings. One day near the end of the unit, you will want to have a lively interactive discussion to allow your students to report on what they have learned and discovered on their own about the topic. For example, Judy Eby once planned and taught a unit called Aviation and Map-making. This unit began with students making maps of their school and neighborhoods. Then the class examined maps made by the early explorers who traveled the globe by ship and created maps of the new worlds they discovered. The students had compared the early maps with modern maps and laughed at how inaccurate the early maps appeared. As a culmination of this unit plan, Eby hired a pilot and a 10-seat airplane to take the students on short flights over their school and neighborhood. They took photos of the ground and then created new aerial maps based on their photos.

Let's imagine a discussion taking place a few days after the students' flights. The general topic of discussion is "How has aviation changed map-making?"

To promote linguistic intelligence, questions involving vocabulary might be asked: "What is a map legend? What is the difference between latitude and longitude?" Logical-mathematical intelligence can be stimulated by asking questions about the map scales: "How accurate are the first maps you made? Does the entire map have the same scale or does it vary? How accurate are the scales of the aerial maps you are making? Why are they likely to be more consistent?"

This whole project was an excellent example of a school program that develops visual-spatial intelligence. There can be many discussion questions in which students refer to their maps or show something on their photos. "Can you show us an example of how your map is more accurate now than it was before the aerial photo experience?"

Bodily kinesthetic intelligence was involved in creating the first maps. Students can be asked to describe the process they used to walk around the school or their neighborhood and find ways to see the big picture of what they were drawing. "Did you have to climb on something high and look down at the area in order to draw it accurately? Did you pace off the distances and then convert them to inches or centimeters?"

Musical intelligence does not come easily to this unit. If it is not appropriate, there is no need to include it just for the sake of including it. Other units may have many musical applications. It would be a stretch, but you might ask students to create short songs about their experience in the air or sing a song or two from early American history that refers to maps or travels or distances.

Naturalist intelligence can be promoted by referring to the land and its uses. "In your view, is the land near our school used well or are there things that you would like to do differently? By looking at your photos and maps, what do you appreciate about the world that you didn't seem to notice before?"

To promote interpersonal intelligence, the discussion could turn to how well people worked together to create their maps. If a cooperative learning model was used, the maps may have been the work of a small committee rather than an individual. "How well did your group work together on the first map you made? Did you work more effectively or less effectively on the second maps?"

During the evaluation phase of this unit, the teacher can tap into students' intrapersonal intelligence by conducting an interactive assessment of what each student accomplished. "What are you most proud of accomplishing during this unit? What new interests have you developed during this experience? What do you want to improve?"

ROLE OF THE TEACHER IN LEADING DISCUSSIONS

PRAXIS
Strategies for encouraging student involvement are tested in PRAXIS™ Exam Section 2a: Instruction and Assessment.

Discussions that promote the use of multiple intelligences and critical or creative thinking can be exciting classroom events for both students and teachers, but beginning teachers may find it difficult to elicit responses from students who are not used to taking part in such activities. What if you ask a wonderful question and the pupils do not respond? There is nothing quite so demoralizing for a teacher as a lack of response from students.

"Now boys and girls, how do you think the sound got onto this tape?"

No response. Interminable silence. Finally the teacher leaps in to break the tension and gives the answer. Everybody, including the teacher, visibly relaxes. Whew! Let's not try that again.

This example of a nondiscussion is more common than is desirable. Students in your classroom may not have had opportunities to think creatively and express their own ideas. If not, they may be reluctant to do so at first. They may believe that you expect one right answer, just as most of their teachers have in the past. Because they do not know the one right answer, they may prefer to remain quiet rather than embarrass themselves by giving a wrong answer. Your response to their silence will tell them a great deal. If you jump in with your own response, they will learn that their own responses were not really wanted after all.

Scaffolding is a necessary component of teaching critical thinking and discussion strategies to students. Be explicit about what you do expect from them in a discussion. Tell them that there are no wrong answers and that all opinions are valued. If they still hesitate, provide cues and prompts without providing answers. Simplify or rephrase the question so that they are able to answer it. If the question "How do you think the sound got onto this tape?" gets no response, rephrase it. "What sounds do you hear on this tape? Can you imagine how those sounds were captured on a piece of plastic like this? Do you think machinery was used? What kinds of machines are able to copy sounds?" These supporting questions provide scaffolds for thinking and talking about unknown and unfamiliar ideas.

Another consideration in leading discussions is to *value* silence rather than fear it. Silence can indicate that students are truly engaged in reflection. By allowing a few moments of silence, a teacher may find that the resulting discussions are much more creative and productive. Students need time to process the question. They need time to bring forward the necessary schema to their working memories and to consider the question in light of what they already know about the topic. Some students need more time than others to see connections between new ideas and already stored information and to generate a response of their own.

Some teachers consciously use *wait time*, requiring a short period of silence after each significant question is asked. Students are taught to listen quietly, then think quietly for several seconds and not raise their hands to respond until the wait time has passed. Rowe (1974) found that when teachers used a wait time of 3 to 5 seconds, more students were able to generate a response to the question. Without a planned wait time, the same group of fast-thinking students is likely to dominate all discussions. With the wait time, even students who are more hesitant will have an opportunity to consider what it is they do believe before hearing the opinions of others.

Lyman (1989) recommends that teachers employ a system called *listen, think, pair, share* to improve both the quantity and the quality of discussion responses. This technique employs a structured wait time at two different points in the discussion. When a question is asked, wait time goes into effect while students jot down ideas and think about their responses. Students are then expected to discuss their ideas in pairs for a minute. Then a general discussion takes place. After each student makes a contribution, other members of the class are expected to employ a second wait time of 3 to 5 seconds to process what their classmate has said before they raise their hands to respond.

The quantity and quality of students' responses may be improved by introducing the questions early in the class period, followed by reading, a lecture, or another type of presentation and actual discussion of the questions themselves. This strategy follows the principle of using the question as an advance organizer. Giving students the question before presentation of new material alerts them to what to listen or read for and allows sufficient time for them to process the information they receive in terms of the question. When teachers use this technique, they rarely experience a silent response.

Another strategy that promotes highly interactive discussions involves the physical setup in the classroom. To facilitate critical and creative thinking, students must be able to hear and see one another during the discussion. Arranging the chairs in a circle, rectangle, U-shape, or semicircle ensures that each student feels like a contributing member of a group.

Meyers (1986) notes that a hospitable classroom environment is the most important factor in engaging students' attention and interest and promoting their creative responses during discussion:

> Much of the success in teaching critical thinking rests with the tone that teachers set in their classrooms. Students must be led gently into the active roles of discussing, dialoguing, and problem-solving. They will watch very carefully to see how respectfully teachers field comments and will quickly pick up nonverbal cues that show how open teachers really are to student questions and contributions. (p. 67)

Reflective teachers are critical and creative thinkers themselves. They welcome opportunities to model their own thinking strategies for their students and plan experiences that encourage the development of their students' higher-level thinking processes. They are likely to make even the simplest discussion an exercise in problem solving, reasoning, logic, and creative and independent thinking. They examine the subjects taught in the curriculum in search of ways to allow their students to learn to think and communicate their ideas. They plan discussions involving the creation and testing of hypotheses in science. They promote thinking that avoids stereotypes and egocentricity in social studies. They teach their students to suspend judgment when they lack sufficient evidence in discussions of math problems. They promote flexible, original thinking in discussions of literature. Discussions in every part of the curriculum can be crafted in ways that teach individuals to think reflectively, critically, and creatively.

Communicating with Parents

Helping students feel comfortable and confident enough to actively participate in class discussions can be greatly enhanced if parents understand the goal of participation and encourage their children to become engaged in the process. A combination of communication strategies is often needed to convey the importance of home–school cooperation.

Introduce the topic at a parent meeting early in the year. Help parents understand the importance of their children participating in class discussions; the engagement, higher-level, and problem-solving thinking skills that they gain from these types of discussions; and the need for their involvement at home. Many parents think of their role in discussions as providing the answer. Help them to understand that students quickly learn to turn off thinking and just wait for the answer when they are conditioned to that type of parental role.

Help parents learn to provide scaffolding questions by engaging them in an activity where they have to generate such questions. In other words, just as you are training your students to engage in invigorating discussions, teach your students' parents to participate as providers of scaffolding. Tell the parents that you will be working on learning discussions all year and that one of their responsibilities should be to ask, "Did you have any good discussions in school today?" By having the students recall and recount the discussions, they will have a second opportunity to explore the ways in which the ideas were generated and the solutions (if any) that were generated through brainstorming.

Ask the parents to involve their children in these same types of discussions at home. Discussions around the dinner table can give all the children in the family confidence in engaging in higher-level discussions and problem solving. Everyday problems or challenges, community problems, or current events can serve as topics for these types of discussions.

Periodically during the year, send home a class newsletter that includes some news about the ways in which you are using class discussions to address problems, current events, or creative challenges. These articles will serve as reminders to the parents to ask about class discussions and to engage their family in these types of discussions. The newsletter items can serve as a starting point for family discussions.

GUIDED GROUP EXPLORATION

To give the class practice in generating scaffolding questions, provide an experience with this goal.

1. Divide the class into small groups. Give each group a discussion topic that has a variety of objectives. Also, give each group some transparency film and transparency markers.
2. Ask the groups to generate scaffolding questions they could use to stimulate thinking and discussion, write their topic and scaffolding questions on their transparencies, and be prepared to give a short presentation about their results.
3. Give the groups time to work, discuss, and create their transparencies.
4. Bring the groups back together to share their results.

REFLECTIVE ACTION ACTIVITY FOR YOUR PROFESSIONAL PORTFOLIO

Your task is to write a short paragraph on how you would plan a class discussion following a lesson on a topic of your choice

Points to consider:
1. Capture attention by means of a
   - Question.
   - Film clip.
   - Story or case description.

   Give a description of how you would capture students' attention.
2. Ask questions.
   - Ask open-ended questions that are directed to the whole group.
   - What will you do if no one answers?
3. What happens if an answer is wrong?
   - How can the student find the correct answer?
   - What happens if the answer is partly right?
4. Keep talking on the topic.
   - Summarize what the class has done.
   - Summarize what the class needs to do next.

   How will you present this summary: on whiteboard, butcher's paper, or the overhead projector?
5. When an audience member's comment is off the point, say something like, "Thanks for giving us that information Emma. Let's think about it in relation to . . . . ."
6. Use the whiteboard or overhead transparency to summarize the discussion.
   - Advantages of this are . . . .
   - Disadvantages of this are . . . .
7. What will you do if the discussion gets out of control or off the topic?
8. What will you do if some people don't contribute to the discussion?
9. What will you do if one person becomes the "class clown" and dominates the discussion with his or her negative contributions?
10. What will you do if students don't do the reading and feel it's okay to talk "off the top of their heads".

References

Anderson, L., Kratwohl, D., Airasian, P., Cruikshank, K., Mayer, R., Pintrich, P., Raths, J., & Wittrock, M. (Eds.) (2001) *A taxonomy for learning, teaching, and assessing: A revision of Bloom's taxonomy of educational objectives*. New York: Longman Publishers.

Bloom, B. (1981). *All our children learning*. New York: McGraw-Hill.

Bloom, B., Engelhart, M., Furst, E., Hill, W., & Krathwohl, D. (1956). *Taxonomy of educational objectives: Cognitive domain*. New York: Longman.

Doyle, W. (1986). Classroom organization and management. In M. Wittrock (Ed.), *Handbook of research on teaching* (3rd ed.), (pp. 392–420). Upper Saddle River, NJ: Merrill/Prentice Hall.

Einstein, A., & Infeld, L. (1938). *The evolution of physics*. New York: Simon & Schuster.

Gagne, E. (1985). *The cognitive psychology of school learning*. Boston: Little, Brown.

Gordon, W., & Poze, T. (1975). *Strange and familiar*. Cambridge MA: Porpoise.

Guilford, J. (1967). *The nature of human intelligence*. New York: McGraw-Hill.

James, W. (2009). *Principles of psychology*. Scotts Valley, CA: IAM.

Lipman, M. (1988). Critical thinking—what can it be? *Educational Leadership, 46*(1), 38–43.

Lyman, F. (1989). Rechoreographing the middle-level minuet. *Early Adolescence Magazine, 4*(1), 22–24.

Meyers, C. (1986). *Teaching students to think critically*. San Francisco: Jossey-Bass.

Paul, R. (1988). *31 Principles of critical thinking*. Rohnert Park, CA: Center for Critical Thinking and Moral Critique.

Piirto, J. (2004). *Understanding creativity*. Scottsdale, Arizona: Great Potential Press.

Rowe, M. (1974). Wait time and reward as instructional variables, their influence on language, logic and fate control. Part 1: Wait time. *Journal of Research on Science Teaching, 11*, 81–94.

Torrance, E. (1966). *Torrance tests of creative thinking*. Bensenville, IL: Scholastic Testing Service.

Vasquez, V. (2003). Getting beyond "I like the book": Creating space for critical literacy in K–6 classrooms. Newark, DE: International Reading Association.

Now go to Topics #7 and 9: Strategies for Teaching and Group Interaction Models in the MyEducationLab (www.myeducationlab.com) for your course, where you can:

- Find learning outcomes for these topics along with the national standards that connect to these outcomes.
- Complete Assignments and Activities that can help you more deeply understand the chapter content.
- Apply and practice your understanding of the core teaching skills identified in the chapter with the Building Teaching Skills and Dispositions learning units.

CHAPTER 9

Balancing Standards and Creative Activities: The Importance of the Arts

As standards-based education is becoming the norm in American education, reflective teachers have become concerned. They recognize the need for a balance between a carefully sequenced, standards-based lesson with clearly defined objectives and the students' need to experience creative activities that stretch the imagination and provide authentic opportunities for problem solving and innovation (Burke-Adams 2007).

Elliot Eisner, a professor in education and art at Stanford University, maintains that lessons in the arts accomplish a number of outcomes for students:

- They teach children to make judgments about qualitative relationships. Other areas of the curriculum value rules and correct answers, but in the arts, students learn to make judgments, choices, and decisions.
- The arts teach students that problems can have more than one solution and that questions can have more than one right answer.
- The arts teach that there are many ways to see and interpret the world.
- Learning in the arts requires students to surrender to anticipated possibilities and to engage in complex problem solving.
- In the arts, students find that words cannot always capture the essence of what we know.
- The arts teach the promise of subtlety. Students learn that small differences can have large effects.
- The arts teach students to think thoroughly and to find ways to make images become real.
- The arts support students in expressing their emotions and finding their own poetry.

- The place of arts in the curriculum symbolizes to students what adults believe is important. (Adapted from Eisner, retrieved from www.oregonfoto.org)

Creative adults often talk about their imaginative childhood experiences. Giving a child the chance to play without the invading eyes of adults is one way adults can be supportive of the child's creativity. *Play* is a child's *work* during the early years. It is during play that they learn to imagine, pretend, and even create original dialogue. Children who have created dialogue for favorite toys find writing dialogue for characters in their original plays and stories much easier. When children have engaged in creative play, they move much more naturally into artistic and learning endeavors such as drawing, music, and writing. Children who play with blocks, Legos©, and Lincoln Logs© know much more about how things work and their spatial relationships. They often can delve into scientific experimentation without fear. Creativity is often nurtured in an environment that provides time and place for solitude, private thought, and experimentation.

You may think, "But I also need to ensure the child's safety." This is a natural concern, especially in today's society. As teachers and parents, the answer to this concern lies in finding a secluded place within earshot but one that gives the child a sense of privacy for his or her creative play. In a busy classroom, this can be a table set apart that is blocked off by using a screen or portable bulletin board. It can also be a tent set up indoors or just outside the classroom but within sight. A large, empty cardboard box filled with throw pillows is a great privacy place. Allowing the children to paint the outside of the box with their own designs gives them ownership.

One teacher had a dad who did construction work, and he built a loft in the classroom. He put up a see-through fence around the edge of the loft to make it safe and carpeted it (with a remnant purchased for $10) to make it quiet. The children called it the writing loft and equipped it with some small tables and writing materials. The students did a lot of writing that year. The area under the loft was called the Hidey Hole and contained tables and art materials. The second-graders tended to write their stories in the loft and then come down to the Hidey Hole and illustrate them, using a wide range of art materials.

Because time to think and experiment will always be scarce in classrooms, it is important that parents understand the child's need for privacy and time to explore new concepts. Teachers can help by discussing this need at parent meetings and giving parents suggestions for finding private space for their children's creative endeavors. At home, especially in large families, it is often difficult to find secluded places for creative activities. Families will need support to understand the importance of this need for a small, private space that belongs to each child. When you are creating, you sometimes need to leave your project unfinished, which provides incubation time for creative thought. The child needs to know that his or her projects will be safe when left behind.

Some of the same suggestions for secluded areas in classrooms also work in the home setting:

- Adrienne recalls that one of her sons did a lot of writing under the dining room table, an area that was rarely used except on holidays. In a family with five sons, this was his creative solution for private space.

- Another son had a set of bunk beds in his room, slept on the top bunk, and removed the bottom bed to create a private space for his creative projects. He curtained off the bottom area using old drapes he found in a storage closet. He moved a card table and folding chair into his private space, but he usually worked stretched out on the rug.

- A third son set up a work space in the garage because his projects always seemed to involve power tools. He found two old two-drawer filing cabinets and an old door and set up a workbench. The filing cabinets gave him storage space, and he was close to power outlets and a water supply for cleanup.

All of these arrangements require patience, understanding, and valuing of creative projects on the part of the rest of the family. They are often not the neatest areas in the house.

ENCOURAGE CREATIVITY—PROVIDE MATERIALS

Materials from Homes

Providing materials for the creative child sometimes requires some creativity on the part of teachers and parents. Art and writing materials, dancing lessons, music lessons all cost money. Some materials are provided by schools, but many of the materials end up being paid for by the teachers. Enlist parents in saving items that would normally be thrown away but could be used instead for creative projects. Include a Classroom Needs section in your classroom newsletter and ask parents to donate useful items for the classroom. Items that are commonly saved for classroom use include the following:

- Empty paper towel and toilet tissue rolls—for paper sculptures, finger puppets.
- Empty egg cartons—for 3D animals, mixing paint colors, containers for small beads and other decorative items.
- Leftover gift wrap and wallpaper—for collages, book covers for publishing books.
- Scrap paper of all kinds—for writing drafts, paper sculptures.
- Newspaper—for papier-mâché, to protect desks and carpets.
- Small plastic containers (yogurt, photographic film)—for storing small items such as buttons and beads or for mixing paint.

Materials from Merchants

Learn to ask for items from merchants who will be discarding them. Leave an empty cardboard box at a local print shop with your phone number on the box, and ask the manager to put any paper scraps into the box for use with your kindergarten class. Make it a practice to go by the print shop every week to claim the paper scraps so that the manager is never inconvenienced. One teacher reports that she put paper scraps in one of the art centers and suggested that the students might want to make fancy bookmarks. The first girl who went to that center made "book bracelets." She drew illustrations from her favorite books on each scrap and then taped them together to make bracelets. Before the end of the day, all the students were wearing book bracelets.

Your local print shop may keep a big bag of "holes" from their hole punch machine. Because the print shop is punching holes in many colors of paper, the paper circles are multicolored. The children can use them to create texture in their artwork.

Other Sources of Materials

Some schools have projects where they ask for donations of musical instruments for the music program. They are often amazed at the number of instruments that are stored away and not being used. At least one school found a retired musician who was willing to give music lessons as a volunteer. It is important to keep your community in mind. Service clubs are often looking for projects, and all they ask is that you come and speak to the service club and explain your project. They also like to see the results of their donations, so make a habit of taking a lot of pictures.

Remind parents that art and writing materials make wonderful birthday gifts. Before major gift-giving holidays, you might include gift suggestions in your class newsletter. Busy parents often get caught up in a shopping mode led by television advertising instead of sound child development theory. A gentle reminder that art and writing materials (such as clay, paint, paper, markers, and writing tablets) inspire creative activities is often appreciated. Legos™, blocks, Lincoln Logs™, and magnetic rods all serve to encourage scientific experimentation. Delores Durkin's research (1975) found that all the children who entered kindergarten already knowing how to read had toy chalkboards at home with which to experiment.

PRAXIS
Approaches for diverse learning styles are tested in PRAXIS™ Exam Section 1b: Students as Learners.

SETTING A CREATIVE TONE

The atmosphere of a school or home can support creativity. When you walk through the halls of a school that values and supports creativity, it is obvious. Products of creative work are displayed everywhere. Children's art, sculpture, writing, and science experiments, both completed and in progress, are in evidence.

For children to extend their creative potential, the potential has to be nurtured. Adults who work with children can set a creative tone by modeling creative behaviors, challenging creative thought, and exposing children to the creative works of others, including themselves.

It has been said that what we love, we will pass along to our children. Mister Rogers of television fame was a good example of this adage. At a national conference of the National Association of Education of Young Children (NAEYC) in Anaheim, California, the topic of his speech was passing along our passions. He talked about exposing children to art forms that they might never experience without our influence. He showed film clips from his program *Mr. Roger's Neighborhood*, where he had guests who demonstrated playing the cello or performing modern dance. We may never know or come to appreciate how many children were led into creative pursuits by watching his enormously popular program.

A large elementary school in Titusville, Florida, was built around a lovely indoor courtyard. Due to budget cutbacks, the school had no art teacher, and some of the teachers were not comfortable teaching art. The primary specialist tried to support them as best she could, but her time was spread too thin. As a way of providing the school with a creative atmosphere, the primary specialist invited local artists, starting with some of the parents, to work in the courtyard about once a week. They would set up and paint or sculpt in the courtyard, and the teachers would bring their classes through to watch and to ask questions. The children were fascinated with the processes they observed. The teachers planned follow-up art activities in their classrooms. One of the dads built some wonderful picture frames that had slots in the sides so the pictures could be changed regularly. Each classroom was responsible for choosing an art product to be displayed in the courtyard monthly, using these lovely frames. The first of each month, the artist of the month was called to the courtyard to have his or her picture taken with the framed artwork. This exposure to creative tone prompted the teachers to incorporate more creative expression into their curricula.

CREATIVE ATMOSPHERE

Developing a creative atmosphere at your school is vital to the students with creative potential; it also opens avenues of expression for all the students. Many of today's students have not had exposure to many forms of creative expression, and the school can open these doors for them. Explore possibilities by contacting local orchestras, ballet companies or dance schools, theatre groups, and artists to see if they have any children's programs. Local groups are often available to come to the schools and provide programming that is appropriate for children.

Technology is another way that creative activities can be made available to students while still addressing state standards. When a school acquired one computer per classroom, many of the teachers were uncomfortable using it in the classroom, so the principal planned after-school workshops to teach them how to use a free word-processing program. The parent-teacher association (PTA) purchased rolling carts for each of the computers and storage disks for each student. The computers were housed in each classroom until 1:30 each day. When the kindergarteners went home at 1:30, a "computer mover" student from each class moved the computers to a large multipurpose room that

also housed two kindergarten classes. The kindergarten teachers then taught a computer lab for the school from 2:00 to 3:30 each day. The computer lab was used for publishing student work. The students could work on the computer in their classroom during the mornings if they had time, and they could bring their storage disks to the computer lab during the time their class was scheduled or during after-school computer time. They got to publish their writing in the computer lab. Parent volunteers were available to help students make covers for their books (using donated materials such as contact or wallpaper as covers).

At the end of the school year, an English teacher from the nearby high school was invited to bring one of her creative writing classes to the elementary school for a writer's conference. The elementary students shared their books in small groups, and the high school students shared some of their writings. The high school students answered questions and gave encouragement to the younger budding writers. The elementary students were excited about the experience, and many of them participated in a summer writer's workshop that year. The high school students told their teachers how impressed they were with the writing done by the younger students, and several of them volunteered during the summer workshop.

HOW TO ENCOURAGE CREATIVITY IN STUDENTS

Teachers can do several things to foster creativity in their students and to provide a balance between the structure needed to achieve standards and the open-ended teaching and thought process needed for creative thinking. Here is a list of ideas:

1. *Be a role model.* Teachers and parents can set a wonderful example by involving themselves in creative activities and sharing their passions with the children. When you are teaching writing, share your writing with your students. Use your own writing as an example when teaching revision and editing. It is empowering for students to see that their teacher's writing can be improved and that teachers want their feedback before making decisions about what to revise.

2. *Expose children to the creative works of others.* Teachers can support parents by helping them become aware of creative projects that are part of the community. Use your class newsletter to let them know of art fairs, music festivals, theatre productions, and other artistic endeavors in your local area. Many of these activities are free or of very low cost. If your community theatre doesn't have a student ticket price, approach them and ask about providing one to the community.

In larger cities, art galleries and museums are often available for field trips. The teachers are usually the ones who choose the field trips to be taken. Unfortunately, the current trend is that field trips are eliminated because of cost and liability issues. As teachers and parents, we need to serve as advocates for our children, especially in these areas. Children who have never seen great art, heard professional symphonies, experienced live opera or ballet, or attended the theatre are much less likely to participate in these activities as adults. They won't know how to enjoy these beautiful artistic expressions without having some early experiences and instruction.

3. *Implement interdisciplinary work and authentic problem-solving challenges.* Units of study that integrate different disciplines and allow students to approach a topic from many different perspectives provide more opportunities for creative thinking and activities (Erez, 2004). Open-ended projects and assignments that give students choices allow them to express themselves using their strongest intelligences and passions (Ritchhart, 2004).

Projects that encourage students to design new products for everyday common use allow them to use creative thinking in problem solving. A helpful Web site for creative problem solving can be found at http://www.LGReal.org.

4. *Find time for students to engage in extension and/or enrichment projects.* In today's fast-paced classrooms where meeting basic standards is vital, finding time for extensive study to delve into projects in depth is difficult. Teachers who value creative activities are innovative in finding the time. Some teachers plan extended day activities a day or two each week. With parental permission, the students stay "after school" to participate in activities that allow them to explore some of their academic topics in more depth and integrate them with art, music, science, and technology. In some schools, teams of teachers work together to provide these experiences, each leading students in activities according to the teacher's areas of expertise. Do not overlook community resources for these types of activities. Local colleges often have professors or students who can be enlisted to lead challenging activities. As volunteerism and community involvement become more popular, many businesses are giving their employees time to volunteer as club leaders after school.

5. *Utilize technology.* Many computer programs foster creative activities. Support students in using word processing programs for writing. Concept maps, graphic software, and CAD/CAM applications all support creative production. Students can use multimedia such as PowerPoint to support oral presentations. Using digital cameras and video production programs to produce videos and graphic displays encourages students to write scripts for their productions and design costumes and props appropriate for different times in history (Herrell & Fowler, 1997).

6. *Make a conscience effort to differentiate your instruction.* Use both sequential and creative modes of instruction to meet the individual needs of your students. This balance is a critical piece in providing equitable opportunities for all students to demonstrate their strengths (Burke-Adams, 2007).

7. *Value and appreciate the uniqueness of your students.* Some of our most creative scientists, musicians, and artists were not successful in school because of the limited definition of what it meant to be a "good student" in past times. In today's schools, and with Gardner's research on multiple intelligences (1983) and our understanding of the importance of authentic problem solving, teachers can celebrate innovative thought and unique solutions. They might, quite possibly, be supporting the next Albert Einstein!

THE SELF-FULFILLING PROPHECY

Children and adolescents are extremely perceptive. They understand and react to subtle differences in adult expectations. This effect has come to be known as the self-fulfilling prophecy. The process appears to work like this: (1) The teacher makes a decision about the behavior and achievement to be expected from a certain student; (2) the teacher treats students differently depending on the expectations for each one; (3) this treatment communicates to the student what the teacher expects and affects the student's self-concept, achievement motivation, and aspirations either positively or negatively; (4) if the treatment is consistent over time, it may permanently shape the child's achievement and behavior. High-expectation students tend to achieve at higher and higher levels, whereas the achievement of low-expectation students tends to decline.

What is it that teachers do to communicate their high or low expectations for various students? This is the question that interested Good and Brophy (2002), who found that some teachers treat low achievers this way:

1. Seat them far away from the teacher.
2. Call on them less often.
3. Wait less time for them to answer questions.
4. Criticize them more frequently.
5. Praise them less frequently.
6. Provide them with less detailed feedback.
7. Demand less work and effort from them. (p. 55)

STEREOTYPES STIFLE CREATIVITY

The Marlboro man and Barbie (of doll fame) are probably not the most appropriate creative models. On a continuum from extremely masculine to extremely feminine, creative children and adults tend to fall somewhere in the middle (Piirto, 2004). Rigid sex roles tend to limit creative behavior and discourage sensitivity. In a world where boys don't cry and girls don't climb, children's opportunities for creativity are limited. To be successful in maintaining the discipline and hard work necessary to succeed in the arts, children must become very self-sufficient and yet maintain their sensitivity. This requires being able to work like a man and feel like a woman. As teachers and parents who value creativity in our children, we need to guard against stereotyping of any type, but we need to know that gender stereotyping, in particular, often stifles creativity.

As we have said before, adults have very powerful influences over the atmosphere in the classroom and at home. To encourage creative children, they have several important responsibilities. In addition to modeling and valuing creative behavior, and exposing children and adolescents to high-level creative expression through art galleries, ballet, music, and theatre productions, they can also:

- Talk to children about their ideas and the dedication and hard work that is involved in producing creative products.
- Avoid reinforcing sex-role stereotypes.
- Encourage conversation and support children in learning to express themselves.
- Never accept "pat answers."
- Advocate for creative programs for children in your community.
- Join the library and take children often.

Become aware of the creative programs available near you, and take your children regularly. As a parent or a teacher, you have the power to encourage or kill the creative potential in your students and children. That is a very frightening thought.

Adrienne tells this story. "My mother, both a parent and a teacher, supported me through dance lessons, art lessons, piano lessons, and many art projects. She took me to the theatre, the ballet, concerts, and we went to the public library every Monday night. I thank her for all that support and appreciate her contributions to my love of the arts. But she did one thing that discouraged me. She told me that I couldn't carry a tune. All my life, I have been afraid to join in on sing-alongs. I sing *very* quietly in church. When my church choir director asked me why I didn't join the choir, I said, 'Oh, you wouldn't want me to spoil your beautiful music.' And yet I love to sing. I sing along to the radio in the privacy of my car but would never consider singing if anyone else were listening. Can I sing? I don't think I can. After all, my mother, whom I cherished, told me I couldn't. That is the power that parents and teachers have over the students and children they teach and love."

As adults, responsible for the tender sensibilities of children, we must be very aware of the impact of our words and actions. When working with children, remember the difference between words of praise and words of encouragement. Choose words that focus on the child's feelings and efforts. If a child shows a picture that can't be deciphered, say, "Tell me about your picture," hoping that the child will give a clue about what is represented. This is hard to do. We have stored scripts in our minds, and we tend to revert to those scripts when responding to children. In order to use words of encouragement, we have to reprogram.

Instead of saying, "I really like your picture" (*praise*), say, "You must be very proud of that picture. You worked very hard on it" (*encouragement*). Turning the discussion to the child's feelings and sense of self-worth supports his or her incentive and motivation. It also gives the child the recognition for a job well done.

WAYS TO DEMONSTRATE VALUING CREATIVITY

Besides words of recognition and encouragement, adults can demonstrate that they value children's creative efforts in several other ways:

- Display art in the home and classroom.
- Find time to read students' writings.
- Respond when students write to us in a dialogue journal.
- Help students publish their writings, and then include the books they've written in the class library.
- At home, keep a portfolio of their work, or display it on the refrigerator.
- Frame some of their work and hang it on the classroom wall.

All of this shows children that we value their creativity and serves to encourage their efforts. But there is one more thing that serves to demonstrate the value we place on these efforts, and that is *providing our time and attention*.

Spending time with children, actually participating in creative work, sends a very powerful message to the child. When adults sit down and create along with children, it encourages them in a very real way. Children are aware of how busy teachers and parents are. They want more of our time and attention. Working together on creative projects is a wonderful way to spend that elusive "quality time" and also establish the family creative mythology we discussed above.

CORE ATTITUDES IN CREATIVE THOUGHT

In studying creative people and the creative process over the past 50 years, researchers have identified a number of attitudes that creative people have in common (Piirto, 2004). Creative people, at least those who are productive and successful in bringing their creative ideas to fruition, posses an attitude of naïveté or openness. They have an attitude of self discipline, often working long and arduous hours, days, months, and even years in the pursuit of creating something very unique and special. They are risk takers, willing to brave public opinion and even public censure for their unique ideas. If they work in a collaborative way with other creative people, they practice a mutual trust and respect for one another's ideas. These attitudes sometimes seem unreasonable to the onlooker. Creative people must often get beyond the opinions of others to bring their creative projects to fruition.

Naïveté is a term that literally means "uncritical." It is the ability to see uniqueness in very common things. Vincent Van Gogh, for example, is said to have been able to see drawings and pictures in everything he viewed, even shabby huts or dusty rooms. Naïveté is the ability to see, in a non-judgemental fashion, interesting textures, lines, color values, designs, or combinations in common objects that the ordinary person would look at but not really see.

The gift of observation has often been linked to this creative attitude of naïveté, and observation is surely a part of it. It seems to be much more than simple observation, however. The creative person does observe, but he or she seems to see unusual potential or may simply delight in things (or ideas) that are odd or strange. There are elements of acceptance and curiosity inherent in naïveté, too. To quote Igor Stravinsky, "[T]he true creator may be recognized by his ability always to find about him, in the commonest and humblest thing, items worthy of note" (p. 192).

To teach this attitude to students, teachers must model an openness and acceptance of the unusual. Ironically, many teachers reveal that they find the creative student's unusual approaches to tasks and discussions in the classroom disruptive (Torrance, 1963). To foster openness, creative approaches and unique problem solving in a classroom setting require teachers who are open and accepting of unique thought processes and who validate these unusual points of view and observations. Secondary teachers often feel that they have so many curriculum topics to address that they cannot take the time to encourage creativity beyond the writing classroom. One high school science research teacher encouraged his students to "get creative" when logging their progress in their science project journals. He took a few minutes of class time to brainstorm some of the ways they could prepare their project journals to document their work and yet make the journals more interesting. One of the best projects he received that year was from two young men who built a homemade greenhouse and experimented with plant growth at various temperatures and humidity settings. Their log was a video journal complete with music specially selected to set the mood. Their opening music was the theme from Star Wars, with scenes of the building of the rather scary-looking greenhouse made from plastic sheeting and two-by-fours. When the team set up their display board at the fair, they included a small television set and played their video journal for the judges, who were very impressed.

Self-discipline is another attribute of creative people. People may have self-discipline in many areas. Some have self-discipline in controlling their diets. Others are very disciplined in maintaining a healthy exercise program. Creative people in the arts and sciences are very disciplined in their creative work. The successful inventor usually has many, many versions of his or her invention before discovering the one that works. Writers may write thousands of words and end up publishing a very small percentage of them. Albert Einstein is quoted as saying, "I know quite certainly that I myself have no special talent. Curiosity, obsession, and dogged endurance combined with self-criticism have brought me my ideas" (Piirto, 2004, p. 47). Author Sydney Harris agrees that self-discipline contributes to success and is quoted as saying, "Self-discipline without talent can often achieve astonishing results, whereas talent without self-discipline dooms itself to failure" (quotations.about.com). Great creators are known for their great productivity. Choreographer Agnes de Mille noted that "all artists—indeed all great careerists—submit themselves, as well as their friends, to life-long, relentless discipline, largely self-imposed and never for any reason relinquished" (de Mille, 1991, p.158).

Parents and teachers have long struggled with the challenge of fostering self-discipline in their children and students. Many adults still struggle with a lack of self-discipline in themselves. In a fast-paced world of instant gratification, what type of activities lead students to the development of self-discipline? A number of books and articles on self-discipline and ways to develop it have been published. Most of them begin with a similar strategy: *start small*. Begin with a small task that you dread, and spend a few minutes getting started. Then try to develop a habit of doing small things regularly for the practice of self-discipline. But this type of self-discipline is not quite the same thing as the self-discipline that Einstein mentioned. Einstein was talking about obsession: being so involved and interested in something that he was able to work on it again and again until he felt that he had it right, mastered it, or found a solution to a difficult problem.

Parents and teachers can support children in the development of self-discipline in several ways:

- First, they can model it. They can demonstrate the self-discipline of staying with projects until their completion and then share the exhilaration of having completed a task that took time and commitment.
- Second, they can include their children in these activities and also find pursuits that will fascinate and engage the students.

Another important contribution parents and teachers can make is genuine interest in and celebration of the child's efforts. Notice when a child has spent a lot of time and effort on a project. Understand the difference between praise and encouragement. If you are trying to inspire self-discipline, then the object of your encouragement should be the time and effort the child put into the project rather than the quality of the result. With practice, effort, and self-discipline, the products will improve. Your encouragement will also foster the child's self-confidence, and thus a very powerful cycle is begun.

We know that our children are being exposed to life in 7-minute segments, the time between television commercials. To develop self-discipline, they have to become actively involved and

PRAXIS

This section prepares you for PRAXIS™ Exam Section 1b: Students as Diverse Learners, and Section3b: Cultural and Gender Differences.

engaged in life. They have to be exposed to a number of interesting topics and then be given time to explore them in depth. In today's busy homes and classrooms, children rarely have the opportunity to engage in an activity that requires time and perseverance.

Creative people are, almost by definition, risk takers. Creative risk taking is not the same as taking physical risks. Creative risks involve exposing your innermost thoughts, feelings, and passions to a world that may not accept them or even understand them. To quote the noted social psychologist, Dean Keith Simonton, "Great creators are great risk-takers besides" (1995, p. 255). The risk that the creative person takes is public censure and rejection. Because artists and writers, poets, and inventors put so much of themselves, their heartfelt feelings as well as their efforts, into their work, the risk they take is very real. It is also a necessity for them to practice their art. Creative people have often been quoted on the topic of risk taking, possibly because this attitude is so vital to their ability to express themselves in their chosen field, whether it is painting, poetry, writing essays, dancing, or inventing.

One second-grade teacher encourages her students to share the books they have read by creating a project based on the book when they finish reading it. Most of her students draw pictures, create timelines, make posters, or build dioramas. One year she had a student who was taking modern dance lessons, and the student wanted to choreograph a dance showing the events in the story she had read. The teacher encouraged her, knowing that she would be taking the risk of being laughed at by her peers (especially the boys). The little girl dressed up in costume as the heroine of the story and danced to music she had selected to help create the context of the story, which was set in the old West. The class was enthralled. The creative child was given positive feedback from her teacher and her peers. She had been given a chance to take a creative risk and it had paid off.

An important aspect of the process of valuing the child's creativity is focusing on the core attitudes shared by creative people. Children should be introduced to the concept of hard work and practice in enhancing creative potential. Become aware of the children's favorite authors, illustrators, and musicians. Look for information about these creative people, and share your knowledge about their training, the number of creative works they have produced, and their work ethic. A number of authors of children's books have now published autobiographies. Read these autobiographies to students, and discuss how the authors all continue to work to perfect their art. The task of the parent or teacher in encouraging a creative child involves supporting the child in taking creative risks.

Several approaches for encouraging students to complete projects can be incorporated into the school setting:

- Schedule blocks of time for reading and writing that allow students to get beyond the superficial. Encourage students to keep drafts of their writing in a writing folder and to work on more than one project at a time. Often they will need to leave one project and work on another to allow time for the incubation of ideas.
- Avoid changing activities like learning stations on a set schedule. Allow the students to move to a new station when they have completed their work in the first one (and cleaned up, of course).
- Encourage students to complete projects. Have conferences with them to check on their progress. Teach them strategies to use when they get stuck.

CREATIVITY IN THE LANGUAGE ARTS

When we think of creative activities in the language arts, we almost automatically think of writing. There are now six recognized language arts: reading, writing, speaking, listening, viewing, and visually representing. All six of these language arts can be used for creative activities. Reading should involve reading with expression, using different voices for different characters, maybe even using accents or unique speech patterns to define characters. Speaking activities can include some extemporaneous speaking to encourage fluency and flexibility in oral expression. It can also involve assignments where the speaker must convince the listener of a point of view or lead him or her to change an opinion. Viewing and visually representing give learners the opportunity to create visuals to accompany their oral presentations or to explain by speech or other means the feelings that a visual image evokes.

In this age of technology, we have a new way to engage in creative writing with our children. If children are going to become writers, they need time to develop writing skills. Writer's workshop classrooms support the students as they become better writers. If you structure the workshop to address standards in language arts and other academic subjects like social studies, you can meet a number of standards in the process. Having students read books related to social studies and then write reader's theatre scripts, plays, or simulation journals incorporates creative writing into the study of history and geography.

Students can work together to write and publish their books. They can write the About the Author page and place a copy of their school pictures in their books. The teacher can demonstrate appreciation of their efforts by letting them read the book to the class and questioning them about where they got their ideas. Allowing the students enough time to complete in-depth projects like this is another way of fostering creativity in the classroom.

Email Stories

An email is another way to use students' natural interest in using the computer to support creativity and the language arts standards. The teacher starts a story and emails it a student. The first student adds to the story and sends it to another student or back to the teacher. The story is exchanged several times before it is complete. When it is finished, the teacher publishes it by printing it out on the computer and making it into a book. Pictures of the authors can be included in the back, along with a brief About the Author section. The children keep the books in their personal libraries but also share them with their teacher and classmates. For additional suggestions for creative activities in language arts, see Figure 9.1.

CREATIVE ACTIVITIES IN MATHEMATICS

We think of mathematics as the one discipline where there is always a correct answer. While this is usually true, students can be challenged to think of situations in which the answer might change. For instance, why is it that when you mix 1 cup of water with 1 cup of alcohol, the result is less than 2 cups of liquid? Don't 1 and 1 always equal 2? Students have great imaginations and can usually find some ways in which the right answer might be different.

Another way to introduce creative thought into the use of mathematics is to combine math with another discipline such as writing. One fifth-grade teacher introduced the concept of math riddles by reading the book *One Riddle, One Answer* (Thompson, 2000), in which the emperor found a husband for the princess by posing a mathematical riddle. The teacher then gave a short lesson on how to write math riddles and allowed the students to write their own. The students were so fascinated by the topic that they continued writing riddles through their lunch period. After lunch, students presented their riddles, and the class enjoyed another period of creative mathematical thought as the students attempted to solve them. They were so excited by this application of mathematics that the teacher kept a learning center in the classroom for several weeks. At the center, they wrote math riddles and left them for others to solve. As a result of reading this one book aloud and giving the students opportunities to extend their knowledge in math, the students published a book of math riddles that they shared with the other fifth-grade classes.

There are a number of mathematics-based stories that can be used with students to challenge their understanding of math principles and to encourage students to include math in their creative projects. See Figure 9.2 for a list of some of these books.

Language Arts Activity	Activity	Adaptations
Speaking	Painting a verbal picture	Students create a visual (picture, clay sculpture, or diagram). The visuals are displayed without names attached, and each student must create a verbal picture by describing his or her product so that others can identify it. Can also be done using art prints.
Listening	Re-creating something you have heard	Teacher or student describes a picture that the others cannot see. The students re-create the picture strictly by listening to the description.
Reading	Making a character come alive	Using published or class-written reader's theater scripts, each student assumes a character and creates a way of depicting that character with gestures, voice, and movements so that the other students can identify the character readily. Teachers can provide additional motivation by offering "Oscars of the Day."
Writing	Writing reader's theatre scripts for favorite books	This can be done as a class project to introduce the format. Then students can write their own scripts as they read books and involve their peers in producing the scripts.
Viewing	Viewing an art print and creating a story to explain what the artists were thinking or feeling	This can be done in writing or verbally. Once students become more comfortable with expressing new ideas verbally, this activity becomes a wonderful way to encourage extemporaneous storytelling.
Visually representing	Listening to music and creating a verbal picture	Teacher plays a musical piece, and students respond in writing, creating a story behind the music. They tell what the composer was thinking or feeling. This activity presents another opportunity for extemporaneous speaking when it is done verbally.
Literary response	Reading and creating a response using a variety of media	After reading a book, students create a product to convey the essence of the book. Some suggestions include the following: • Create a diorama of the setting. • Create a script for a favorite scene. • Write a new ending. • Create a mural of the plot. • Create a timeline of the plot. • Create a simulated journal of the events from one character's perspective. • Compose a song that tells the story. • Create a comic strip of the main events. • Design a response format of your own.

Figure 9.1   Suggested activities in language arts.

Demi, (1997). *One grain of rice: A mathematical folktale.* New York: Scholastic. ISBN: 0-590-93998-X.

Friedman, Aileen. (1994). *The King's Commissioners.* New York: Scholastic. ISBN: 0-590-48989-5.

Murphy, Stuart J. (1996). *Too many kangaroo things to do!* New York: HarperCollins (a book about multiplying). ISBN: 0-06-446712-0.

Murphy, Stuart J. (1998). *A fair bear share.* New York: HarperCollins (a book about regrouping). ISBN: 0-06-446714-7.

Neuschwander, Cindy. (1997). *Sir Cumference and the first round table: A math adventure.* Watertown, MA: Charlesbridge. ISBN: 1-57091-152-5.

Neuschwander, Cindy. (1999). *Sir Cumference and the dragon of Pi: A math adventure.* Watertown, MA: Charlesbridge. ISBN: 1-57091-164-9.

Neuschwander, Cindy. (2001). *Sir Cumference and great knight of Angleland: A math adventure.* Watertown, MA: Charlesbridge. ISBN: 1-57091-169-X.

Piligard, Virginia. (2000). *The warlord's puzzle.* Gretna, LA: Pelican Publishing. ISBN 1-56554-495-1.

Thompson, Lauren. (2001). *One riddle, one answer.* New York: Scholastic. ISBN: 0-590-31335-5

Figure 9.2 Children's books to encourage creative applications in mathematics.

CREATIVE ACTIVITIES IN SOCIAL SCIENCES

The social sciences give many opportunities for creative projects as well as integration with other areas of the curriculum. For example, a unit of study on the three branches of government led one fifth-grade teacher to challenge her students to design their own island country. They had to create a topographical map of their island showing all the landforms and create a legend so that other students could read the map. They designed an economic plan for their country and found ways for the people to obtain food, water, supplies, and ways to make a living. They had to decide what form of government their island would have, how the laws would be made and enforced, and how they would balance power in the government. During the course of this project, the students addressed social studies standards in mapping, government, and economics. They also addressed standards in music and art when they designed a national anthem and state flag. For additional suggestions for creative activities in social studies, see Figure 9.3.

CREATIVE ACTIVITIES IN SCIENCE

Science is an extremely creative discipline. Great inventions are important in history and are almost all scientifically based. Students can be encouraged to become creative in science by involving them in explorations in elaboration. Introduce a simple object, and invite the students to change it slightly to make it serve a different function.

A science teacher added a new twist to a science fair project by allowing the students make a video documenting their project: where the idea came from, how it was planned, and each of the steps along the way (including the mistakes.) The students were extremely creative in making their tape because the teacher added one caveat: Make it interesting!

For additional books about inspiring creative activities in science, see Figure 9.4.

Activity	Standards Addressed	Adaptations
Online simulations	History, geography, economics	www.simulations.com www.jimcrowhistory.org
Virtual field trips	History, geography	www.uen.org
Debates	History, economics, current events	Slave owner versus abolitionists, prohibitionists versus bar owners, hawks versus doves.
Illustrated concepts	History, economics, current events	Define a concept in writing and then illustrate it; make a class book. An example is the Bill of Rights.
Timelines	History	Clothesline timelines, picture timelines, artifact timelines.
Creative note taking	All areas of curriculum	Flap books, foldables, graphic organizers (See the Appendix for directions.)
Edible maps	Geography	Create a map using edible materials (graham crackers and icing, for example).
Exploring the Internet	All areas of curriculum	www.brainpop.com www.nationalgeographic.com www.history.com (great speeches)

Figure 9.3 Suggested activities in the social sciences.
Source: Dr. Angela Fiske, Florida State University, personal communication.

Casey, S. (2005). *Kids inventing! Handbook for young inventors.* Hoboken, NJ: Jossey-Bass.

Erlbach, A. (1989). *The kids' invention book.* Minneapolis, MN: Lerner.

Harper, C. M. (2001). *Imaginative inventions: The who, what, where, when, and why of roller skates, potato chips, marbles, and pie (and more!)* New York: Little, Brown Young Readers.

Hauser, J. F. (1999). *Gizmos and gadgets: Creating science contraptions that work (and knowing why.)* Charlotte VT: Williamson.

Jones, C. (1994). *Mistakes that worked.* New York: Doubleday.

Panati, C. (1989). *Extraordinary origins of everyday things.* New York: Harper and Row.

Thimmesh, C. (2002). *Girls think of everything: Stories of ingenious inventions by women.* New York: Houghton Mifflin.

Tucker, T. (1998). *Brainstorm! The stories of twenty American kid inventors.* New York: Farrar, Straus, & Giroux.

Wulffson, D. (1999). *The kid who invented the Popsicle: And other surprising stories about inventions.* New York: Puffin.

Figure 9.4 Books to inspire creativity in science.

CREATIVE ACTIVITIES IN THE VISUAL AND PERFORMING ARTS

Visual and performing arts are usually the first areas that come to mind when you think about creativity. With the combination of stress on meeting academic standards and tight budgets across the nation, these programs are all too often the first to be cut back or eliminated altogether. There is a movement toward finding innovative ways to reintroduce the arts into education in many areas of the country. The *San Diego Union-Tribune* featured several California school districts that were finding ways to raise funds to support the arts in the schools. The money raised was used for teacher training, art docents, resident art and music teachers, and arts education curricula.

Another approach is being used in Hawaii, where the local arts council and the school district have found ways to integrate the visual and performing arts into almost every aspect of the academic curriculum. The results have been extremely positive. This integration is helping raise test scores and increase student motivation. The arts council/school district collaboration has made an arts toolkit available with lessons for all grade levels and all academic disciplines. This toolkit can be downloaded from http://arts.k12.hi.us.

HUMOR AND CREATIVITY

What does humor in the classroom have to do with creativity? Humor is a very abstract form of language. It often requires using language in unique ways. Understanding humor requires a facility with the manipulation of ideas and concepts that develops over time. Some children cannot understand certain types of jokes until they attain certain sophistication in their language development. Intelligent children sometimes have highly developed abilities to design and understand humor. This "off the wall" humor may be a sign of intelligence, but it can often be misunderstood by the majority of the children in the class and, sometimes, by the teacher.

When you have children in your classroom who enjoy playing with language to create jokes, consider ways to channel that talent. They can have time to share their jokes, just as you would give students time to share any other form of writing. Always stress the importance of not using jokes to demean or hurt others.

Children love humor, and creative children enjoy it more than most. When teachers think of humor in the classroom, they tend to become a little cautious. We have all heard humor in the classroom that is sarcastic and hurtful. Humor in the classroom should be a case of joint enjoyment and laughter, not humor at anyone's expense. There are questions that you, as a teacher, should ask yourself. Are you naturally a humorous person? Do you enjoy your students? Have you found that you can tease them without hurting their feelings?

Bryant and Zillman (1989) studied humor in the classroom and found that elementary teachers used humor more often than did middle school and high school teachers. They also found that humor used with older students tended to be more sarcastic and hurtful.

STYLES OF HUMOR-ORIENTED TEACHING

Diane Loomans and Karen Kolberg (2002) have written a book called *The Laughing Classroom*, which is filled with motivating strategies for teachers to use in all areas of the curriculum. They identify four different styles of humor-oriented teaching:

- The Joy Master is a teacher who inspires students to become warmhearted and humane toward one another. She might use a strategy such as creative debate in which students are assigned a role and debate an issue. Abe Lincoln may be debating on one side and Charlie Chaplin on the other.
- The Fun-Meister uses slapstick and clowning as a motivational technique. When teaching a mathematical operation, the teacher may pretend to make mistakes so that

students catch them, thereby giving the students a reason to monitor the teacher's demonstration more carefully. Peals of laughter may fill the room as the students point out the teacher's error. This style of teaching can have its dark side, however, because Fun-Meisters sometimes mock others, including their students, causing students to laugh at one another's mistakes.

- The Life Mocker is almost entirely negative from the students' viewpoint. Teachers who are cynical and sarcastic may cause a few laughs, but the students may experience this style as coldhearted and dehumanizing.
- The Joke Maker has a way with telling stories and jokes that are always entertaining for his students. These stories can be very instructive and provide insight as examples of an abstract concept. Occasionally, teachers can use jokes or stories that are experienced as insults or stereotypes, which have a negative impact on students.

The Laughing Classroom is an excellent resource for teachers at all grade levels, and it can assist you in planning humorous activities that are supportive, positive, and healing.

CREATIVITY TRAINING

Creativity training classes are being offered for teachers and students of all ages. Some school districts have invested in this training for teachers, especially teachers who will be teaching in gifted programs. Several different programs are available. Some of the better-known creativity training courses are listed below:

- Creative Problem Solving (CPS) is the oldest of the training courses and is the foundation of programs such as Future Problem Solving and Odyssey of the Mind. In this program, groups of students work together to solve problems through the use of divergent and convergent processes such as problem finding and solution finding." (http://en.wikipedia.org/wiki/Creative_problem_solving)
- Gordon's Synectics is based on putting unlike things together to form a new object. It is a popular teaching approach in textbooks about models of classroom instruction. (http://www.writedesignonline.com/organizers/synectics.htm)
- Meeker's Divergent Production Exercises are found in *Sourcebooks*, which are workbooks at the basic and advanced levels. The workbooks contain exercises in all of Guilford's divergent production factors. Divergent production involves the identification of novel and unique uses for common objects and stimuli of creative problem-solving strategies. (http://en.wikipedia.org/wiki/J._P._Guilford)
- Torrance's programs are available from the Torrance Center for Creativity at the University of Georgia (http://en.wikipedia.org/wiki/Ellis_Paul_Torrance). The Torrance Center for Creativity and Talent Development is a service, research, and instructional center concerned with the identification and development of creative potential. Many of the materials were developed by Torrance's graduate students.
- Taylor's Talents Unlimited (http://inventors.about.com/od/creativity/a/Calvin_Taylor.htm) is a program to help teachers recognize and nurture the multiple talents of children based on Taylor's talent totem poles: academic, productive thinking, communicating, forecasting, decision making, planning, and designing.
- Starko's *Schools of Curious Delight* is a book written by a professor of elementary education, who gives suggestions to teachers about ways to infuse creativity training into the curriculum.

Some have raised concern about the approaches used in some of the creativity training courses. Some people find it odd that workbook exercises would be used to teach creativity. Some of the researchers at the Buffalo Creativity Studies program are now looking at creativity training in relation to personality types. Torrance (1983) studied the creativity training programs and found that most of them focused on six approaches:

1. Teaching specific, creative problem-solving skills.
2. Direct teaching of problem solving and pattern recognition.
3. Using guided fantasy and imagery.
4. Using thematic fantasy.
5. Using creative writing.
6. Using quality circles for quality control.

Some of these training exercises are taken from the more popular approaches to creativity training. The fantasy exercises encourage students to imagine sights, sounds, and tastes as they hear a fantasy story read aloud. The quality circles approach originated in Japan and involved employees working in small volunteer groups to brainstorm ways to improve production and solve problems.

In some school districts, creativity training is being used as a way of differentiating instruction for gifted students. Many of the publishers of reading textbooks are now including some creativity training exercises in their teaching materials. It is a concept that is growing in popularity, but the results of such training are still unknown. Torrance (1983) listed the results of creativity training in elementary and secondary schools as follows:

1. Increased satisfaction.
2. Evidence that academic achievement is not affected by creative performance.
3. Writing more creatively in different genres.
4. Growth in personality and healthy self-concept.
5. Improvement in attitudes toward mathematics.
6. An openness to pursuing creative choices.

Attitudinal and conceptual changes are difficult to measure. Because creativity involves emotional risk taking, there are certain factors that must be included in any creativity training. The effect must be valued as well as the importance of building trust between the group experiencing the training and the leader. Piirto (2004) suggests that maybe *training* is not the correct word. She suggests *creativity experiencing* or *creativity simulation* as possible alternatives.

Communicating with Parents

When you talk with parents, make it clear to them that they are constantly creating a family mythology. Explain to them that this is a very powerful aspect of family dynamics that can help students understand the core values in their family. For parents, the family mythology (Piirto, 2004) is important. When you begin sentences, "In our family . . . ," you are creating a mythology related to your family beliefs and values. For example, "In our family, we go to college." Many of you knew from kindergarten that you would attend college, and there was never a question about it. Think about the message that children get from the choices parents make. For example, "In our family, we went to art museums, the ballet, and the symphony." This part of a family mythology is passed along to each generation. If you, as a parent, are interested in something and share that interest with your children, they are much more likely to show an interest in it or similar pursuits. If you are raising boys, you may have to point out that athletes use ballet training in their sports to help the boys appreciate ballet and other forms of dance as adults. As a teacher, you can use your class newsletter to support parents in finding inexpensive ways to expose their children to and involve their children in a variety of activities in your community. If parents are aware of the power of their influence, it helps them when making these types of choices.

Playing Catch Up

If you are teaching upper elementary or secondary grades, and if you have students in your class who have not been exposed to the arts or have had teachers who did not value unique approaches to learning, you may have to do some work to adjust attitudes toward the arts. For example, one local ballet company gave a performance at an elementary school. The company was comprised of six female dancers and two males, all teenagers. After the performance, the dancers fielded questions from the audience. One sixth-grade boy directed his question to one of the male dancers: "Don't you think that ballet dancing is a sissy thing for men to do?" The dancer's response was classic: "I started studying ballet because I wanted to learn to move quickly and exactly to improve my broken-field running in football. But I stayed with it because I enjoy the weight lifting I do lifting beautiful girls better than the weight lifting I do with barbells."

Students who have had no exposure to classical music will benefit from instruction in the different aspects of this type of music and the ways in which classical themes have been incorporated into popular music over the years. Students with little exposure to the aspects of art will also need to be taught that line, form, color, and movement all have a part in creating visually pleasing products. As with most subjects, some basic instruction is important.

Changing attitudes toward risk taking is more difficult. If your students always ask questions like "How long does the research paper have to be?" or even "Is this the right answer?" you have some catching up to do. Students need to feel comfortable making decisions about how long a paper has to be to convey the important aspects of a topic and when there may be more than one correct answer. Even more importantly, they need to understand that you, the teacher, value unique responses and don't want everyone's answer to be the same unless there happens to be only one correct answer.

GUIDED GROUP EXPLORATION

1. Divide the class into several groups.
2. Draw samples of geometric shapes on the board and discuss them with the class. Present the students with the definition of each shape and one example of each in use.
3. Then ask the students to brainstorm as many applications of each shape as possible. Have them present their findings to the class. You can make this a contest, with rewards for the most number of applications that each group discovers. You can include a prize for the group that lists the most shapes.

REFLECTIVE ACTION ACTIVITY
FOR YOUR PROFESSIONAL PORTFOLIO

A parade is a public march or procession honoring a certain occasion. There are countless themes for parades, many of which have become celebrated traditions. Paintings on cave walls depicted the earliest parades believed to be celebrations of hunters arriving home. The first recorded use of a float was in Athens during a sixth-century parade in honor of the god Dionysus.

Floats have changed since then, especially concerning how they are powered. But what if animals or modern inventions could not be used? We would have to use our own power to move floats in parades.

Design and write a lesson plan for a lesson in which the class chooses a theme for a parade related to something being studied in the classroom. Divide the class into groups and design floats (one for each group) to be entered into the parade. As a culmination activity, the groups might also build a model of the float and share it with the class.

References

Abbott, K., Lewis, M. (2007). *Humor in the classroom: Cultivating camaraderie to maximize learning.* Abbott Communications. Retrieved May 8, 2007, from http://www.abbottcom.com/Humor_in_the_classroom.htm

Bryant, J., and Zillman, D. (1989). Using humor to promote learning in the classroom. In P. McGee (Ed.) *Humor and children's development* (pp. 49–78). Binghamton, NY: Haworth Press.

Burke-Adams, A. (2007). The benefits of equalizing standards and creativity: Discovering a balance in instruction. *Gifted Child Today, 30,* 58–63.

Durkin, D. (1975). A six-year study of children who learned to read in school at the age of four. *Reading Research Quarterly, 10,* 9–61.

Encouraging your child to write creatively. (2006). Scribble Pad. Retrieved May 7, 2007, from http://www.scribblepad.co.uk/EncouragingYourChildToWriteCreatively.html

Erez, R. (2004). Freedom and creativity: An approach to science education for excellent students and its realization in the Israeli arts and science academy's curriculum. *Journal of Secondary Gifted Education, 15.* 133–140.

Good, T., & Brophy, J. (2002). *Looking in classrooms* (9th ed.). Boston: Allyn & Bacon.

Loomans, D. & Kolberg, K. (2002). *The laughing classroom.* Tiburon, CA: H J Kramer.

Piirto, J. (2004). *Understanding creativity.* Scottsdale, AR: Great Potential Press.

Ritchhart, R. (2004). Creative teaching in the shadows of the standards. *Independent School, 63*(2), 32–41.

Stutz, E. (1998). *The Link Between Play and Peace.* Retrieved May 8, 2007, from http://www.users.globalnet.co.uk/~estutz/linkp&p.html

Thompson, L. (2000). *One riddle, one answer.* New York: Scholastic.

 Now go to Topic #7: Strategies for Teaching in the MyEducationLab (www.myeducationlab.com <http://www.myeducationlab.com/>) for your course, where you can:

- Find learning outcomes for this topic along with the national standards that connect to these outcomes.
- Complete Assignments and Activities that can help you more deeply understand the chapter content.
- Apply and practice your understanding of the core teaching skills identified in the chapter with the Building Teaching Skills and Dispositions learning units.

CHAPTER

10

Assessing and Reporting Student Accomplishments

■ ■

What is good work? As a teacher, you may find evaluating students' accomplishments among the most difficult judgments you have to make. You have worked hard to create authentic learning experiences. Now, how can you create an assessment system that allows students to demonstrate what they have learned? How can you create an assessment system that allows students a range of possibilities for demonstrating their own particular strengths and talents? How can you create an assessment system that is fair and that your students can understand?

PRAXIS
This chapter prepares you for PRAXIS™ Exam Section 2c: Assessment Strategies.

Educators committed to providing authentic learning for their students are also searching for meaningful and useful assessment systems. They want assessment systems that provide the kinds of information and feedback that allow students to move ahead and develop their skills and knowledge base.

Teachers use assessment devices in their classrooms for two very different purposes. On the one hand, teachers give students tests that will be used to assess the progress of the class as a whole. Teachers want information on how their students are doing on average as a guide for making judgments about what to teach and how to teach it most effectively. Teachers use test data for the purpose of planning for the group as a whole.

The second purpose of assessment is to inform teachers of individual student progress. Professional teachers are astute observers of students—tracking their movements, their words, and their minds. Teachers use a variety of assessment devices to collect information on individual student progress, and they recognize that each assessment tool has its own strengths and weaknesses. These assessments may be formative in nature, given during a sequence of instruction to help determine what learning is taking place and whether more instruction might be needed to assist the students in mastering needed material before further progress can be made. Summative assessments are typically given at the end of a unit of study or sequence of lessons to determine how well individual students have mastered the material presented.

> Professional teachers create their own assessment tools, including but not limited to portfolios, videos, demonstrations, and exhibitions. In addition, they use more traditional methods of assessment such as quizzes and exams. Teachers use questions and group discussions to determine how well students are responding to the lesson. They also talk with individual students in conference to learn more about each student's needs and accomplishments.

EFFECTIVE WAYS OF USING ASSESSMENT

All teachers give tests of some type. Giving and scoring tests provide information that is valuable in planning future instruction. School districts and state departments of education are requiring more and more assessment but there is evidence that this data is not always used in ways that improve instruction (Hoerr, 2009). One important aspect of using assessment results is the practice of data disaggregation. Instead of simply scoring the tests and entering a grade in your grade book, look at the number of students who got each question right *and* more importantly, *why* they missed the question, if they did. This is called error analysis. It is a vital step in determining what to teach next and which students need more instruction before moving to the next step.

If more than 30% of your students missed an item, you will want to re-teach the content using different or additional examples. If only a few of your students missed the item, you can work with them in a small group to solidify their knowledge, *but* if they all missed the item for different reasons, you will want to provide more guided practice for the group so you can monitor their thought processes and help them to learn to think more productively in testing situations.

> You will also want to group your students for instruction so that they are all receiving instruction that will move them toward "continuous improvement." This is the basic premise of the Continuous Improvement Model or CIM (Davenport & Anderson, 2002). Using test data allows you to make informed decisions based on hard data, what the student was able to do on a given test.

It is important to note that data analysis takes time and training. Many schools do this activity after school ends for the year or right before fall semester begins. Other schools schedule data analysis days at the ends of marking periods. Teachers and anyone else involved in data analysis should be trained. Many districts require a data analyst specialist at each school. Training is provided and time allotted for that person to work with faculty. Students and parents should also be involved in training so that they understand the test results they receive. We will explore this in more depth later in this session.

An important aspect of disaggregating the data is to look at individual test items to see what percentage of the students were able to answer correctly. You will also want to look at responses that are partially correct. These responses often provide good insight into where the student's thinking went wrong. Again, if a majority of your students missed an item, you'll want to re-teach that material, preferably with a new teaching approach. If some of your students are making careless errors, you'll want to use those as teaching points and focus on things such as proofreading one's work or going back to spot check answers before submitting a test paper.

LOOKING FOR IMPORTANT PATTERNS IN THE DATA

As data is disaggregated, it can be examined for patterns. Individual student's data can be examined for patterns such as the types of math concepts that need to re-taught or writing conventions that are not yet mastered.

Programs can be evaluated based on the scores and progress made by students enrolled in those programs, such as ESOL. If patterns appear that indicate that a majority of students at a certain grade level are struggling with inference in reading, plans can be made to increase the emphasis in this area. One of the most valuable patterns to look for an indication that certain skills or concepts are not being understood by the students. This often means that teachers can use some additional training and support in those areas.

IMPROVING TEACHING STRATEGIES

Meyers and Rust stress the importance of helping teachers learn how to "assess their own work and its impact on their students" (2000, p. 34). To be successful, school leaders need to engage in conversations with teachers using assessment data to diagnose strengths as well as areas in which the teachers need to modify their instruction. In addition, providing the opportunity for teacher collaboration and discussion about practice, using assessment data as a springboard, has been a powerful tool for improvement.

For example, the Barbour County School District in West Virginia uses class-based profiles generated from SAT-9 data that include information about the performance of individual students on each concept tested. These data sheets are analyzed to identify areas of strength and weakness for individual students as well as for groups of students:

> The data not only help teachers see specific areas of difficulty for each student, it also helps teachers and principals to pinpoint objectives that either need to be covered more thoroughly or taught in a different way. (Cawelti & Protheroe 2001)

THE PURPOSES AND APPROACHES USED FOR PRIORITIZING INSTRUCTION BASED ON THE DATA

As we look at the data related to the assessment of individual students and groups of students, we must begin to prioritize instruction. For students who met the standards and have just a few skills or concepts to master, of course, we will address those standards. For the students who pass enough items to meet the minimal passing score, their remediation and priorities are again, not difficult to identify.

For the students with more material to master, prioritizing becomes vital. At this point we need to begin to group students. We need to make charts (for our own sanity) so that we can see clearly which students need to be included in small-group instruction to address skills and concepts they have not yet mastered.

You may remember that we discussed tutorials and enrichment activities in an earlier chapter. If there are limited numbers of students in the grade level who need tutorials on the same concepts or skills, they can be placed together in a tutorial group. If you have a number of students in your class that need work in a certain area, you can teach them in a small-group setting, making sure that you are teaching for mastery and giving them guided practice. Guided practice means you are giving them experience in actually using the skills being taught under your supervision before you ask them to use the skills in independent practice. This gives you, the teacher, the opportunity to observe them and identify the point at which their understanding breaks down.

In CIM and other effective teaching models, teachers assume that all students can be successful with the right instruction. By using assessment results and grouping students for additional instruction as needed, teachers can provide the support students need to continue to make progress. This assessment can take many forms; standardized tests, teacher-made tests, and even simple observation. None of these assessment forms support student success unless they guide teachers in making informed decisions about effective instruction.

HOW TEACHERS SELECT AND USE
ASSESSMENT PROCEDURES

One piece of the authentic learning puzzle is to be sure to link your grading and reporting criteria with the criteria used in the learning process. When students know what the criteria for success are and see how they are linked to the learning experiences in the classroom, the learning environment seems fair to them (Guskey & Bailey, 2000). Varying evaluation procedures is also seen as beneficial. No one evaluation strategy works well for all subjects, grade levels, or student learning styles. For that reason, students should have a variety of ways to earn their grades.

Imagine you are a teacher planning a unit on astronomy for your classroom. You have gathered some interesting learning materials, including filmstrips on the solar system, National Aeronautics and Space Administration (NASA) material on the space shuttles and telescopes, and many exciting books with vivid illustrations. You have planned a field trip to an observatory and have invited an astronomer to visit the classroom. You have worked out a timeline for several weeks' worth of individual and group investigations and projects.

Now, it is time for you to think about evaluation for yourself and to clarify your values regarding complex evaluation issues. How will you know what students have learned at the end of this unit? What do you expect them to learn? What techniques will you use to find out whether they have learned what you expect? What about the possibility that they may learn something different from what you expect or even that some students who become very actively engaged in the study may learn more than you expect? How will you know what they learned? How will you assign students science grades at the end of this unit? How will you communicate to the students' parents what each has gained from it?

The following sections describe a variety of assessment devices. Each one has a variety of uses and applications. Each one provides answers to different questions that teachers have about evaluation. Reflective teachers will consider each alternative and decide whether and how to use such measures in their own classrooms. Recognizing that this introductory text can provide only minimal information about each assessment method, the reflective teacher will want to search actively for more information about certain methods in order to fully understand their value and use before incorporating them into a program that affects children's lives.

INFORMAL OBSERVATIONS

Teachers use informal observation intuitively from the first moment the students enter the classroom at the beginning of the term. They watch groups to see how students relate to one another; they watch individuals to spot patterns of behavior that are either unusually disruptive or extremely productive. To manage a classroom effectively, with it teachers are alert to the overt and covert actions of their students at all times.

Informal observations also have academic implications. Teachers who observe their students while teaching a lesson are able to evaluate their understanding. Spotting a blank look, a nervous pencil tapping, or a grimace of discomfort on a student's face, the teacher can stop the lesson, check for understanding, and reteach the material to meet the needs of the students who did not understand.

As students read aloud, primary teachers observe and listen for patterns of errors in decoding words. They may also listen to the expression in the student's voice to determine whether the student comprehends the material or is simply saying words aloud. They listen for signs that indicate whether the student is interested in or bored with the material. An additional tool in informal observation is asking the student pertinent questions to check for understanding and determine the student's thought processes. This one-to-one interaction provides data and information that cannot be measured in any paper-and-pencil test.

By observing the student read, asking a few questions, and comparing the results with other students of the same grade or age, the teacher can assess many factors, including (1) the extent to which the student is able to use phonics and context clues to decode reading material, (2) the student's approximate reading level in terms of sight vocabulary, and (3) the student's comprehension level. In addition, the reflective teacher uses the informal observation to gather information about the student's affective qualities, including confidence level, interest in the subject or in reading itself, the amount of effort the student is willing to give to the task, and expectations the student has about success or failure in the subject.

By observing as students write or by reading what they have written, teachers can gather similar data about children's writing abilities, interests, and expectations. As students work out unfamiliar math problems, teachers are careful to observe who works quickly and who is struggling. Then they can gather the struggling students together for an extra tutoring session.

In the astronomy unit, the teacher may observe as students take part in discussions to determine the extent to which various students understand the concepts. When students are visiting the observatory, the teacher watches them to learn about their interests in various aspects of the topic. When an astronomer visits the classroom, the teacher listens to the students' questions to assess the depth of understanding they have achieved.

Informal observations are one of the most powerful assessment devices the teacher can use to gather new information about children's learning patterns and needs. Teachers may gather data about a student from academic and psychological tests, but in the end, teachers rely on informal observation to understand the test data and make a final evaluation about appropriate placement or a grade value for a student's work.

PERFORMANCE TASKS TO SHOW MASTERY OF OBJECTIVES

In contrast to informal evaluations, which provide useful subjective information, behavioral objectives are relatively formal and provide useful objective data about what students have learned. Do not assume that teachers choose one or the other of these two devices. Many reflective teachers know that it is valuable to gather both objective and subjective data. They may choose behavioral objectives as a means of gathering hard data about what students have achieved during classroom learning experiences and compare those data with the subjective information they have gathered during their informal observations.

To plan an assessment system based on students showing mastery of certain specified outcomes or objectives, the teacher must begin before teaching the lesson. By preplanning a unit with specific outcomes or a lesson with very concrete behavioral objectives, the teacher specifies the skills that students should be able to demonstrate at the conclusion of the lesson and the criterion for success. Teachers then plan learning experiences that are linked with the outcomes. After each objective has been taught and students have had an opportunity to practice the new skill, a quiz, worksheet, or other assessment product asks students to demonstrate that they have mastered the new skill and can perform it with few errors.

When each lesson is introduced, the teacher describes the prespecified criterion for success to the students. The criterion for success may be specified as a percentage or as a minimum number of correct responses. For example, the following behavioral objective specifies 80% (or 16 of the 20 possible items) as the acceptable demonstration of mastery of this objective.

Spelling Objective: When the teacher reads the list of 20 spelling words aloud, students will write 80% of the words, using correct spelling and legible handwriting.

A criterion-referenced test such as the weekly spelling test common in many classrooms demonstrates whether the students have mastered the new skill. To record student achievement, teachers may write the percentage of correct responses that each student attained in a grade book.

For more complex objectives, teachers design performance tasks that require students to demonstrate what they have learned. Marzano (2000) describes a system that allows teachers to design performance tasks that measure growth in communication skills, information processing, and other complex acts. For example, students may present oral reports on a NASA satellite launch, and the teacher may evaluate their knowledge and communication skills by using a scoring rubric. A scoring rubric consists of a fixed scale and a list of the characteristics for describing performance for each of the score points on the scale. Because rubrics describe levels of performance, they provide important information to teachers, parents, and others interested in what students know and are able to do. Perhaps most importantly, rubrics provide a clear statement to students, teachers, and parents on what is considered important and worth learning, even before the learning has occurred. Teachers may choose to use a rubric such as the following:

Rubric for communication skills and oral presentations

4. Clearly and effectively communicates the main idea or theme and provides support that contains rich, vivid, and powerful detail.
3. Clearly communicates the main idea or theme and provides suitable support and detail.
2. Communicates important information but without a clear theme or overall structure.
1. Communicates information in isolated pieces in a random fashion.

CRITERION-REFERENCED QUIZZES AND TESTS

Quizzes, such as the matching quiz described below, are frequently used with behavioral objectives to determine whether students are successfully gaining each new skill or bit of knowledge in a unit of study. Quizzes are generally short, consisting of only a few questions or items, and are thought of as formative assessments, providing teachers with a way to know whether the students are learning the material day by day.

Tests, however, may consist of many items and are generally thought of as summative assessments. Tests are often given at the end of a unit and contain a variety of items that measure students' achievement of content and skills that have been taught during a period.

In both cases, the term *criterion-referenced* refers directly to the criterion established for each behavioral objective. Each item on a criterion-referenced test should match a preestablished criterion. Criterion referencing provides objective data about material that all students in the class have had an equal opportunity to learn.

Objective tests may take a variety of forms. The most common are matching, true-false, multiple-choice, and short-answer or completion forms. Matching items are those that provide both the question and response. Students have only to recognize the correct response for each item and draw a line to connect the two. Items appear in a column on one side of the paper, and the responses appear in a different order on the other side. In terms of Bloom's revised taxonomy, matching items is an excellent way of measuring understanding-level objectives that require students to recognize correct responses. An example of a matching quiz related to the astronomy unit might look like this:

Jupiter	Planet with rings and many moons
Earth	Planet closest to the sun
Mercury	Planet that is three-fifths water
Saturn	Largest planet

To construct fair matching items, each right-column response must be clearly identified with only one item on the left. In our astronomy test, for example, descriptions of the planets need to contain unambiguous elements so that only one matches each planet. If several responses are vaguely correct, the reliability and therefore the objectivity of the test decline.

True-false items are also knowledge-level items, consisting of a statement that students must recognize as either true or false. These items are difficult to write because they must be factual and objective if they are to provide useful data. If items contain unsupported opinions or generalizations, the students must guess what the teacher intended. For our astronomy unit, we might construct a quiz with true-false statements such as these:

True	False	The sun orbits the Earth.
True	False	Venus is smaller than Jupiter.
True	False	Mars is closer to the sun than Neptune.

These items are reliable because the correct responses are not likely to change in our lifetime. They are also valid because every item is an element directly related to our objective of teaching students about the physical characteristics of the solar system. As examples of less reliable and less valid items, consider these:

True   False   Venus is a more interesting planet than Uranus.
True   False   The sun will never stop shining on the Earth.

Multiple-choice items also measure knowledge-level objectives because they call for the student to recognize a fact or idea. A multiple-choice item contains a question, problem, or unfinished statement followed by several responses, including the correct answer and several "distractors". The directions tell the student to mark the one correct answer. While college admissions tests may contain several near-right responses and students are expected to use reasoning to determine which one is best, classroom tests should probably be constructed with only one correct response. As in other objective measures, the reliability and validity of each item must be considered. Two examples of valid and reliable items that fit the astronomy unit are the following:

1. Which planet is known as the red planet?
   A. Venus
   B. Orion
   C. Mars
   D. Jupiter
2. It would take longest to travel from Earth to:
   A. Neptune
   B. Mercury
   C. Venus
   D. Saturn

Short-answer or completion items supply a question or an unfinished statement, and students are expected to supply a word, phrase, number, or symbol. These items are used primarily to test students' knowledge of specific facts and terminology. Two examples of short-answer questions for our astronomy unit are the following:

1. The planet Saturn has _____ rings around it.
2. Which planet has the most moons?

The advantage of the four types of objective items that comprise most criterion-referenced tests is that they objectively measure students' knowledge of the basic content of a subject. They can be written to match directly the criteria of the teacher's objectives for the lessons. They are also relatively easy to correct, and the scores are easily recorded and can be averaged together to provide the basis for report card grades.

The disadvantage of such items is that they only measure students' understanding of basic understanding-level content and skills. They do not provide information about what students comprehend, how they would apply the knowledge they have gained, what they would create, or how they analyze and evaluate the ideas they have learned.

MASTERY LEARNING ASSESSMENT

Some teachers prefer to use a teaching strategy known as *mastery learning* to motivate students to learn a sequence of skills. In mastery learning, individual students work through a series of learning experiences at their own pace and demonstrate mastery as they complete each objective. The teacher uses the information gained on the tests to provide helpful feedback for reteaching rather than as a record of achievement. Summative evaluations occur only at the end of a unit of study, when students are expected to demonstrate mastery of a whole sequence or unit of learning. Grades of unit tests are recorded and become the basis for determining students' grades.

For the astronomy unit, the teacher could write outcome statements such as these:

Outcome 1: After viewing the filmstrip on the solar system, the students match pictures of each planet with its name, with no more than one error.

Outcome 2: Students will draw and label an illustration of the solar system with the sun and the planets in their respective orbits, with 100% accuracy.

Together, these two outcomes will inform the teacher about whether students have learned the names, distinctive visual elements, and locations of the planets in the solar system. To measure whether students have mastered this content, the teacher simply carries out the tasks described in the objectives after students have had sufficient opportunity to learn the material. The teacher prepares a matching quiz with a column of names of the planets and another column of pictures of the planets. For those who do not achieve the criterion of specified correct answers, the teacher can provide a reteaching experience or require students to do additional reading on their own. They can be retested until they achieve the criterion.

On another occasion, the teacher distributes blank paper and asks students to draw and label the solar system. From these two objectives and others like them, the teacher can begin to answer the question, "How will I know what they have learned?" Also, the data gathered from this assessment system are more readily translated into letter grades than are the data from informal observations.

ESSAYS EVALUATED WITH RUBRIC GUIDELINES

PRAXIS
Scoring methods are assessed in PRAXIS™ Exam Section 2c: Assessment Strategies.

Essays have the exact opposite advantages and disadvantages of criterion-referenced tests. They tend to be subjective rather than objective. Unless they are given specific criteria upon which to base their ratings, two or more teachers rarely evaluate an essay the same way. Essays are also time consuming to read and mark.

However, essays provide teachers with an excellent means of knowing what students comprehend, how they would apply their new learning, and how they analyze and evaluate the ideas and concepts. Essays also provide students with opportunities to be creative by asking them to synthesize a number of previously unrelated notions into an original expression of their own. Essays can answer the question, "How much more have they learned than what I taught in this unit?"

To improve the way teachers rate essays, many school systems employ a rubric guide that specifies what an essay must contain and how it must appear on the page to earn a specific mark or grade. Teachers who use a rubric to guide their assessment of essays usually limit the topic of the essay with specific parameters and may even specify what must be included in the response. For example, in the astronomy unit, the teacher may want to assess whether students can describe the concept of outer space in their own words. This will provide information about how much students truly comprehend about the subject rather than what they simply remember.

A teacher might present students with the following guidelines for writing their essay on the solar system.

Write a two-paragraph essay in your own words comparing the Earth's atmosphere with outer space. Tell why humans cannot live in outer space without life support. Use examples and provide evidence to support your ideas.

These guidelines are fairly explicit in terms of both length and content. For these reasons, this form of essay is relatively objective. To make it even more likely that two or more teachers would look for similar elements when correcting the papers, school systems may provide teachers with rubric evaluation samples of student work, along with specific descriptions for measuring success on a particular essay topic. Here is an example:

Grade Characteristics of Essay

A Paragraphs are well organized and contain at least six sentences. Facts are accurate and evidence is clearly given to support the student's viewpoints.

B Paragraphs contain at least four sentences. Most facts are accurate. Examples are given to support ideas.

C Paragraphs contain at least three sentences. Some facts are accurate, although one or more errors are present. One example is given.

D Paper contains only one paragraph. Some facts are accurate, though no evidence or examples are given to support them.

F Unconnected sentences contain few accurate facts. Many errors are stated. No examples given.

This format for essay evaluation is especially useful for assessing students' levels of comprehension on a topic. It also provides an opportunity for students to demonstrate their ability to analyze the topic, but it limits the use of synthesis and evaluation. If students are provided with the rubric system before they begin writing, they are more likely to know what the teacher expects of them and thus be able to deliver it.

For other purposes, the extended-response essay gives students more freedom to express ideas and opinions and to use synthesis-level thinking skills to transform knowledge into a creative new idea. In the astronomy unit, the teacher may hope that students will gain a sense of responsibility for the Earth after studying its place in the universe. This affective goal for the unit may also be expressed as a series of problem-solving or expressive objectives; for example,

> At the end of the unit, students will write an essay entitled "The Big Blue Marble," in which they express their own hopes and fears for the future of the Earth. The essays will be edited, rewritten, illustrated, and displayed for parents to view on parent's night.

This extended-response essay calls on students to integrate all that they have learned in this unit and combine it with previous learning from geography and social studies units. Their individual experiences and outside readings are likely to affect their responses as well. Objectivity in marking this essay is very low. It is quite likely that teachers will view the responses differently. Nevertheless, within a single classroom, a teacher can say or state a set of criteria or expectations that can lead students to write a successful essay. In this instance, as stated in the objective, students will have an opportunity to receive critical feedback and make corrections on their essays before the final products are displayed.

Despite the lack of objectivity of extended-response essays, there is good reason to include them in an educational program. They provide invaluable information about the creativity, values, philosophy, and maturity of students. Moreover, they encourage students to become more creative and give them practice in making difficult judgments. One of the most effective ways to provide students with the information they need to succeed is to provide them with the rubric descriptions prior to the time they write their essays. Another very effective technique in preparing them to write their own essays is to have them use the rubric criteria descriptions you have given them to evaluate a mock essay that you have written. This can be very useful as a whole-class activity. When students can see the criteria upon which their work will be evaluated, they are able to meet the expectations with much greater degrees of success than when they try to guess what the teacher expects or wants from them.

ORAL REPORTS AND EXAMINATIONS

Like essays, oral reports can be restricted or unrestricted depending on the type of assessment the teacher wants to generate. To increase objectivity and communicate expectations to students, teachers can create rubric systems describing the length and format of the oral report as well as what must be included. Examples of restricted oral reports include book reports in which students are expected to describe the main characters, the setting, the plot, and their favorite part of the story. In a restricted oral examination, teachers may ask questions that students must answer within specified parameters. In the astronomy unit, an oral examination may be scheduled for a certain day. Students are told to prepare for it by reading material supplied by NASA on the U.S. space program. In the examination, teachers ask questions taken from the reading material, and students are expected to respond in their own words; for example:

Tell how the astronauts prepared for weightlessness.
Describe the food astronauts eat in space.

As teachers listen to the students' responses, it is possible for them to make a judgment about whether their answers are right or wrong. It is also possible to assess whether the students have a poor, average, or unusually good understanding of the ideas they speak about. Teachers' evaluation of the students' responses can be recorded in some form, to be shared with the students later.

Unrestricted oral reports allow students more opportunities to speak about matters of great interest and importance to them. They encourage students to use their imagination to generate synthesis-level responses or to be persuasive about a matter of opinion or judgment. Some examples for topics include the following:

Describe the space journey you'd like to take.
Tell us what you think should be NASA's next big undertaking.

Debate is a form of oral examination because it provides students with an opportunity to prepare to speak about a subject by learning a great deal of content and evidence for opinions prior to the event. During the debate, teachers can assess the students' energy and effort used in gathering information, as well as their understanding of the topic.

In evaluating oral presentations, teachers may write comments as they listen, or they may video the presentations so that they can evaluate them more comprehensively later. Students may also be involved in evaluating their own efforts. They can view the video and discuss with the teacher what they did well and what they need to improve.

DESIGNING AUTHENTIC ASSESSMENT TASKS

It is possible to construct assessment tasks that measure student performance in terms of using higher-level thinking skills of analysis and evaluation, as well as critical thinking skills of observation and inference and problem-solving strategies such as the creation and testing of hypotheses. These tests can be constructed as paper-and-pencil exams, presenting a situation or dilemma and asking students to respond to it in various ways. Such tests may consist of a passage to be read that describes a problem or dilemma. Maps, charts, graphs, or other forms of data might also be available on the test. The test items then consist of questions that allow the student to observe, infer, formulate a hypothesis, design methods of testing the hypothesis, and speculate about the possible outcome.

Another common method of assessing students' authentic learning is to encourage them to do independent research on one aspect of a unit theme and to create a product that shows what they have learned. This method allows students to demonstrate their knowledge, comprehension, and all four of the higher-level thinking skills on a topic. This assessment technique is appropriate for every area of the curriculum. Students can do independent research or make an independent investigation in math, science, social studies, literature, music, or art. This method lends itself especially well to interdisciplinary units.

The strategy is for the teacher to introduce a unit or theme and provide some teacher-centered instruction on it at the outset. Readings may be assigned, and quizzes and worksheets

Characteristics of Each Level	Products Associated with Each Level
Remembering Level Can recognize and recall specific terms, facts, and symbols.	**Remembering Level** Worksheets, labeling diagrams, memorizing poems or lists, responding to flashcards.
Understanding Level Constructing meaning from oral, written, and graphic messages.	**Understanding Level** Paraphrasing information, giving examples, sorting or classifying by a given criteria, summarizing orally or in writing.
Applying Level Using knowledge or procedures.	**Applying Level** Completing a math calculation, diagramming or illustrating, writing and solving story problems, using writing skills to create a paragraph.
Analyzing Level Breaking material apart and showing how the parts relate to one another.	**Analyzing Level** Showing cause and effect, differences and similarities; determining the author's point of view; finding relevant numbers in a word problem; comparing and contrasting.
Evaluating Level Making judgments based on criteria and standards.	**Evaluating Level** Ranking or prioritizing, choosing the best solution from two or more possibilities, writing critiques.
Creating Level Putting elements together to create a functional whole or creating new material.	**Creating Level** Planning, researching, and writing a report, creating a new example, generating and supporting hypotheses.

Figure 10.1 Student products related to the revised Bloom's taxonomy.
Source: Adapted from Anderson et al. (2001).

may be used to assess the extent to which the students are developing a knowledge base about the topic. Essays or oral presentations may be assigned to assess whether students comprehend the main ideas and concepts of the topic. Finally, each student selects one aspect of the main topic on the basis of individual preference or interest and begins to research that subtopic independently. Each student decides on a final product that will demonstrate what has been learned and achieved during the independent study.

The kinds of products that students might create as a result of this type of investigation are limitless. Many teachers prefer to plan their evaluations of student accomplishment to correspond with the revised Bloom's taxonomy. Specific student products are appropriate for learning objectives at all six levels. A sample of them can be found in Figure 10.1.

Teachers may evaluate these student products using a rubric checklist or rating scale. Specific rubric systems may be specified so that students know exactly what their product must demonstrate to earn a high mark or positive evaluation from the teacher. Reflective teachers who wish to encourage critical thinking and reflection among their students are also likely to involve the students in self-evaluation of their products. When students evaluate their work critically, they are learning how to become more independent and responsible for revising and improving their work without an outside evaluator.

RUBRICS, CHECKLISTS, AND RATING SCALES

When teachers wish to assess students' products or presentations, they can tell the students their reactions in a conference or write comments on a piece of paper and give these comments to the students. These methods suffice for informing the students, in a general way, whether they have met the teacher's expectations for the product, and they may be adequate for evaluating an unrestricted product or presentation.

When the teacher has specified the criteria for a product or presentation and several important elements must be included, the teacher may choose to create a rubric or checklist to use for notation when listening, for example, to a speech. This is frequently done when the objective involves the use of effective speaking skills in a presentation. In preparing the students for the speech, the teacher will likely specify several important elements that the students should incorporate, such as maintaining eye contact with the audience, using appropriate volume to be heard by everyone in the room, and speaking rather than reading during the presentation. By preparing a simple checklist with these items on it, the teacher can quickly and accurately record whether each student used these skills in his or her presentation. To make the whole system even more valuable, the teacher can share the rubrics with the students ahead of time so that students can make much better judgments about what to study, what to include, or how to present the information they have learned.

Rubrics and checklists can record mastery of many basic skills in the primary grades. Each item on the checklist can correspond directly to a behavioral objective. Together, the items on a checklist provide an overview of a sequence of objectives. Kindergarten teachers frequently employ checklists to record the letter recognition of each pupil, letter by letter. Primary teachers use checklists to record mastery of basic math operations. Intermediate and middle school teachers may use checklists to record whether students have demonstrated fundamental research skills. In our example of the astronomy unit, the teacher may combine a goal of developing research and study skills with the goal of content mastery. To record the accomplishment of these skills, the teacher may use a checklist such as the one shown in Figure 10.2.

Checklists provide useful and efficient means of recording information about the accomplishments of individual students. They are also very valuable during a student–teacher conference. Both teacher and student can quickly see what has been achieved and what still lies ahead. Checklists are also valuable when teachers confer with parents about the student's progress along a set of learning objectives.

Rating scales are used in circumstances similar to those of checklists. They provide additional information, however, in the form of a rating of how well the student achieved each element or skill on the list. Rating scales are useful in providing students with feedback that rates their performance on an objective. In the astronomy unit, for example, students' products may be turned in and evaluated by the teacher, who uses a rating scale of important elements. In many classrooms, teachers involve the student in their own evaluation of the product and the

Name _____	Grade _____

This is a record of research and study skills demonstrated by this student. The teacher's initials and date indicate when the skill was successfully demonstrated.

Date	Initials	Skill Area
_____	_____	A. Located a book on astronomy in the card catalog
_____	_____	B. Located a book on astronomy on the library shelves
_____	_____	C. Used the table of contents to find a topic
_____	_____	D. Used the index to find a subtopic
_____	_____	E. Orally interpreted a graph or chart
_____	_____	F. Took notes on a chapter in a book on astronomy
_____	_____	G. Summarized the chapter from notes
_____	_____	H. Wrote a bibliographic entry for the book

Figure 10.2 Astronomy unit checklist of research and study skills.

Name _____ Grade _____

To the student: Please evaluate your own product, using the following scale:

O = OUTSTANDING; one of my best efforts
S = SATISFACTORY; I accomplished what I set out to do
N = NEEDS IMPROVEMENT; I need to revise and improve this element

Student's Rating	Skill Area	Teacher's Rating
_____	Did adequate research and information gathering	_____
_____	Elements of the model are accurate in shape	_____
_____	Elements of the model are accurate in scale (except for orbits of planets)	_____
_____	Labeling is accurate and legible	_____
_____	Legend is accurate and legible	_____
_____	Model is visually interesting and pleasing	_____

Figure 10.3 Rating scale for the solar system model in the astronomy unit.

efforts expended in creating them. In Figure 10.3, a rating scale is structured so that both the student and the teacher rate the finished product.

A rubric system is similar to a checklist, but it also employs detailed descriptions of the specific levels of mastery the teacher hopes that students will attain. Student products are then compared to the levels of mastery described in the rubric system. Figure 10.4 shows a rubric system that allows the teacher to compare student products related to the astronomy research project against a set of specific criteria. As has been suggested before, if students are given this

To the student: Read these criteria before you begin your research so that you will know how to earn the level you want to attain.

Turn in a 5–10 page booklet on the solar system. The booklet may contain a combination of words, pictures, graphs, and any other types of illustrations that show an understanding of the physical elements of the planets, moons, and sun that make up our solar system. The booklet will be evaluated according to the following criteria.

Level 4: The student clearly and completely identifies the important planets and moons of the solar system and shows how they are related to the sun and each other in size and space. There is a combination of verbal descriptions and visual illustrations that make the distinguishing features of each planet very evident. The writing is well organized and references are given for sources of information. At least four references are provided.

Level 3: The student clearly identifies the planets and some of the most important moons of the solar system. Relationships of size and space are given, though they may be distorted in some cases. Verbal information is fairly well organized and illustrations are useful in distinguishing among the planets. At least two references are given as sources of information.

Level 2: The student correctly names the nine planets and shows that they travel around the sun. Relationships among planets are not accurate. The booklet uses more pictures than words. Only one source of information is provided.

Level 1: The student incorrectly labels planets and shows little understanding of their relationship to the sun and to each other. Verbal information is given as captions for illustrations only. No source of information is given.

Figure 10.4 Rubric grading evaluation system for the astronomy research project.

rubric system prior to beginning the unit, they are empowered to make better choices about how to use their time, what to study, and how to present the material they have learned.

You will often see rubrics with four levels of quality, as shown in Figure 10.4. What do the levels 4 through 1 mean? Are they the same as the grades A, B, C, and D? Andrade (2000) observes that "satisfactory labels are hard to come by, although it is obvious at a glance that a 4 is what everyone should try to achieve and a 1 is something to avoid. Some teachers indicate a cutoff point on the rubric, for instance, by drawing a box around the level that is considered acceptable.

How do you, as a classroom teacher, learn how to create fair and useful rubrics for your classroom assignments? Andrade (2000) suggests that you look at other models of rubrics, but then *involve your own students in the process.* She envisions the teacher and students discussing the criteria together, listing the most important criteria, and then writing descriptions of the various levels of quality. One method Andrade suggests for creating rubrics uses these four sentence stems: Yes; Yes, but; No, but; and No. For example, if the criterion is "Briefly summarize the plot of the story," the four levels might be the following:

Level 4—"Yes, I briefly summarized the plot."

Level 3—"Yes, I summarized the plot, but I also included some unnecessary details or left out key information."

Level 2—"No, I didn't summarize the plot, but I did include some details from the story."

Level 1—"No, I didn't summarize the plot." (Andrade, 2000, 14)

LEARNING CONTRACTS

A learning contract is a device that can be thought of both as a teaching strategy and a means of assessment. The learning contract described in Chapter 7 lists several required activities and a number of options for the unit on settling the western United States. Teachers using this strategy meet with individual students to agree on a suitable number and type of optional activities. The activities on the contract then provide the structure for daily learning experiences. When the unit is complete, the contract is used as the basis for assessing what each student has accomplished. Just as in adult life, students are held accountable for meeting the terms of their contracts. If they succeed, they can expect a positive evaluation. If they have not met the terms of their contract, they can expect to have to explain why and describe what they will do to honor their contract.

Learning contracts can take several forms and can even be structured so that the student makes a contract to receive a certain grade for a specified amount of work. A point system can be employed to allow students to select from among options and earn the grade they desire. For example, a learning contract with a built-in point system for earning a grade for the astronomy unit is shown in Figure 10.5.

Learning contracts also serve as the basis for recording accomplishments. In the sample learning contract for the astronomy unit, the parent is also required to sign the contract, agreeing to support the student's efforts. This strategy is an efficient way to communicate with parents about the goals and expectations of the class. Later, during parent-teacher conferences, the parent can see the work that was accomplished. If a student did not complete the contract, the parent can see what was left undone.

PORTFOLIOS OF STUDENT PRODUCTS

Portfolios are collections of work samples designed to illustrate a person's accomplishments in a talent area. Photographers collect portfolios of their best photos; artists collect their artwork; composers collect their compositions. Assessment portfolios are used to document what a student has achieved in school. To use this technique, teachers collect samples of each student's work and put them in separate file folders with the students' names on them. Some teachers collect many types of work in a single portfolio, one for each student; others have

---

Astronomy Unit Learning Contract

I, _____ , a student in the fifth grade at
_____ School, do hereby contract to complete the following tasks during my
investigation of the solar system.

Furthermore, I agree to complete these tasks by _____ .

I understand that I am agreeing to earn _____ points, which will earn a
grade of _____ if my work is evaluated to be acceptable. I understand that the point values listed below are the maximum number that can be
earned for each task and that fewer points may be awarded.

Points Needed to Earn Specific Grades

> 90 = A	> 80 = B	> 70 = C	> 60 = D	< 60 = F

_____ 10 pts Read chapter 7 in the science text. Do exercises, pp. 145–146.

_____ 10 pts Matching quiz

_____ 10 pts True-false quiz

_____ 10 pts Multiple-choice quiz

_____ 10 pts Short-answer quiz

_____ 15 pts Drawing of the solar system, labeled correctly

_____ 20 pts Model of the solar system, labeled and scaled to size

_____ 10 pts Essay on Earth's atmosphere and outer space

_____ 10 pts Essay on "The Big Blue Marble"

_____ 05 pts Per answer on NASA oral exam

_____ 10 pts Oral report on "A Space Journey I'd Like to Take"

_____ 10 pts Finished Checklist on Research Skills

Signed this day _____ , 20 _____ at _____ School.

_____   _____
      student signature   teacher signature

_____   _____
      parent signature   witness signature

Figure 10.5 Sample learning contract.

writing portfolios that contain only writing samples, math portfolios filled with worksheets and tests, and other portfolios for other subject areas.

It is important to understand that a collection of student work in a folder is not a portfolio assessment. As an assessment tool, a portfolio contains a selection of work samples, anecdotal records, tests, and other materials that document the student's progress. The student's progress must then be analyzed and summarized by the teacher and the student. There should be a statement of goals written jointly by the student and teacher. Students can select samples of work to be included in the portfolio and write brief explanations of the reason the item was selected and the progress it shows. Often there are summary sheets that document the students' growth.

Portfolio assessment allows students to demonstrate their content knowledge without being dependent on English fluency or reading ability. Portfolios allow the teacher and student to approach the anxiety-laden process of evaluation more comfortably because it celebrates progress rather than weaknesses.

Portfolios may be kept for a long or short time. Many teachers collect writing samples in the first week of school, then periodically throughout the school year. In some cases the teacher may assign a writing topic during the first week and then assign the very same topic during the last week of school. When the two samples on the same topic are compared, the growth and development of the students' writing abilities is plain for everyone to see.

A short-term portfolio may be collected for the duration of a learning unit. For example, in the astronomy unit, all of the student's work, including quizzes, essays, pictures, and photos of the model solar system, can be collected in a portfolio to document that student's accomplishment during the unit. If a contract was used during the unit, the contract is included in the portfolio along with the work samples. In the following reflective action story, Diane Leonard, a first-grade teacher, shares her experience on developing portfolios.

✳ REFLECTIVE ACTION CASE STUDY ✳

Teacher's Reflection on Portfolio Assessment

Diane Leonard, First-Grade Teacher, Balderas Elementary School, Fresno, California

Teacher Begins to Plan

I teach in an inner-city school, where the vast majority of the students are from lower socioeconomic settings and are second-language English learners. I notice that my students respond best when I can give them concrete examples and model what I want them to do.

Teacher Considers What Students Already Know

Because my students are all second-language learners, I feel it's important to document and celebrate their growth. First-graders' work changes rapidly, and I've found collecting samples of their work showing the growth they've made to be a good way to communicate with their parents, many of whom speak very little English. It also helps me to focus on exactly what they need to be taught based on where they are in relation to the achievement of standards.

Teacher Has Expectations

I needed a system to accomplish several things at once. I need to be able to relate the students' progress to their achievement of the standards. I need to be able to clearly summarize the growth they make on their report cards. I need to be able to show their parents the progress that their children are making, and I need to be able to give 6-year-olds concrete examples of things they can be working on to improve their own learning. I had heard about portfolios, but no one at my school was actually using them. I wanted to find out more about them, so I went on a search for resources.

Teacher Does Research and Invites Feedback

Because I was in a master's program at my university, I decided that researching and implementing portfolios in my classroom might be a good project. I did a literature review on portfolio assessment and decided that I could implement this approach and create my master's project at the same time. Because my undergraduate major had been video production, I decided to document each step of my implementation on video. I hoped that the implementation would be successful and then I could share the process and the product with my colleagues.

Reflective Teachers Use Withitness

I started with a small piece of portfolio assessment by setting up storage boxes in my classroom. Each child had an individual portfolio labeled with his or her name. I collected baseline examples of their writing, drawing, cutting, and reading (a running record). I made video clips of each step of the process and shared the video with three of my colleagues. Their input into the ongoing process helped me to clarify the elements in the video, make adjustments, and include explanations of the process.

Afterward, Teacher Reflects on the Event

As I continued my refinement of the portfolios and sharing with my colleagues, it became obvious that this was more than just a classroom problem, it was a schoolwide challenge. Because I had included my colleagues in the process, several of them asked if they could implement portfolio assessment in their classrooms, based on my model. By the end of the school year, all of the first-grade teachers were using portfolio assessment. This gave us the opportunity to sit together and help each other evaluate the products in the portfolios in relation to the first-grade content standards. It also gave us an opportunity to share ideas for lessons that would help our students move toward meeting the standards.

Teacher Creates a New Action Plan

The first-grade teachers who had implemented portfolio assessment and collaborative scoring asked the principal if we could share this approach with the entire faculty. The principal set up a series of faculty meetings so we could share the implementation video and talk about the success of the collaborative approach in implementing the process.

Portfolios may be used at all grade levels and for any subject or course a student takes. When portfolios are meant to be used to document student accomplishment, they must be organized so that they reveal the development of a skill or the growing understanding of a set of ideas. To demonstrate growth and change, Wolf (1989) suggests collecting "biographies of works, a range of works and reflections" (p. 37).

The biography of a work consists of several drafts of a work, showing the student's initial conception of the project, the first attempts, and the final product. By collecting these items, the teacher can document the growth and development of the student. Wolf (1989) further recommends that, after completing this collection, the teacher may ask the student to reexamine all the stages of the work and reflect on the process and the products from beginning to end. The student's reflection may be done in writing or captured as an audio recording (and later transcribed onto paper) and should then be included in the portfolio itself. This self-evaluation process is valuable in helping the student develop metacognitive abilities that can then be applied to future self-assessments in academic or real-life settings.

Wolf (1989) also suggests that teachers deliberately collect a range of works, meaning a diverse collection, consisting of journals, essays, poems, drawings, charts, graphs, letters, tests, and samples of daily work. When using the portfolio as a basis for a parent-teacher conference, this range allows the teacher to discuss and document many different aspects of the student's school accomplishments.

Primary teachers must take responsibility for setting up a system for assisting the children in collecting and filing items in their portfolios. Colored portfolios in storage boxes or bins can be used so that the younger students do not have to search the whole box to locate their own folios. The teacher should take care to put similar names in different colored folders to assist the children in locating their personal work. Each item entered into the portfolio should be date-stamped, and even young children can be taught to put their work in chronological order by date in the folder. This adds another dimension to the portfolio because it adds authentic learning tasks (alphabetizing and filing in chronological order) to the process of maintaining the portfolios. The portfolios should contain periodic representative examples of the child's sequential improvement and advancement through the learning process. At the higher levels, however, students may be asked to assume more responsibility for choosing representative examples that document their growth and learning. The teacher may suggest items to be included, and the student may decide on others. At the end of a people and nature unit, for example, each student may have a portfolio containing the tests, lab reports, essays, creative writing, and charts created for the unit. Portfolios are especially powerful in documenting the growth of English learners through representative samples of class work when the teacher encourages students to document their understandings in less traditional ways. Diagrams, illustrations, recordings, multimedia presentations, and the like, can be included to document content knowledge growth without being bound by the student's English writing ability. Students' growth in English language development, both oral and written, is also documented in the portfolio.

Portfolios of student work are an excellent way to communicate with parents about students' accomplishments. When the parent and teacher look at the representative writing samples together, they can both reflect on the student's growth and better understand what the student's strengths and weaknesses are at a glance. When a parent sees the signed contract and the completed work, both parent and teacher are looking at the same evidence to support the resulting grades.

Some teachers, and even entire schools, schedule portfolio days toward the end of the school year. Each student selects his or her best work for the year and prepares a short presentation to talk about the work, what it represents in the way of effort and accomplishment. Parents and community members are invited to the school to hear the students talk about their work and to ask questions of the students. In schools where portfolio days are a regular part of the school schedule, teachers help the students to plan by being made aware of these presentation days in advance so that they have an opportunity to carefully select the work they will present and to write and practice their presentations. Teachers may also choose to assess the students' oral presentation skills as part of the portfolio day.

VIDEO RECORDS

When the purpose of evaluation is to record the accomplishment of a student and allow later analysis and more comprehensive evaluation, a video is an excellent way to capture and store a variety of learning events. Speeches can be easily captured on video. So can dramas, skits, presentations, and displays of students' products.

Videos are also excellent ways to communicate to parents the accomplishments of a student or the entire class. They allow all interested parties to view the final products or performances of a unit of study. Teachers can store on tape a whole year's worth of accomplishments.

Video recordings also provide teachers with data they need to evaluate their own plans. By reviewing a video of a classroom learning event, reflective teachers can gain new understandings about what students need from their learning environment to be successful.

Video elements can also be successfully incorporated into computer-based presentations. Programs like PowerPoint provide excellent opportunities for students to display their work in a number of formats as videos, photographs, documents, and audio recordings. Elements of the presentation can then be easily manipulated, edited, and combined as students progress through their studies.

GRADING COOPERATIVE GROUP PROJECTS AND PRODUCTS

Many of the assessment methods described in this chapter can be adapted for cooperative groups. Evaluation of cooperative group efforts should include an assessment of both a task that requires a group effort to complete and an assessment of individual efforts to ensure that each member of the group takes responsibility for doing personal reading and preparation.

For example, to adapt the astronomy unit for use by cooperative groups, each group can function as a study team with directions to assist one another in reading and preparing for the quizzes. Group scores can be computed and recorded for each quiz at the same time that individual scores are recorded.

The contract system works well with cooperative groups. When used in this way, there is one contract per group instead of per individual. Each group negotiates what they will accomplish together. Evaluations can include peer assessments, with members of the group providing critical feedback for one another.

Assessment of student accomplishment is a complex and multifaceted undertaking. There isn't one best way to assess what students have learned or accomplished in school. Some methods work better than others at various grade levels. Some work better than others with different individuals. This chapter has provided you with a number of assessment methods so you can develop a repertoire of assessment devices to use as the basis for making judgments about the accomplishments of your students.

REPORTING STUDENT ACCOMPLISHMENTS

Report cards. These two words are likely to elicit memories filled with anxiety and a variety of other conflicting emotions for most people. In your many years of schooling, you have probably received more than 50 report cards. You probably viewed many with relief and happiness and proudly displayed them to your parents; others may have caused torment and disbelief. On occasion, you may have questioned the teacher's fairness or integrity; you may have questioned whether the teacher really got to know you or understood the effort you put into your work. Perhaps you have even approached a teacher and challenged the grade you received, showing evidence of why the assigned grade was unjustified.

Eight or nine weeks into your first school year of teaching, you will face the task of deciding on and recording report card grades for your students. Many first-year teachers consider the responsibility one of their most difficult challenges. Experienced teachers often report that the task does not seem to get easier as the years pass. In fact, many reflective teachers find that the more they know about grades and children, the more difficult it is to sum up the work and efforts of a student in a single letter grade.

Reflective teachers struggle with many conflicting ideas, thoughts, and concerns when they confront existing evaluation systems. Systems using letter grades are likely to be based on the assumption that students vary in ability and acquire learning by passively receiving knowledge from the teacher. From this assumption, it is logical to conclude that students should be evaluated by determining what they have learned and how this compares to other students of the same age. Categorizing and rank ordering of students is the next step and is done by assigning letter grades to label their respective categories of ability. Teachers with this perspective can be overheard saying, "John is an A student, and Sally is a C student."

Reflective, caring teachers are often very uncomfortable with such statements. They recognize the complex mix of environmental, nutritional, genetic, and experiential factors that contribute to each student's success or lack of success in school. According to their view of teaching and learning, it is the teachers' responsibility to diagnose their students' needs and plan a series of learning experiences, scaffolding each student's learning as needed, in order for them to experience success. The competitive nature of letter grades contrasts sharply with this philosophy.

Due to the time-consuming nature of the task of correcting students' work and the complexities of the evaluation processes described previously, it is easy to see why school personnel have resorted to a form of shorthand to record and report student progress. Most teachers have too many students and too little time to hold discussions with each student's parents or to write extensive narratives of each student's learning on a regular basis. Schools use standardized shorthand methods known as grades and test scores to communicate with parents, future teachers, college admissions personnel, and future employers (Oakes & Lipton, 1990).

The practice of awarding letter grades as measures of individual achievement has been part of the U.S. educational scene for many decades. In the 1960s and 1970s, personnel in some school districts attempted to replace conventional report cards with detailed anecdotal records, describing what each student had accomplished in each subject area during the course or term. But these attempts to change the prevailing evaluation system met with opposition from parents, who insisted on a return to the letter grade system with which they had grown up. Parents were not satisfied with a description of their own child's achievements. They wanted to know how their child compared with other students. They expressed concern that these records would not be accepted at the most prestigious colleges.

In response to these debates, school boards and administrators in most school districts arrived at a compromise. They reestablished the letter grade report cards for the intermediate and upper elementary grades, but they retained the use of anecdotal report cards for the primary grades. As more and more states have adopted standards-based education, reporting systems are being developed to reflect the student's progress toward meeting the standard in each content area. Thus, if you are planning to teach at the primary grades (kindergarten through the second or third grade), you may be expected to write anecdotal report cards describing and documenting the progress each student in your classroom has made toward meeting the content standards for that grade. If you are planning to teach at higher levels (upper elementary, middle, or high school), you may still be expected to compute letter grades for the students' report cards. However, the letter grade computation may include reference to the student's progress toward achievement of standards in a standards-based system.

ELECTRONIC MANAGEMENT SYSTEMS

Electronic management systems can be categorized into two basic functional groups: a student information system and a learning management system. A student information system is deployed by administration at their school, district, or even state level. These systems are designed to keep track of all the pertinent information on a student: the student's address, demographical information, coursework, attendance, lunch programs, grades, and even individualized educational plan (IEP) information. Companies like Excelsior Software (http://www.excelsiorsoftware.com/) and Schoolmaster (http://www.schoolmaster.com/) provide the software and other services to meet an organization's student information needs. Most teachers in the classroom might use only a portion of the software or services provided, like the grade book or attendance function of the software.

Many districts and states have also developed proprietary student information systems. Learning management systems, such as Blackboard or Moodle, can be deployed at the classroom, school, district, or even state level; they provide tools to manage the electronic educational environment. These systems allow the teacher to post grades, assignments, video, and electronic messages. They also allow students to submit assignments and to view their graded assignments and cumulative grades. In some cases, parents have access to their children's grades and the teachers' comments. Some of these programs also have options to allow and encourage communication between teachers and parents. In some instances where learning management systems are being used along with student information systems, the systems can share and transfer pertinent information about the students from teachers to administrators as well as parents.

Some districts are now requiring teachers to post grades at the middle of the term for students so that parents do not have to wait until the end of the 6- or 9-week grading period to view their children's progress. If parents have consistent access to the grading of assignments, they can contribute to solving problems earlier in the grading period. They will know when they need to confer with the teacher to determine what type of assistance is needed, and they can talk with their child to provide help or motivation.

COMPUTATION OF GRADES

At the end of the astronomy unit described earlier, the grades for all of the reports, tests, and projects may be recorded in the teachers' grade books, as shown in Figure 10.6. Computation of the final grades for this curriculum unit involves a straightforward computation of an

Name of Student	Graded Objectives					Average Score	Report Card Grade
	1	2	3	4	5		
Lisa	A	B	B	A	C		
	4 +	3 +	3 +	4 +	2	= 16/5 = 3.2	B
Peter	B	C	A	C	D		
	3 +	2 +	4 +	2 +	1	= 12/5 = 2.4	C+
Alejandro	B	A	A	B	A		
	3 +	4 +	4 +	3 +	4	= 18/5 = 3.6	A–

A = 4 points
B = 3
C = 2
D = 1
F = 0

Figure 10.6 Teacher's grade book.

average grade by awarding numerical equivalents to each letter grade, adding the seven items, and dividing the total score by 7. The average scores can then be assigned a letter grade. After they are computed, the grades are recorded in the student's cumulative folder and on the report cards that are sent home to parents. Intermediate report cards are likely to use letter grades to sum up the student's achievement in each academic subject. Some report cards may also provide checklists of subskills beneath the letter grade as a means of explaining to parents how the letter grade was determined.

WRITING ANECDOTAL RECORDS

In most school districts, teachers are responsible for writing three or four report cards per year. These report cards contain descriptions of each student's current level of accomplishment in each of the major areas of the curriculum, plus a summary of the student's work habits and social adjustment to school and peers. At the primary grades, report cards usually consist of either anecdotal records or checklists of skills rather than letter grades. Some school districts may use both. The advantage of this double format is that it allows teachers to describe and report their direct observations of a student's actual behaviors and accomplishments with sufficient detail so that parents understand the student's strengths and deficiencies. This is especially useful for skill areas such as listening, speaking, writing, study habits, social skills, and interests (Linn & Gronlund, 2000).

When a concern about a student arises, the teacher's daily observations of the student's work habits and social interactions can be important sources of data to help parents or other school personnel understand the student's particular needs and strengths. These observations may be augmented by written anecdotal records of what the teacher observes. For example, if a student comes to school late, appears tired, and has difficulty sitting still at her desk, the teacher may want to document these observations by keeping a short anecdotal record for a week, recording how late the student is every morning and describing episodes of falling asleep or inattentiveness. When this written record is shown to the parents, they are more likely to cooperate with the teacher in seeking answers to the problem than if the teacher simply reports orally that the student is "always late and too tired to work."

To be used to their best advantage, anecdotal records should be limited to observations of specific skills, social problems, or behavioral concerns. If a teacher sets out to record every behavior and event in a student's school day, the process will become too tiring and difficult to be feasible. Instead, when a student is exhibiting a particular behavior or deficiency in a skill area, the teacher can focus on daily descriptions of that one area and be successful in producing a useful document.

The major limitation or disadvantage of the anecdotal record is teachers' tendency to project their own value judgments into the description of a student's behavior or accomplishment. This is due, in part, to the tendency to observe what fits one's preconceived notions. For example, nonreflective teachers may tend to notice more desirable qualities in those pupils they like best and more undesirable qualities in those they like least. The recommended way to avoid this tendency is to keep descriptions of observed incidents separate from your interpretation. First, state exactly what happened in nonjudgmental words. Then, if you wish to add your interpretation of the event, do so in a separate paragraph and label it as such (Linn & Gronlund, 2000).

In general, a single observation is seldom as meaningful as a series of events in understanding a student's behavior. Therefore, anecdotal records should contain brief descriptions of related incidents over time to provide a reliable picture of a student's behavior.

INVOLVING STUDENTS IN EVALUATION PROCEDURES

For reflective teachers, the natural extension of the teaching process is the interactive evaluation process that encourages students to become active evaluators of their own efforts and products. The current writing programs organized around periodic student-teacher conferences and the grouping of students who edit one another's work are excellent examples of this type of evaluation. In classrooms that feature such writing programs, the teacher's role in evaluation is to confer with the students about their current writing projects and to ask questions that engage them in analyzing what they have written.

Teachers may use open-ended questions designed to gather information on what the student has intended to do in a piece of writing. When the teacher has a sufficient understanding of the student's goal, the teacher and student may begin to zero in on ways to improve the quality of the writing so that it more nearly matches the student's purpose. This may mean correcting the mechanics of the writing so that it can be understood by others, or guiding the student to rethink the way a passage is written and to consider new ways of stating the ideas.

The editing groups used in such writing programs encourage students to learn how to listen to and respect the work their peers are creating. Typically, students in a group each read aloud from a current piece of writing and then answer questions about the content from the other students in the group. Through this type of interactive evaluation, students may be learning how to work cooperatively, accept critical feedback, and write better at the same time.

This interactive evaluation system can be used in other parts of the curriculum, too. The question "What did you learn?" should form the core of the classroom evaluation. The more often this question is asked, the easier it is for students to identify and receive the help they need. It is a question children can learn to ask themselves (Oakes & Lipton, 1990, p. 132).

Providing students with self-evaluation checklists or rating scales assists them in learning more specific types of questions about their own progress and achievement. Checklists and rating scales that ask the student to evaluate specific outcomes may be developed for any learning activity, especially a unit of study that takes place over several weeks. Teacher evaluations may be entered on the same form to allow students and their parents to compare the student's self-evaluation with the teacher's assessment of the student's accomplishments. For example, in Figure 10.7, students are allowed to assess themselves after completing a research unit on leadership.

Interactive evaluation procedures are designed to breed success and enhance students' metacognitive capacities. They are as much a part of the learning process as they are a part of the assessment process. In fact, the long-term goals of most caring, reflective teachers are likely to emphasize the development of independence, self-responsibility, self-discipline, and self-evaluation as important affective goals of education. These goals are achieved through the development of metacognitive processes as children learn to understand how to succeed in any learning environment.

Leadership Unit

Student/Teacher Evaluation

Name of student _____ Grade _____ Date _____

Leader selected for research _____

The student completes the left side of this evaluation and then the teacher will complete the right side. Afterward, student and teacher discuss the accomplishments made by the student, decide on areas that need to be improved, and plan goals for future learning experiences.

O = Outstanding   S = Satisfactory   N = Needs Improvement

Student Evaluation: **Teacher Evaluation:**

_____   I completed the readings and assignments for this unit on time.   _____

_____   I showed responsibility by bringing appropriate materials to class.   _____

_____   I showed growth in my planning, decision-making, and organizational skills.   _____

_____   I have gained skills in doing research and taking notes to gather information.   _____

_____   I used a variety of relevant and challenging resources to learn about my subject.   _____

_____   I improved my ability to speak in public.   _____

_____   I gained confidence in my ability to speak in public.   _____

_____   I gained independence in working on my own to achieve a goal.   _____

_____   I am able to evaluate my own accomplishments and identify what
        I need to improve with accuracy and honesty.

The most important thing I learned in this unit was:

Regarding my work in this unit, I am most proud of:

Figure 10.7 Interactive student–teacher evaluation for a leadership unit.

Communicating with Parents

You need to inform parents about the types of assessments that you will be using in your classroom. Make sure they understand that although "letter grades" are a great way to provide a snapshot of a child's work, they do not necessarily paint a complete picture of a student's progress. Use parent-teacher conferences to inform them of the variety and types of assessments you are using with their child. Show them examples and explain the importance of looking at a child's work through a multitude of lenses and not basing judgments on a single assessment. Talk with them about their role in creating a positive level of expectations, avoiding inappropriate and severe criticism, and providing positive reinforcement for successes in and outside school. Encourage them to join you as a team in finding the best way to teach and assess their child.

Playing Catch Up

When students are not working on grade level and their test scores are poor, they can often become very discouraged. As the teacher, you must find ways to help them to acquire the basic skills they need in order to make progress and begin to catch up. Standardized tests can be overwhelming for these students, and using portfolio assessment becomes a method to help them to begin to see the progress they are making. If you take baseline examples at the beginning of the year and store them in the students' portfolios, they can look back to see the work they did at the beginning and celebrate the growth they are making.

It is important to confer with students who are behind and set goals for them so that they can begin to see exactly what they need to accomplish in order to begin to catch up. If the teacher sits and reviews work with the students, they can set some learning goals together and begin to chart progress. It is important to confer frequently, to review the learning goals that have been set and the progress that has been made. Placing a progress chart in the front of the portfolio so that the student can see evidence of the progress helps to motivate most students, too.

Some schools have begun to schedule extended-day programs so that students who need additional instruction can be given the time after the other students have been dismissed or early in the morning before the others arrive. This should not be conveyed as punishment but an opportunity for the student to get the extra attention and instruction that is needed. If extended-day programs are scheduled, it is important that the students have an opportunity to practice their skills in a relaxed, informal way so that they don't see this extra time as just "more school." Some schools have provided enrichment type activities: computer time, math games, email writing groups, and special approaches that provide the skill development the students need by using a different approach from what they have been engaged in during regular school hours. One teacher even provided videos of sit-coms with closed captioning so that the students got to watch a funny television show while practicing their reading skills. It is important to find additional instructional time for the students who need to accelerate their learning in order to become more successful in the grade-appropriate learning activities.

GUIDED GROUP EXPLORATION

1. Divide the class into groups.
2. Have each group design a 4-point rubric for assessing a student portfolio on a social studies unit. The group may decide on the grade level, but remember to guide your assessment with the grade-level standards for the chosen grade.
3. Have each group present their rubric to the class, followed by a short discussion of each rubric.

REFLECTIVE ACTION ACTIVITY FOR YOUR PROFESSIONAL PORTFOLIO

Write a 10-question criterion-referenced test for a unit on the solar system or another unit of your choosing. You may choose your grade level. Be sure to base the questions on the appropriate subject matter standards for the chosen grade level.

References

Anderson, L., Krathwohl, D. (eds.). (2001) A taxonomy for learning, teaching, and assessing: A revision of Bloom's taxonomy of educational objectives. New York: Addison Wesley Longwood.

Andrade, H. (2000). What do we mean by results? Using rubrics to promote thinking and learning. *Educational Leadership, 57*(5), 11–14.

Cawelti, G., & Protheroe, N. (2001). *High student achievement: How six school districts changed into high-performance systems.* Arlington, VA: Educational Research Service.

Davenport, P. & Anderson, G. (2002). *Closing the achievement gap: NO EXCUSES.* Houston, TX: American Productivity and Quality Center.

Hoerr, T. (2009). Data that count. *Educational Leadership, 66*(1), 93–94.

Guskey, T., & Bailey, J. (2000). *Developing grading and reporting systems for student learning.* Berkeley, CA: Corwin Press.

Linn, R., & Gronlund, N. (2000). *Measurement and assessment in teaching* (8th ed.). Upper Saddle River, NJ: Prentice Hall.

Marzano, R. (2000). *Transforming classroom grading.* Alexandria, VA: Association for Supervision and Curriculum Development.

Meyers, E., & O'Donnell Rust, F. (2000, June 30). The test doesn't tell all: How teachers know that their students are learning. *Education Week*: 34, 37.

Oakes, J., & Lipton, M. (1990). *Making the best of schools.* New Haven, CT: Yale University Press.

Wolf, D. (1989). Portfolio assessment: Sampling student work. *Educational Leadership, 46*(7), 35–39.

Now go to Topic #6: Assessment in the MyEducationLab (www.myeducationlab.com <http://www.myeducationlab.com/>) for your course, where you can:

- Find learning outcomes for this topic along with the national standards that connect to these outcomes.
- Complete Assignments and Activities that can help you more deeply understand the chapter content.
- Apply and practice your understanding of the core teaching skills identified in the chapter with the Building Teaching Skills and Dispositions learning units.

Integrating Technology into the Curriculum

PREPARING STUDENTS TO THRIVE IN A HIGH-TECH WORLD

How do we prepare our students to thrive in the high-tech world of the 21st century? We learned how to do research in encyclopedias and libraries. Now we must teach our students how to do research on the Internet. We learned to make political and economic decisions by reading the newspaper and watching television newscasts to inform our votes. Although our students will continue to gather information from these same sources, much of their information is now gained online, and they may have to sort out opinion from fact when offered hundreds of different points of view from around the world.

We learned how to read, write, and do arithmetic from books and workbooks, but now we will use the latest CDs and computer programs to assist our students in learning the basics. Then we will enrich their curricula with an amazing array of high-tech ideas such as those found on www.schoolnotes.com, a site that allows teachers to share curriculum ideas and teaching strategies with one another. Another useful networking site is called Teachers Helping Teachers, located at www.pacificnet.net/~mandel/.

Of one thing we can be certain: nothing is going to stay the same very long in our future. How do we prepare our students to cope with change so that they can be flexible and yet have an underlying set of values to guide their decision making? How do we prepare them to respond creatively to the opportunities that come with the changing priorities of our world, without losing their sense of self?

In January 2000, Ravi Chhatpar, a recent college graduate, went to a job interview at an Internet firm in Boston. He was taken aback when, instead of talking about his education and experience, he was asked to build something with Legos™. He was given 5 minutes to build whatever he wanted, and then he and the interviewers would talk about his creation. Other job seekers are being asked to solve mathematical brainteasers and riddles to demonstrate their capacity to think under pressure. Another strategy is to ask a candidate to participate in a group game that tests the ability of the candidate to collaborate with others.

If our curriculum is going to keep pace with and prepare our students to thrive on the changes in our social and economic environment, it must go beyond the teaching of facts and concepts to involve students in problem solving and help them use multiple sources of information. The responsibility for making that a reality depends largely on your problem-solving skills, your ability to collaborate with others, and your capacity to think creatively and design new learning experiences that will generate enthusiastic responses from your students.

Imagine that you are a parent of a middle school student whose class has gone to a national park for several days to take part in an outdoor education experience. You might wonder what they are doing and feel somewhat disconnected from your child. However, if your child is spending the week visiting Yellowstone Park on a geology field trip with John Graves's class from Bozeman, Montana, you could monitor the daily activities of the class online at a site he created to keep the parents and the world informed about the class's explorations and adventures.

In the fall of 2003, you would have learned from the Web journal written by John's students that they climbed and hiked for 5.2 miles. On their webpage, they posted pictures of a snake and a brand new elk calf that they observed. You could also view their pictures of travertine terraces and of travertine being deposited around the base of living trees. This outdoor education experience and the way it is being reported to the entire world online is evidence of the significant change taking place in the way that educational experiences are structured and documented. The students' field trip is taking place along ancient ground, while they examine history and earth science with their own eyes. Yet their laptop computers allow them to communicate with their parents, other classmates, and educators around the world in real time.

Professional teachers are responsible for maintaining a repertoire of curricular strategies and resources in their classrooms. This repertoire should include primary sources, models, reproductions, textbooks, videos computer software, and musical recordings. Professional teachers are expected to keep abreast of technological developments that can add richness and depth to their teaching/learning experiences. Being able to engage students in making use of the rapidly expanding field of computer technology and how to use the computer to enhance their own teaching are both essential to the professional teacher.

As you read about or select a strategy to try in a laboratory or classroom, you will find that some of them work for you and others do not. You will need to reflect on what works for you and your students and why. As you think about what works, it is quite acceptable for you to combine, adapt, modify, and add your own unique strategies to the ones you read about or observe. Through this process of practice and reflection, you will discover, create, and refine your own unique teaching style.

Technology is a valuable tool and can play a pivotal role in education, but it is just that, a tool. It will never replace the types of spontaneous, invigorating class discussions that take place between students and teacher when they are actively engaged in puzzling out some dilemma or discussing the relative merits of an abstract idea such as liberty. The most effective teaching is still a human experience and great teachers thrive and take advantage of these teacher–student interactions.

In today's classroom, however, that interaction may be initiated and conducted through technological formats including online discussion boards and chat rooms. Teachers and their students may email one another after school hours, or parents may be monitoring what is happening in their children's classes by logging on to class webpages.

USING TECHNOLOGY TO TRACK HOW TEACHERS MEET STATE STANDARDS

Greenberg Elementary School opened in August 2000 as an inner-city school whose focus was to create an instructional environment in which standards and students' needs were the driving forces behind teaching practices. This was to be in contrast to the curriculum-driven situations found in many traditional school settings.

Early in the development of the school practices, the need for a means of monitoring students' progress through the standards, and in particular the elements that form the details of these standards, was identified. Because the number of elements tracked for each student was much more complex than the traditional grading system of average performance percentages, the management of tracking student progress threatened to become an impediment to the real objective, which was to use this information to inform instruction and also improve the match between student instructional needs and teacher planning and instruction.

Darrell Blanks, a fifth-grade teacher and the school's math coach, developed a database file using Microsoft Access with the hope of supporting teachers at his school in documenting students' achievement of standards. The teachers at Greenberg are linked via their computers to Darrell's system, where they can enter each child's progress in the meeting of grade-level content standards, element by element. Once the teachers enter the data, they can access class reports that show exactly which of their students have met each element of each standard. This allows them to form small groups for more focused instruction. The program also links the standards to suggested assessments and teaching strategies for each standard.

Once the data have been entered, the teachers can print standards-based report cards, which indicate to the parents the child's progress in meeting standards and what percentage of the elements are met for each standard. Although Greenberg does not assign letter grades to these percentages, it would be an easy task to do. Teachers can assign a letter grade to a certain percentage of elements met if they choose to do so. The administration and teachers at Greenberg have decided that, in their students' case, the reporting of progress in relation to the standards is more appropriate than letter grades.

Carolyn Calmes, principal of Greenberg, says, "This system allows me to generate tracking sheets that tell me what percentage of the students are meeting standards at any given time. I can print tracking sheets for individual students, classes, grade levels, or tracks." (Greenberg has four attendance tracks as a year-round school.) The data that is entered by the teachers can also be used to document the students' academic progress toward meeting the requirements for promotion to the next grade level.

When it comes time to report progress to the students' parents, the teacher enters the data in English, but the ACCESS program offers choices of printing the report cards in English or in other languages, such as Spanish or Hmong. This system permits teachers to communicate effectively with all parents about the important matter of student achievement and promotion requirements.

Darrell, Carolyn, and the teachers are continually upgrading the system. Darrell is responsive to teacher and administration input and is always refining the system to make it more teacher-friendly. The Greenberg team wants the standards to drive instruction. They also want to be able to compare students' progress in meeting the standards to their individual reading levels and test scores. The comparison of these more traditional progress monitors with the progress in meeting standards can be done using Darrell's program and serves as a method for alerting teachers when there appears to be a mismatch. This also gives the administration the ability to survey progress and schedule staff development without waiting for centralized services to process information from standardized test scores or burden teachers with data collection activities.

REASONS TO INCORPORATE TECHNOLOGY INTO YOUR CURRICULUM

Although it is true that excellent teaching can take place with little assistance from current technology, most reflective teachers are enjoying the new doors and windows that computers have opened for extending students' learning experiences beyond the classroom walls. We view technology as an essential ingredient in a well-run classroom for the following reasons.

1. *Technology adds variety to classroom experiences.* Using a variety of teaching methodologies with students in any class is important. Integrating the appropriate technology into your classroom will provide more options. For example, students can use word processing to

create final drafts of written materials, use video cameras to capture class projects, create PowerPoint presentations covering a broad span of topics, search the Internet for material related to assigned investigations, engage e-pals in electronic conversations, electronically scan work into e-portfolios, take virtual tours of other classrooms and locations to broaden their views of global community, and perform a host of additional activities. Students become more engaged in the curriculum when it offers novel ways to explore and learn. Bringing the world to their doorstep through electronic means offers them more excitement and brings their learning into the real world of application and understanding.

2. ***Technology mirrors the world beyond the classroom.*** The classroom environment should reflect what is happening beyond the classroom. Our students will be continually challenged by technological innovations throughout their lives. We must make certain that they are computer literate and confident in their interactions with a technological world.

3. ***Technology is an effective teaching tool.*** To enhance learning, technological devices can add to teachers' presentations and make subject matter more meaningful in new and unusual ways. Students can see changes to variables and subsequent ramifications at the click of a mouse. The what-ifs can be explored in seconds. Students can generate their own patterns and make judgments when large blocks of data are gathered from many sources and displayed on computer screens.

4. ***Learning to master technology prepares students to cope with change.*** Robert Lauriston (1999), editor of *The PC Bible*, feels that "there's nothing on the horizon that seems likely to make current PCs obsolete any time soon" (p. 25). In every historical era, there have been skeptics who believe that, because technology changes so rapidly, school curricula are perpetually out of date and will never keep up. Nonetheless, we believe that by using the most up-to-date technological methods available, teachers are helping their students envision the future and prepare themselves for living in a world in which change is occurring more rapidly than ever before. Teachers who keep current themselves and use the most up-to-date technological equipment in their classrooms are modeling for students that there is immense value in technology. Students who become accustomed to using technology will be motivated to adapt to the times and keep current with future technological advances.

MANAGING YOUR CLASSROOM WITH (AND FOR) TECHNOLOGY

Technology can assist teachers in classroom management, but at the same time, technology creates new classroom management issues. As a means of making teachers' professional lives more manageable, the market provides excellent software packages that can be adapted or are designed for seating charts, grades, attendance, lesson plans, room inventories, rubrics, test masters, word processing, spreadsheets, and other classroom needs. Keeping a computer file of these important daily functions saves office space and paper and creates a much more efficient method of handling student information. Many teachers have developed classroom management systems that include having students do their homework on computers. They may turn in their papers by emailing their homework to the teacher or uploading it to a learning management system. Independent or group projects can be done by students working on their home or school computers. Some schools now provide laptop computers for each student.

When there is a computer laboratory in the school, the classroom teacher and the computer specialist may frequently confer about what the students need to accomplish when they come into the laboratory. Occasionally, the computer specialist will initiate and manage a series of curriculum-related experiences for each grade level.

Having computer activities in a centralized laboratory has certain advantages. The teacher working in the lab is likely to be more familiar with various programs and can efficiently select and instruct students in their use. Computer programs can be stored in the lab and distributed easily when students need them. On the negative side, when the entire school must be scheduled for time in the lab, each class may get only an hour or two per week to spend working with the computers.

Media center computers are managed by media center personnel. They may designate one or more computers to be used for CD-ROM research stations. Students use these computers when they want to search for information on the CD-ROM encyclopedia, atlas, or other database. Other computers in the media center may be available for a variety of uses, including word processing, tutoring programs, and literature-based software packages. When the media center has a collection of software programs available, students may be allowed to check them out and use them on a computer in the room, getting assistance from media center personnel when needed.

Just appearing above the technological horizon is a new technology that may revolutionize the way we think about teaching and learning. The Smart Spaces Laboratory (http://www.nist.gov/smartspace/) provides a potential for people to be able to interact with one another in a life-size and real-time setting. Through the Internet, a teacher and students may be separated by thousands of miles, but they will be able to interact as if they were in the same room. For example, a social studies teacher attending a conference in San Francisco could deliver a lecture to her students in New York City. During the teaching session, the teacher in San Francisco will see her class projected onto a wall in a room at the conference center and students will see her projected on a wall in the classroom. The teacher will appear to her students as if she is really there. A teacher can lecture, perform demonstrations, and view her virtual wall to see student responses. The teacher can respond to questions as they are asked, and students' body language and other important feedback cues will be clearly visible in a real-time, lifelike setting.

Does one have to be a technological "super geek" to deliver these presentations? No. Through implicit computing, small nested computers around your neck and on your clothes will activate all commands through voice recognition. Universities are researching this technology today. Although the Smart Spaces Laboratory does not appear to be imminently available, we should be aware of its possibilities and respect its potential.

Similar technologies are currently available in the form of course management and delivery systems such as Blackboard (http://www.blackboard.com) and Moodle (http://moodle.org). These systems allow for much of the same types of interactions between students and instructors as was mentioned in the previous example. Assignments may easily be passed back and forth between student and instructor. Chat rooms and discussion boards allow for high levels of interaction between and among students and instructors. Assignments may be posted on the site for students to access and review 24 hours a day, 7 days a week. Virtual classrooms allow instructors to be located away from the physical classroom yet conduct the class session in real time by having all the students signed onto the site at the same time. Individual lessons may also be posted to the website so that students who are unable to attend the face-to-face lessons may access them at a later time as if they were actually (or virtually, in this case) attending the class.

When teachers have more than one computer in a classroom for use by the students and the teacher, they may designate one or more computers for a specific use. In the primary grades, rotating schedules are often created that allow each child to use a computer to accomplish a specified task for the week. For example, while studying addition, students may rotate through four to six stations that allow them to practice addition. In a primary classroom, one of the stations may be a computer with a program such as Number Muncher (MECC), an addition (math) learning activity.

In the upper grades, schedules are often created so that students can sign up to use a computer. Cliff Gilkey, for example, has four computers in his classroom. He has collected a variety of software programs over the years. For some projects, he uses a rotation system that allows one cooperative group to use the computers at a time. He tries to keep the computers busy as much as possible during the day, so he rotates students to the computers for one task or another. During free time, students can choose to use the computer to play educational games.

A video camera can also be used to record lessons for students who are absent. Also, for teacher absences, a video camera can be used to record a lesson and then allow a substitute

PRAXIS

Computer use in the classroom is assessed in Praxis™ Exam Section 2a: Instructional Strategies.

teacher to show the material at a later time. Important concepts that are difficult to perform in class can be recorded and played over several times for student comprehension. Intricate events that are videoed as they unfold over time can be replayed one frame at a time. Making a video of student laboratory work and pertinent class presentation discussions, and then showing vignettes, can be an invaluable review session at the end of a unit. However, make sure that parents agree to the video recording of their children and that signed permission slips are kept on file.

The information recorded by a digital camera can be downloaded into a computer and then either printed or projected on a television screen. These pictures can be displayed in the classroom at a nominal cost. The pictures from a digital camera can also be used to document accomplishments for teacher and student portfolios. Digital photographs can be printed out on transparencies using inexpensive inkjet printers, and the transparencies can be projected using a simple overhead projector, thus enhancing the image and providing visual input to aid in understanding and comprehension. Students also enjoy seeing themselves in videos and being projected as larger than life on the overhead screen. They can use these relatively simple technologies to create projects and enhance oral reports presented in class.

If your school district has a photocopy network, you can add to your classroom management system by preparing and binding handouts for each unit of study. At the middle school or high school level, teachers can plan a packet of handouts for each semester. The typical bound handout may include a calendar of events, unit objectives, homework assignments with due dates, lab experiments, review sheets, supplementary reading materials, and pictures of key transparencies. Each page of the handout can be perforated for easy removal. Students are less likely to lose a bound packet of material compared to individual sheets, which might end up in the wrong folder or be lost. Using colored divider sheets between the units of study lets students easily locate material and allows them to see upcoming work at a glance. Classroom packets are extremely helpful for teachers when students are absent and want to be able to keep up with class assignments. Of course, such a packet can also exist in a paperless version on a class website available to the students and parents.

ENHANCING YOUR INSTRUCTIONAL STRATEGIES WITH PRODUCTIVITY SOFTWARE

Word-Processing Programs

Word-processing programs are among the most versatile software available for classrooms. Early experiences, especially in the primary grades, may be devoted to simple writing assignments with a dual purpose: composing and learning keyboarding. Many programs are available to teach students how to type and use the special function keys on the keyboard. As students learn to identify letters and numbers, they can often begin to type them before they can hold a pencil and write them on paper.

Learning to operate a keyboard also provides new opportunities for older students with special needs related to small motor functioning. Students with visual and motor difficulties that prevent them from writing neatly or cause them to erase and redo their work can now create neat papers. The delete key may save students from embarrassment and frustration, just as it does for teachers.

When students master keyboarding skills, they are free to compose many types of verbal products, including letters, stories, poems, essays, reports, and plays. Studies have shown that students write longer pieces with a word-processing program than they do by hand. The other major benefit is that the word-processing program greatly simplifies the editing and revision processes. Students can learn to use spell checkers, grammar checkers, and thesaurus programs. Their motivation to write is increased in part not only because of the attraction of working on a computer, but also because the final printed products are neat and relatively error-free. Rather than experiencing writing as drudgery, students are likely to feel pride and success related to the writing process when they are allowed to compose and edit using a word-processing program.

Students with limited English proficiency benefit from writing and composing with a word processor. By pairing a proficient English speaker with a less proficient student, the two can work together at the computer to compose and illustrate stories and poems. In the process, they are communicating orally as well as in writing, giving the less proficient English speaker an opportunity to use the new language in a meaningful context.

Using word-processing programs or more specialized desktop publishing programs, students can create newspapers, magazines, posters, invitations to events, and other materials that have the appeal of a professionally published product. Many teachers employ these media to help students create gifts for families, such as published books of poetry or calendars illustrated by the class.

Presentation Software

Several programs such as PowerPoint™, Notebook™, and Keynote™ are available for use by teachers and students to enhance their presentations. This software is fairly easy to use, can be kept for multiple years, and can be modified or updated as needed. Many teachers have reported that their lessons seem more organized when they prepare them as a slide show and teach from the presentation slides. Most of these programs also allow the teacher to print handouts of the presentation. The students can take notes on the handouts and use them to study for exams.

Data Manipulation

Spreadsheets.   Spreadsheets are programs designed to organize and manipulate numerical and textual data and are valuable to teachers and students alike. Their greatest strengths lie in the manipulation of numerical data, charting, graphing, etc. They can be used by teachers for everyday tasks like maintaining records, preparing performance checklists, or analyzing grading trends. Students can be taught to use spreadsheets to organize data for writing research projects or monitoring their own progress.

Spreadsheets are programs designed to organize and manipulate numerical data and are valuable to teachers and students alike. They can be used by teachers to maintain records, prepare performance checklists, or analyze grading trends. Students can be taught to use spreadsheets to organize data for written in research projects or monitor their own progress.

Databases.   Databases are computer programs that allow the user to store, organize, and manipulate information, including both text and numerical data (Roblyer, 2006). Databases are extremely valuable to both teachers and students as they research topics and prepare lessons or research papers. Databases allow the user to reduce data redundancy, save time in locating and updating data, compare data, and examine data. For a more in-depth discussion of the use of productivity software, see *Integrating Educational Software into Teaching* by M.D. Roblyer (2006).

Educational Software.   Computer programs are available for classroom use that can diagnose students' skill levels in math, reading, vocabulary, and other basic skills and prescribe lessons at the appropriate level. In "teaching" the lessons, computers make excellent tutors because they are endlessly patient in waiting for a student response and give the appropriate feedback without emotional side effects. Like manipulatives in mathematics, many computer games provide students with realistic or simulated experiences that allow them to experiment, observe relationships, test hypotheses, and use data to reach conclusions supported by evidence.

How do you select the best program for your students from the thousands of software packages available today? You will find many resources for evaluating software at the website called Superkids (http://www.superkids.com). This website provides reviews and ratings of software programs in terms of educational value and ease of use.

Some gamelike programs are useful in expanding students' experiences beyond the classroom by simulating journeys, laboratories, foreign countries, earlier periods of history, and the future. Many of these programs increase students' decision-making and problem-solving abilities by offering them opportunities to make choices and get immediate feedback on the consequences of their decisions.

EXTENDING CLASSROOM EXPERIENCES BEYOND THE CLASSROOM

Teachers can use both low- and high-tech ways to grab students' attention and keep it before and after they leave the classroom. Dawn Morden, a sixth-grade teacher in Altoona, Pennsylvania, wanted to provide more relevant, authentic learning experiences to motivate her students to learn social studies. She noticed that her students seemed uninterested in the social studies text because they saw little relationship between the text and their own lives. Dawn and a colleague, Connie Letscher, teamed up to create an interdisciplinary, technology-based project called "Crossroads to the World."

They begin with literature that stimulates students' interest in traveling, then introduce computer programs that simulate travel, such as Oregon Trail© (MECC) and Where in the World is Carmen Sandiego©? (Broderbund). They have also subscribed to an online educational telecommunications network, WorldClassroom (http://www.clipper-worldclassroom.org/learning/learningFun.htm) that allows students in Altoona to communicate with people all over the world. When students make contacts in other parts of the world, they share first-hand information about their communities. Turning next to word-processing programs, students write letters to their new friends.

Each student selects a travel destination and writes business letters or email messages to chambers of commerce, tourist bureaus, and embassies to gather information about that destination. To prepare their budget for the trip, they use a spreadsheet. They consult online newspapers and other media to learn about current events or natural disasters in their chosen destinations. Before their journeys, they plan a bon voyage party, complete with party invitations to friends and family, using Print Shop© (Broderbund).

During the virtual travel, students gather information using CD-ROMs, DVDs, and other more traditional resources. They document their trips by keeping a daily log on audiotape or a word processor.

Yen-Ling Shen is a sixth-grade teacher in Barrington, Rhode Island. She likes to introduce her students to her ancestral land of China and a study of ancient China and its geography by showing a PowerPoint presentation of photos taken while she was there visiting relatives. She then has the students explore maps of the ancient land and trade routes. Yen-Ling uses technology in several ways while preparing and teaching her unit:

- She researches Internet sites for information.
- She prepares overhead slides using the computer.
- She shows photos she has integrated into PowerPoint presentations using the computer and a projector.
- She shows KidPix paintings using a computer and projector (http://en.wikipedia.org/wiki/Kid_Pix).
- She prepares handouts for the students on the computer.
- She uses the scanner to create color transparencies from relevant illustrations and travel folders.

During the unit of study, her students use technology in the following ways.

- They research information using Internet sites predesignated by Yen-Ling.
- They create slides using KidPix paint.
- They write summaries using a word processor.
- They print out their summaries on the computer.

Yen-Ling's learning goals for this unit include the students' discovery of China's geography and its early settlements, and an understanding and respect for those whose way of life is different from their own.

Through a series of explorations and the use of technology, Yen-Ling is able to address history and social science standards related to the structures of early Chinese civilizations (geographic, economic, religious, and social). She addresses visual arts standards by having the students use various observational drawing skills to depict a variety of subject matter as well as creating a drawing using various tints, shades, and intensives. Yen-Ling addresses English/language arts standards by exploring the organizational features of electronic text (bulletin boards, databases, keyword searches, email addresses). The students also gain experience in composing documents with appropriate formatting by using word-processing skills and principles of design (margins, tabs, spacing, columns, and page orientation). They also research their topics using a variety of resources, and compose and organize informational text. Yen-Ling addresses technology standards by giving the students experience in using a variety of technologies, including word processing, Internet research, and multimedia presentations. She concludes her unit of study by inviting the parents to an evening where the students share maps and reports they have created using technology and PowerPoint visuals.

Mrs. Mary Grimble, a fourth-grade teacher at an urban Minnesota elementary school, was starting a unit on birds when she saw Apple's advertising campaign touting their new iPhone™. The ad focused on the many applications ("apps") that were available on the phone for a number of topics that the public might find interesting. One of those apps was a bird-watching field guide. Mrs. Grimble figured that she could use the technology to help her students better understand identifying and classifying birds. Her school had a number of iTouch mobile devices, and she decided to use 15 of these devices to help her students make the connection to the outside world with what they were learning in the classroom. She divided her class into pairs and had them identify the birds that they saw as they walked around a lake across the street from her school, using the apps available on the iTouch devices. Not only were they able to identify and classify the birds they saw but even some that they could hear but couldn't see. When they heard the birdcalls, they compared them to birdcalls that the software provided and were able to identify many birds that didn't venture out from the brush. They used their knowledge of birds that they might find in the area to confirm their identifications and entered them into their research model.

Computer-Assisted Research Projects

CD-ROM discs, DVDs, and online databases are fast replacing the traditional encyclopedia in most school media centers. Students are able to type in a keyword to call up an article on almost any subject. For many topics, they also see a picture or even a short video of the subject they are researching.

Cliff Gilkey, a teacher in a multi-age fourth-, fifth-, and sixth-grade class at Frank Paul Elementary School in Salinas, California, was searching for a method to engage the interest of his students, many from families of migrant workers, with limited English proficiency. The social studies material he had available neither matched his students' interests nor gave them positive role models. To meet these needs, Cliff created the Local Heroes Project, a social studies investigation and oral history of local Hispanic, African-American, and Vietnamese leaders (such as political figures, businesspeople, researchers, and teachers).

The students decided that they would produce videos and publish booklets about the local heroes and that students in other classes could use these materials, too. Students were asked to identify local heroes that they would like to know more about. The heroes they selected included a Mexican-American school board member, a Latina news anchor, an African-American police chief, the Cuban-American city manager, and a Miwok Indian leader.

For this project, students worked in teams of three or four. They developed a set of interview questions by reading and analyzing biographies to see what other biographers included. After preparing the interview questions, they set up appointments to meet the individual local heroes they wanted to interview. One student asked questions as another operated the video camera. They transcribed the words of their heroes using word processors so that they could create booklets about each hero.

This year, Cliff plans to do the project again with even more technology at his command. He has a new HyperStudio™ program that will allow the students to create multimedia presentations and a video companion they plan to use to create special effects and credits for their video production.

Sheila Fitzgerald, an American history teacher at Eden Prairie High School, in Eden Prairie, Minnesota, was working on a lesson unit where her students could collect information on different decades in American history. She wanted to provide flexibility by allowing her students to have a place where they could collect and produce information on different eras within U.S. history. In some instances she wanted to foreshadow upcoming lessons by asking students to find three or four pictures from an era and provide as much information that they could find about this period in history. For example, the students might find 1950s pictures of people like Rosa Parks, Jackie Robinson, and the Little Rock Nine, and they could describe what they knew about how these people or events contributed to desegregation. The students might also find additional images or references to an era about which they would like to know more. Ms. Fitzgerald also saw this approach as a way to track how the students were constructing knowledge as the unit progressed. Students would collect images, stories, or other materials and use Google Sites™ (http://www.google.com/sites/help/intl/en/overview. html) to produce a website covering the subject. Google Sites™ is a free website and wiki builder that allows the students to post their knowledge online as well as work collaboratively if the project warranted. A wiki is a website that uses wiki software, which allows the easy creation and editing of any number of interlinked webpages. Students expanded the project and began to write questions for quizzes using Smart Technologies Notebook (http://smarttech. com/) software, the same software that Ms. Fitzgerald used with her interactive whiteboard. The students, as she explains, were "really constructing knowledge throughout the process. I could see what they were learning, how that learning progressed, and how they became teachers to one another."

Science teachers at a Minnesota suburban high school took the approach of letting students teach one another about environmental issues affecting our planet. The teachers instructed the students to research the main issues adversely affecting the Earth's environment. The students were to produce a 3- to 5-minute video outlining the issues that they found during their research. Then the students were instructed to post these videos onto the class's Moodle site, where all of the students were to view and post insights, questions, and critiques to their videos. The students used *Photostory 3* (http://www.microsoft.com/windowsxp/ using/digitalphotography/PhotoStory/default.mspx) a free program available from Microsoft Corporation that allows pictures to be imported as well as text and voice narrations to be added to the videos. The science teachers also asked the students to vote for what the students felt were the top three issues affecting the environment. The students used Moodle to post their final videos on a forum page that allowed other students to place comments as well as record their voting. The classes then would discuss these issues further during class time. As the students produced and viewed one another's videos, the teachers noted that many students started to connect many of the environmental issues that they were researching with other issues students were researching. The teachers also noted that it seemed that viewing the issues from their peers' point of view helped them synthesize how some concepts were having a global affect on the environment.

Computer Literacy Program at Beardsley School

Another district that has encouraged and supported teachers in their efforts to infuse technology into the curriculum is Crystal Lake District 47, Crystal Lake, Illinois. Diane Jensen brings a great deal of expertise to her computer technology instructor position at Hannah Beardsley Middle School (grades 6–8) in Crystal Lake. Teaching is a second career for Diane, who was a managing editor of 13 community newspapers when she retired at age 40. The lack of excitement she experienced while in the workplace encouraged her to go back to college and pursue a career in teaching. She has never looked back and immensely enjoys her teaching assignment.

Diane's main responsibility is teaching computer technology skills to students in seventh and eighth grades. Because her students' different levels of keyboarding skills can present a problem, one focus of the sixth-grade program is to ensure a minimum level of keyboarding competency for all students.

The first topic in her 9-week course for seventh-graders is file management, which is important for data storage and retrieval. Then a PowerPoint assignment called About Me helps Diane learn more about the students while the students become familiar with this presentation program. Included in this assignment is information about their family plus their activities, hobbies, and dreams for the future. Once finished, students take this project one more step by making presentations to their classmates.

The major project for seventh-graders is a report and presentation on an endangered species, which is a collaborative effort with seventh-grade science teachers, Fran Hicks and Ann Min. The science teachers evaluate the content of the project; Diane evaluates its technical side. "I like to say I grade the style and pizzazz, whereas the science teachers grade the substance," she says. Before students get started, they are given two rubrics for grading the project: one from their science teacher and one from Diane. That way everyone knows what is expected.

Working with seventh- and eighth-grade language arts teachers, Diane uses Inspiration™ (http://www.inspiration.com/)—a webbing and graphic organizing software program—to teach her students how to create a book report. Using circles, rectangles, clouds, and a host of other graphics and symbols available in Inspiration™, students craft a concept flowchart using arrows that are drawn between main and complementary ideas. With the click of a mouse, Inspiration™ transforms this right-brain activity into a traditional outline complete with Roman numerals and subcategories.

Diane believes computers can enhance the education of all students, including students with special needs. Some students in special education do very well on computer tasks. Diane does not allow labels to interfere with how she treats her students. "Several years ago one of my best students was in special education for support and I didn't even know it," she says. "Because some students have a hard time getting ideas on paper, which could result from having trouble with their handwriting, the computer somewhat standardizes each writing assignment. When writing second or third drafts, students readily appreciate, like all of us, that we do not have to rewrite what is correct. By copying and pasting, only the mistakes have to be corrected. Also, there is a creative side to using computers, especially in PowerPoint presentations and webpage designs. The computer is seen as less frustrating for many students. I always like to think I teach children, not the curriculum."

One teaching technique Diane uses to improve efficiency and independence involves placing a red plastic cup upside down on top of the computer. For example, when working on computer tasks, Diane encourages students to be self-directed, with her as the guide on the side. If students do have questions, then instead of raising their hands or shouting out distress signals, they place the cup on top of their computer and continue to troubleshoot. The students say that it's like turning on a red light to signal they need help. "I use this approach so students can keep working even though they need my help in one area. I don't know very many people who can keyboard efficiently with one hand up in the air and the other one on the keys," she quips. "Sometimes students can remedy their own problems in seconds after the cup alert. Also, neighbors seeing the cup can assist, thereby encouraging students to see themselves as drivers rather than passengers."

The eighth-grade curriculum emphasizes telecommunications. The major project involves students creating their own webpages featuring a social studies topic. Geography is the focus for some of the students; a Civil War battle might be the focus for others. Like with the PowerPoint science project, this is a collaborative effort and students earn a grade for both classes.

The eighth-grade telecommunications curriculum includes history of the Internet, email usage, the substance of a URL address and its purpose, vocabulary pertinent to telecommunications, search engines, and netiquette. Students often surf chat rooms outside the classroom, so Diane makes them aware of the dangers associated with this type of activity. That is one reason why she and the school's police liaison officer, Terri Nowak, co-teach a lesson on Internet safety and computer crimes. "Young people in this age group think they're invincible and nothing will happen to them. We try to break down that myth. They also think there's nothing wrong with loading someone else's program onto their computer. Hopefully they'll understand that it is tantamount to stealing," says Diane.

Beyond the classroom, Diane works with middle school students who apply what they have learned in the classroom to a real-world experience: the school newspaper. Four to five times a year, *The Beardsley Roar Newspaper* provides faculty, parents, and students with first-class journalism, complete with photos, coupons, advertisements, news and features, editorials, sports, and a Dear Hannah column. The tabloid format of the newspaper is published on actual newsprint at a nearby printing plant. Readers pay 25 cents a copy or $1 for a 1-year subscription. This is an after-school club activity, and students are responsible for all content, including advertisements. The activity is entirely self-supporting. The school newspaper provides a sense of community for the school, with the latest issue 20 pages long. The Dear Hannah advice column reveals an openness and sensitivity that rivals national publications. One entry reads:

> Dear Hannah,
> I'm having trouble with my parents. You see, they are going through a divorce and I don't know what to do. I'm so upset about it that I barely talk to them anymore. I know they are starting to worry, but I just can't talk to them because I am so mad. How can I fix my problem?
> Divorce
>
> Dear Divorce,
> Your voice will come back, but for now use your writing skills. Instead of talking to your parents, write to them about how you feel. You might learn writing is a powerful thing. It is often easier to write out your feelings than to say them.
> Hannah

In addition to mentoring the computer skills of their students, technology support faculty assist other faculty members as they develop programs and curricula that make use of technology. Sarah Youngberry is a math teacher at Eden Prairie High School in Eden Prairie, Minnesota who expects, and gets, quality work from her students. In the following case study, Sarah recalls how she supports students in enhancing and monitoring their own learning. New technology and the support of her colleagues allow her to keep growing as a teacher. She interacts as a part of a team to develop courses of study that engage her students in a creative and active search for knowledge and hold them accountable for their learning.

✱ REFLECTIVE ACTION CASE STUDY ✱

A high school teacher supports her students in monitoring and enhancing their own learning

Sarah Youngberry, math teacher, Eden Prairie High School, Eden Prairie, Minnesota

A Teacher Begins to Plan

Sarah Youngberry noticed that her Algebra 2 students' test results did not always match the learning that they were able to demonstrate in class. She wanted to find a way to help them monitor their own mistakes and enhance their ability to succeed on math tests.

Teacher Considers What the Students Already Know

Sarah knew that her students were proficient in basic math principles, but she also knew that they weren't all functioning at the same level. She also recognized their frustration when their tests scores didn't demonstrate their understanding.

Teacher does research and invites feedback

Sarah went to her colleague, Jennifer Nelson, former math teacher and now technology coach at Eden Prairie. Working together Sarah and Jennifer designed a one-page structured feedback form for the students to analyze their test results when they got their tests back. The form asked the students to analyze each item they missed on the test and determine the cause of the error. They were asked to note whether the error was caused by (1) simple arithmetic error, (2) an incorrect application of a concept, or (3) not understanding the concept being tested. This allowed the students to figure out what they don't know. Sarah then produced review worksheets with practice problems the students could work through and she provided time for them to ask further questions.

Sarah and Jennifer discussed this process after the first use of the review worksheets. Jennifer suggested that they produce some instructional videos that allowed the students to receive more instruction matched to their individual needs. Sarah agreed that the students needed something more than the review sheets because they were all working on different concepts and at different paces.

Teacher has expectations

Because Sarah uses Moodle (http://moodle.org), an open source (a software program that can be freely used under the General Public License) learning management system that allows teachers to create online courses for their students, Jennifer suggested that the instructional videos they make be made available through Moodle. Sarah would create the videos and upload them to her Moodle course, along with other course content like syllabi, online links covering course content, and other course material. The students would have access to these materials from anywhere they could access the Internet.

Making the videos

Because Sarah had access to an interactive whiteboard (http://smarttech.com), along with presentation software from Smart Technologies, she was able to write out and work problems using the software. Using the technology, she would work the problems and record them using Jing, a screen capture program (http://www.jingproject.com). This program allows the user to capture what is displayed on the computer or smartboard screen and also narrate what is being captured on the screen. This program also allows Sarah to make the videos as she is explaining concepts in class. If she does this in class, however, she has to remember the 5-minute limit on Jing. Because of the 5-minute time limit as well as the possibility that questions would interrupt her recording, Sarah does the recordings without students in the room during her planning period or before or after school.

Teacher invites feedback

Once Sarah had posted the videos on Moodle, she began to track the usage of them. Through tracking, she realized that the students who were accessing the videos were doing better on the tests but that some students were accessing the videos on a very limited basis. When she discussed this with her class, she found that some students had limited access to the Internet.

Teacher reflects again

Reflecting on the feedback from her students, Sarah realized that she needed to find a way to make the videos more available to the students who did not have Internet access at home.

Teacher creates new action plan

At that time, the Eden Prairie School District had made an investment in a podcast server by Apple (http://www.apple.com/mac/). With the podcast server, Sarah could upload the videos and then make the videos available through iTunes (http://www.apple.com/itunes/). Those students who had a mobile phone or other mobile device could subscribe to the video podcast and view it on their mobile device. The high school also invested in Apple iTouches (http://www.apple.com/tunes/), which could be synchronized with the videos and podcast. This was another way to distribute the videos to the students. Most of the students have cell phones, so this approach made the videos more widely available. The access part of this really has to do with students getting the videos to their mobile devices and viewing them at a later time. They still needed Internet access to get the video, but they just didn't need to be connected to the Internet to view them, as was the case Moodle. The students can download the video at school using the school's wireless access and then view the video on their cell phone at a later time.

Teacher reflects on the plan

Sarah found that the videos made a big difference in the students' understanding of the concepts being taught. The ability to watch the videos numerous times and at their own pace resulted in dramatic improvement in the students' comprehension and test scores. Because Jing allows a screen capture video of 5 minutes only, it limits the amount of content that can be included in a single video. This provides an opportunity for the students to repeat short segments of instruction several times easily.

How to implement this idea if your school has less technology available

Most schools have video cameras, and the videos can be made using a basic video camera. Copies of the videos can be made available to the students for checkout. If students do not have video players at home, one could be made available in the school media center so students could use it before and after school or at various times throughout the day.

Tracking the Return of Spring on the Internet

When one enters Ann Min's seventh- and eighth-grade physical and life science room, the place is filled with science. It's easy to understand why she is one of the first middle school science teachers in Illinois to attain the coveted National Board Certified Teacher designation. Ann challenges her students each day to hypothesize, evaluate, and reach a consensus when finalizing answers. The Internet plays a pivotal role in her seventh-grade life science curriculum called Cycles. Beginning on Groundhog Day, she coordinates her curriculum unit called The Return of Spring with the Annenberg Foundation's online program entitled, "Journey North" at http://www.learner.org/jnorth/current.html.

On campus, students are assigned to teams that monitor the return of springlike conditions around Hannah Beardsley Middle School. Teams monitor tulips, monarch butterflies, earthworms, and robins. By recording soil temperature as a function of days, number of hours of sunlight each day, arrival dates of certain birds, and emergent dates for assigned plants, correlations can be made between measured variables. The student teams fill out a template of information and then log on to the Internet. The Annenberg Foundation's webpage processes the information and shares it with the world. Each group identifies its position by latitude and longitude. After downloading information weekly from the Internet, the seventh-graders tape little robin stickers onto a huge map of the United States at locations where robins were sighted. Because this map is located in the hallway, all students in the school are able to see a wave of springlike happenings starting in the south and traveling north. To heighten interest in scientific observation skills, the Annenberg Foundation picks 10 mystery schools. Students are asked to locate these mystery schools by observing weekly data from their positions.

The monarch butterfly study also has an international component. Each fall, Ann has her students mail paper butterflies to middle school students in Mexico. "The fall mailing, of course, symbolizes monarch butterflies heading south for the winter," Ann explains. When the monarch line hits the city in the spring, the middle school students in Mexico mail the butterflies back to her students. But Ann adds a twist to this. "Our students have to write in Spanish to the students in Mexico, and the students in Mexico write in English to the students at our school." This project is then truly international and interdisciplinary.

THE ADVANTAGES OF TEACHER-TO-TEACHER NETWORKING

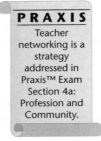

PRAXIS
Teacher networking is a strategy addressed in Praxis™ Exam Section 4a: Profession and Community.

A major premise of the reflective action model presented in this text is that teachers learn a great deal by interacting with respected colleagues. We encourage beginning teachers to ask for feedback when they have questions or problems. One of the best methods teachers use today to interact and exchange ideas is networking. Although networking still occurs on the telephone or in meetings, the Internet has created many more exciting opportunities for "meeting" people and exchanging ideas.

Today, teachers and their students can belong to a community of learners who are willing to share ideas, explain complex issues, or suggest alternative solutions. Whereas most other forms of networking may involve travel expenses or long-distance phone charges, most of the information from Internet networks is free. For example, at http://www.teachers.net, you are greeted with this welcome message: "Take part in a nationwide Mentor Support Center, bringing together hundreds of thousands of educators in an environment specially designed to foster peer support and development. Take advantage of this incredible panel of experts and friends; you won't find teacher support like this anywhere else on Earth!" At this site, you can choose from a variety of chat boards including the following topics:

General Interest Forum

English Center

Tech Center

Teacher Chatboard

Administrators Chatboard

- Pre-School (Early Childhood)
- Kindergarten
- Primary Elementary
- Upper Elementary
- Middle School
- High School
- College Professors
- Multi-age Classroom
- Beginning Teachers
- Student Teachers
- Substitute Teachers
- Golden Apples
- Retired Teachers

- Gifted/Talented Ed
- Special Education
- Adult Education
- Private School
- Montessori
- Professional Readings
- Classroom Discipline
- Classroom Management
- Counseling

Curriculum Chatboards

- Math Teacher
- Science Teacher
- Social Studies/Geography

Music Teacher

Fine Arts and Art Education

PE/Coaching

Health

Brain-Compatible Learning

Reading and Writing

High School English

Books and Literature

Remedial Reading

Accelerated Reading

4 Blocks Literacy

Building Blocks (Kindergarten)

6 Traits Writing

Library/Media Specialists

Language Center

ESL/EFL

French Teacher

Spanish Teacher

Travel/Study Abroad

Project Center

Project Switchboard

Learning Centers

Grant Writing

Career Support Center

JobTalk Support Board

Teacher Job Listings

At http://www.teachnet.org, you can search for lesson plans, grant information, online courses for teachers, and other resources to support teachers in search of successful teaching practices.

New teachers are sure to receive many responses from fellow teachers willing to share their valuable resources and expertise. Perhaps not all the responses will be useful or match the teachers' teaching style. It is the responsibility of the teacher who requests the information to reflect on all the responses and make use of the material that is most appropriate and usable. This is true of all Internet exchanges today. There is always more information than you can possibly use, and you must be willing to consider each source to determine its value.

We encourage teachers at all levels and in all subjects to join networking groups to help support and promote excellent teaching techniques. It is only when we work together and pool our resources that the students of this nation will have the best education possible.

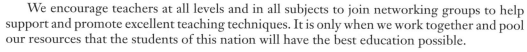

Communicating with Parents

Student-designed and -executed classroom newsletters are a great way to keep parents and administrators informed about what's going on in the classroom. You can also include a feature called Teacher's Corner to make sure important information about expectations, standards, classroom needs, upcoming studies, etc., are clearly communicated to parents and guardians at home. Having students doing the work also provides them with a real-life connection to their learning and is a great motivator.

Playing Catch Up

In this case, it might be the teacher who needs to do some catching up. The Internet is filled with information for teachers and students. It is up to the teacher to develop the skills to access these valuable resources and to make them available to her students. In the event that you feel unskilled in this area, you should immediately seek help to improve your abilities and knowledge relative to Internet access. Check out workshops that might be available at your school or a nearby university, college, or community college. Many school districts also offer classes to help you become computer literate and access the Internet through adult education courses, usually at minimal or no cost to you. And, of course, there are online courses. So get out there and learn and have some fun. It's all there waiting for you!

GUIDED GROUP EXPLORATION

1. Divide the class into groups.
2. Assign each group a different content area at the elementary, middle, or secondary level.
3. Each group should sign on to the Teachers Network website (www.teachersnet.org).
4. Go to the Lesson Plans section of the website.
5. Each group should search its assigned area for a lesson plan that contains an exciting and appropriate use of technology.
6. Have the groups share the lesson plans with the rest of the class.

REFLECTIVE ACTION ACTIVITY FOR YOUR PROFESSIONAL PORTFOLIO

Professional teachers should keep abreast of technological developments that can be used in their classrooms for many purposes. Teachers should be able to demonstrate that they know how to engage students in the rapidly expanding field of computer technology, as well as how to use the computer to enhance their own teaching.

Lesson plans are available in almost unlimited quantity (and quality) on the Internet. However, they don't become truly usable to you until you adapt them to your own teaching style, as well as to the learning styles and needs of your students.

Go to the website mentioned on the first page of this chapter (www.pacificnet.net/~mandel) and choose a lesson plan that is not specifically designed with imbedded use of technology. Adapt the lesson plan you find to the format used in this text and add appropriate technology to enhance the learning and teaching process. You may want to use the following format for planning your technology integration:

Preparation—Identify objectives to be taught (including technology objectives). Plan ways to demonstrate skills to be taught. Plan how you will gather the materials you will need (noting sources.) Plan the management strategies you will use, the sequence of delivery and activities, how to close, and how you will evaluate (including the design of a scoring rubric, if needed).

Specific plans for delivery—Plan your opening (motivation) and your closure (review or celebration). Make a concise list of all you plan to do and how you will provide guided practice.

Independent practice—What will the students do to practice what you have just taught?

Evaluation—Specifically, how will you evaluate all your objectives?

References

Lauriston, R. (1998). *The PC bible*. Berkeley, CA: Peachpit Press.

Roblyer, M. (2006). *Integrating educational technology into teaching* (4th ed.). Upper Saddle Piver, NJ: Pearson Education

Now go to Topic #14: Integrating Technology in the MyEducationLab (www.myeducationlab.com <http://www.myeducationlab.com/>) for your course, where you can:

- Find learning outcomes for this topic along with the national standards that connect to these outcomes.
- Complete Assignments and Activities that can help you more deeply understand the chapter content.
- Apply and practice your understanding of the core teaching skills identified in the chapter with the Building Teaching Skills and Dispositions learning units.

Reflecting on Teaching and the School Community

■■■■■■■■■■■■■■■■■■■■■■■■■■■■■■■■■■

The teacher's role in the school community becomes more complex each day. Most school districts are undergoing some form of reform or systemic change that calls on teachers to take more responsibility for decision making beyond their own classrooms. School reform can be compared to piloting an airplane and conducting a major overhaul while in flight. While attempting to maintain a stable environment for students and faculty, many schools are overhauling their curricula, schedules, student evaluation systems, and administrative relationships.

The motivation for many of these changes appears to be a shift in what people see as the basic purpose of schools. When reforms appear to be succeeding, teachers share in the glory. When reforms appear to be failing to meet their objectives, principals, teachers, and other staff must respond by working harder and longer hours to accomplish the many complex tasks needed to turn things around. They must also be able to reduce a natural tendency to become defensive when hearing criticism. Instead, teachers must be able to examine what it is the community wants them to accomplish and how to communicate to the community what they themselves view as important. This process is likely to generate conflict. It is probably unavoidable and may perhaps be necessary to induce change. Reflective teachers, however, are not afraid of conflict. They recognize that conflict is part of any important change, and they are willing to use their reflective action skills to perceive the needs of all members of the school community. Teachers can demonstrate their commitment to being active members of their school community in two ways. One way is to take an active role in collaborating with other professional educators. The second way is to look for ways to collaborate with parents.

The ability to work collaboratively with other professionals may be demonstrated by sharing responsibilities for developing curriculum or planning other aspects of the instructional program of the school. Teachers may work in grade-level or subject-matter teams to establish goals and coordinate learning experiences that will achieve these goals. Teachers may work together to strengthen their teaching proficiency. They may observe one another and engage in discussions about teaching and learning strategies. They may collaborate in trying new instructional strategies. All of these opportunities for collaboration are viewed as important. The days of teachers working as solo performers is a narrow and outdated concept. The new image of the professional teacher is a team player who seeks opportunities to share knowledge and ideas with colleagues.

Reflective, caring teachers also recognize that they share responsibility with parents for educating students. They communicate frequently with parents and guardians, listening as often as they speak, in order to learn parents' perspectives and to enlist their support in fostering good learning habits. Professional teachers recognize that circumstances can complicate parent-teacher relationships; some examples include cultural and language differences or the variation among parents in the amount and type of support they are willing to provide for their children. Nevertheless, reflective teachers demonstrate that they value and welcome parental input into their children's educational needs and experiences.

NO CHILD LEFT BEHIND

In 2002, the federal government passed the No Child Left Behind legislation (http://www.ed. gov/policy/elsec/leg/esea02/index.html), which is intended to motivate every public school in the nation to make improvements that will result in higher achievement for its students. One federal mandate in this legislation forces each state to identify schools that are not showing positive results, but the large number of schools identified as needing improvement under the No Child Left Behind Act has alarmed many state education officials. In late 2003, Claudio Sanchez, of National Public Radio, interviewed the staff and parents of one such school in Virginia. He reported that teachers and parents at Maury Elementary in Alexandria, Virginia, could not believe their school had been sanctioned by the federal government. He attended a parent-teacher association (PTA) meeting in the school's cafeteria, which was originally planned as a discussion about fundraising to help a family with rent and medical expenses, as well as for classroom supplies and a book fair.

The parents and teachers at the meeting called the federal sanctions a huge distraction rather than a motivation to improve. Tonya Kelly, PTA treasurer, said at the meeting, "What's the point of shaming a school if all it does is demoralize people? It's just the negative press that we get. It's like you're fighting an uphill battle all the time. The teachers here are great. It's a wonderful school, and it's just that we have so many negative numbers out there, it's hard to get past that."

Kelly said that her son, a first-grader, was thriving at this school, but during the past 2 years, fewer than half of the students had passed the state's reading and math tests. That's why Maury Elementary was sanctioned. Under the new federal law, its academic progress was termed "inadequate." When parents heard this news just 2 weeks before the start of school, 20 of them pulled their children out. We can only guess that these may have been some of the highest achieving students, further complicating the school's challenge to improve.

Kristene Ruscello, principal at Maury Elementary, believed that the federal government should have given them another chance. She didn't deny Maury Elementary had struggled. She was the third principal in the last five years. But the year before, Maury turned a big corner and the students' math, English, and history scores increased significantly.

Rebecca Perry, Alexandria's public schools superintendent at the time, was convinced that most of the parents of the children who left Maury were spooked by the negative publicity. "Just because the federal government says so, it must be true. I believe in accountability, but this is ridiculous."

No Child Left Behind did not take into account all that had been done to help Maury Elementary, says Perry. "We had already gone to a great deal of effort to hire a whole new staff. This fall, class size is down to 14, the school has three extra reading specialists and two

> **PRAXIS**
> This chapter prepares you for PRAXIS™ Exam Section 4b: The Larger Community.

new resource teachers. We're paying every teacher a bonus to go the extra mile, and we'd already started making great progress."

What No Child Left Behind did not take into account was that 80% of the children who attend Maury lived in poverty. Most were bused in from one of Alexandria's largest public housing projects. Many of the students started school already behind in basic skills, some so far back that it takes years for them to catch up to meet Virginia's unusually high academic standards, reports Claudio Sanchez.

Mark Christie, a past president of Virginia's State Board of Education, says the No Child Left Behind Act expects dramatic improvement or else. That fact, says Christie, punishes states that are trying to push kids to meet higher academic standards gradually. No Child Left Behind is undermining the cause of standards and accountability because its rating system is so strict and uncompromising, and it is shaking public confidence in the whole cause of standards and accountability. After all, he says, "Virginia's fourth-graders had the second-highest gains in math nationally last year. And even with an increase in non-English-speaking students, reading scores are also up overall. And yet, nearly half of Virginia schools are not meeting the federal guidelines for adequate yearly progress."

The U.S. Department of Education officials say that the problem is that the state of Virginia is not testing everybody. Under the new law, every school must test 95% of its students, including disabled and non-English-speaking children. It must also break down test scores by race, ethnicity, and income. If 40% or more of the children in any one of these groups does not pass the state's reading and math test, the entire school fails.

Gene Hickok, undersecretary of the U.S. Department of Education, says that Virginia and many other states need to change their testing procedures. "They have not been testing limited English proficiency kids; they've been letting them opt out for a number of years. A lot of school districts choose not to assess those children because their scores bring down the average score in the district or in the school. And this is a law that says, 'No, you must test them.'" Hickok believes that you cannot close the huge achievement gap between low-income and wealthy kids or the gap among black, white, and Latino students if you do not test them. If there is a gap, says Hickok, parents have a right to know what their school is doing about it.

The good news is that Maury Elementary and thousands of other schools placed under federal sanctions have restructured and the students are making good progress. In the case of Maury Elementary, the school was "reconstituted" meaning the faculty was restructured, a new principal was assigned and the staff, faculty, and administration worked together to examine the school's strengths and weaknesses. Using the data from required state assessments, programs were designed to support the progress of every student. Five years later, the school met all state standards for student achievement.

This story provides both sides of a difficult dilemma that you will face as beginning teachers. When you are hired as a teacher, the school you select may be struggling to meet federal mandates or raise test scores. You will be on the frontline of meeting the expectations in these and other guidelines. As a teacher, you will have both the opportunity and the responsibility to create the curriculum and the classroom conditions that will motivate your students to achieve success on the standardized tests and other measures that determine how your school is evaluated.

Although educators across the nation initially reacted negatively to the No Child Left Behind Act, some districts found ways to ensure children's progress. CIM (Continuous Improvement Model) is one example of ways to address the concerns of children entering school with limited background experiences and/or limited English proficiency. By using the required assessments to identify areas of need and planning instruction that incorporates review, active learning, and frequent formative assessment, the CIM model provides support for students who have not typically been successful in school. Tutorials and enrichment activities add approaches for additional instruction for those who need it. Using community resources and experts for facilitating the enrichment programs provides opportunities for all students to make continuous progress.

Providing enrichment activities for students is a goal that is an important part of the Continuous Improvement Model (Davenport & Anderson, 2002.) In this model time is set aside each day to provide extra instruction (tutorials) for the students who are struggling with meeting standards. At the same time, students who have mastered standards are provided with enrichment activities. People with specialized expertise are recruited from the community to serve as facilitators for these enrichment activities, while teachers are freed up to focus on planning for and teaching the students who need extra instruction in order to master basics. Finding community facilitators involves tapping into community resources by approaching local businesses and universities for experts. Many businesses have programs in place to release employees for school-community collaborations. These people serve as valuable resources for enrichment programs. They present a real-world connection to knowledge that is not commonly addressed in school settings. Some examples of these collaborations:

Topic of study	Experts	Who to contact for support
Investing in the stock market	Investment bankers Financial planners Business Professors	Banks, Universities, Investment Companies
Knowledge Base for Building a House	Contractors Architects Electricians Decorators	Local businesses Habitat for Humanity
Saving the environment	Environmental scientists Water systems engineers Recycling engineers Utility Consultants	Electric Company Water Company Science Professors Recycling Pants
Creative Science & Math	High school science & math teachers Science & Math Professors Engineers	High Schools Colleges Engineering Firms

The Basics of Enrichment Planning

To plan an enrichment program for your students there are a number of considerations :

1. What are the specific interests, strengths, and needs of your students? Gather this information through surveys, interest inventories, class discussions.
2. What are the time constraints? Will you be able to expand your in-school program to allow more time for in-depth exploration? Can your students stay after school? If the program needs to be limited to time available during the school day, can you break projects into small steps that can be done within the time constraints?
3. Have you approached your administrator for approval, resources, and a commitment?
4. What is your expertise? What areas of interest and expertise do the rest of the team possess?
5. What resources are available in your school and community? Do you need to write a grant for funding? Are there local businesses that you can contact for support? Are there other teachers on our faculty with expertise in the area you will be addressing? Are there parents who can provide expertise?
6. Once these questions are answered, you are ready to sit down with your team members and plan the activities.

Because one school had a number of computers available and the mastery students were interested in learning more about computers and the Internet, the enrichment activities centered on Internet usage. The instructors focused on ethical Internet usage and then had the students work in small groups to plan and research in-depth studies and PowerPoint presentation to be presented in their classrooms. After their introduction to the Internet, the teachers involved them in an electronic scavenger hunt to give them practice in searching for specific resources online.

Another school used the instructional focus currently being addressed the enrichment students researched more in-depth information about the topic and created "Want to Know

More? Booklets" for their classrooms. They researched and wrote the text and used visuals downloaded from the Internet to create the illustrations. Because the enrichment groups are not all from the same classroom, these booklets were shared in all the grade-level classrooms. The students were extremely innovative in making real-world connections. For example: one group interviewed their parents and community members and wrote booklets with examples of how the use of incorrect grammar in real-life situations can cause miscommunication, loss of opportunities, and social mishaps. It is very important that the enrichment activities NOT be neglected in order to focus more attention on the tutorials. Both are equally important. The enrichment program, properly implemented, can be a powerful incentive for students to pass the basic standards while providing them the opportunity to work with real-life community experts in different fields of study.

TWO-WAY COMMUNICATION WITH PARENTS

Parents do have a right to know how their children's school is evaluated as well as how the curriculum meets the needs of the students. For beginning teachers, the thought of interacting effectively with parents is not always a high priority, however. They are struggling to cope with all the planning and preparation for teaching the many subjects in the elementary curriculum and for establishing a welcoming classroom environment for their students.

At the beginning of Chapter 4, Diane Leonard described the many thoughts, feelings, and decisions she had to make on her first day of teaching. In the week prior to that first day, Diane spent a lot of time in her classroom setting up bulletin boards and learning centers. As she worked that week, many of her new students *and their parents* who had come to the school for registration stopped by her classroom to see the "new teacher." Some stood outside her door looking in quietly until she approached them and introduced herself. Others came into the room and looked around, excited to see the brightly decorated walls. The children were all interested in trying to discern whether the new teacher was "nice" and whether they thought they would be happy in her class. Their visits, before the first day of school had even arrived, alerted Diane to the fact that she had more than just the needs of 20 or more students to consider. She realized that she had to use withitness and concern for their parents' needs, too.

Some parents of primary children may be especially reluctant to see the beginning of school because, for them, it marks an end to an important phase in their lives. For 5 years, they have had complete jurisdiction over the lives of their children. Now they recognize that the teacher may have almost as much influence over their children as they have. I have observed the parent of a first-grader, for example, standing outside the school after dropping off the child, saying tearfully, "But we've had lunch together every day of his life."

For the majority of parents, many of whom work outside the home and whose children have gone to daycare centers and preschools, this leave-taking may not be so abrupt, but it is still a significant event in their own lives, as well as those of their children. Many parents feel a strong interest in, and responsibility for, determining whether a particular classroom is a healthy and welcoming environment for their children. For this reason, parents of primary schoolchildren are likely to come to school, on one pretext or another, during the first days of school, just to see for themselves that their children are in good hands.

Beginning teachers may feel somewhat overwhelmed by these visits. All of their available energy has gone into planning the curriculum, moving furniture, decorating the classroom, and meeting and becoming acquainted with other teachers in the school. When a parent suddenly shows up, unannounced, it can be unsettling, especially if the parent wants to ask questions when the students are present. When this occurs, it is necessary for the teacher to suggest politely, but assertively, another time for this impromptu conference: "I'm sorry, Mrs. Jones, I would love to talk with you, but all of my attention is needed in the class right now. Could we talk about this after school or tomorrow morning at 8:15?"

On many occasions throughout the school year, the teacher is expected to communicate with parents either singly or in large groups. In addition, many classroom teachers invite parents to become involved in the life of the classroom. Some students come from single-parent families, blended families (in which divorced parents have remarried and have children with previous and current spouses), families with foster parents, and guardians. Teachers meet students who do not have the same last names as their parents. Teachers must recognize that the home lives they may have themselves experienced may be different from those of their students. When the term *parents* is mentioned in this chapter, it is meant to refer to the people who are being contacted or are meeting with the teacher on behalf of a particular child.

Fall Open House

When parents come to visit the classroom early in the year, one method of deflecting their concerns is to suggest that they will be able to have many of their questions answered within a few weeks at the annual fall open house (sometimes called back to school night). This event is planned especially for that purpose in many school districts.

The fall open house is usually held on an evening in late September. To prepare for the event, teachers are asked to be ready to describe their goals for the year and give an overall picture of the school's curriculum at that grade level. The event usually begins in the school auditorium or other large meeting rooms, where the principal welcomes everyone to the school and describes the important events that the entire school has planned for the coming year. The teachers, counselors, other administrators, and sometimes the president of the parent-teacher organization are introduced. Special attention is usually given to introducing any new teachers on the faculty. At the conclusion of this general meeting, the teachers are released to go to their classrooms and make themselves ready for the open house. After a few minutes, the visitors are dismissed from the general meeting to find their children's classrooms. Some schools may ring a bell periodically so that parents who have more than one child in a school have an opportunity to move from classroom to classroom in order to meet all of their children's teachers.

When the parents assemble in the classroom, the teacher makes a short presentation to the entire group and describes what is planned for the year. A time for questions and answers of interest to the entire group is also likely to occur. Because most school districts intend the fall open house to be a time for general discussions of goals and curriculum, there is no planned opportunity for individual parents to ask teachers for specific information about their child's achievement or behavior. If parents approach the teacher and begin to discuss personal concerns, it is expected that the teacher will suggest an alternate time and place for an individual conference.

Parent-Teacher Conferences

Conferences between individual parents and teachers vary greatly in purpose. Some are primarily used for diagnosing a problem or concern, and others are set up to report to the parents about a child's progress in school. If either the teacher or the parent has a serious concern about a child, one or the other may arrange a conference in the first weeks of school. When teachers observe unusually aggressive, passive, depressed, or antisocial behavior in a child, for example, they are wise to call home immediately and set up a conference right away to gain information about the nature of the child's problems. This is especially true when a child's behavior disrupts other students in the class or interferes with the learning process.

Setting up a conference sends an important signal to a student who is exhibiting unusual or unacceptable behavior. It tells the student that the teacher has withitness and is going to take action to correct the problem rather than let it go. It allows the teacher to seek information about the underlying reasons for the observed behavior. In a conference of this type, it is recommended that the student join the conference at some point with the parents to gain a better understanding of the adults' views of the behavior.

When the conference takes place, the teacher should describe the behavior and, if possible, supplement the oral description with written anecdotal reports of examples of the behavior. The specificity (date, time, and specific behavior) of anecdotal records sends a clear message to the parents and to the student that the teacher is acutely aware of specific behaviors. The teacher should express concern about the behavior and then ask both the student and the parents to explain why it is occurring. Good and Brophy (2002) point out how students usually cannot explain fully why they act as they do, and teachers should not expect them to be able to do this. If the students had such insight, they probably would not be behaving badly in the first place. Instead, the hope is that clues or helpful information will emerge from the discussion.

When the parents discuss their own views of the child's behavior, the teacher may gain significant insight by learning about the home environment. For example, the parents may agree that they have observed the same behavior at home and that it seems to be related to a crisis the family is dealing with, such as a death, divorce, drugs, lost job, or move. When the teacher, the child, and the parents confront this matter together, they can begin to put together a workable plan to help support the student during this difficult period and, at the same time, help the child gain awareness about the effects of the behavior on others.

Conferences do not always result in such harmonious cooperation. Parents may not present much useful information. On occasion, they may become defensive or resentful of the suggestion that their child's behavior is unacceptable. In their family, this behavior may be okay. For example, a fifth-grade teacher was alarmed to see a boy walk into her class on the first day of school wearing a T-shirt that read, "Born to Raise Hell!" True to the message on the shirt, the child fought with other children at least once a day. When the parents were called in for a conference and the teacher described this behavior to them, the father replied, "So what? I tell my kids not to let anyone get the best of them." From the words and the father's tone of voice, the teacher learned that fighting was an acceptable behavior for resolving conflict in that family. No happy resolution was discovered in this conference, but it did give the teacher some additional insight into the source and the depth of the boy's difficulties in social interactions with his peers.

At times, a teacher may need to involve others in the conference. Counselors may need to be present to suggest alternative ways of dealing with problems. If the teacher, parents, and counselor cannot effectively address a problem with the student, additional professional help may need to be offered to the parents. At times, parents admit that they cannot even handle their child at home.

Interpreters may also be needed for parents who are not proficient English speakers. If you are using an interpreter, it is important to remember to maintain eye contact with the parent, and not conduct the conference focusing on the interpreter. The use of older children as interpreters, while convenient and sometimes the only choice available, is not recommended. There is a chance that it is demeaning to the parent, and it may also result in some purposeful miscommunication by the child, depending on the content and repercussions of the conversation.

Conferences designed for reporting student progress rather than for diagnostic purposes usually take place in the late fall to coincide with the end of the first grading period and the first report card. In many districts, the parents are asked to come to the school for a conference with the teacher shortly after report cards are sent home. Thus, the parents have an opportunity to look at the report card and think about the questions and concerns they may want to raise at the conference. Some school districts require parents to come to the school to pick up the child's report card and have a conference with the teacher. In this case, the teacher explains the grades and observations to the parent as the parent views the report card for the first time. This second strategy is used primarily to make sure that parents attend the conference.

Report card conferences are generally 15 to 30 minutes in length. They may be offered during the day and in the early evening so that parents who work during the day may choose an evening conference. Usually one or two school days are used for the fall conferences. In some school districts, the entire process is repeated in the spring. In the elementary school, a schedule of 30 conferences over a period of one or two days is a tiring experience for most teachers, who may find that conference days are more exhausting than regular teaching days. This is due primarily to the tension caused by the teachers' recognition that they are responsible for the smooth flow of conversation and information. When this feeling of responsibility is multiplied by a factor of 30 or more in a few short days, it is easy to see how draining it can be.

To minimize the tension, it is extremely important that teachers plan each conference carefully. Prior to the event, reflective teachers often write a page of notes about each student, highlighting the accomplishments and the matters of concern that the teacher wants to discuss with the parents. It is important for the teacher to be able to identify the child correctly in the conference. Teachers have mentioned embarrassing moments when parents have a puzzled look on their faces, only to discover that they were talking about another student and not the child of the parents meeting with them!

In addition to planning what you want to say about each child, it is a good idea to make a general plan for how you will conduct your conferences. The primary purpose of report card conferences is for you to inform the parents about the child's progress in your class, but the conference is also designed to elicit information from the parents that may help you help the child. The parents may also have concerns that they wish to discuss. To accomplish all of these tasks in 20 minutes can be difficult. You must act as the timekeeper and allot a reasonable amount of time to each purpose. The parent will not be concerned about taking more time, but you will because you will be aware that the next set of parents is waiting outside the door for their appointment with you.

Linn and Gronlund (2000) suggest considering the following elements for planning your conferences:

1. Make plans for each conference. For each child, list the points you want to cover and the questions you want to ask.
2. Begin the conference in a positive manner. Making a positive statement about the child, such as "Betty really enjoys helping others" or "Derek is an expert on dinosaurs," is likely to create a cooperative and friendly atmosphere.
3. Present the student's strong points before describing areas needing improvement. Present samples of work and focus on what the child can do and what he or she still has to learn. Try to use the word "and" instead of "but" when moving from one area to the other. It makes for a much more positive transition. For example, "Betty's research work on the project was outstanding, and we are going to continue working on her presentation skills as well."
4. Encourage parents to participate and share information. You must be willing to listen as well as talk. They may have questions and concerns about the school and about their child's behavior that need to be brought out into the open before constructive, cooperative action can take place.
5. Plan a course of action cooperatively. Guide the discussion toward a series of steps that can be taken by the teacher and the parents to assist the child. At the end of the conference, review these steps with the parents.
6. End the conference with a positive comment. Thank the parents for coming and say something positive about the student such as "Erik has such a good sense of humor and I enjoy having him in my class."

The regularly scheduled report card conferences may be the only time you will meet with the parents of most of your students. For those whose behavior or learning problems are quite serious, you will need to continue to contact the parents by telephone or in follow-up conferences to monitor whether the cooperative plan of action is being implemented and what effects it is having.

Talking to Parents about Underachievement

Effective two-way communication with parents is essential for assisting students with severe problems. An excellent resource (for both teachers and parents) for working with children whose behavior interferes with their learning in school is Rimm's (1995) *Why Bright Children Get Poor Grades*. This book describes many of the most feared behavior problems that teachers must face: hyperactivity, passiveness, perfectionism, rebellion, bullying, and manipulative behaviors. Rimm believes these behaviors cause children to achieve much less than they are capable of in school. In her studies of underachievement, Rimm has discovered that children learned most of these behaviors in response to some elements of their home environment. Changing the behavior takes a concerted effort by the parents to isolate the causes and create new procedures to help children learn healthier, more productive behavior patterns that can lead to success.

Often it is the teacher who spots the self-defeating behavior. Parents have been living with the child for so long that they may not see the child's behavior as unusual, and they may not be able to recognize how it affects the child's school achievement. Some examples of home situations that may lead to underachievment include the following:

> *The overwelcome child.* Although it has long been recognized that an unwelcome or rejected child is likely to have problems in life, it is also likely that excessive attention can cause achievement and emotional problems. When parents overprotect and overindulge, the child may develop a pattern of not taking initiative and of waiting for others to do his or her bidding.
>
> *Child with early health problem.* When children are born with allergies, birth defects, or other disabilities and parents respond by investing themselves almost totally in the child's well-being, a set of behaviors similar to those of the overwelcome child can develop.
>
> *Particular sibling combinations.* Birth order and sibling rivalry affect all children, but some combinations may be particularly damaging to a child's achievement. A student who is the sibling of a child with severe health problems or considered to be extremely gifted may feel left out or inadequate in comparison to the sibling. This can lead to the development of attention-getting behavior patterns, such as clowning or mischief making that may prevent the child from achieving fully.
>
> *Specific marital problems.* A single parent may develop a very close relationship with the child as a result of seeing the child as the only purpose for living. The parent may treat the child more like a spouse or a partner than a child, thus giving the child too much power. The child may learn to expect power and may not be willing to give it up to conform to the requirements of school. (Rimm, 1995)

These are only four of the many possible situations that can cause children to develop behaviors that may prevent them from achieving well in school. When a teacher spots a child who is exhibiting overly dependent or overly aggressive behaviors, it is important to confer with the child's parents—to report the problem and to learn how the behavior first developed and how the parents are responding to it. The first step toward a positive behavior change is for the teacher to describe and give examples of the behavior and its effects on the child's achievement. The parents may deny that the behavior exists or that it is serious, but if the teacher can establish a cooperative two-way dialogue with the parents, it may lead to new insights for everyone.

If parents do acknowledge the behavior, the next step is for you to describe the changes you are going to make at school to support the development of new, more positive behavior patterns and to suggest modifications that the parents might make at home. Together with the parents, set some reasonable goals for the child in terms of both behaviors and grades. Discuss methods of helping the child reach these goals, and agree on a plan that fits the child and the situation.

Rimm cautions that children will not change their behavior just because the adults in their lives want them to do so. The child must want to break the underachieving patterns and substitute them for behaviors that lead to success. Both the teacher and the parents must also confer with the child, describing the behaviors and their effects in words the child can understand and accept. When the teacher, parents, and child have the same goal and are working together on a plan of action tailored to fit the needs of the child, it is quite possible that the child will succeed.

Independent contracts are also useful support systems for helping children change behavior. A contract can specify work the child is to accomplish, with deadlines and expectations for success. It can also be used to specify behavioral expectations. When the teacher negotiates the contract with the child ahead of time, the child has an intrinsic incentive to complete it—after all, the child helped to create it and decide what would be required. A sense of ownership is likely to increase the likelihood of the contract being fulfilled (see Figure 12.1).

The teacher may employ additional extrinsic incentives if these seem useful in a given circumstance. It is most often recommended that students receive a reward that supports

Student's Name: _____ Teacher: _____ Date: _____
Behavior:
___ Good   ___ Fair   ___ Poor
Issues in Behavior Today: _____ _____
Attitude:
___ Good   ___ Fair   ___ Poor
Issues in Attitude Today: _____
Work:
___ Completed   ___ Mostly Completed   ___ Very Incomplete
Work to Be Completed at Home Tonight: _____ _____
Teacher Comments: _____
Student Comments: _____
Parent's Comments: _____
Teacher's Signature: _____ Date: _____
Student's Signature: _____ Date: _____
Parent's Signature: _____ Date: _____

Figure 12.1 Daily evaluation form.

academics. For example, a student could earn points toward additional time at learning an activity or a game. The major point is that the reward is something a student really would like to receive. Some activities that a teacher assumes would be rewarding may not be rewarding to students. The types of rewards should vary by grade level.

This type of plan may be created as a result of a successful parent-teacher conference, a visit by the teacher to the student's home, or a telephone conversation, followed by written documents specifying what the teacher expects, what the parents agree to take responsibility for, and what the student agrees to do to earn the agreed-upon incentive. For example, if the teacher observes that a student is not turning in homework, the teacher may call the students' parents and ask for a conference at school or suggest that the teacher come to visit the home to discuss the matter. Alerting the parents to this concern is likely to result in a discussion of probable causes. The parents may or may not accept the teacher's perceptions of the problem and its negative consequences for their child's achievement. After a frank discussion of conditions at home that may support or interfere with the student doing homework, the parents may come to recognize that the major cause might be the fact that the child and the family watch a great deal of television, beginning right after school and continuing up to bedtime. If the parents express a willingness to do their part to help change the child's behavior, then together they can draft an agreement or contract specifying when the student will do homework and when he or she can watch television. It is a good idea for the teacher to follow up on this type of agreement by sending the parents daily reports specifying whether the homework is actually being turned in. These daily reports are likely to help everyone remember the commitment they have made. Later, when the student appears to have learned the new pattern of behavior and is more

---

Student's Name: _____ **Week of:** _____

Rating Scale: 5 = Excellent, 4 = Good, 3 = Acceptable, 2 = Fair, 1 = Poor

Monday: ___ Behavior ___ Attitude ___ Work quantity ___ Work quality

Tuesday: ___ Behavior ___ Attitude ___ Work quantity ___ Work quality

Wednesday: ___ Behavior ___ Attitude ___ Work quantity ___ Work quality

Thursday: ___ Behavior ___ Attitude ___ Work quantity ___ Work quality

Friday: ___ Behavior ___ Attitude ___ Work quantity ___ Work quality

Overall Week's Rating: _____

Teacher's Signature: _____

Student's Signature: _____

Parent's Signature: _____

Figure 12.2 Weekly evaluation form.

consistent about turning in homework, the reports can be sent home weekly instead of daily (see Figure 12.2).

When a student is beginning to show more responsibility and independence, the teacher may choose to involve the student in writing a study plan contract, such as the one in Figure 12.3. This contract describes what the goal is and how the student plans to accomplish the goal. It may specify a reward or positive consequence that the student wants to earn when the goal is reached.

One final caution about conducting parent-teacher conferences: Occasionally, participants in the conference may reveal a family problem that is unusual and extremely serious. The students or parents may describe extreme poverty, desertion, or physical or sexual abuse to a teacher as a desperate attempt to get help. The classroom teacher is well advised not to try to deal with such problems alone. If this happens to you, ask the parent to allow you to discuss this matter with the school's social services personnel and immediately contact the principal, school psychologist, social worker, and other members of the crisis team to assist in the matter. Remember that there are legal responsibilities involved in suspicion of neglect or child abuse: The teacher is mandated by law to report such suspicions.

I _____ agree to spend _____ minutes each evening doing homework. I will work without complaint, without TV or radio, for that amount of time and try my best to complete my homework assignments during that time. If I finish before my allotted time, I agree to read for the rest of the allotted time.

I _____ agree to accept the work completed during the allotted time without penalty if it is not complete as long as _____ has put forth honest effort to complete the assignments.

This contract may be revised with the mutual consent of both the student and the teacher.

Teacher's Signature: _____ Date: _____

Student's Signature: _____ Date: _____

Figure 12.3 Sample study plan contract.

THROUGH THE EYES OF PARENTS

When parents send their children to school, they have many hopes and fears for their children's future. They want to be able to trust the school to create a safe, stable, nurturing environment for the children. They want their children's developing sense of self to be enhanced and their individual talents to be appreciated. But many parents feel left out of the decision-making process within their children's schools. If teachers describe their goals or programs using educational jargon unfamiliar to the parents, the parents may be reluctant to attend conferences or meetings at the school.

When parents are involved in establishing the school's vision statement and are invited to participate in advisory groups, they may contribute many valuable ideas. In Jefferson County, Colorado, a school created a parent-teacher focus group to provide teachers with feedback on how to increase student self-esteem. At first, teachers were reluctant to have the parent observers visit their classrooms, but team members worked collaboratively to design a set of guidelines for the observations and agreed to provide teachers with copies of their observation notes after each visit. A parent-teacher retreat was held to build trust and clarify roles and expectations. After observing classrooms and playgrounds, the parent observers worked with faculty to develop a statement of their beliefs about how the schools could enhance students' self-esteem. Their statement of beliefs includes the following:

Provide experiences that allow for individual differences.

Provide opportunities to express creativity.

View mistakes as learning opportunities.

Provide a safe/clean learning environment. (Meadows, 1993, p. 32)

Although these recommendations were not new to the faculty, they were helpful in clarifying what the community wanted and expected from their school. From the team effort, both teachers and parents had a better understanding of the complexity of education.

In some communities, parents take a very active role in governance. Parents serve as members of school boards or advisory groups that work closely with the school administrators to make the important decisions about school funding and hiring and firing of personnel. On occasion, some parents have strong views about a single issue and may try to influence school boards or administrators to provide a certain program or modify an existing program to coincide with the parents' values or philosophy. When this occurs, opinions can become strongly stated, and conflict is likely to arise among parent factions and faculty. For the beginning teacher, it is important to try to learn as much about the values of a school community as possible prior to submitting an application for employment or accepting a teaching contract. If your own values and philosophy differ greatly from that of the majority of the school governance teams, then you are unlikely to feel at home teaching in that school district.

Teaching and Learning in a Multicultural Community

When the language, culture, and values of the parents match those of the teachers in a child's school, communication is likely to be relatively clear and agreements relatively simple to achieve. When the culture of a child's home differs significantly from the culture of the teacher, the teacher must be especially willing to listen as well as talk during parent-teacher conferences.

Before the *Brown v. Board of Education* Supreme Court decision in 1954, children who were racially different from the white majority were often segregated in separate (and inferior) schools. Since that time, federal mandates have required school systems to integrate both the student bodies and the faculties and administrators of their schools. But federal laws have not been able to mitigate the subtler forms of racism that still exist in some educational settings.

Although the United States is known as a nation of immigrants and a melting pot of cultures, the traditionally accepted cultural norm has mirrored the philosophy of the white Anglo-Saxon majority. Other cultures have been known as minority cultures. The prevailing

PRAXIS
Strategies for encouraging home/school partnerships are addressed in PRAXIS™ Exam Section 4b: Profession and Community.

belief is that children from minority cultures must be taught the language and habits of the majority. Florio-Ruane (2001) found that when the home culture's practices and values are not acknowledged or incorporated by the school, parents may not feel capable of supporting children in their academic pursuits (Florio-Ruane, 2001).

Reflective teachers are aware that their own values and expectations may vary considerably from those of the families in their school community. Rather than assume that the children and their parents should be taught to mimic the language, behavior, and norms of the teacher's culture, however, reflective teachers strive to gain a better understanding of the various cultures that comprise the school community and to celebrate these differences by incorporating them into the curriculum.

In parent-teacher conferences, the reflective teacher is likely to ask with great interest about the home environment and the parents' cultural values as a means of better understanding the various cultures and conveying respect to the parents. When parents sense this respect from the teacher, they are more likely to return it and to believe that the teacher shares their own concerns for their child. The teacher may need to be especially encouraging to parents of other cultures, urging them to share their own concerns and ask questions. People from many cultures were not raised to ask questions of teachers and may be reluctant to do so. If the teacher encourages them to ask questions or make suggestions for the child's benefit, they may feel comfortable enough to speak up. This two-way communication and mutual understanding can lead to a more productive arrangement to work together in supporting the child's achievement at home and at school.

Hodkinson (2003) points out that people from various cultures see the world differently and have different perspectives, needs, and values. While some teachers may expect students to speak up and show their individuality, students from many other nations have great difficulty doing so. This type of behavior, known as "putting yourself forward" in Asian cultures, is considered to be a negative character trait. Some students are taught not to meet another person's eye, especially someone with as much authority as a teacher. Teachers must be aware that their own way of doing things and the expectations they were brought up to emulate may not be shared by their students.

The classroom teacher must demonstrate a willingness to assist culturally diverse children and their parents as they make the difficult transition from one land to another. One of the best ways to accomplish this is to show sensitivity and respect for the various cultures of all the children in the class. Each year, the teacher may plan a special unit of study on the contribution of the cultures represented by the class members. Parents can be invited to participate in the learning experience by visiting the classroom and sharing with children the achievements, crafts, and food of their countries. They can teach the children the songs and games of their homelands. When teachers involve the parents in their children's education, they send a powerful message that the school cares about them. A teacher should not feel offended, however, if the parent does not want to be involved. The teacher may interpret this as parental disinterest, even though, in some cultures, parents have been taught that the school is responsible for their youngster's education, and they should not be involved in the process on the school campus.

Visits to Students' Homes

When teachers care sufficiently about understanding the particular home and cultural environments that surround their students, one way they can seek information is to visit the children and their families in their homes. Teachers may do this by sending home a newsletter early in the year, announcing that the teacher would enjoy meeting the parents and seeing the children in their homes and that invitations to do so will gladly be received. This gives the parents an opportunity to invite the teacher when it is convenient for them.

The visit will probably take place after school or during the evening. No agendas need to be established for such a visit; in fact, doing so would be counterproductive. The visit is not a structured parent-teacher conference; it is simply an opportunity for the teacher to understand more fully the conditions in which the child lives. The teacher may be invited to share the family's meal, look at their photographs, and hear some of their family stories. As a result, the child and the parents are more likely to feel that they are respected members of the school community. Such visits should always be conducted with an eye to safety and comfort. You may want to ask a colleague or an administrator to accompany you on these visits.

On occasion, it may become necessary for school personnel to make a more structured visit with an agenda. This may occur if a child is having extreme problems and is being referred for special services and a psychological evaluation. In that case, the school social worker or psychologist may visit the home to determine if some factor in the home environment may be causing the child's problems.

Newsletters and Notes

Many elementary teachers communicate with parents by sending home handwritten notes describing a particular behavior or accomplishment of their child. In some classrooms, a note from the teacher signifies only bad news that is sent home when the teacher wants to describe an incident or pattern of misbehavior, a poor test result, or excessive tardiness. More recently, many reflective teachers have considered how to use the home note to encourage good behavior and reward achievement. Many teachers now send home notes or emails describing a special accomplishment, an improvement in classwork, or an act of friendliness or generosity shown by the child.

To ensure that all children benefit from this system, the teacher may send a note of good news home to a certain number of children per week until every child has had one. Others prefer not to use a schedule but to send a note or email whenever they observe a child doing something especially well. Without a schedule, however, it is important that teachers be careful to include all the children in the process and not favor some students over others.

In some classrooms, teachers prepare and send home classroom newsletters describing the important events planned for that week or month. The newsletter may contain items describing completed projects and new ones just getting underway. In the newsletter, the teacher can request parent volunteers for various projects and write notes of appreciation to parents who have recently helped out in some way. If your parents have access to the Internet, a class website is a very effective tool for communication and allows for posting of exemplary work while saving paper.

In primary classrooms, the teacher generally takes full responsibility for creating the newsletter. But in intermediate and upper-level classrooms, many teachers allow students to help write the items. They may use a computer program designed for creating newspaper formats. In this case, the production of the newsletter becomes more than just a method of communicating with parents; it also becomes an enriching learning experience.

Telephone Calls

The telephone provides an important link between school and home. Teachers often call students' homes for the same reasons that they write notes or emails. Some use a telephone call to report a child's misbehavior and poor achievement and to enlist the support and assistance of parents in correcting the problems. Other teachers try to call home to report both positive and negative news. It is often of great value to make the first call to a parent a positive interaction. Tell them how excited you are to have their child in your class. Be prepared to mention one or two specific things that have occurred since the beginning of school that reflect the positive impression that their child has made on you. Remind them that you are seeking their assistance in making this a successful year for their son or daughter in your classroom. Ask if there is anything in particular that might make this a really positive year for their child in your classroom. If a call must be made to a parent to report a problem or concern, we recommend that you follow up a few days later with a second telephone call to (hopefully!) report that the student is making progress in solving the problem.

Teachers are often on the receiving end of telephone calls or emails from students' parents. Parents may call to clarify something about an assignment or an announcement that they cannot understand from their child's description. If parents hear confusing stories about something that happened during the school day, they may call the teacher to find out what really

PRAXIS
Effective communication strategies are assessed in PRAXIS™ Exam Section 3a: Communication Techniques.

occurred. Responding to these promptly and in an open and informative manner promotes a positive pattern of communication between home and school.

Occasionally parents call in anger or frustration. They may disagree with the contents of the curriculum, the way a test was graded, or the way a classroom incident was handled. The teacher receiving one of these calls may easily become defensive and angry, too. Dealing effectively with these calls involves the use of mature, well-developed communication skills. It is difficult, but very important, to listen empathetically to what the parent says. The instinctive reaction of most teachers is to break into the parent's statements and present their own side of the situation, but it is more productive if the teacher's initial responses encourage the parent to describe the problem in more detail and express personal feelings.

After the parent has had an opportunity to fully describe the reason for the telephone call, the teacher's side of the story can be presented in a quiet, nonthreatening, and nondefensive voice. In a situation such as this, the teacher has the responsibility for attempting to resolve the conflict and creating a mutually acceptable solution. For example, suppose a fight occurs in the classroom during the day and Dean punches John in the face and bloodies his lip. The first thing the teacher may decide to do is send John to the nurse. Then the teacher may talk to Dean to find out what prompted the fight. Suppose that Dean claims he was provoked by John's name calling, and many children in the class support that claim. When John returns from the nurse, the teacher tells him that both he and Dean will have to stay in during recess because of the fighting. John seethes with anger for the rest of the day. After school, the teacher is called to the telephone to find John's very angry parent on the other end. "Why did you keep my son in for recess when he got hit by that bully? And why didn't you call me immediately when he got hit? Did you know he was bleeding? I'm going to come in right now and talk to your principal about this matter, and you will be sorry you treated my son this way!"

The instinctive reaction for most teachers is to jump in and explain after the first few words are spoken. If the parent continues to question the teacher's judgment, the teacher may soon feel as angry as the parent does. But reflective teachers recognize that there will be days like this in the classroom with 30 students and one adult. They will try to keep their feelings under control and say something to soothe the parent's hurt pride and upset feelings: "I'm glad you called, Mrs. Jones. I can understand how you feel. Tell me how John's lip is now." This type of comment will help the teacher gather information and gain time to formulate a good response. Not all such problems can be readily resolved. Perhaps the teacher and the parent will continue to have different points of view no matter how much they discuss it. If this is the case, it is necessary to acknowledge it and end the conversation with a comment such as "I recognize how you feel about this situation. I'm sorry John got hurt today, and I'll do my best to see that he is not involved in any more fights this year."

You should be aware, however, that many schools currently participate in zero-tolerance programs that involve clearly specified reactions and consequences related to certain behaviors on the school grounds or during the school day. Be sure you are familiar with your school's policies regarding misbehaviors and the procedures to be followed in those cases. There may be times when you have little or limited choice as to how you handle a given situation.

The key point of this section is expressed in the phrase *reflective teachers recognize that there will be days like this*. Every school year has days like these. Values clash and feelings are hurt. The beginning teacher may be shocked the first time it happens and overreact by feeling angry, guilty, or defensive. When incidents such as these occur in your classroom, try to remember that every teacher experiences conflict. Conflict is unavoidable in this career, and the first step in learning how to handle it is learning to expect and accept it as part of the job. Feel free to discuss your feelings and concerns with your administrators and colleagues. They are there to help you through these all-important initial years.

Spring Open House and Other Special Events

In the fall, the purpose of most conferences and open house events is to allow parents and teachers to get to know each other, communicate their goals for their children, and make plans for accomplishing these goals. As the year goes by, the focus of most meetings between parents and teachers is for the teacher to demonstrate to the parents how these goals are being met.

Many classroom teachers invite parents frequently, perhaps as often as once a month, to attend exhibits, plays, assemblies, or other occasions for students to display what they are learning and what they have accomplished. Some of these events may be schoolwide assemblies, such as Thanksgiving plays, concerts, feasts, winter pageants, midwinter cultural fairs, and spring open houses in which collections of student work are displayed throughout the school.

Individual teachers may also invite their students' parents to school to view the performances or an exhibit of products resulting from a unit of study. These events are usually highly prized by students and parents, and they are an excellent way for the teacher to interact and communicate continually with the parents.

Consider, however, how some parents might feel if they attend a spring open house and find that their own child's work is not displayed. In some competitive classrooms, teachers tend to display only the papers with "100%" written across the top. For those children who rarely get perfect papers, this can be a discouraging experience; for their parents, it is likely to be equally discouraging. If classroom displays include examples of students' work, it is important to display the best works of every student in approximately equal numbers.

To avoid creating a competitive environment, you may want to display students' work inside their portfolios on their desks so that each parent can view the work done by his or her own child alone. General classroom displays can consist of group projects and murals so that every child and parent can take equal pride in the classroom.

COMMUNITY INVOLVEMENT IN CLASSROOM ACTIVITIES

Parents as Volunteers

Parents volunteer to do many things in schools to benefit their own children and the larger community. Many parents enjoy being members of an all-school organization known as the parent-teacher association (PTA) or parent-teacher organization (PTO). These organizations have regularly scheduled meetings and yearly fundraising events to serve the needs of the school. In most cases, parents do the greatest part of the work on the committees, although teachers are usually represented, too.

Many elementary schools encourage parents to volunteer their time during the school day to assist teachers in educational or extracurricular programs. Parents can serve as coaches (academic as well as athletic), assistant coaches, or referees for some sports events such as all-school field-day events. They often serve as helpers on class field trips, accompanying the class on the bus ride and throughout the day. Usually, teachers ask each adult to be responsible for a small group of children during the trip, reducing the adult-to-child ratio from 28:1 down to 4:1 or 5:1.

In the classroom, many primary teachers invite parent volunteers to serve as assistants in the reading and language arts program. A parent can work with one small group while the teacher works with another or with the rest of the class. In this way, parents can serve many important functions. They can read aloud to a group of children or listen to an individual or a small group of children read aloud to them. Parents can write the words as a child dictates a story or can edit a piece of writing done by a child. Parents can listen to book reports and keep records of the number and type of books each child has read.

With the advent of computers in the classroom, many teachers appreciate the help of parents who are knowledgeable about computers. Parents can volunteer to work with groups of children as they learn to operate a computer or to monitor students' progress as they work with tutorial or problem-solving computer programs.

During individualized mathematics or spelling programs, or those structured on a mastery learning model, parents can serve as assistants who correct formative tests and provide feedback to students. They can also help to organize the large amounts of paperwork, filing, and record keeping that often accompany individualized instructional programs.

Having parents volunteer in your classroom has many benefits, and you will often find knowledgeable and experienced parents who enjoy this type of work. Many parents have interrupted their own careers to raise children and look forward to having a regular volunteer job.

Not all teachers, however, enjoy having parent volunteers in their classrooms. Some teachers are reluctant to have parents view the ups and downs that occur in any school day. Other teachers are not comfortable with parent volunteers because the teacher must be ready with activities and materials when the parent arrives. For some teachers, this is a burden that outweighs the benefit of having the extra help. It is true that working with parent volunteers means greater responsibility for the teacher, who must manage the other adults as well as the students in the class.

Whether or not you wish to use parents as volunteers in your classroom is one of those issues that you will need to reflect on, considering the benefits against the costs. One of the best ways to gather information about the efficacy of this practice in your classroom is to try it out with one subject area and a knowledgeable, experienced parent volunteer to see if it is a system you want to employ.

To increase the likelihood that the practice will work in your room, you and the parent volunteer should discuss in advance what you expect the parent to do and agree on the times the parent will visit. Usually parents are responsible only for routine tasks or monitoring students as they work on a program planned by you and your colleagues. When these matters are clarified, you will probably find the volunteer effort to be very productive, allowing you to reduce the amount of time you spend on routine tasks. Be sure you have a schedule for volunteers in your classroom to allow yourself the time and opportunity to prepare for them.

Community Resources

Parents with special interests, abilities, careers, and accomplishments can also enrich your program by speaking to the class about their specialties. A unit on community helpers can certainly benefit from visits by parents who are nurses, police officers, firefighters, and others who perform community services. Parents who are manufacturers or waste haulers can provide their input during a unit on ecology. When the class is studying economics, parents who work as merchants can describe the theory of supply and demand to the class.

During the first parent-teacher conference in the fall, you may be able to discover what talents and/or experiences your students' parents possess and create a community resources file to draw on throughout the year. In some schools, these files are kept for schoolwide use, and parents listed in the file have volunteered to come to any classroom in the school to share their knowledge and experience with the children. The file may also contain names of adults in the community who are not parents of children attending the school but who are willing to visit as a service to the community.

Some schools seek financial contributions from the community to fund music, art, or other programs that have been eliminated from their school budgets. Booster clubs are often formed by parents, and other community members raise money to finance sports teams, the arts, or technological programs that require additional equipment and resources.

Some districts have established an educational foundation that is run by an administrator. People in the community donate money to the foundation and teachers apply for mini-grants to be used within their department or classroom. These are often great ways to fund materials for a special project or possibly a field trip for the class. If your school does not have such a foundation, it might be worthwhile to encourage one.

Getting a foundation started can be an arduous task. A wall of donors prominently displayed in a conspicuous place within the school, with plaques indicating the range of support for donating families, is an effective procedure for encouraging funding. Auctions and other enjoyable pastimes may be occasions for bringing together families from the school community for a fun evening as well as fundraising.

Occasionally, parents may approach a teacher and offer to pay for something or contribute something of value to the class. A parent who works in a scientific or technological field may approach a high school science teacher, for example, and say, "I would like to donate a used cathode ray oscilloscope or a used computer to the department. Can you use one?" It is very hard to turn down this type of request when you may need the equipment and there are no funds available from other sources. It is important that you check with your administration before accepting an offer of this type or before making an appeal for funding at an open house or parent conference.

There should never be confusion about whether money or gifts have been exchanged for grades. To reduce this fear for yourself and for the administration, send a letter to each parent stating that, in the past, some parents have approached you to donate certain items or money, and therefore you would like to inform all parents about the procedures to be followed for classroom donations. Items of value or donations of money should be sent to the school office with a letter stating which department or class should receive the money. The teacher is not to be informed who donated the money or equipment. A ledger should be kept with all receipts so that at any time during the year, appropriate personnel can check how much money was collected and what was purchased. An administrator should be asked to oversee the fund. This procedure standardizes all gift-giving practices for your class or department so that everyone is protected. If an anonymous gift comes to your class, you could recognize the gift in your newsletter home, thereby alerting the donor that the gift had been received and was greatly appreciated.

CHARACTER AND MORAL EDUCATION PROGRAMS

The interaction between home and school becomes more complex and controversial when the school's objective changes from supporting the child's academic development to supporting the child's moral development. Nevertheless, schools in the 21st century are likely to be at the center of a growing concern about the need for greater emphasis on moral education. This concern grows out of awareness that schools must take more responsibility for countering the influence of drugs, violence on television and other media, the fragmentation of the family, and the publicity about questionable ethical practices in business and industry.

When teachers and parents discuss the schools' role in teaching values, there is general agreement that, due to the enormous temptations and distractions facing children today, schools must take an active role in teaching children about the nature of right and wrong. The ever-increasing social, religious, and ethnic diversity of the schools also makes it difficult to agree on a specific set of values.

Gardner (1999) explored the concept of a moral intelligence, but he chose not to include it as one of the multiple intelligences he describes because of the difficulty in defining it. He is able to state that "central to a moral domain is a concern with those rules, behaviors, and attitudes that govern the sanctity of life."

Lickona (2002) recommends that school–parent support groups think locally rather than globally in order to achieve a meaningful set of moral values. Within the school community, we hope that you as teachers will take an active role in trying to (1) arrive at a consensus about the moral values most important to your community, and (2) write or implement a moral education curriculum that will be taught at school and in the home at the same time.

Saterlie (1992) illustrates how such a parent–school partnership can be formed and what it can produce. As a school administrator, she describes the Baltimore public schools' experience in which school administrators created a community task force to participate in an open dialogue on community values. They purposely invited people with different religious and political beliefs to serve on the task force. After extensive reading and debate, the task force was able to agree on a common core of values appropriate for a democratic and pluralistic society. They are compassion, courtesy, critical inquiry, due process, equality of opportunity, freedom of thought and action, honesty, human worth and dignity, integrity, justice, knowledge, loyalty, objectivity, order, patriotism, rational consent, reasoned argument, respect for others' rights, responsible citizenship, rule of law, self-respect, tolerance, and truth. After identifying these community-acknowledged values, the task force wrote outcome statements for development of these moral values. The board of education then discussed and ratified their report. The PTA developed a brochure on the values education program and distributed it to all parents in the system.

The method used to implement this program allowed each of the 148 schools in the district to appoint its own values committee, which was encouraged to select certain task force–identified values to emphasize in its own school projects. This encouraged a creative response from most schools. Some addressed additional values such as computer ethics or academic honesty, as well as those identified by the task force. The Baltimore model linked parents, schools, and the community in a unified examination of moral and ethical issues to strengthen the character of students, which in turn will contribute to strengthening a free society (Saterlie, 1992).

As a beginning teacher, you may find that your school district is undertaking similar measures, and you may wish to become an active part of the task force that identifies the values of your community and creates school programs to educate students in them. If you find that your school district has not yet considered such a challenge, perhaps you can be the one who initiates the idea. Reflective individuals who are committed to upholding the moral values of the community can serve as important role models for the students they teach.

TEACHERS MENTORING AND COACHING ONE ANOTHER

In recent history, the school principal was responsible for observing and evaluating teachers' classroom performance. The top-down hierarchy implied that only administrators could and should supervise teachers and make recommendations about improving their performance.

Currently, there is a growing consensus that teachers' growth and development is enhanced when they think of themselves as members of professional communities who take responsibility for teaching each other, learning together, and focusing on the successes and challenges of educating their students (Shaps, Watson, & Lewis, 1996). The idea of belonging to a community changes the way teachers think about their own learning. It tends to break the pattern of isolation that individual teachers used to experience when they went into their classrooms and closed the doors to the outside world. In supportive communities, teachers buoy up one other, share teaching strategies, try new ways of teaching, and ask for and receive feedback, which leads them to be able to redesign their curriculum and methods of instruction. Teachers in professional communities learn how to reflect on their abilities and gain confidence for changing their practice to better meet student needs (Lieberman, 1995).

One promising approach being implemented in a number of schools is the formation of professional book clubs. Groups of teachers purchase copies of professional books, read assigned chapters, and meet to discuss the possibilities of using the ideas contained in the book in their classrooms. We may be prejudiced, but we believe that this book could be used effectively in that context. By discussing the issues raised in these chapters, teachers can provide the feedback and support for one another that reflective teachers seek in order to improve their practice.

Being part of a teaching community encourages the type of reflective action that we have recommended throughout this book. When teachers seek other, more experienced teachers to discuss their classroom dilemmas and ask for feedback, they are demonstrating their willingness to reflect on their own practice in an effort to improve it.

In many school systems today, teachers are sharing their own perspectives with each other as part of the evaluation process. Experienced classroom teachers, sometimes called *coaches* or *mentor teachers*, observe less experienced teachers as they work with children in their classrooms. Afterward, the two teachers discuss the observed classroom events. This practice allows the mentor teacher to provide critical feedback and to share personal knowledge with colleagues. It also encourages the beginning teachers to reflect on what they do, the effects of their actions, and decisions and ways to improve their teaching.

In Watsonville, California, teachers in two schools created a program called Professional Partnerships to decrease isolation and build collegial support systems. In this program, two teachers selected each other on a voluntary basis to become teaching partners. They observed one another's classrooms each month for a minimum of 30 minutes each visit. The partners meet prior to each observation to define the focus of the lesson and then discuss the visit afterward.

Quarterly, the partners meet with the principal and two additional teachers in the school, who serve as facilitators. Here is how two of the teacher partners described the project:

> My partner is coming to visit so I don't let things slide. My area of interest is improving the quality of student interactions. But I've also improved management, groupings, and materials because everything surrounding the lesson affected what I wanted to have happen.

> The post-conferences give me a chance to talk about the details of the lesson that I couldn't pay attention to while I was teaching. My partner always gives me new ideas. I feel very supported, and I'm making changes. (Stobbe, 1993, p. 41)

Teachers are also actively involved in selecting the type of staff development they need to accomplish the goals they have established for themselves. When teachers get interested in a new curriculum such as Critical Literacy or mathematics programs that emphasize problem solving, they are likely to propose conferences they would like to attend and to arrange to bring in consultants knowledgeable about the new methods.

Another powerful new result of being part of a professional community of teachers is the increase in the role of the teacher as a researcher. Asking questions of one another and generating ideas often leads teachers to investigate areas of concern. Informally, and quite naturally, they often begin doing active research to improve their own instructional practices. When they learn something valuable about their own efforts, they are increasingly taking the role of collaborating with other educators to communicate what they have found. To share the results of their investigations, many teachers are writing about their experiences and describing the investigations they have made. They submit their papers to journals and take part as presenters in local and regional conferences.

INTERACTING WITH COLLEAGUES IN CREATING PROFESSIONAL PORTFOLIOS

Beginning teachers are frequently interested in creating professional portfolios as a means of demonstrating their knowledge, awareness of issues, ability to communicate, and reflectiveness on the important issues of K–12 education. Many school systems engage experienced teachers as mentor coaches and ask beginning teachers to create professional portfolios that document their accomplishments and strengths. Judy Eby has worked with beginning teachers as a mentor coach and finds that the most valuable aspect of creating the professional portfolio is not the product itself, but the growth that occurs during the process of selecting what to include, reflecting on each document and work sample, and talking with other colleagues and the mentor coach about the experiences that resulted in each document or page of the portfolio.

In this text, we have encouraged the creation of a professional portfolio and have offered specific suggestions of what might be included. We also highly recommend that you view your portfolio as a work in progress, changing it weekly or monthly as new ideas or accomplishments occur. We also heartily recommend that you share your portfolio with other trusted colleagues and look at theirs. The ideas you will gain from one another will enable you to make your portfolio more interesting and useful as a means of communicating your strengths.

We hope that you have a mentor coach when you begin teaching, and that your mentor will assist you in collecting artifacts and documents for your portfolio. A mentor can be asked to photograph your classroom while you are teaching so that you can include the photos in your portfolio. You may also ask your mentor to record you while you present your first unit, teach with manipulatives, or lead a lively discussion. These videos are wonderful additions to your portfolio, and viewing them allows you to see yourself from a totally different perspective.

Many states are now mandating beginning teacher programs in all districts, whereby new teachers are involved in an induction process. Through this process, the beginning teachers are assigned support personnel to assist them in areas that they (the teachers themselves) identify as areas needing more training or attention. New teachers are encouraged to write a professional development plan outlining the steps, courses, and professional development workshops and seminars they will participate in over the first 2 to 3 years of their teaching. These programs have met with high approval from new teachers and are responsible for a dramatic increase in the number of teachers remaining in the profession after their initial 3 years of teaching.

If there are no mentor coaches in your district during your first year of teaching, you should find one for yourself. In the first few weeks of teaching, listen and watch for the teachers who have the most in common with your philosophy or curriculum orientation. Approach one and ask the teacher to serve as your informal mentor. The teacher is likely to be delighted with this invitation because it offers both of you the opportunity to grow and learn. You will learn from the experience of your chosen coach, and the mentor will learn what's new from you. We hope that you will share this book with your instructional coach and work on the professional portfolio pages together.

THE POWERFUL IMPACT A TEACHER CAN HAVE

At the center of all this change is the teacher and the growing power, responsibility, and respect that the teacher has earned. Good and Brophy (2002) report that since the early 1970s, there has been a surge of activity in research on teaching. Much of it has been predicated on a deceptively simple thesis: Effective school learning requires good teaching, and *good teachers* are those who exercise good judgment in constructing the education of their students. As we expressed in Chapter 1, we believe that good teachers may have their own hopes and expectations when they enter the profession, but they choose to use withitness and reflective action to put the needs of their students above their own. Not satisfied with their own self-perceptions, they consciously seek respected colleagues to ask for feedback on their actions and plans. We hope that we have made our case in this text that there is a strong, undeniable link between *reflective* and *effective* teachers.

As we discussed in Chapter 2, research shows that the most effective teachers are good classroom managers. This management skill grows directly out of reflective, relational, and democratic leadership from the first day of school. As shown in Chapter 10, the role of the teacher includes the responsibility for making accurate assessments of students' needs. Students from all cultures, ethnic groups, and economic conditions can thrive in the classroom of a caring and relational teacher who uses formal and informal sources of information as a means of ensuring that all students in the class can achieve success.

Throughout the research on effective teaching and effective schools, the attribute of *teacher clarity* continues to surface. Effective teachers are clear about what they intend to accomplish through their instruction, and they keep these goals in mind both in designing instruction and in communicating its purposes to the students (Good & Brophy, 2002). Clarity in articulating the goals and outcomes expected of students is described in Chapter 3, while clarity in presentation skills requires the strategies described in Chapter 6.

It is also becoming apparent that it is very effective to combine or integrate subjects into multidisciplinary units of study, as described in Chapters 4 and 9. Rather than being textbook technicians, reflective teachers prefer to create their own learning experiences working either individually or with teammates. They frequently focus on interesting themes or topics in which students use and develop their reading, writing, and research skills as they gain new knowledge about a variety of subjects.

Another common element identified throughout the literature on effective teaching is that effective teachers create learning experiences in which students are not simply passive recipients of fact-based knowledge; instead, they teach their students how to use many *cognitive processes*, how to organize information in new ways, and how to solve problems for themselves. It takes a reflective, relational teacher to recognize and select the appropriate teaching strategies that will engage students in active learning, as described in Chapters 7, 8, and 9.

Reflective teachers are eager to use a variety of assessment techniques, such as those described in Chapter 10, rather than rely on one objective method. This is an especially effective practice because it allows students with a variety of learning styles to demonstrate their accomplishments and succeed. Effective practitioners are also talented at providing students with useful, timely, and detailed *critical feedback* so that students know what is expected and what they must do to succeed. We also know that simply being a good evaluator is not enough; the most effective teachers are those who encourage their students to take an active role in the evaluation of their own learning by teaching them how to apply *metacognitive strategies* to become independent and self-reliant, able to monitor and regulate their own learning.

In addition to their responsibilities to their students, effective teachers are able to communicate well with the parents and other members of the school community in order to support the moral development of students, as described throughout this text.

The teacher's role in the educational community is changing. Teaching shows considerable promise of becoming a highly respected profession in the United States during the 21st century. This is largely due to the efforts of reflective teachers who are asking the important questions about how they can improve classroom events and children's lives. Alone or in collaboration, reflective teachers are seeking new alternatives and selecting the ones they believe might improve their teaching. They are taking responsibility for evaluating their classroom practices by gathering data from their own observations and from the current research and knowledge base on teaching and learning. They are disseminating what works for them in faculty meetings, workshops, conferences, and articles in professional journals. The result is a new emphasis on inquiry, reflection, and building a knowledge base about the most successful and effective practices that create a stimulating and healthy learning community.

A single teacher can exert a powerful influence on the community and has the potential to literally change the lives of students in perceptible ways. Chaos theory in physics tells us that only slight changes to the initial conditions of two identical dynamic systems will result in two completely different outcomes as time proceeds. The classic example is a pinball machine where each pinball is as identical to the others as we can possibly make them. No matter how precise we try to produce the same initial conditions for each release and operate each flipper the same way, minute variations along the path of each ball result in different scores and different paths. No two games are identical.

Our teaching influences others just like the pinball machine, as we "touch" each student's life. A teacher's acts of kindness or courage take on huge proportions months or even years down the road. What each individual does today to improve the lives of the next generation is the most lasting contribution any of us can make. National Basketball Association (NBA) superstar Michael Jordan's greatest contribution to society will not be his feats on the basketball court, but how he interacts with other people. A teacher has the opportunity to make a direct impact on the lives of many more young people than basketball stars or business executives do. Although we may not experience the notoriety of a film star or receive the signing bonuses of a professional athlete, teaching is being seen as the most important profession in society. Just imagine the life your students will live 10 years from now if you do your best to instill in each one the following goals:

1. To be a lifelong learner.
2. To erase the fear of failure, learn from mistakes, and know that sometimes we have to fail to succeed.
3. To explore meaningful and productive paths in life.

The profession of teaching can lead us to conclude that yes, it's a wonderful life, like we saw in the movie starring Jimmy Stewart. Occasionally, when a student comes back to visit you after 5 or 10 years, you may be given the opportunity to understand the impact your life has had on others; that your influence was significant; and that the caring, reflective actions you worked so hard to achieve in your classroom are, indeed, very much appreciated.

Playing Catch Up

Throughout this text, we have made suggestions for ways in which you, the teacher, can provide remedial help for students who have areas in their background knowledge that are not strong or whose skills are not up to grade level. Whenever you find that you must play catch up with students, it is vital that you share your concerns, your catch up plans, and your goals with the child's parents. The parents can often be involved in supporting the catch up plan.

Some suggestions for activities that parents can do at home to help the child catch up and be able to participate in the classroom activities more fully might include the following:

1. Reading with the student for 15 to 20 minutes each night. This could include background reading in informational books to help the child better understand the topics being studied in science, for example, or social studies if this is an area of concern. Be sure to provide the parents with appropriate reading material such as books that the child is capable of reading with a little support.

2. Suggestions for videos or television programs that the student and parent can view together and discuss. For example, before a study of the Antarctic, the parents could view *The March of the Penguins* with the student to build background knowledge.

3. Suggestions for local activities that would be beneficial in building background knowledge for future classroom studies such as Native American pow-wows, multicultural festivals, local museum exhibits, or traveling exhibits that are scheduled in your area.

4. Suggestions for local theatre, art, storytelling, and music productions that are appropriate for students.

GUIDED GROUP EXPLORATION

1. Divide the class into groups.
2. One member of the group should volunteer to be a "teacher" and the remaining members of the group will act as "parents" and "students."
3. Assign a scenario (see the list below) to each group and have them role-play a parent-teacher conference using their assigned scenario.
4. Bring the class back together and have each group report about the issues and resolutions that occurred during the group's role play.

Suggested scenarios:

a. Jenny's grades have taken a dramatic nosedive, and the teacher has asked Jenny's parents and Jenny to come in and discuss what can be done.

b. Andy refuses to do his homework. Contracts and withdrawing privileges have been tried unsuccessfully. A meeting with Andy's parents and Andy has been requested for the purpose of finding a solution.

c. Susie is constantly off task and out of her seat. She seems oblivious to the teacher's requests to focus, and she doesn't respond to traditional management strategies.

d. Lakisha excels in all her subject areas and is reading three grade levels above her grade placement. She finishes all assignments quickly and spends most of her time reading a library book. Her parents have requested a conference with the teacher because they don't feel she is being challenged in the classroom.

e. Reynaldo, a fifth-grader, is extremely talented in art. The problem is he spends most of his time drawing. His teacher has requested to meet with Reynaldo and his parents. They arrive at the meeting accompanied by Reynaldo's grandmother, a great fan of his artwork, who is carrying several framed pieces he did especially for her.

REFLECTIVE ACTION ACTIVITY FOR YOUR PROFESSIONAL PORTFOLIO

PRAXIS
The use of professional development to support ongoing personal reflection is tested in PRAXIS™ Exam Section 4a.

Demonstrate Your Commitment to Collaborative Teaching

Arrange to attend a faculty meeting or another decision-making body at a school you are visiting. How are decisions made? Do teachers work as colleagues to propose programs or solve problems? Does the administrator respect the ideas of the faculty members? Visualize yourself as a member of this faculty. What responsibilities would you be willing to assume?

Are you a person who is comfortable or uncomfortable with decision-making power? If you work in a school district that encourages teachers to take responsibility for many important decisions, will you welcome this as an opportunity or look on it as a burden? Would you prefer to make decisions about your own classroom independently, or would you rather share the power and the responsibility with your teammates?

Ask several experienced teachers to tell you stories of their interactions with other faculty members at their schools. If there are mentor teachers at the schools you visit, talk with them about the way teachers coach one another in that setting. What are the advantages of having teachers visit one another's classrooms to offer support and suggestions? What are the possible disadvantages or fears related to these visits? In your view, how can these fears or disadvantages be minimized?

You may have learned from your discussions with colleagues that it is difficult or impossible for teachers to please every student, every colleague, or every administrator. When a controversial issue arises in a school community, your point of view will be welcomed by some, but not all, of your colleagues on the faculty. If you accept that condition, how can you present your opinions to others on your faculty who may have opinions that differ from yours?

Choose an educational issue or dilemma that you are observing in the schools you visit. Create an action plan to approach this problem that you would propose to your colleagues if you were a full-time faculty member at the school. Include a method for gathering information from a variety of people who make up the school community.

Show your action plan to an experienced teacher. Get feedback on how to improve your plan or make it more realistic. What will you do if other teachers are reluctant to discuss your plan? What will you do if they think your issue is of little interest or value? What will you do if they disagree with you? Revise your plan and include it in your portfolio, along with your reflective analysis of the collaborative process you used to achieve your goals.

References

Davenport, P. & Anderson, G. (2002). *Closing the achievement gap: NO EXCUSES*. Houston, TX: American Productivity and Quality Center.

Florio-Ruane, S. (2001). *Teacher education and cultural imagination: Autobiography, conversation, and narrative*. Mahwah, NJ: Lawrence Erlbaum & Associates.

Gardner, H. (1999). *Intelligence reframed: Multiple intelligences for the 21st century*. New York: Perseus Books.

Good, T., & Brophy, J. (2002). *Looking in classrooms* (9th ed.). Boston: Allyn & Bacon.

Hodkinson, H. (2003). Educational demographics: What teachers should know. In A. Ornstein et al. (Eds.), *Contemporary issues in curriculum*. Boston: Pearson Education.

Lickona, T. (1992). *Educating for character: How our schools can teach respect and responsibility* (pp. 23–37). New York: Bantam.

Lieberman, A. (1995). Practices that support teacher development: Transforming conceptions of professional learning. *Phi Delta Kappan, 76*, 591–596.

Linn, R., & Gronlund, N. (2000). *Measurement and assessment in teaching* (8th ed.). Upper Saddle River, NJ: Prentice Hall.

Meadows, B. (1993). Through the eyes of parents. *Educational Leadership, 51*(2), 31–34.

Rimm, S. (2008). *Why bright children get poor grades*. Scottsdale, AZ: Great Potential Press.

Saterlie, M. (1992). Schools, parents, and communities working together. In T. Lickona, *Educating for character: How our schools can teach respect and responsibility*. New York: Bantam.

Shaps, E., Watson, M., & Lewis, C. (1996). A sense of community is key to effectiveness in fostering character education. *Journal of Staff Development, 17*(2), 42–47.

Stobbe, C. (1993). Professional partnerships. *Educational Leadership, 51*(2), 40–41.

 Now go to Topic #15: Collaborating with Colleagues and Families in the MyEducationLab (www.myeducationlab.com <http://www.myeducationlab.com/>) for your course, where you can:

- Find learning outcomes for this topic along with the national standards that connect to these outcomes.
- Complete Assignments and Activities that can help you more deeply understand the chapter content.
- Apply and practice your understanding of the core teaching skills identified in the chapter with the Building Teaching Skills and Dispositions learning units.

NAME INDEX

SUBJECT INDEX